GLOBALIZATION OF MANAGEMENT EDUCATION:
Changing International Structures, Adaptive Strategies, and the Impact on Institutions

GLOBALIZATION OF MANAGEMENT EDUCATION: Changing International Structures, Adaptive Strategies, and the Impact on Institutions

Report of the AACSB International Globalization of Management Education Task Force

AACSB International –
The Association to Advance Collegiate Schools of Business
777 South Harbour Island Boulevard
Suite 750
Tampa, Florida 33602-5730 USA
Tel: + 1-813-769-6500
Fax: + 1-813-769-6559
www.aacsb.edu

ⅲ AACSB
INTERNATIONAL

United Kingdom • North America • Japan
India • Malaysia • China

Emerald Group Publishing Limited
Howard House, Wagon Lane, Bingley BD16 1WA, UK

First edition 2011

British Library Cataloguing in Publication Data
A catalogue record for this book is available from the British Library

ISBN: 978-0-85724-941-8

Emerald Group Publishing
Limited, Howard House,
Environmental Management
System has been certified by
ISOQAR to ISO 14001:2004
standards

Awarded in recognition of
Emerald's production
department's adherence to
quality systems and processes
when preparing scholarly
journals for print

INVESTOR IN PEOPLE

Globalization of Management Education Task Force

Robert F. Bruner (Chair)
Dean and Charles C. Abbott
Professor of Business
Administration
Darden Graduate School of Business
Administration, University of
Virginia

Arnoud De Meyer
President
Singapore Management University

Pankaj Ghemawat
Anselmo Rubiralta Professor of
Global Strategy
IESE Business School

Jaime Alonso Gomez
Distinguished Professor,
International Strategy and
Management
Instituto Tecnológico y de Estudios
Superiores de
Monterrey - Campus Monterrey

Stefanie Lenway
Eli and Edythe L. Broad Dean,
Eli Broad College of Business,
Michigan State University

M. Rammohan Rao
Professor and Dean Emeritus
Indian School of Business

Edward A. Snyder
George Shultz Professor of
Economics
Booth School of Business,
The University of Chicago

Pierre Tapie
Groupe ESSEC President
ESSEC Business School Paris -
Singapore

Hildy Teegen
Dean
Darla Moore School of Business,
University of South Carolina

Peter W. Wolnizer
Dean
The University of Sydney Business
School

Daniel R. LeClair
Senior Vice President and Chief
Knowledge Officer
AACSB International

Juliane Iannarelli
Director, Global Research
AACSB International

Acknowledgements

The vision of current and past members of the AACSB Board of Directors and its Committee on Issues in Management Education has made this report possible. We thank them for the opportunity to serve and for the knowledge gained, and we commend AACSB leadership for empowering us to delve deep into the subject and to be direct about our conclusions, even when they point to huge opportunities to improve. We especially appreciate the support and patience of John Fernandes, AACSB President and CEO, and AACSB previous, current, and future chairs Howard Thomas, Andrew Policano, and Jan Williams.

Such an ambitious report as this one does not happen without research support from many talented people. We thank AACSB research staff, particularly Hanna Drozdowski, Amy Memon, and Colin Nelson for support in gathering and understanding information and examples that are found throughout this report; AACSB knowledge services staff, particularly Jessica Brown and Joe Mondello, for support in developing and administering the AACSB Member Collaboration Survey 2008, as well as for support in analyzing the data; Crystal Jiang of Bryant University College of Business and Masaaki Kotabe of Temple University Fox School of Business for a useful literature review and briefing; Darden student Jonathan Stanewick for analytical support; and Bernard Yeung for collaborating with AACSB and Pankaj Ghemawat on a survey of academic thought leaders.

We wish to recognize contributors to our case studies: Rolf D. Cremer, China Europe International Business School; Blair Sheppard, Duke University, The Fuqua School of Business; Maria Tereza Fleury and Ligia Maura Costa, Fundação Getulio Vargas, Escola de Administração de Empresas de São Paulo; Leonard Cheng, Steve DeKrey, and Kate Chan, Hong Kong University of Science and Technology, School of Business and Management; John Roberts, Stanford University, Graduate School of Business; Bill Kooser, The University of Chicago, Booth School of Business; Michael Houston and Anne D'Angelo King, University of Minnesota, Carlson School of Management; and William R. Folks Jr., University of South Carolina, Moore School of Business.

Countless other business school leaders have made thoughtful contributions to the report. Many of them delivered conference presentations and wrote articles that were helpful. Their names appear in footnotes throughout this report. Others inspired us through other, less formal channels: on the phone, in the hallways at events around the world, and through e-mail. Though they are too many to name, we thank them all and hope that each can see in our words the contributions they have made.

Finally, we thank Emerald Group Publishing, especially Bill Russell, for demonstrating an unwavering commitment to management education and for not hesitating to step up when we called for their expertise and assistance in publishing the report. We thank Lee Davidson for editing the report and Duncan Elliott for managing the design process.

Contents

Foreword

A common question frequently posed to those of us who have been dean for as long as I have is, "How have business schools changed over the past two decades?" My response is simple: the difference is night and day. Today, business schools are expected to be much more customer-focused, entrepreneurial, and self-reliant. And perhaps most important, today business schools need to be more global. They depend on "selling their products" to an increasingly global market that demands students who are prepared to implement global strategy and who possess international experience, cultural awareness, and the ability to work in cross-cultural environments. Through significant curricular change and the development of collaborations that cross the globe, business schools must create an educational experience that develops global leaders who can react swiftly and effectively to far-reaching shifts in international economic dynamics.

Two decades ago, over half of today's staff positions likely did not even exist in many business schools. Our staff members in career services, student recruitment processes, exchange programs, advertising and branding initiatives, and international alumni and corporate relations, to name a few areas, have taken on added complexity and responsibilities as the global nature of the business school operation has expanded. The faculty are called upon both in their research and teaching environments to focus on the issues that confront organizations that are expanding their global footprint. Globalization has been moving all of us in management education to do almost everything differently. Strategically, the implications of globalization continue to reveal themselves; a new and fundamentally different global landscape continues to emerge. An endless stream of new opportunities is available for us to rethink the scope of our missions, join forces with other institutions, finance our activities, and strengthen the quality and scope of our business schools.

Recognizing the significance of the global dynamic that faced our members, three years ago the AACSB Board Directors appointed the Globalization of Management Education Task Force to study the globalization of management education and to consider what it means to business schools. To say the least, it was a broadly defined charge but, not surprisingly, Bob Bruner and the Task Force did not shrink from the charge or try to minimize the breadth and depth of research it demanded. They embraced its enormous scope, and the result is nothing less than what we believe is the most definitive report on globalization in our field.

The report is written for anyone who works in or has an interest in business schools or higher education. The report helps leadership to strategically position and prioritize the globalization of management education; at the same time, the report serves, at an operational level, as a reference guide for faculty and administrative staff. It describes macro-level trends, clearly articulates why the globalization of management education is important, and explores ongoing debates about its benefits and costs. The report describes current business school activity and offers suggestions for how they can respond to change more effectively. It considers how management educators can work together and coordinate efforts to accelerate and improve the globalization of management education.

The globalization of management education can bring enormous benefit to society. But change does not happen because of words on a page—the report is a call to action. The Task Force urges all management educators to lead within their institutions to instill in future managers a global mindset, generate more international research into the theory, practice, and teaching of management, and to leverage the global environment to create new value in our society. To think that each business school acting alone is sufficient, however, would overlook the enormous potential for industry-wide leadership to guide and coordinate change. Organizations like AACSB can and will play an important role in shaping the future of management education.

On behalf of AACSB, I commend and thank the Task Force for the very significant time commitment that went into creating this provocative report that is both visionary and useful. This report will stand the test of time and will help all of us navigate the challenges brought on by globalization. In the future, we will all look back and certainly agree that this report had a powerful and constructive impact on the direction of management of management education.

Andrew J. Policano
Chair, Board of Directors, AACSB International,
Dean, The Paul Merage School of Business,
University of California, Irvine

Chapter 1

Introduction

Globalization is one of the most significant forces of change for business. Our children and grandchildren will likely feel the effects of a wave of globalization that seems yet in its infancy. Appropriately, globalization has commanded the attention of legions of writers, consultants, and advisers, who have stepped forward to assist managers as they wrestle with globalization. Governments have also increased their attention in an effort to create "national champions" and to advance the growth of their economies. To date, the accumulated books, articles, proceedings, and speeches published on the globalization of business rise to a mountain of material.

Yet comparatively little is known about the globalization of management education.[1] At no other point in history have business schools invested so much energy into seeking new means of expanding their international networks, incorporating international perspectives into learning experiences and faculty research, and establishing (or maintaining) a globally recognized brand. The motives for this heightened initiative are numerous and include the pursuit of revenue, reputation, access, impact, and influence. A report published in 2007 by the Global Foundation for Management Education details some of the emerging challenges (growth, localization, quality assurance, scholarship, and resources)—clearly, the costs and risks to schools are numerous. The complexities of globalization were amplified by the financial crisis that began in early 2007, the aftershocks of which will be felt for years to come. Large gaps remain in our knowledge about the globalization of management education: scale, scope, curriculum, modes of collaboration, and impact.

---

[1]In this report, we use "management education" to reflect an awareness that the need for effective managerial talent extends beyond the for-profit business environment to not-for-profits and government agencies—essentially to any organizational form that requires the effective management of resources in order to achieve a desired objective.

Globalization seems likely to transform management education at least on par with major inflection points in the past, such as the turn from application to research in the 1950s as advocated by the report of Gordon and Howell[2] and the turn toward humanism in 1988 as advocated by the report of Porter and McKibbin.[3] It is likely to overshadow more recent developments such as the rise of rankings beginning in 1988; the turn toward leadership development in the 1990s;[4] and the debates over the profession of management in the 2000s.[5] Globalization of management education re-opens decades-old debates and layers upon them new complexity, broader scope, and greater scale. Given the pace and direction of change, it seems inevitable that the future global field of management education will differ vastly from what it is today. Leaders in academia, business, and government need to understand the consequences of these imminent changes.

This report aims to complement and extend the stream of critical reflection on management education by illuminating the opportunities and challenges presented by globalization. The spirit of the report is to both encourage and support business schools' globalization efforts. In some respects, the report raises caution and points of concern; in other respects, the report calls for action by academic leaders and organizations that support management education. In all respects, this volume seeks to fill a gap in research and knowledge about higher education in management around the world. Clearly, in a rapidly evolving field such as this, more research is needed. Serving the aims identified by the Task Force is made daunting by the scarcity of data, the accelerating pace of change, and the sheer scope of activity in the global field of management education. But the original research presented in this volume, supplemented with numerous secondary sources and authorities consulted, pioneers a range of insights about a field in rapid transformation. Already, the insights presented here are sufficient to motivate reviews of curricula, global outreach strategies, accreditation policies, and government regulations. Overall, the Task Force

---

[2]Gordon, Robert Aaron, and James Edwin Howell, *Higher Education for Business*, Columbia University Press, New York, 1959.

[3]Porter, Lyman W., Lawrence E. McKibbin, and the American Assembly of Collegiate Schools of Business, *Management Education and Development: Drift or Thrust into the 21st Century?* McGraw-Hill Book Company, New York, 1988, ch. 1, pp. 12–14.

[4]See, for instance Pfeffer, Jeffrey, and Christina R. Fong, "The Business School 'Business': Some Lessons from the U.S. Experience," *Journal of Management Studies,* Vol. 41, No. 8 (2004), pp. 1501–20.

[5]See, for instance Khurana, Rakesh, *From Higher Aims to Hired Hands: The Social Transformation of American Business Schools and the Unfulfilled Promise of Management as a Profession*, Princeton University Press, Princeton, NJ, 2007.

aspires to accelerate innovation and adoption of mechanisms that support the *effective* globalization of management education.

In general, this report is an industry study that looks at recent trends from both a macroscopic perspective of supply and demand and a more microscopic perspective that considers the responses of schools. In the following chapters, we aim to accomplish the following goals:

- **Macro: Large trends in supply and demand.** We seek to explore the demographics of the field, the trends of change, and its drivers. This "industry" is characterized by a very large number of players, most of whom are local in reach and orientation. Entry is relatively easy. But the field of management education is highly segmented along many dimensions including mission, size, financial resources, and reputation. Mobility across borders is relatively high for students, and low but growing for faculty and institutions. Institutions confront geographic mobility barriers from regulation, reputation, culture, and capital.
- **Micro: Conduct of players.** We seek to explore the behavior that globalization elicits. Institutions respond to globalization as a threat and as an opportunity. Globalization may summon new competitors for students, faculty, or capital. At the same time, globalization may open opportunities to expand programs, increase revenues, and build brands. As a result, globalization has stimulated a new wave of competition among institutions as they jockey for position; of particular interest are curriculum strategies and the use of strategic alliances, joint ventures, exchange programs, and operating agreements to leverage the reach of schools across borders.
- **Implications.** We seek to explore the consequences of the emerging supply and demand, the trends, and the behavior of players. By connecting the points raised in earlier chapters, we call management educators to collective action aimed at elevating the achievement of business school globalization efforts, and in turn the ability of business schools to support positive economic and social change. The call to action includes roles for individuals within the bounds of their respective schools, as well as in concert with others across the industry. The organizations—governmental and supranational— that influence and support higher education, or management education specifically, also have significant roles to play. Ultimately, this chapter aims to serve as a launch pad for additional attention and action.

1.1. Importance and Urgency of the Subject

Our view is that globalization is a driver of change that cannot be ignored. It is a trajectory that inextricably links both the business community and business schools. The course of globalization will continue as long as people are driven to look across borders for resources, ideas, efficiencies, and services. Business schools that fail to adapt to that reality do so at their own peril. A review of the status and trends of globalization of management education is important and timely, for several reasons:

> **The profession we serve.** The general mission of business schools is to educate and prepare talent to serve customers, firms, and markets. As the field of business administration evolves, the academy must evolve as well. In Section 1.3, we detail some of the evidence of globalization by business; the reality is that this change is not evolutionary, of a slow and silent nature. In some respects it is discontinuous, fast, and prominent. Such change has called for nimble response by firms and their leaders. The same response is required of the academy. Business schools mirror the profession they serve. The spectacular globalization of business since World War II has created a significant demand for administrative talent educated in the challenges and opportunities of globalization.
>
> **Globalization is a disruptive force of change in management education.** Our research suggests that globalization is changing former assumptions, practices, and strategies. Among the schools we studied, globalization was motivated by strategic objectives related to many trends within the global business and economic environment as well as those related to globalization trends within higher education. We find that business schools globalize for many reasons: a sense of mission or professional obligation, networking (to build connectivity with other schools), signaling and brand-building, satisfying demand, generating revenues, and, ultimately, self-transformation. At the same time, globalization requires resources that elude many schools.
>
> **Quality of the learning experience for students.** Unfortunately, present efforts by business schools to globalize typically include a series of independent and fragmented activities. These activities are mostly focused on student and/or faculty diversity and the establishment of cross-border partnerships for student exchange. The Task Force is concerned that business schools are not responding to globalization in a coherent way, i.e., they tend to focus on collecting an array of activities (e.g., exchange programs) with insufficient emphasis on learning experiences and intended outcomes. Accreditors of academic institutions should set standards of excellence consistent with this new world. By these

standards, business schools hold one another accountable for practices and policies that best serve their constituents. Expectations for the incorporation of global perspectives into the curriculum, for the intellectual capital of faculty to keep pace with the evolution of business practices in a global business environment, and for schools to ensure consistent quality across all programs and locations can provide a framework for this quality assurance, yet the methods through which schools meet these expectations are likely to evolve substantially in the years to come.

The impact that business schools have on globalization itself. Business schools' responses to globalization are only half of the story. We are also interested in the role of business schools as drivers of globalization, which we believe is a central enabler of increased prosperity around the world. During times when public sentiment leans toward protectionism, business schools and their alumni must advocate the benefits of a globalization effort fueled by lower barriers to trade. These benefits extend to trade in higher education, which has the potential to increase access to and the quality of education received by the world's labor force. Economic growth in regions currently underserved by management education depends on sufficient investment in management education to satisfy the regions' talent needs.

Furthermore, globalization of management education is a key enabler of globalization in many other fields. Increased connectivity across countries has facilitated the transfer of ideas and collaborative development of innovations in fields as diverse as archaeology, engineering, and medicine. These discoveries are fueled by the fact that the same laws of physics, mathematical principles, and biological systems that underlie basic research and innovation within the hard sciences are constant across every country and world region. The same cannot be said for management, the application of which is heavily influenced by contextual factors such as culture, social norms, and national regulations or policy. Business leaders are called on to create the organizational processes and settings that enable innovations in the hard sciences to be developed and implemented in a contextually complex society. In short, managers who can lead in a global context are a critical resource for innovation and economic development.

Challenges to globalization. In the eyes of most knowledgeable analysts, globalization has delivered vast benefits to society. Free trade and the gains from comparative advantage—understood since David Ricardo's seminal work in 1817—have offered incentives for integration of business across countries and markets. Undeniably, the train has left the station: we now are well down the track toward a truly global business economy.

Yet, a succession of economic crises over the past two decades spawned a small but headline-grabbing chorus of criticism.[6] Some critics blamed the onset and spread of the financial crisis on the wave of globalization over the past generation. That business schools have a hand in globalization is a popular charge. The financial crisis spawned some op-ed columns alleging that the crisis was due to MBA graduates of leading schools.[7,8] Management educators and their institutions should respond—but after research and reflective consideration. For business schools, globalization presents both a challenge and an opportunity. The events of this past decade warrant careful research and adjustment of curricula in an effort to convey a richer under-standing of the evidence and impact of globalization.

---

[6]The Tequila Crisis (Mexico, 1995), the Asian Flu Crisis (1997), the Russian Bond Default (1998), the Argentine crisis (2001), and the Subprime Crisis (2007–09) challenged the notion that the capitalist model would deliver widespread prosperity. Stormy protests threatened meetings of the World Trade Organization, G8, G20, and other groups in venues as diverse as Geneva, Davos, Prague, Genoa, Quebec City, Seattle, Heilingendamm, and London. After a 50-year process of trade liberalization, the Doha Round of negotiations collapsed in 2006 as developed and developing countries resisted abandoning protections for favored industries.

[7]See, for instance, Holland, Kelley, "Is it time to retrain business schools?" *New York Times*, March 14, 2009, electronic document, http://www.nytimes.com/2009/03/15/business/15school.html, accessed January 31, 2010; Stewart, Matthew, "RIP, MBA." *The Big Money*, March 25, 2009 electronic document, http://www.thebigmoney.com/articles/judgments/2009/03/25/rip-mba, accessed January 31, 2010; Plumer, Bradford, "The MBA Frayed," *The New Republic*, April 1, 2009, electronic document, http://www.tnr.com/article/politics/mba-frayed, accessed January 31, 2010; Green, Charles H., "Wall Street Run Amok, Why Harvard's to Blame," *BusinessWeek*, October 5, 2009, electronic document, http://www.businessweek.com/bschools/content/oct2009/bs2009105_376904.htm, accessed January 31, 2010; *Harvard Business Review*, "How to Fix Business Schools," compendium of commentaries, electronic documents, http://blogs.hbr.org/how-to-fix-business-schools/, accessed January 31, 2010; Broughton, Philip D., "Harvard's Masters of the Apocalypse," *The Times of London*, March 1, 2009, electronic document, http://www.timesonline.co.uk/tol/news/uk/education/article5821706.ece, accessed January 31, 2010; and Alvarez, Paz, "Las Escuelas de Negocios, Contra las Cuerdas," CincoDías.com, April 4, 2009, electronic document, http://www.cincodias.com/articulo/Directivos/escuelas-negocios-cuerdas/20090404cdscdidir_1/cdspor/, accessed January 31, 2010.

[8]George Soros argued that academics and economists had to pay the price for optimistic convictions about markets and institutions. "Economists have to accept a reduction of their status," *New Paradigm for Financial Markets: The Credit Crisis of 2008 and What it Means*, PublicAffairs, New York, 2008, p. 75.

1.2.   What is "Globalization"? What Does It Mean to Be "Global"?

Globalization is a process of change. We use "globalization" to refer to a *process*[9] of change within educational institutions extending the reach of educational engagement beyond one's home borders and deepening the richness of understanding about the increasingly global foundation of business. The end results of the globalization of management education process should be 1) greater competence and confidence of graduates for doing business with global impact; 2) more research insights into the global complexity of the managers, enterprises, and markets studied; and 3) ultimately better service of the global management profession.

Defining a "global" business school. We think that whether a school is "global" is determined first by the outcomes it achieves, second by the processes it engages, and last by the places it inhabits. Actions and locations are useful means toward the end goal of globalization, but ultimately schools are judged by the outcomes they achieve. A global school of management:

- prepares students to perform competently and confidently in a world of global business competition and inherently global issues.
- generates research insights about trends and best practices in global management.
- leverages diverse cultures and practices in pursuit of innovation and continuous improvement.

---

[9]Conventional definitions suggest that globalization pushes an enterprise, its products, and its services across national borders; it promotes interaction and engagement on a global scale; it advances networking, communication, and execution of transactions; it spreads trade, investment, capital, and technology; and it integrates nations politically, economically, and culturally. Many writers use "internationalization" almost interchangeably with "globalization," though some definitions have gained traction within the international higher education literature. Knight, for example, argues that "globalisation can be thought of as the catalyst while internationalisation is the response, albeit a response in a proactive way." Knight, J., "Internationalisation of higher education," in J. Knight (ed.), *Quality and Internationalisation in Higher Education*, OECD, Paris, France, 1999, p. 14. Naidoo writes that internationalization of education consists of "policy-based responses that education institutions adopt as a result of the impact of globalization." Naidoo, Vikash, "International Education: A Tertiary-level Industry Update," *Journal of Research in International Education*, Vol. 5, No. 3 (2006), p. 324. Beamish defined internationalization as "the evolving awareness and acknowledgement by the manager/organization/country of the impact of non-domestic forces on its economic future and the translation of the latter into new attitudes and behavior regarding the establishment and conduct of transactions with those in, and from other countries." Beamish, P.W., "Internationalization as strategic change at the Western business school," in S. Tamer Cavusgil (ed.), *Internationalizing Business Education: Meeting the Challenge*, International Business Series, Michigan State University Press, East Lansing, MI, 1993.

There is no tipping point at which a school becomes "global." Today's commonly used indicators, which tend to center on international diversity and the number of international partnerships, can be misleading. The above framework allows for schools to prepare students to be globally competent without necessarily having an internationally diverse student body. Similarly, it is possible for a school with an internationally diverse student body to fail to achieve these outcomes. World literature contains prominent examples of cosmopolitan travelers who remain quite provincial in attitude and outlook, of professionals who cease to be effective when they cross borders, and of colossal cultural clashes within multinational organizations.

Getting to "global." Is globalization an end in itself or simply a means to an end? Our analysis has led us to believe that when a school's underlying objective is to be perceived as "global," the school is more likely to engage in a fragmented and disjointed set of activities or costly operations that bring little to no real added value to the stakeholders being served.

In fact, a claim of being "global" is relatively easy for a school to make. A school that simply rents space on several continents, recruits a handful of students from different countries, or inserts modules into its curriculum that cover the cultures of different nations can likely state, accurately, that its educational delivery, student profile, or pedagogy is "global." But is this really the goal that business schools are trying to achieve? For some of the world's business schools, it seems so.

Our definition, however, takes the perspective that business schools globalize as a means of achieving other objectives, which differ significantly among schools. Business schools educate young adults, mid-career professionals, and seasoned executives. They serve, through the students they educate and other forms of outreach, community-serving family businesses, small and medium enterprises, and multinational corporations. Each school's mission and environment provide a unique set of circumstances that require a customized approach to globalization.

In this sense, successful globalization does not necessarily require a global "footprint" of facilities or a network of alliances outside of the home country. As our findings reveal, facilities and networks can help immensely toward achieving the learning, research, and innovation-related aspects of our above framework—but only if they exist as infrastructure to support a broader focus on students, research, and culture. In legitimizing a wide range of strategies for schools, however, we acknowledge the difficulty of measuring or ranking how "global" a business school is. Measures that focus on inputs/activities will inevitably ignore highly responsive and substantive approaches taken by schools that do not align well with those measures. Decision-makers must measure outcomes, though this process is not easily accomplished.

1.3. Globalization of Business and Business Schools

The relationship between the business profession and the business academy is largely symbiotic: they support each other in various ways that advance the welfare of society. When one gets materially ahead of the other, it is a moment for reflection, action, and realignment. The Task Force judges that globalization has created such a moment in the relationship between business and business schools.

Thus, as context for this report's focus on globalization within the business academy, some acknowledgement of the globalization trends within the business profession are important. We begin by presenting some indicators of economic globalization by focusing on indicators of cross-border trade, and corresponding shifts in the global economic landscape. These trends are widely documented and analyzed in other texts, and thus are presented only briefly in order to frame later discussions of the impact on derived demand for global management education.

We also are interested in the trends of firms that, like many business schools, are seeking to operate effectively in this globalizing business environment. Some academics discount comparisons of academic institutions to firms or suggestions that the strategies and actions of the two should parallel one another.[10] While we do not deny that significant differences exist between the two environments, we also point to many similarities shared in the globalization efforts of each establishment. Both of these dimensions must be explored and should not be underestimated.

1.3.1. Globalization Indicators

Business has been, arguably, the visible hand of globalization over the past several decades. Thus, evidence of globalization in business provides insights into the dramatic impact of globalization on the business profession, and the subsequent impact on demand for global management education. Business schools, after all, are driven by their missions to meet the needs of this market.

We can get a rough indication of the advance of globalization since World War II by tracing the growth of total world exports. From 1960 to 2007,

---

[10]Only 7 percent of AACSB member business school deans were corporate executives in their most recent position. Perhaps this low number is a testament to the differences between the two establishments.

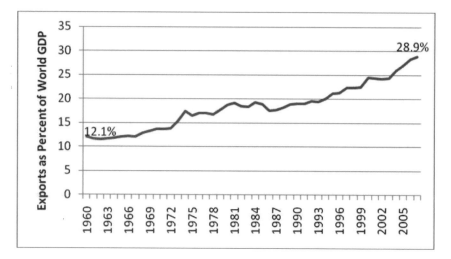

Figure 1.1: Ratio of World Exports of Goods and Commercial Services to GDP, 1960–2007.

Source: World Bank WDI & Global Development Finance Database.[11]

total world exports as a percentage of global gross domestic product (GDP) more than doubled, from 12.1 percent to 28.9 percent (as shown in Figure 1.1). In fact, by this measure, we can discern that the pace of globalization has been accelerating.[11]

Another clear trend related to globalization is the growing contribution to global GDP that has come from emerging markets. The International Monetary Fund (IMF) reports that Europe and the U.S. have steadily lost significant shares of global GDP to developing regions such as Asia and will continue to do so into the foreseeable future.[12] All signs point to a world economy with falling U.S. and European shares of world GDP, incremental demand, and sales to global firms. Companies must cultivate executives and managers skilled in overcoming distribution and service challenges to reach new markets and shift research and development (R&D), innovation, and

---

[11]World Bank, World Development Indicators and Global Development Finance online database, 2010, electronic document, http://databank.worldbank.org/ddp/home.do?Step=1&id=4, accessed August 26, 2010.
[12]Beinhocker, Eric, Ian Davis, and Lenny Mendonca, "The 10 Trends You Have to Watch," *Harvard Business Review*, Vol. 87, No. 7/8 (2009), pp. 55–60.

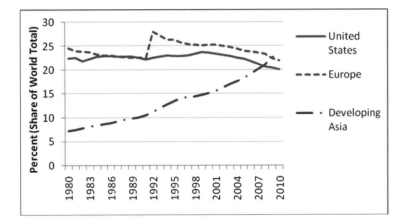

Figure 1.2: Changing Regional Shares of Global GDP Based on Purchasing Power Parity.
Source: IMF, World Economic Outlook Database, April 2010.[13]

design activities, over to new, emerging regions.[14] The future of the world economy strongly favors business managers who can contribute to the great needs for talent in regions such as developing Asia, as Figure 1.2 suggests.

Likewise, the composition of the firms within the Fortune Global 500 has been changing. From 2005 until 2010, the percentage of corporations from the Global 500 that were from the "BRIC" economies (Brazil, Russia, India, and China) and a handful of other emerging economies[15] has grown from 8.2 percent to 17.4 percent. The portion of Fortune Global 500 companies based in the U.S. decreased from 35.2 percent to 27.8 percent, or an average of approximately seven firms per year between 2005 and 2010.

Global economic development has also been accompanied by a general increase in global prosperity. The expansion of the middle class in many countries has made higher education more affordable for a larger portion of the population and has resulted in markets for numerous goods and services. India and China stand out in particular as two of the BRIC countries where this market growth has occurred. Surjit Bhalla notes that in

---

[14]Beinhocker, Eric, Ian Davis, and Lenny Mendonca, "The 10 Trends You Have to Watch," *Harvard Business Review*, Vol. 87, No. 7/8 (2009), pp. 55–60.
[15]Specifically, those economies that the International Monetary Fund defines as "Newly industrialized Asian economies," namely Chinese Taipei, Hong Kong, Singapore, and South Korea.

2006, the middle-class population in Asia rose to 60 percent of the world's total middle-class population—a significant increase from approximately 20 percent in 1980.[16] While the correct approach to defining what constitutes a "middle class" is hotly debated, almost all approaches point to the expansion of this group of the population, particularly within emerging markets.[17]

Similar indicators of globalization in management education also exist. For example, global "exports" of students are increasing and projected to continue to grow, especially among students of business. Measures of multinational activity by educational providers in the form of collaborative partnerships, branch campuses, and involvement in international networks show burgeoning activity, but also suggest many untapped opportunities. Demands for a more highly educated labor market in emerging economies, in particular, are likely to lead to educational providers in those countries taking a more significant role in the global field of management education. These and other indicators are explored in more detail in Chapter 2.

What is perhaps more important is that the globalization of business has led to substantial derived demand for global management education. Indicators of globalization in business are likely to underestimate the corresponding needs for knowledge, skills, and attitudes that align with current and future needs of the business profession. We touch briefly in Chapter 2 on indicators that corporations desire more global skill sets among their employees, and then we devote Chapter 4 in its entirety to exploring schools' curriculum-based responses to meeting these needs.

1.3.2. Shaping Globalization Strategy

In addition to looking at evidence of globalization in business, we also conducted a comprehensive academic literature review to uncover the major themes of international business research; this information likewise suggests insights into the globalization of management education.[18] Many of these insights are confirmed through an examination of a series of case studies of

---

[16]Bhalla, Surjit S., "Second Among Equals: The Middle Class Kingdoms of India and China," 2007, electronic document, http://www.oxusinvestments.com/files/pdf/NE20090106.pdf, accessed August 23, 2010. Cited in Parker, John, "Burgeoning bourgeoisie," *Economist*, February 12, 2009, electronic document, http://www.economist.com/node/13063298, accessed February 1, 2010.

[17]With regard to India, for example, "In 2005, says the reputable National Council for Applied Economic Research, the middle-class share of the population was only about 5%. By 2015, it forecasts, it will have risen to 20%; by 2025, to over 40%." Parker, John, "Burgeoning bourgeoisie," *Economist*, February 12, 2009, electronic document, http://www.economist.com/node/13063298, accessed February 1, 2010.

[18]The Task Force thanks Crystal Jiang, Assistant Professor of Management at Bryant University, College of Business, and Masaaki Kotabe, The Washburn Chair Professor of International Business and Marketing at Temple University, The Fox School of Business, for their literature review and for briefing us on these themes. Section 1.3.2 draws on their summary document.

business schools and their globalization strategies, included as an Appendix to this report.[19]

The literature reveals four broad trends that characterize the globalization of business in recent years: 1) the deepening of integration, 2) fusion of markets, 3) shift to networked organizations, and 4) migration to cyberspace. At the policy level, these trends have changed the relationship between states and firms, lessened the importance of access to territory, and raised serious questions about the continued viability of economic governance exercised through territorially defined national markets. At the operational level, these tendencies have meant new organizational models and structural dynamics, new strategies, and a need for new capabilities among employees.

Compared to the business environment, higher education tends to be more tightly rooted in tradition, and tends to encounter more inertia than business in the face of change. Still, whether proactively or reluctantly, business schools are confronting and responding to these trends. Higher education systems are becoming more integrated as student interest in international mobility increases, calling for efforts to harmonize previously incompatible educational models. Boundaries of markets served are blurring—programs that once recruited a majority of students nationally now enroll a blend of students originating from (and sometimes still living in) multiple continents. Collaborative partnerships between schools and cross-border extensions of a school's operations are changing the organizational and hierarchical structures of business schools. The Internet today plays a critical role as an enabler of global connections and operations—supporting communication, facilitating new methods of educational delivery, and connecting remote colleagues through organizational networks.

At a micro level, our review of the growing body of international business research uncovered several meaningful themes that complement these four broad trends, including motivations for globalization; semi-globalization and standardization vs. adaptation strategies; competition, cooperation, and "co-opetition"; and the role of technology in the evolution of firm and subsidiary relationships. In the pages that follow, we briefly discuss these four themes and their parallels in management education globalization.[20]

---

[19]China Europe International Business School (China); Duke University, The Fuqua School of Business (U.S.); ESSEC Business School Paris-Singapore (France/Singapore); Fundação Getulio Vargas-São Paulo, Escola de Administração de Empresas de São Paulo (Brazil); Hong Kong University of Science and Technology, School of Business and Management (China); Stanford University, Graduate School of Business (U.S.); The University of Chicago, Booth School of Business (U.S.); University of Minnesota, Carlson School of Management (U.S.); and University of South Carolina, Moore School of Business (U.S.).

Motivations for globalization. For firms, globalization might offer any of several advantages. For example, some companies seek to globalize in order to enhance their comparative and competitive positioning. Sometimes companies derive benefits from locating their operations closer to large pools of potential customers; at other times, an international move is preemptive and designed to establish or maintain a competitive position. Production and cost factors also motivate globalization. Firms might seek arrangements that allow specialization in different value-adding activities or improved economic efficiency from greater scale and scope; for instance, expansion beyond the home country might optimize an inefficient supply chain. And yet other firms might seek enhanced internal organizational (e.g., knowledge, managerial, etc.) capabilities beyond simply exploiting the advantages of multiple locations worldwide.

Although each of these motives could apply to business schools, our intuition suggests that order of importance may shift dramatically as we move from firms to business schools, with a greater emphasis placed on mission than on competition. For example, in a 2004 study by AACSB, the European Foundation for Management Development (EFMD), and the Canadian Federation of Business School Deans (CFBSD), the number one reason given by deans for forming strategic program alliances was to enhance the educational experience for their students.[21] Though financial motivations ranked low back then, it is clear that the pursuit of higher revenues and lower costs has become more important as traditional sources of funding, such as government support, have not kept pace with rising costs.

Semi-globalization and standardization versus adaptation strategies. Through popular literature by Thomas Friedman and other writers, conventional wisdom has grown increasingly aware of a global movement toward a more level international playing field. Technological innovations, privatization, liberalization of trade, changes in government policies, advances in communication, and other trends have all contributed to an increasingly globalized world. The world has seen growing numbers of multinational

---

[20]The Task Force notes that scholars of multinational enterprises are in a unique position to use their expertise to contribute to another growing body of research—that of the internationalization of higher education—with a particular focus on effective strategies for multinational institutions of higher education.

[21]AACSB International, Canadian Federation of Business School Deans, and European Foundation for Management Development, 2004–05 Alliances Survey Results, internal communication to survey participants, 2005.

corporations, joint ventures, alliances, and international sourcing, all demanding new sets of border-transcending capabilities from business leaders.

The same development applies to management education as well. Measurable and significant trends within the global economy have driven the integration of higher education across borders. Harmonization of degree structures (e.g., the Bologna Accord), the reduction of language barriers, technological innovation, and other trends contribute to a (generally) increasing ease of mobility among students and higher education providers. The result is increased interest in the phenomenon of globalization within the broader higher education community, and among business schools as an extension of that community.

But as Task Force member Pankaj Ghemawat argues, to say that the world is "semi-globalized" is more accurate. He writes, "Most types of economic activity that can be conducted either within or across borders are still quite localized by country."[22] Ghemawat's analysis of indicators that include cross-border migration, telephone calls, private charitable giving, patenting, stock investment, and trade as a fraction of gross domestic product has led him to a "10 percent presumption"—the supposition that on any given dimension, the actual level of globalization is somewhere around only 10 percent of all activity. Across countries and regions, we see different stages of economic development, different industries dominating and needs for varying skill sets, different socio-cultural factors influencing individual and societal behavior, and a web of varying laws, legislation, and policies that govern business practices.

The asymmetries between countries are not insignificant for firms that operate internationally, or for the business schools that supply the management talent demanded in each setting. Firms often must deal with problems such as government corruption, limited intellectual property rights, legal systems of differing sophistication levels, as well as the hidden rules that no contractual agreement can capture in firms' strategic alliance agreements. Khanna, Palepu, and Sinha suggest that companies match their strategies to each country's contexts (e.g., political and social systems, openness, product markets, labor markets, and capital markets), so they can take advantage of a location's unique strengths.[23]

Similarly, the world of higher education is also far from flat. Across countries and regions, we see variances in national policies and regulations

---

[22]Ghemawat, Pankaj, *Redefining Global Strategy: Crossing Borders in a World Where Differences Still Matter*, Harvard Business School Press, Cambridge, MA, 2007, p. 10.
[23]Khanna, T., K. Palepu, and J. Sinha, "Strategies that fit emerging markets," *Harvard Business Review*, Vol. 83 (2005), pp. 63–76.

affecting higher education operations, varying higher education degree structures, differences in faculty models, and variations in supply and demand. The vast majority of business schools around the world still serve a predominantly local set of stakeholders, and those that venture across national borders face an array of different economic, cultural, political, and legal contexts in the markets they enter. This semi-globalization in the world of higher education has implications for business schools as they develop strategies for the delivery of management education, whether through international recruitment of students and faculty, cross-border delivery of degrees, collaborative initiatives with foreign schools, or other means. In a semi-global world, one size does not fit all aspects of curriculum, and the phrase "global best practice" is an oxymoron.

The diversity of economic, cultural, political, and legal climates across (and within) countries has led to much research attention focused on the issue of a standardized strategy versus customized strategy to suit the specific needs of individual foreign markets. A substantial body of literature has been developed to explore just *how* firms might balance the simultaneous demands for supply-side efficiency and demand-side customization.[24] Additionally, a greater availability of market research as well as greater transparency of regulatory frameworks in various countries mean that corporations today have easier access to information that will influence decisions to standardize, adapt, or customize strategy across borders (particularly in new, emerging markets).

The tension between standardization and customization or adaptation is also evident in management education. Business schools that generate efficiencies through standardization reach larger student populations and potentially broaden their impact. At the same time, concerns are often raised (rightly so, this Task Force believes) when too much standardization is applied beyond the provision of basic skills training. The schools in the case studies pursue different approaches in striking this balance, and we devote special attention in Chapter 5 to exploring their strategies.

Competition, cooperation, and co-opetition.   Due in part to globalization, the relationships between organizations have become increasingly complex, and characterizing relationships as either competitive or cooperative has

---

[24]See, for example: Prahalad, C.K., and Yves L. Doz, *The Multinational Mission, Balancing Global Integration with Local Responsiveness*, Free Press, New York, and Collier Macmillan, London, 1987; Porter, M., *Competition in Global Industries*, Harvard Business School Press, Cambridge, MA, 1986; and Kotabe, Maasaki, "To kill two birds with one stone: Revising the integration-responsiveness framework," in M. Hitt and J. Cheng (eds.), *Managing transnational firms*, Elsevier, New York, 2002, pp. 59–69.

become more difficult. Many involve both competition and cooperation. For example, a version of "co-opetition" in the international business literature refers to firms' cooperating to create a bigger business pie while competing to divide it up.[25]

In the international business literature, a strategic alliance is defined as a structure that connects two or more organizations in an effort to achieve strategically significant goals that are mutually beneficial.[26] Research points to many potential benefits of alliances, such as the fact that alliances speed up learning and innovation processes[27] and that cross-border R&D alliances produce the strongest effect on firms' technology learning.[28]

Strategic alliances have thus become central to competitive success in fast-changing global markets. Rapid environmental changes, such as intensification of competition, acceleration of technology advancements, enlargement of required investment, and globalization of markets, call for strategic responses and capabilities that firms may not be able to deliver on their own. This challenge is especially notable in high-technology (i.e., knowledge-intensive) industries, in which the new technology and product development level is remarkably high and the lifecycle of products is relatively short. Reflecting these circumstances, the number of strategic alliances has increased in the past decade, with tens of thousands of strategic alliances reported worldwide in recent years. Joint R&D ventures are an efficient way to shorten the development time by combining technological resources with partners, with less individual cost. Global competition also brings about global cooperation.[29]

What is meant by competition in management education is not always clear. Within a set of schools, there might be some level of competition for prospective students in a particular segment. For example, schools might compete for the brightest prospects interested in full-time MBA programs. However, schools also compete for contracts with companies for custom programs, resources from potential donors, and the best potential faculty

---

[25]Luo, Y., "Toward coopetition within a multinational enterprise: a perspective from foreign subsidiaries," *Journal of World Business*, Vol. 40, No. 1 (2005), pp. 71–90.

[26]Murray, E., and J.F. Mahon, "Strategic Alliances: Gateway to the New Europe?" *Long Range Planning*, Vol. 26, No. 4 (1993), pp. 102–11.

[27]Doz, I.L., and G. Hamel, "The use of alliances in implementing technology strategies," in Tushman, M.L., and P. Anderson (eds.), *Managing Strategic Innovation and Change*, Oxford University Press, New York, 1997, pp. 556–80.

[28]Kim, C.S., and A.C. Inkpen, "Cross-border R&D alliances, Absorptive Capacity and Technology Learning," *Journal of International Management,* Vol. 11 (2005), pp. 313–29.

[29]In the past decades, companies have found it more profitable to compete through cooperation. See, for example, Parkhe, A., "Building Trust in International Alliances," *Journal of World Business*, Vol. 33, No. 4 (1998), pp. 417–37.

members. Though nearly all competition stills occurs between schools based in the same country, globalization has increased competition as well as increased the portion of competition that is international. Furthermore, while the world has seen the emergence of a few large education providers seeking to obtain a large market share in the multinational environment, more business schools seem to be focused on "brand share" than on enlarging their pool of consumers. And unlike in the business world where increasing market share is often viewed as a sign of success, in the world of higher education, market share and perceptions of quality tend *not* to be directly proportional to each other.

Despite the rise in competition, or perhaps because of it, a growing number of schools have approached globalization by seeking to distinguish themselves in local and global environments through strategic partnerships with schools abroad. Their goal is to acquire, mobilize, and utilize resources and competencies in new ways and new contexts. Partnerships or alliances can take on many forms; they may be unilateral relationships between two educational institutions, or multilateral relationships within the framework of a consortium. In addition to educational institutions, partners may also include various for-profit, not-for-profit, governmental, non-governmental, and other types of organizations.[30] As we shall show, much of this collaboration takes place among schools that are alike and potentially competitive with one another.

Most cross-border business school alliances today focus on educational delivery, and are established to provide the infrastructure to deliver a program (or part of a program) in a location that is closer to a target student market or a particular industry cluster or socioeconomic context of focus. Fewer alliances support collaborative R&D in the form of joint-discipline-based, practice-oriented, or pedagogical research. The Task Force believes that greater engagement in this area will advance innovation in educational delivery and our understanding of business in a global context.

Finally, both for firms and for educational institutions, a central ingredient to strong international programs is the establishment of mean-ingful relationships based on common values and goals and a sense of trust between partners. Trust functions as a central organizing principle in alliance management. As noted by Parkhe, building trust in international alliances involves an understanding of the relationship, accrual of trust over time (patience), awareness of each partner's strategic direction, knowledge

---

[30]Wood, V., "Globalization and higher education: Eight common perceptions from university leaders," Institution of International Education, electronic document, http://www.iienetwork. org/page/84658/, accessed June 19, 2009.

of asymmetry in alliance value creation and value appreciation, and attention to staffing issues, such as effective selection, placement, and retention of personnel.[31] An alliance partner must be sensitive to the strengths and natural tendencies of the partner institution and ensure that the partnerships formed and initiatives undertaken are beneficial to the relationship.

The role of technology in the evolution of firm and subsidiary relationships. In addition to shaping the relationships between organizations, globalization is also leading to shifts in the relationships between firm headquarters and subsidiaries. In recent years, the traditional perception of firms as a bundle of dyadic, hierarchical headquarter-subsidiary relationships has been considered obsolete. More and more researchers view a firm as a network with diverse, differentiated, and complex inter- and intra-relationships.[32] Subsidiaries are considered nodes within those networks.[33]

Gradually, scholars have also begun to recognize how firms leverage resources across large geographic markets. The paradigm has shifted from that of a hierarchy or federation-based focus to a network-based focus. In this context, firms are emphasizing an integrated strategy and organization, gradually introducing interdependence across operations, and finding alternatives to units' traditional independence in strategy, resources, and organization.[34]

This trend has been largely supported by the emergence of the Internet, which has made the physical and psychological distance between countries (and therefore between the units and/or employees located there) less prominent. Information technology has made global

---

[31]Parkhe, A., "Building Trust in International Alliances," *Journal of World Business*, Vol. 33, No. 4 (1998), pp. 417–37.

[32]See, for example: Andersson, U., and M. Forsgren, "In search of centre of excellence: Network embeddedness and subsidiary roles in multinational corporations," *Management International Review*, Vol. 40, No. 4 (2000), pp. 329–50; Gupta, A., and V. Govindarajan, "Knowledge flows and the structure of control within multinational corporations," *Academy of Management Review*, Vol. 16, No. 4 (1991), pp. 768–92; Nohria, N., and S. Ghoshal, *The differentiated network: organizing multinational corporations for value creation*, Jossey-Bass, San Francisco, 1997; and O'Donnell, S.W., "Managing foreign subsidiaries: agents of headquarters, or an interdependent network?" *Strategic Management Journal*, Vol. 21, No. 5 (2000), pp. 525–48.

[33]Andersson, U., M. Forsgren, and U. Holm, "The strategic impact of external networks: subsidiary performance and competence development in the multinational corporation," *Strategic Management Journal*, Vol. 23 (2002), pp. 979–96.

[34]Malnight, T., "The transition from decentralized to network-based MNC structures: an evolutionary perspective," *Journal of International Business Studies*, Vol. 27, No. 1 (1996), pp. 43–65.

hierarchies increasingly obsolete in that firms can efficiently manage projects virtually in an instant around the globe. Warrington et al. present evidence that the Internet has "provided marketers with new ways of promoting, communicating, and distributing information and product."[35] As Yip and Dempster found, the Internet helps companies to be both global and local simultaneously.[36]

As organizational hierarchies become more flat, subsidiaries in foreign markets play increasingly active roles; they are empowered to be more active contributors to a firm's knowledge base and to also develop new technologies.[37] This more dynamic approach allows for two-directional information flows from three sources: each unit's own existing knowledge, each unit's ongoing R&D, and specialized resources local to each unit.[38] As a result, subsidiaries have the potential to make a great contribution to the competitive advantage of the whole firm.

---

[35]Warrington, T., N. Abgrab, and H. Caldwell, "Building trust to develop competitive advantage in e-business relationships," *Competitiveness Review*, Vol. 10, No. 2 (2000), pp. 160–68.

[36]Yip, G., and A. Dempster, "Using the Internet to enhance global strategy," *European Management Journal,* Vol. 23, No. 1 (2005), pp. 1–13.

[37]Cantwell, J.A., "The globalisation of technology: What remains of the product cycle model?" *Cambridge Journal of Economics*, Vol. 19 (1995), pp. 155–74; Cantwell, J.A., and L. Piscitello, "The emergence of corporate international networks for the accumulation of dispersed technological competencies," *Management International Review*, Vol. 39 (1999), pp. 123–47; Håkanson, L., and R. Nobel, "Technology Characteristics and Reverse Technology Transfer," *Management International Review*, Special Issue 40, No. 1 (2000), pp. 29–48; Kuemmerle, W., "The drivers of foreign direct investment into research and development: an empirical investigation," *Journal of International Business Studies*, Vol. 30, No. 1 (1999), pp. 1–24.

[38]For more on firm and subsidiary relationships, particularly related to knowledge acquisition and R&D, see Kuemmerle, W., "The drivers of foreign direct investment into research and development: an empirical investigation," *Journal of International Business Studies*, Vol. 30, No. 1 (1999), pp. 1–24; Forsgren, M., U. Holm, and J. Johanson, "Internationalization of the Second Degree: The Emergence of the European-Based Centres in Swedish Firms," in Stephen Young and James Hamill (eds.), *Europe and the Multinationals: Issues and Responses for the 1990s*, Edward Elgar, Aldershot, England, 1992; Johanson, J., and J. Vahlne, "The internationalization process of the firm: a model of knowledge management and increasing foreign market commitments," *Journal of International Business Studies*, Vol. 7 (1977), pp. 22–32; Porter, M.E., *The competitive advantage of nations*, Macmillan, London, 1990; Sölvell, Ö., and I. Zander, "Organization of the Dynamic Multinational Enterprise: The Home Based and the Heterarchical MNE," *Journal of International Studies of Management & Organization*, Vol. 25, Nos. 1–2 (1995), pp. 17–38; Birkinshaw, J., and N. Hood, "Multinational subsidiary evolution: capability and charter change in foreign-owned subsidiary companies," *Academy of Management Review*, Vol. 23, No. 4 (1998), pp. 773–95; and Malnight, T., "The transition from decentralized to network-based MNC structures: an evolutionary perspective," *Journal of International Business Studies*, Vol. 27, No. 1 (1996), pp. 43–65.

The Internet has also rapidly modified the way higher education is structured, generated, and distributed, both globally and locally.[39] Branch offices or campuses can function in much the same way as firms' subsidiary (or networked) units as described above, enhancing opportunities and capabilities for organizational learning. Information technology has already shaped teaching and learning through advances in development of distance learning and now also affects the management of academic institutions.[40] In fact, the ease with which a firm headquarters can interact with subsidiary or networked units also encourages more international activity. Opportunities arise for individuals and groups distributed around the world to contribute to knowledge creation and assimilation.

1.4. Overview of the Chapters and a Summary of Some Key Findings

The contrast between globalization's push toward widespread connected-ness and harmonization and the pull of distinguishing cultures and traditions is what makes the study of globalization so fascinating. The former leads us to study broad trends impacting an industry on a worldwide scale, but the latter reminds us that the same global trend can have different impacts on and elicit different responses from individual players. Similarly, a macro view can reveal overarching issues and opportunities, but a micro view can give us insights into actionable responses.

It is with the juxtaposition of the two views in mind that the following chapters are organized. Chapters 2 and 3 present a macro view of the globalization of management education. Data are presented showing that the globalization of management education is well under way, but also that significant opportunities remain. Furthermore, globalization is highly complex and its impacts are uneven. Together, these two chapters aim to call business school leaders to attention—to think about what is happening and how best to navigate the complexities that globalization presents.

Chapters 4 and 5 provide insights to help guide individual school strategy development and implementation. Every business school with an over-arching objective to provide education that is current and relevant must deal with globalization, yet the ways in which they do so will (and should) vary

---

[39]Bloland, H.G., "Whatever Happened to Postmodernism in Higher Education?: No Requiem in the New Millennium," *Journal of Higher Education*, Vol. 76, No. 2 (2005), pp. 121–50.
[40]Altbach, Philip, "Globalization and the University: Myths and realities in an unequal world," *Tertiary Education and Management*, Vol. 10, No. 1 (2004), pp. 3–25.

according to mission, context, and resources. A comprehensive strategy begins with learning objectives and their implications for curriculum development and faculty research, but also looks more broadly at supporting strategies, processes, and resources (including physical, financial, and human capital).

Finally, Chapter 6 argues that although globalization may be inevitable, the pace and benefits/costs will depend on leaders across the management education industry, as well as on leaders in higher education more broadly. The chapter discusses what can be done in order to steer the best possible course.

The outline that follows is intended to convey the main themes of each section and also to guide readers to the section(s) most relevant to their specific interests and needs.

1.4.1. Chapter 2: The Global Nature of Management Education

Those readers with a thirst for data will find an abundance in Chapter 2, which attempts to describe the current level of globalization within management education along several dimensions. Our effort to describe the global management education landscape reveals much that is known and unknown regarding the thousands of management education providers around the world. Yet it calls—loudly—for business school leaders to pay attention, not because of *how much* is going on, but because of the broad, complex, and highly dynamic nature of what is happening.

The chapter begins with a brief examination of the emergence of management education around the word. This historical perspective is important because it enables us to see current trends as part of a longer trajectory. Globalization of management education is not a new phenomenon of the twenty-first century. In fact, since its emergence, management education has been linked to growth in international trade and globalization. Furthermore, the state of the industry today exists because of the cross-border diffusion of models and ideas that has occurred throughout the twentieth century.

The remainder of the chapter focuses on pulling together data from numerous sources to describe the globalization of management education today, with indicators of changes in *demand* from management education consumers and shifts in the number and connectedness of the institutions that *supply* it.

On the demand side, the proportion of the population seeking higher education is increasing in nearly every country. This trend affects providers of higher education in all disciplines, and affects both undergraduate- and graduate-level education (though the impact on the latter lags the impact on the former). Across countries, increases or decreases in the overall size of the population can augment or minimize the effect of the growing emphasis on attaining higher education credentials.

Yet savvy industry analysts and business school leaders will not be content with simply knowing where demand is increasing and by how much. They will instead look at demand for *different types* of management education—such as undergraduate- versus graduate-level education, or emphases on particular industries and skill sets. These aspects cannot easily be measured, but consideration of economic and labor market developments in various regions does suggest ways in which shifts are occurring.

On the supply side, the data point to several characteristics that are emerging to define the globalization of management education. The first of these is the sheer volume of *local* management education providers that have emerged to service the growing demand for management education around the world.

The second feature is the extent to which the impact of these providers grows when one considers that many have developed mechanisms for extending their reach and influence across national borders. Data from an AACSB survey of member institutions[41] is presented, which reveals that four out of every five survey participants reported that their school maintained one or more collaborative agreements with other business schools.

A still greater number of management education providers—at least one in five of the global total—have taken a proactive step toward affiliating themselves with an international network of schools. Though some affiliations may be established through simple paperwork and the payment of a membership fee, we see this as an indication that business schools—for networking, developmental, reputational, recruitment, or other purposes— are looking beyond their own national borders in a strategic way.

These and other trends suggest that, while substantial global growth in management education providers will continue in some regions of the world, management education's next phase of development will be characterized less by the proliferation of providers than by the development of strategic connections between them. Given the numerous forces working to shape management education today and our hypothesis (and hope) that business school collaborations will become more strategic, the analysis in this section

---

[41]AACSB International, AACSB Member Collaboration Survey 2008, Internal survey data, 2008.

also provides a useful reference point for comparison against future "maps" of the global management education landscape.

1.4.2. Chapter 3: The Fault Lines of Management Education Globalization

Because the data presented in Chapter 2 fail to tell the whole story of the dynamics shaping globalization of management education today, Chapter 3 builds on the indicators described in the previous chapter to provide some perspectives about what makes globalization so complex. It argues that the outcomes of globalization in the aggregate are good, but that impacts are likely to be asymmetric. The chapter explores asymmetries along four dimensions: economics, culture, public policy, and positioning.

Economic imbalances play a significant role in the globalization of management education. Resource constraints at the individual (e.g., student) or organizational (e.g., business school) level impact student and faculty recruitment, and may place limitations on the globalization strategies that a school can adopt. These constraints are aggravated or alleviated by broader economic realities; imbalances in exchange rates, average GDP/capita, and academic salary norms impact the rate of brain drain (or brain gain) for schools and communities.

Globalization also has a tendency to highlight differences in culture and tradition across communities, with many implications for globalization of higher education. Concerns that globally dominant practices are adopted at the expense of a loss of cultural identity are common. Differences in traditional learning and teaching styles have implications for culturally diverse classrooms, while differences in work styles and organizational decision-making frameworks cause difficulty for schools with cross-border partnerships or operations. Even definitions of quality vary based on values and traditions, with implications for international accreditation frameworks.

Ironically, some of the most significant opportunities and obstacles are presented at the national level, through policies and regulations impacting higher education delivery, individual mobility, and resource allocation. From a national perspective, generally two drivers of such policies exist: higher education as a component of global trade and higher education as a component of national competitiveness. The past several years have seen initiatives (through policy changes, marketing campaigns, and the provision of financial or other incentives) by many countries to attract foreign students or education providers, but we have also seen the notable absence or reversal of such initiatives in other countries. National regulations of local and foreign higher education providers fall along a spectrum ranging from relatively laissez-faire to very strict. The complexities of broad variation across and sudden changes within national settings challenge schools to develop sustainable and far-reaching internationalization strategies.

The strategies that schools employ are also significant in that they help to determine the positioning of the school relative to others. With the rise in individual mobility across borders and the development of faster and broader distribution channels for information (including global rankings), it is increasingly likely that a business school may not necessarily share the same geographic location with its peers and competitors. This environment calls for schools to have a well-defined mission and to be acutely aware of their unique strengths as a foundation for differentiation.

1.4.3. *Chapter 4: Responses to Forces of Change: A Focus on Curricular Content*

Chapters 4 and 5 shift the focus of analysis to the micro level by looking at what individual business schools are doing, and could be doing, to better respond to the evolving circumstances described in the previous chapters.

Chapter 4 argues that while curriculum development is the most important area in which business schools should focus their globalization-related efforts, evidence suggests that business schools are not yet doing enough to globalize their curricula. Given the interconnectedness of the world's economies, we believe that business, in each of its various fields and disciplines, cannot be taught, understood, or conducted in an entirely local context. By nature, therefore, business schools have a responsibility to ensure a minimum level of global awareness or engagement among students and faculty, and to go beyond that threshold as appropriate, given the specific needs of the stakeholders served.

Over the past several decades, business schools have made efforts to internationalize the content of their degree programs, but in many cases they have struggled to do so consistently, comprehensively, or effectively. An analysis of a sample of business schools suggests that, with some exceptions, schools place a greater emphasis on the incorporation of global experiential learning opportunities than on the development and integration of global content within the curriculum. Motivational, structural, and cognitive barriers all play a role in impeding development in this dimension.

The chapter aims to provide schools with guidance for advancing curriculum development in a way that more effectively provides students with the knowledge and perspectives called for by today's rapidly evolving business environment. We do not go so far as to argue that there is a global "canon" that all schools should include in their educational programs; the curriculum will most certainly vary according to the mission of the school and the student population served. We do, however, call upon survey results from academic thought leaders that suggest that efforts to bridge the gap should focus on cross-country differences and their business implications. Additionally, we explore curriculum design models in order to guide schools in determining just how to incorporate these new dimensions. And we look at the vital role of course content—an area where we believe a large gap currently exists—and the supplemental role of various experiential learning activities as part of a comprehensive curriculum design.

It is our hope that this chapter will motivate more schools to shift, rebalance, or refocus content to incorporate appropriate international and intercultural dimensions, or to more effectively balance discussion of ideas and their applications in local and global contexts.

1.4.4. Chapter 5: Responses to Forces of Change: A Focus on Structures and Processes

Chapter 5 focuses on business school strategies related to the structures and processes that often complement attention to curricula. The chapter draws upon data from the AACSB survey of member schools' collaborations and from a series of case studies of the internationalization efforts of various business schools, in an effort to explore the common threads and unique approaches of schools with different missions and objectives. Specifically, the chapter focuses on strategies related to collaborative agreements, collaborative degree program structures, establishment of a global "footprint," and a school's most important asset—its faculty. The chapter concludes with insights taken from the case studies to guide schools in implementation. Among the findings are the following:

First, in webs of partnerships, some connections are stronger than others. Many of the schools we studied maintain numerous basic-level partnership agreements, but over time they have begun to focus on strengthening relationships with a core set of partner schools. Their experiences provide insights for other schools regarding the formation of mission-appropriate partnerships that support globalization strategies. Essential to the strengthening of partnerships is trust: partners base a deepening relationship on a sense of trust that is earned and proved over time.

Second, globalization of faculty is about much more than country of origin. Ensuring that faculty members are able to competently and confidently engage the world beyond their home school's borders is an important part of the globalization strategies at the schools we studied. This task requires more than simply recruiting individuals who have lived and worked in another country; it also calls for ongoing professional development opportunities that broaden faculty members' perspectives and experiences.

Third, schools utilize a mix of standardization, adaptation, and customization strategies. Like the businesses they study, business schools must determine the appropriate mix of standardization, adaptation, and customization when exploring new ventures. Many globally-oriented programs manifest as adaptations of domestic programs to a joint venture or international sphere. In fact, product line extensions were common among the schools we studied, indicating that schools see a clear benefit in sticking to a model that "works" and replicating it with perhaps some slight alterations in other contexts. At the same time, schools made strategic decisions about the adaptations needed in order to best meet the needs of the stakeholders served.

Fourth, business schools seek a balance between "local" and "global" dimensions. The schools we studied manage the contradiction that they are at once local and global, seeking to strike an appropriate balance between the two characterizations. That balance, and the means by which it is achieved, varies for each school according to its own mission and context.

Finally, exploration and experimentation serve as a foundation for building. For all of the schools we studied, globalization has been a continuous process fueled by experimentation, learning by doing, and efforts to build upon and fine-tune incremental successes. Optional programs become mandatory. Unsuccessful initiatives are discontinued or modified. These adjustments require ongoing self-analysis and a willingness to admit shortcomings.

1.4.5. Chapter 6: Summary and Implications

Chapter 6 serves multiple purposes. It brings together and synthesizes important ideas from other chapters and, as a consequence, can serve as a useful summary of the report and "bookend" to Chapter 1. Chapter 6 also intends to elevate discussion to a higher level and, as a result, reveal new insights and opportunities to lead change. Most importantly, the chapter is a call to action for management educators to lead the globalization of management education within their schools and across the industry.

The globalization of management education matters because of the economic and social benefits it can bring. These benefits are more likely to be achieved, and to be achieved more responsibly, when business schools produce graduates with a global mindset and intellectual contributions that advance the knowledge, practice, and teaching of international business and management. There are also more direct benefits to management education stakeholders, including students, employers, and faculty, because globalization expands the degree program choices available to them and can improve quality by intensifying international competition and increasing benchmarking opportunities. The globalization of management education also matters because it informs critical debates that will shape the future of globalization in society.

Anyone that has read the previous chapters will not be surprised by the conclusion that business schools have not achieved their full potential in globalization. According to the Task Force, with respect to learning outcomes, there remain unmet expectations and with respect to intellectual capital, the foundations are weak. The degree to which the globalization of management education has elevated overall quality is too early to tell, and there are several factors conspiring to create an uncertain future.

Why has there been limited progress? Pressure and motivation for globalization has intensified, but globalization is still new and complicated, and it is costly and risky. There are regulations and norms that are significant barriers to change and externalities that suggest a natural tendency to under-invest in globalization activities. By reviewing the range of impediments to change, the Task Force begins to show that current barriers are not insurmountable and to shift attention to opportunities for proactive, industry-level leadership to accelerate and improve the globalization of management education.

For any business school there are important implications for its mission and purpose, opportunities to exploit complementarities, and requirements to invest in staff capabilities. Much of the discussion in Chapter 6 about implications for management educators draws on material from Chapters 4 and 5, but makes a tighter connection between actions and outcomes. It also begins to view business schools in relation to each other and to consider the shared benefits of individual action; as a consequence, it helps transition to a discussion about opportunities for concerted, collective action.

A major contribution of Chapter 6 is to identify industry-wide initiatives that can accelerate and improve globalization. These initiatives might include joint efforts to collect and share data and information, convene educational meetings, and conduct benchmarking exercises. They also include extending and augmenting quality improvement/assurance mechanisms to assist business schools and society to deal more effectively with globalization. Other industry-wide initiatives could include coordinating efforts to overcome traditions and norms that have been barriers to globalization and collaborating to develop management education capacity around the globe.

The Task Force recognizes that governments (national, regional, and local) and supra-national organizations (such as the World Bank and United Nations) have enormous influence on the globalization of management education. The benefits from globalization may be accelerated or delayed by the policies they adopt in relation to higher education. Accordingly, the Task Force recommends that government entities embrace several underlying principles that both safeguard their constituents and entertain—if not encourage the development of—new opportunities related to quality management education.

The chapter concludes by recommending areas for additional research related to the globalization of management education. This report, necessarily, is the product of numerous trade-offs between depth and breadth of coverage in the vast space of issues that relate—directly and indirectly—to the globalization of management education; furthermore, globalization will continue to evolve in unforeseen ways. The report's call to action, therefore, also includes a call for others to extend the findings of this report in new and deeper directions in order to influence the pace and direction of change.

Chapter 2

The Global Nature of Management Education

Most people today would agree that management education is somewhere along a trajectory of globalization, but few agree on exactly where any individual school—much less the entire industry—falls along that trajectory. Those who argue that business schools have not moved far enough along the path point to inertia, resource constraints, or lack of direction as obstacles that business schools have been too slow to overcome. Others, such as Ben Wildavsky, note that business schools "were early adapters to globalization," relative to schools in other fields.[1]

In fact, business schools have already come a long way in terms of globalization, but the road ahead remains full of untapped and underdeveloped opportunities. And the sheer complexity of today's global management education landscape, coupled with its highly dynamic nature, commands the attention of any individual or institution striving to navigate in this environment.

Our aim in this chapter is to broadly describe some of the many dimensions captured in that trajectory of globalization and provide readers with a shared understanding of some of the indicators showing that management education is globalizing in complex ways. Achieving a consensus on exactly where business schools fall along the trajectory of globalization is neither realistically feasible nor necessary. Such a task is impeded by unavailable or incomparable information and by the natural tendency of individuals to see the world through different lenses. Rather than drill down into any single dimension, therefore, the chapter seeks to provide a sense of the big picture, and to enable business schools to see themselves within the new global paradigm that is emerging.

---

[1]Wildavsky, Ben, *The Great Brain Race: How Global Universities Are Reshaping the World*, Princeton University Press, Princeton, NJ, 2010, p. 120.

The first section of this chapter provides a historical context for under-standing what is happening today and gives an idea of what the early part of the trajectory looks like. This overview of the development of manage-ment education globally reveals that: 1) management education has since its emergence been linked to international trade and globalization; and 2) the state of the industry today exists because of the cross-border diffusion of management education models and ideas that has occurred throughout the past century.

To shift our viewpoint forward, we next move to a series of indicators of contemporary globalization within management education by focusing on the structural characteristics of the industry. This analysis is divided between two sections: In the first, we examine global shifts in the populations, objectives, and mobility of individuals seeking a business degree. In the second, we examine the nature of the supply side of the equation, with a focus on the number and breadth of providers and the growing web of connections between them.

2.1. Early Phase Globalization: The Global Emergence and Diffusion of Management Education Models and Practices

While various sources chronicle the emergence of management education within a particular country or region,[2] to our knowledge no substantial efforts have been made to compile these accounts and to provide a comprehensive analysis of the development of management education globally. Existing accounts do illustrate, however, that the global emergence of management education has been influenced by (and likely has also influenced) the integration of the world's economies that has occurred over the last two centuries.

As business schools began to emerge in various corners of the world, two themes in particular dominated. First, even the earliest business schools were linked to trends in international trade and globalization; in many ways, today's renewed focus on serving the needs of a "global" business environment takes us back full-circle to business schools' roots. Second, the emergence of management education as a global phenomenon would not

---

[2]See, for example, Khurana, Rakesh, *From Higher Aims to Hired Hands: The Social Transformation of American Business Schools and the Unfulfilled Promise of Management as a Profession*, Princeton University Press, Princeton, NJ, 2007; Gupta, Vipm, and Kamala Gollakota, "Critical Challenges for Indian Business Schools as Partners in Development," *Decision*, Vol. 32, No. 2 (2005), pp. 35–56; and Antunes, Don, and Howard Thomas, "The Competitive (Dis)Advantages of European Business Schools," *Long Range Planning*, Vol. 40, No. 3 (2007), pp. 382–404.

have taken place were it not for substantial diffusion of management education models and ideas across borders.

Management education, as we know it today, emerged during a timeframe that Thomas Friedman describes as the world's second wave of globalization, taking place between the years 1800 and 2000:

> In Globalization 2.0 the key agent of change, the dynamic force driving multinational integration, was multinational companies. These multinationals went global for markets and labor, spearheaded first by the expansion of the Dutch and English joint-stock companies and the Industrial Revolution. In the first half of this era, global integration was powered by falling transportation costs, thanks to the steam engine and the railroad, and in the second half by falling telecommunication costs—thanks to the diffusion of the telegraph, telephones, the PC, satellites, fiber-optic cable, and the early version of the World Wide Web. It was during this era that we really saw the birth and maturation of a global economy, in the sense that there was enough movement of goods and information from continent to continent for there to be a global market, with global arbitrage in products and labor.[3]

The "business schools" that emerged throughout Europe and North America during the late eighteenth and early nineteenth centuries were largely technical or vocational in nature. Still, there is evidence that even these schools recognized the importance of including dimensions of "international business" within their curricula. At the Portuguese Aula do Comercio (School of Commerce) established in Lisbon in 1759, for example, one of the four subjects taught in the two-to-three-year course was the "study of weights and measures from different countries … [and] methods for the exchange of currencies."[4]

The late nineteenth century witnessed the emergence of university-based management education in the U.S. model with the 1881 establishment of

---

[3]Friedman, Thomas L., *The World is Flat: A Brief History of the 21st Century*, Picador Press, New York, 2007, p. 9. For a different, but similar take, see also O'Rourke, Kevin H., and Jeffrey G. Williamson, "Once more: When did globalisation begin?" *European Review of Economic History*, Vol. 8, No. 1 (2004), pp. 109–17: "Globalisation became economically meaningful only with the dawn of the nineteenth century, and it came on in a rush" (p. 109).
[4]Rodrigués, Lucia Lima, Delfina Gomes, and Russell Craig, "The Portuguese School of Commerce, 1759–1844: A reflection of the 'Enlightenment,'" *Accounting History*, Vol. 9, No. 3 (2004), p. 60.

The Wharton School at the University of Pennsylvania and its Bachelor of Finance degree program.[5] Some scholars have suggested that this and other early business schools in the United States were launched in pursuit of "higher aims" such as the professionalization of management in an economy that was becoming increasingly complex.[6] While evidence of such a movement does exist, the reality is that these "higher aims" were, at best, an initial motivation for only a handful of the business schools that exist today around the world. Our research reveals that more practical motivations for creating business schools played a significant role, particularly the growing importance of international trade and the implications of effective management for national competitiveness on a global scale.

International trade, for example, was a recurring theme in the missions of early European business schools. In France, ESC Rouen was established in 1871 with the mission "to train business leaders or directors of overseas agencies, consular agents capable of representing France in a suitable manner in its international trade relations."[7] Similarly, the founding documents for Germany's Handelshochschule (HHL) Leipzig, established in 1897, reference the new challenges facing business leaders as a result of increased international competition.[8] The Imperial Export Academy, established in 1898 in Vienna, Austria (now the Vienna University of Economics and Business), reportedly focused its curriculum on preparing students "for employment mainly in international trade."[9]

By the turn of the century, as the Tuck School of Administration and Finance[10] at Dartmouth College was launching the U.S.'s (and the world's) first graduate-level business degree program, undergraduate-level business education was beginning to spread further within Europe and beyond. The University of Birmingham offered the United Kingdom's first "Bachelor of Commerce" degree in 1902, and soon afterward the degree

---

[5]The school reports that its "global network" began with the first class of graduates in 1884—one of whom left the U.S. to begin a career in his native Japan.

[6]Rakesh Khurana suggests this underlying motivation in the sociological perspective introduced in his 2007 book, *From Higher Aims to Hired Hands: The Social Transformation of American Business Schools and the Unfulfilled Promise of Management as a Profession*, Princeton University Press, Princeton, NJ.

[7]Rouen Business School, History: From 1871 until today, electronic document, http://www.rouenbs.fr/en/rouen-business-school/history, accessed May 6, 2010.

[8]Raydt, Herm (ed.), "Zur Begründung einer Handels-Hochschule in Leipzig" (To Justify a Trade School in Leipzig), memorandum on behalf of the Leipzig Chamber of Commerce, 1897, p. 20.

[9]Vienna University of Economics and Business, "WU History," 2009, electronic document, http://www.wu.ac.at/strategy/en/history/, accessed August 18, 2010.

[10]The Tuck School of Administration and Finance is now named the Tuck School of Business.

spread to the (then) British colony of India. There, the first collegiate-level school of commerce, Sydenham College, was established in 1913 in Mumbai (then Bombay), thanks in part to support from the British governor, Lord Sydenham of Combe. The school targeted clerks and supervisors in the banking, transport, and accounting fields and emphasized "basic skills about the principles of trade and commerce."[11]

In China, the first university-level business schools began to appear a few years later (though business training had emerged as early as 1893[12]). Here again, one finds evidence of the influence of then-established Western business schools. Both the first chancellor and the director of academic affairs at the Shanghai University of Commerce,[13] established in 1921, had recently studied at Columbia University in the United States. Though not graduates of the Columbia Business School, they are likely to have observed the development of business education at other U.S. universities and the establishment of the Columbia Business School itself in 1916. In fact, according to the school's website, "in the 1923–1924 academic year, 11 of the 16 Chinese teachers at the Shanghai University of Commerce had earned their degrees from outstanding foreign universities like Harvard University, Columbia University, the University of Pennsylvania, the University of Illinois and Edinburgh University."[14]

In the 1950s, we find the first examples of *direct* involvement by established business schools, primarily located in the U.S., in the development of management education providers in other countries. These early "cross-border collaborations" were primarily intended as capacity building efforts, and in many cases funding was provided by the foreign assistance arm of the U.S. government (which in 1961 became formally known as the U.S. Agency for International Development, or USAID) or through grants from the Ford Foundation. One example was the founding, in 1954, of Fundação Getulio Vargas in São Paulo, Brazil, which emerged through a partnership between Brazilian business leaders and a group of Michigan State University faculty members.

---

[11]Gupta, Vipm, and Kamala Gollakota, "Critical Challenges for Indian Business Schools as Partners in Development," *Decision*, Vol. 32, No. 2 (2005), p. 36.

[12]In 1893, Zhang Zhidong, then governor of Hubei and Hunan Provinces, established the Ziqiang Institute (the predecessor to Wuhan University), the first to include business training among the offered courses of study.

[13]The Shanghai University of Commerce was a predecessor to today's Shanghai University of Finance and Economics.

[14]Shanghai University of Finance and Economics, History of SUFE, 2010, electronic document, http://www.shufe.edu.cn/structure/english/AboutSUFE/HistoryofSUFE.htm, accessed August 17, 2010.

In the same year, Harvard Business School became involved with prominent Turkish businessmen in the development of the Turkish Institute of Business Administration (now the Institute of Business Economy at Istanbul University), and in 1955 the Wharton Business School lent support to the development of the Institute of Business Administration in Pakistan.[15] Faculty members from Harvard Business School would go on to be involved in the development of numerous other business schools including IMEDE[16] (Switzerland, 1957), IESE (Spain, 1958), the Indian Institute of Management-Ahmedabad (India, 1962), INCAE (Costa Rica, 1963), and the Asian Institute of Management (Philippines, 1965). IESE would then "pay it forward" by assisting in the development of many other business schools, primarily in Latin America, over the next several decades. This approach to capacity building continued through the second half of the twentieth century, and many of the newly established "seed" schools went on to influence the development of additional business schools in their respective countries and regions.

Despite all of this activity, as the end of the twentieth century neared, pockets of countries remained where management education was non-existent. However, with the 1989 breakup of the Soviet Union and the fall of communism in Central Asia and Eastern Europe, a new demand for management education surfaced in response to the needs of the new transitional economies of the former Soviet republics and Eastern bloc client states. Many universities in these states had no experience with management education, thus the Western template of business schools became particularly important.[17] In Poland, for example, Western-style business schools did not exist before 1990, but between 1990 and 2005 no fewer than 93 dedicated "business schools" (over two-thirds of which were private) came into existence, while an even greater number of other higher education institutions began offering degrees in business, commerce, and related fields.[18]

A complete account and analysis of the global emergence of management education would be a substantial project that, while valuable, is well beyond the scope of this report. Still, while this "glimpse" at management education's early years is vastly oversimplified, we believe that some understanding of the motivations for the establishment of management education, the methods that

---

[15]Later, the Institute of Business Administration in Pakistan also received developmental assistance from the University of Southern California.

[16]Nestle SA engaged four HBS faculty members to help develop IMEDE. The school merged with IMI in 1990 to form IMD.

[17]Scott, Peter, "Reflections on the Reform of Higher Education in Central and Eastern Europe," *Higher Education in Europe*, Vol. 27, Nos. 1–2 (2002), pp. 137–52.

[18]Leven, Bozena, "Poland's Transition in Business Education," *American Journal of Business Education*, Vol. 3, No. 1 (2010), pp. 53–60.

contribute to its emergence in different parts of the world, and its connection to global economic trends provides an important context for our discussion of the globalization of management education. These themes will remain important for the future evolution of management education in a global context.

2.2. Management Education Today: Characterizing the Global Nature of Students

We begin our analysis of the globalization of management education today by taking into account global shifts in the individuals who seek a business degree and in where they receive it. Market size and needs impact school strategic decisions, particularly with regard to recruiting international students or sending programs or facilities abroad. Supply and demand dynamics (with the added influence of mobility by students and providers) play a major role in globalization generally and also in globalization within education.

The starting point for our characterization of the changing nature of management education consumers is a focus on shifting (for the most part, increasing) higher education access rates and on demographic changes that impact the traditional higher education age population. Because information specific to management education students is more difficult to obtain, we draw primarily upon information regarding the volume of higher education consumers, and assume generally parallel trends among management education consumers as a subset of that group.

This approach, however, provides only a foundation for understanding how, against this baseline, other globalization-related trends impact more specific educational needs. Economic development and integration have implications for the type of management education demanded by a given population. As economies evolve, graduate-level education is likely to become more valued as are "lifelong learning" opportunities for individuals in later stages of their careers. This likelihood has specific effects on demand for management education—which becomes increasingly important as economies get more complex and is an attractive field for employees seeking ongoing professional development.

Finally, what pulls these trends together and makes them particularly relevant for a discussion of globalization of management education is the issue of mobility. Mobility indicators show that student mobility is increasing and that students of business make a relatively high contribution to overall rates of cross-border student mobility.

2.2.1. Higher Education Access and Demographic Changes

Much has been documented about the "massification" of higher education— or the increasing proportion of the adult population with higher education qualifications—in both developed and developing countries. For example, among 78 countries for which the UNESCO[19] Institute for Statistics reported tertiary enrollment data in 2000 and 2008, all but six countries show an increase in enrollment ratios over that short but recent timeframe. At least five countries transitioned from what is considered an "elite" system of higher education to a "mass" system of higher education, while 14 transitioned from "mass" to "universal" systems.[20] In some cases, increases in access rates offset drops in student enrollment caused by decreasing populations of the traditional tertiary education age; in other parts of the world—particularly those where higher education is least developed—rising higher education attainment rates only amplify the added demand from a growing population.

In developing countries, efforts to increase enrollment in primary and secondary education (often led by UNESCO in cooperation with other non-governmental organizations and national governments) have laid a foundation for higher levels of tertiary education attainment. For instance, of the 13 African nations for which UNESCO has the information available for the years 2000 and 2008, all reported increases in the gross enrollment ratio for tertiary education. As noted by the Global Foundation for Management Education (GFME), Sub-Saharan Africa and (to a lesser extent) the Near East and Latin America will see the combined influence of a growing population and increasing higher education participation rates leading to higher demand for tertiary education.[21]

Even in developed countries where tertiary education attainment is already relatively high, we see the impact of national initiatives to make college or university education completion rates even higher. Presumably, these efforts relate to the conviction that a more highly educated population contributes positively to national competitiveness. Organization of Economic Cooperation and Development (OECD) member countries including Australia, England, Sweden, and the United States have all recently announced initiatives to increase the national higher education participation and/or completion rates within a designated timeframe (see box). In some

---

[19]UNESCO is the acronym for the United Nations Educational, Scientific, and Cultural Organization.

[20]"Elite" higher education systems are in countries where less than 15 percent of the tertiary-aged population is enrolled in tertiary education. "Mass" systems have between 15 and 50 percent of the population enrolled, and "universal" systems have more than 50 percent enrolled.

[21]Global Foundation for Management Education, "The Global Management Education Landscape: Shaping the future of business schools," 2008, electronic document, http://www.gfme.org/landscape/reportonlineversion.pdf, accessed January 31, 2010.

countries, increased access is likely to include a substantial focus on associate's degrees, vocational degrees, or their equivalent; the entire impact of these initiatives will not be felt immediately at the bachelor's level and above. Additionally, we leave it to educational scholars to debate whether the increase in access is or is not accompanied by compromises in the quality of education delivered. However, even partial progress toward achieving these objectives would impact the demand for management education relative to the size of the normal student population.

Examples of recent OECD member initiatives to increase higher education participation and/or completion rates:

- Australia—In 2009, then Federal Education Minister (now Prime Minister) Julia Gillard announced reforms intended to support a goal of increasing the proportion of 25 to 34 year olds with undergraduate degrees from 32 percent to 40 percent by 2025.*
- England—In 1999, the Labour Party announced its objective of raising the higher education participation rate of 18–30 year olds from about 43 percent to 50 percent by 2010, mostly through two-year vocational programs.**
- Sweden—The government has set a target that 50 percent of the population born in a given year will have begun university-level education by the age of 25.[†]
- United States—In 2009, President Barack Obama announced his goal for the nation to have the world's highest proportion of college graduates by the year 2020.[‡]

---

*Gillard, Julia, Speech at Universities Australia conference, March 4, 2009, electronic document, http://www.deewr.gov.au/Ministers/Gillard/Media/Speeches/Pages/Article_090304_155721.aspx, accessed August 23, 2010.

**Clark, Tony, OECD Thematic Review of Tertiary Education, Country Report: United Kingdom, 2006, electronic document, http://www.education.gov.uk/research/data/uploadfiles/RR767.pdf, accessed March 31, 2010. P. 19.

[†]Swedish National Agency for Higher Education, OECD Thematic Review of Tertiary Education, Country Background Report for Sweden, 2006, electronic document, http://www.oecd.org/dataoecd/20/29/37524407.pdf, accessed March 31, 2010.

[‡]Obama, Barack, Address to Joint Session of Congress, February 24, 2009, electronic document, http://www.whitehouse.gov/the_press_office/Remarks-of-President-Barack-Obama-Address-to-Joint-Session-of-Congress/, accessed August 23, 2010.

In some regions, increased access to higher education is particularly notable among the female population. (See Table 2.1 for some examples.) Recent reports note that, worldwide, female students of higher education now slightly outnumber their male counterparts.[22] In some countries, this shift is a result of years of efforts to expand access for women to primary and secondary education. In others, it is the result of proactive efforts to encourage women to enroll at the university level. King Abdullah bin Abdul Aziz al-Saud is leading incremental change in Saudi Arabia, for example, by encouraging more women to seek positions in business and law (both traditionally filled by men),[23] and by supporting the development of a new university with an unprecedented level of integration between men and women. According to Philip Altbach et al., initiatives undertaken in Ghana, Kenya, Uganda, and Tanzania have lowered college admission cutoff scores for women in order to increase female enrollment.[24]

Table 2.1: Number of Women Enrolled per 100 Men in Selected Countries.

Country	1988	2005
World	64	105
United States	116	140
Netherlands	81	108
Chile	82	96
Malaysia	87	131
India	47	70
China	55	95
Brazil	106	132
Pakistan	46	88
Bangladesh	25	53
Mexico	66	99

Source: Inside Higher Ed.[25]

---

[22]For example, Fine, Philip, Wagdy Sawahel, and Maya Jarjour, "GLOBAL: Women no longer the second sex," *University World News*, October 25, 2009, electronic document, http://www.universityworldnews.com/article.php?story=20091023110831548, accessed August 20, 2010.

[23]Mills, Andrew, "Reforms to Women's Education Make Slow Progress in Saudi Arabia," *The Chronicle of Higher Education*, August 3, 2009, electronic document, http://chronicle.com/article/Saudi-Universities-Reach/47519/, accessed July 22, 2010.

[24]Altbach, Philip, Liz Reisberg, and Laura E. Rumbley, "Tracking a Global Academic Revolution," *Change*, Vol. 42, No. 2 (2010), pp. 30–39.

[25]Jaschik, Scott, "International 'Leapfrogging,'" *Inside Higher Ed*, October 5, 2009, electronic document, http://www.insidehighered.com/news/2009/10/05/global, accessed August 20, 2010.

On the other hand, demographic changes resulting in smaller populations (or at least, smaller tertiary-education-aged populations) have the potential to temper increases in the percent of individuals seeking higher education qualifications in some countries or regions. In China, for example, the population aged 18 to 22 years is projected to decrease from 124.84 million in 2008 to 87.97 million in 2020. The government's response is to increase tertiary education participation at a rate that will enable enrollments across existing institutions to remain steady at about 27.5 million enrolled per year. The strategy entails raising the participation rate from 22 percent of the 18-to-22-year-old population in 2008 to 31.1 percent in 2020.[26]

In neighboring Japan, the demographic shift has already begun to severely impact some educational providers. Japan is widely recognized as having the world's most rapidly aging population. Since peaking in 1992 at 2.1 million, the number of 18-year-olds has plummeted by more than 700,000. In 2009, the Ministry of Education, Culture, Sports, Science, and Technology (MEXT) estimated that, of the nation's approximately 550 private four-year universities, 47 percent were failing to meet government-set recruitment targets, and a similar percentage was reported to be in debt. Though many private institutions are turning to international students to fill the void, up to one-third of the country's private universities are expected to close or merge within the next ten years.[27]

2.2.2.   Labor Market Demands for Management Education Graduates

Across economies, the pace and direction of economic development influence not only the supply of and demand for higher education graduates generally but also the need for the particular set of knowledge and skills that business schools provide. Increasing demand for management talent must be met by management education providers who understand the appropriate level(s) and orientation(s) of education needed within each region. In a "semi-global" world, considerable variation exists in how these needs are manifest across and within countries. While a

---

[26]Gallagher, Michael, Abrar Hasan, Mary Canning, Howard Newby, Lichia Saner-Yui, and Ian Whitman, "OECD Reviews of Tertiary Education: China," OECD Publishing, 2009, pp. 41–42, electronic document, http://www.oecd.org/dataoecd/42/23/42286617.pdf, accessed February 2, 2010.

[27]McNeill, David, "Enrollment Crisis Threatens Japan's Private Colleges," *The Chronicle of Higher Education*, October 25, 2009, electronic document, http://chronicle.com/article/Enrollment-Crisis-Threatens/48909/, accessed July 22, 2010.

detailed market analysis of the different contexts around the globe is well beyond the scope of this report, we offer some discussion of the ways in which economic contexts affect the dynamics of global management education demand.

First, though actual levels of demand at the undergraduate and graduate levels are difficult to ascertain globally, evidence suggests that demand for graduate programs is on the rise. According to the Graduate Management Admissions Council (GMAC), more prospective students worldwide are taking the Graduate Management Admissions Test (GMAT) to apply to master's and doctoral-level programs. GMAC reports a 15-percent increase in GMAT exams taken worldwide from 2000 to 2008, and a seven-percent increase from 2006 to 2008.[28] GMAC has furthermore reported that 3,710 new graduate management programs were added between 1997 and 2007. In 1997, 74 new programs were added compared to 641 new programs in 2007. Of the total programs added in these ten years, over 80 percent were based outside the United States.[29]

These findings make sense given that macroeconomic trends continue to point to high, sustained economic growth in emerging markets, particularly those in Asia, and that one generally expects indicators of economic growth and development to correspond to increasing demand for trained management talent. According to data from the International Monetary Fund (IMF) (see Figure 2.1), within Asia, the ASEAN-5 (composed of Indonesia, Malaysia, the Philippines, Thailand, and Vietnam) has the fastest projected growth, followed by the Newly Industrialized Asian Economies (composed of Chinese Taipei, Hong Kong SAR, Singapore, and South Korea). Growth in these regions is widely predicted to be twice or more as high as growth in the G7 (United States, Japan, Germany, United Kingdom, France, Italy, and Canada) and the European Union through 2014.

On an individual country basis, the GDP growth leaders are the BRICs (Brazil, Russia, India, and China) and Mexico. China, by far, will remain the largest economy among the large emerging markets followed by Russia, Brazil, India, and Mexico. (See Figure 2.2.) A recent paper published by Goldman Sachs similarly projected that together the BRIC economies have

---

[28]See Chisholm, Alex, and Courtney Defibaugh, World Geographic Trend Report for GMAT Examinees, 2004–2008, Graduate Management Admission Council, Reston, VA, 2009; and Peyton, Johnette, Geographic Trend Report for Examinees Taking the Graduate Management Admission Test, Graduate Management Admission Council, McLean, VA, 2005.

[29]Anderson, Bethanie L., "From Data to Strategy: Understanding Worldwide Trends in Graduate Management Education," Conference Paper for GMAC Annual Industry Conference 2007, electronic document, http://www.gmac.com/NR/rdonlyres/78E0448D-5D01-4E1A-B439-574E4A101B7C/0/Worldwide_Trends_small_v2.pdf, accessed December 28, 2009.

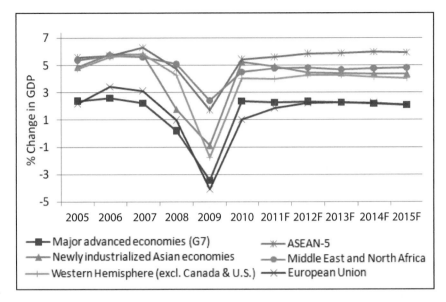

Figure 2.1: Regional Percent Change in GDP, 2005–2015E.
Source: IMF, World Economic Outlook Database, April 2010.[30]

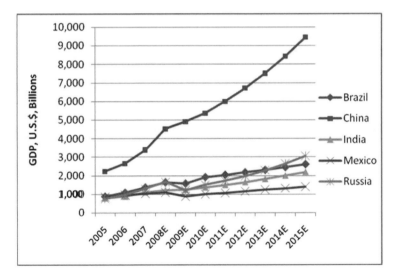

Figure 2.2: Top Five Emerging Market Countries by GDP Growth, 2005 to 2015E.
Source: IMF, World Economic Outlook Database, April 2010.[30]

---

[30]International Monetary Fund, World Economic Outlook Database, April 2010 Edition, electronic document, http://www.imf.org/external/pubs/ft/weo/2010/01/weodata/index.aspx, accessed August 25, 2010.

the potential to be over half the size of the G6 by 2025,[31] and to surpass the G6 in size by 2050 (as measured by GDP).[32] These growth trends suggest considerable opportunity for business schools serving those countries with the greatest anticipated economic growth rates. Increases in demand for graduate-level education are likely to lag increased demand for under-graduate education, as graduate-level education trains a more advanced workforce to serve the needs of a more mature economy.

Second, perhaps more so in developed economies than in emerging economies, a shift from viewing higher education's primary value as advance preparation for a career to recognizing its value as a component of lifelong learning is particularly relevant for management education providers. Mid- to late-career MBA and EMBA degrees, as well as non-degree executive education programs, attract individuals outside the age range typically considered in estimates of the higher education age population. According to a 2006 report by the Executive MBA Council, "more than two-thirds of the Executive MBA Council member programs have entered the market since 1990, and 28 percent since 2000. In the U.S. market, 60 percent of member programs started in the last 16 years, compared to 91 percent for Asia, 83 percent for Latin America and 78 percent for Europe."[33] This growth is likely a result of economic development within these regions as graduate degrees become more valuable assets in increasingly mature, complex economies.

A third important dimension of the economic context is the approach taken by multinationals in the sourcing of talent. In 2003, an estimated 63,000 multinationals were operating around the world (up from only 3,000 in 1990) with an estimated total of 821,000 subsidiaries. Approximately one-fifth of the 90 million people employed by these firms at the time were living in developing countries.[34] Whereas in the past, MNEs operating in the world's emerging economies have relied heavily on expatriate managers or on citizens who have received management training abroad (presuming they return), today local business leaders are leading a push for more and better management education capacity within the countries' own borders. One common driver of this momentum is a need for managers who are equipped to deal with the

---

[31]Here, the G6 refers to the nations of the G7, minus Canada (France, Germany, Italy, Japan, U.S., and U.K.).

[32]Wilson, Dominic, and Roopa Purushothaman, "Dreaming With BRICs: The Path to 2050," *Global Economics Paper No: 99*, The Goldman Sachs Group, Inc., 2003, electronic document, http://www2.goldmansachs.com/ideas/brics/book/99-dreaming.pdf, accessed August 17, 2010.

[33]Executive MBA Council, 2006 Executive MBA Council Survey Results Offer Industry Insights, EMBA Council press release, electronic document, http://www.emba.org/pdf/pressroom/2006_research_results_11_18.pdf, accessed August 17, 2010.

[34]Gabel, Medard, and Henry Bruner, *Global Inc.: An Atlas of the Multinational Corporation*, The New Press, New York, 2003.

unique challenges of emerging markets. For example, the Moscow School of Management, Skolkovo, established in 2006 through a $500 million investment from Russian business leaders, offers an MBA program with a special emphasis on issues such as bribery and corruption that are unlikely to be a focus of business programs in more developed economies.[35]

Finally, we must also consider how the knowledge and skill combination needed across world regions varies by the relative roles of multinational firms, small and medium enterprises, family businesses, and entrepreneurial ventures, as well as how needs vary according to the presence of different industry clusters. For example, as discussed within the Global Entrepreneurship Monitor's *2009 Global Report*, general differences exist in the roles of entrepreneurship within factor-driven, efficiency-driven, and innovation-driven economies.[36] Among the world's knowledge economies, in particular, global economic development has increased demand for managerial skills in specialized industries, such as engineering, healthcare, and the biosciences. Industry clusters in various world regions also influence demand for particular skill sets; for example, the Middle East has seen spectacular success in the financial and real estate sectors.

Deepening global integration also means that all members of the world's labor force—not just employees of multinational enterprises—can benefit from enhanced international and intercultural awareness. Employees of companies with a minimal cross-border presence often must still be able to work comfortably and effectively with international clients, suppliers, and partners. Given that globalization also includes the movement of people to new countries, even employees of companies with no direct cross-border interactions are likely to need to call on intercultural skills in dealing with coworkers and other local business persons. Small businesses with an entirely local focus may feel the impacts of business innovations abroad and of changes in national trade policies.

Though the degree to which firms in other countries experience the same challenge is unclear, evidence does suggest that many U.S. companies are not taking full advantage of international business opportunities. A 2002 survey of large U.S. corporations found that nearly 30 percent of the companies believed they had failed to exploit fully their international

---

[35]Associated Press, "With Help of Russian Business Leaders, M.B.A. School Opens in Moscow," *The New York Times*, September 30, 2009, electronic document, http://www. nytimes.com/2009/10/01/business/global/01iht-mba.html, accessed January 31, 2010.

[36]Bosma, Niels, and Jonathan Levie, 2009 *Global Report*, Global Entrepreneurship Monitor, 2009, electronic document, http://www.gemconsortium.org/download/1282653102864/GEM% 202009%20Global%20Report%20Rev%20140410.pdf, accessed August 24, 2010.

business opportunities due to insufficient personnel with international skills. The firms cited numerous consequences of this deficiency, including missed marketing or business opportunities (21 percent); suffering from a bias toward a U.S. point of view (15 percent); failure to anticipate the needs of international customers (13 percent); failure to take full advantage of expertise available or technological advances occurring abroad (11 percent); and failure to recognize important shifts in host country policies toward foreign-owned corporations (4 percent). A majority of business leaders surveyed—almost 80 percent—expected their overall business to increase notably if they had more internationally competent employees on staff.[37]

2.2.3. *Individual Mobility*

Student mobility continues to increase, with the business and management field proving to be one of the most popular fields for internationally mobile students. The UNESCO Institute for Statistics estimates that, in 2007, about 23 percent of all internationally mobile students studied business and management—a proportion that is greater than that of any other field of study.[38] Similarly, each year since 2004 (the first year for which published data are available), business students have comprised slightly more than one-fifth of all students participating in cross-border study and internship opportunities via the European Union's ERASMUS program.[39] Several trends contribute to growth in individual mobility and to the high participation rate of business students.

First, while higher education trade commitments via the GATS[40] framework have been relatively slow to materialize, many countries have

---

[37]Kedia, Ben L., and Shirley Daniel, "U.S. Business Needs for Employees with International Expertise," conference paper, Conference on Global Challenges and U.S. Higher Education, Duke University, Durham, NC, January 2003, pp. 5, 12–14, and 17, electronic document, http://ducis.jhfc.duke.edu/archives/globalchallenges/pdf/kedia_daniel.pdf, accessed August 17, 2010.

[38]UNESCO Institute for Statistics, "New Trends in International Student Mobility," electronic document, http://www.uis.unesco.org/template/pdf/ged/2009/UIS_press_conference_presentation.pdf, accessed March 30, 2010.

[39]European Commission, Erasmus Statistics, 2010, electronic document, http://ec.europa.eu/education/erasmus/doc920_en.htm, accessed July 22, 2010.

[40]GATS is an acronym for the General Agreement on Trade in Services, a trade liberalization framework among nations.

proclaimed objectives, designated funding, and changed immigration policies in an effort to attract more international students. A sub-section in Chapter 3 on national policies and regulatory environments provides an opportunity to further discuss some of the methods that governments use to influence and shape international student mobility.

Second, trends in cross-border mobility of students at times relate to demographic shifts and resulting implications for supply and demand. This correlation is particularly true for countries that deal with excess capacity of higher education providers established to meet the demands of a once larger student population. In Australia and New Zealand, for example, national-level efforts to recruit international students are a direct response to demographic changes that result in a smaller tertiary-education-aged population. In other cases (particularly the underdeveloped regions of Africa, for example), outbound student mobility is a result of a lack of higher education capacity (if not of providers generally, then of providers deemed of sufficient quality) within the student's home country.

Greater mobility by students is also attributed to new models of cross-border study. In the late 19th and early 20th centuries, only the wealthiest and most connected students had opportunities to travel abroad for education; today, such opportunities are accessible to a much larger portion of the socioeconomic spectrum. At one time, a student interested in studying abroad did so primarily by enrolling at an institution in another country, where he or she pursued a complete degree program. Over time, schools began to facilitate study abroad opportunities in which their own students could take courses at another institution for a semester or more, meaning that a greater proportion of the student population—now including those unable or unwilling to relocate to another country on a long-term basis—could pursue studies in another country.

Today, these two forms of mobility (foreign enrollment and study abroad) are supplemented by shorter-term, often faculty-led study experiences (generally consisting of one to a few weeks in length) designed to complement a particular course or course sequence. While not providing the depth of immersion that might be gained in a longer-term residential experience, these short-term treks have created opportunities for education-related international mobility among student populations that might not otherwise have had the experience. In fact, when UNESCO reports that in 2007 there were more than 2.8 million internationally mobile students worldwide, by definition this number includes only students who were enrolled outside their home country for a year or more.[41] Thus, it is likely to substantially under-represent the level of actual education-related mobility among students, particularly the growing number of students who travel abroad on a shorter-term basis.

Despite its limitations of scope, the data reported by UNESCO on international student mobility still is quite useful, particularly for purposes of determining the direction of cross-border student flows. The top five primary destination countries for students reported by UNESCO are the United States, the United Kingdom, France, Australia, and Germany, which together received more than half (58 percent) of all internationally mobile students worldwide. Language appears to have a role. In fact, six of the countries in which English is the most common language (Australia, Canada, Ireland, New Zealand, the United Kingdom, and the United States) together received 46 percent of the world's internationally mobile students; Germany and France, whose languages are also widely spoken and read, together accounted for another 16 percent of internationally mobile students.

When we compare the UNESCO data to results from a recent AACSB survey of member schools' student exchange agreements, similar patterns emerge in the frequency of country selection (see Table 2.2). Altogether, 157 AACSB member schools in 32 countries report having collaborative agreements to support student exchange with other schools. Nine of the top fifteen locations of AACSB members' student exchange partner institutions also fall among the top fifteen host countries of internationally mobile students according to UNESCO data.

On the other hand, data from GMAC also suggests shifts in the location of individuals taking the GMAT and the locations of schools to which they are sending their test scores. The GMAT has historically been a common basis for admissions decisions at graduate programs in U.S. business schools and at some schools in other parts of the world, and test-taker data can be viewed as a leading indicator of changes in demand for management education. In particular, over the period of 2001 to 2009, the percentage of GMAT scores sent by non-U.S. citizens to U.S. schools decreased markedly and steadily from 75 percent to 61 percent (see Figure 2.3). Similarly, the percentage of scores from Asian GMAT takers sent to U.S. schools decreased from 84.83 percent to

---

[41]UNESCO Institute for Statistics, *Global Education Digest 2009: Comparing Education Statistics Across the World*, Montreal, Quebec, Canada, 2009, electronic document, http://www.uis.unesco.org/template/pdf/ged/2009/GED_2009_EN.pdf, accessed January 31, 2010.

Table 2.2: Attractiveness of Country as Destination for Internationally Mobile Students and as Location of Student Exchange Partner School.

Country	Top 15 Destinations of Internationally Mobile Students:		Top 15 Locations of AACSB Members' Exchange Partners[*]:	
	Number of Students	**Rank**	**Number of Agreements**	**Rank**
Australia	211,526	4	55	12
Austria	43,572	11	46	15
Canada	68,520	7	119	6
China/Chinese Taipei[**]	42,138	12	197	4
Denmark	–	–	50	14
France	246,612	3	284	1
Germany	206,875	5	202	3
India	–	–	71	10
Italy	57,271	10	–	–
Japan	125,877	6	–	–
Mexico	–	–	92	8
Netherlands	–	–	56	11
New Zealand	33,047	14	–	–
Russia	60,288	9	–	–
South Africa	60,552	8	–	–
South Korea	31,943	15	55	12
Spain	–	–	138	5
Sweden	–	–	74	9
Switzerland	38,317	13	–	–
United Kingdom	351,470	2	113	7
United States	595,874	1	233	2

*This indicates only the number of times a student exchange collaboration was reported with a school in each country, not the actual level of activity. Collaborations involving student exchange between two schools in the same country are excluded from this analysis.

**The UNESCO Institute for Statistics reports internationally mobile students to mainland China and Chinese Taipei together as one figure. The 197 exchange agreements reported through the AACSB survey reflect 172 agreements with schools in mainland China and 25 agreements with schools in Chinese Taipei.

Source: UNESCO Institute for Statistics, Global Education Digest 2009; AACSB Member Collaboration Survey 2008.

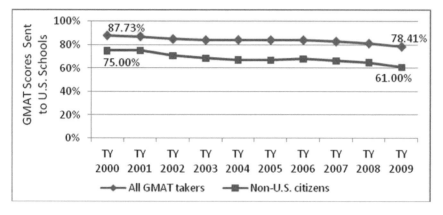

Figure 2.3: Percentage of GMAT Scores Sent to U.S. Schools, Testing Years 2000–2009.
Source: GMAC World Geographic Trend Reports.[42]

67.18 percent. During the same period, the percentage of scores from Asian GMAT takers sent to schools in Asia rose from 4.5 percent to 15.6 percent.[43]

One potential explanation for these trends is an elevation of the perceived quality of schools in Asia by individuals local to the region. Additional analysis would be required to distill how much of the trend might also be explained by other factors, such as increases in the number of schools that

[42]Chisholm, Alex, Courtney Defibaugh, and Hillary Taliaferro, World Geographic Trend Report for GMAT Examinees, 2005–2009, Graduate Management Admission Council, McLean, VA, 2010; Chisholm, Alex, and Courtney Defibaugh, World Geographic Trend Report for GMAT Examinees, 2004–2008, Graduate Management Admission Council, McLean, VA, 2009; Peyton, Johnette, World Geographic Trend Report for GMAT Examinees, 2003–2007, Graduate Management Admission Council, McLean, VA, 2008; Peyton, Johnette, World Geographic Trend Report for GMAT Examinees, 2002–2006, Graduate Management Admission Council, McLean, VA, 2007; Peyton, Johnette, Geographic Trend Report for Examinees Taking the GMAT, 2001–2005, Graduate Management Admission Council, McLean, VA, 2006; Peyton, Johnette, Geographic Trend Report for Examinees Taking the GMAT, 2000–2004, Graduate Management Admission Council, McLean, VA, 2005.

[43]Chisholm, Alex, Courtney Defibaugh, and Hillary Taliaferro, Asian Geographic Trend Report for GMAT Examinees, 2005–2009, Graduate Management Admission Council, McLean, VA, 2010; Chisholm, Alex, and Courtney Defibaugh, Asian Geographic Trend Report for GMAT Examinees, 2004–2008, Graduate Management Admission Council, McLean, VA, 2009; Peyton, Johnette, Asian Geographic Trend Report for GMAT Examinees, 2003–2007, Graduate Management Admission Council, McLean, VA, 2008; Peyton, Johnette, Asian Geographic Trend Report for GMAT Examinees, 2002–2006, Graduate Management Admission Council, McLean, VA, 2007; Peyton, Johnette, Asian Geographic Trend Report for GMAT Examinees, 2001–2005, Graduate Management Admission Council, McLean, VA, 2005.

accept GMAT scores, national restrictions on immigration, etc. We should also note that staying within the same region still allows for mobility between nations. For example, in 2001, only 1.03 percent of GMAT takers from India sent their scores to schools in Asian nations other than India, whereas in 2009, 7.44 percent sent scores.[44]

Before focusing on management education providers, it is worth noting that students are not the only internationally mobile population significant to the globalization of education. Researchers, faculty, and other scholars also work more and more frequently outside their country of origin. Challenges and strategies related to the mobility of academic professionals are discussed at greater length in Chapters 3 and 5, respectively.

2.3. Management Education Today: Characterizing the Global Nature of Providers

As of 2010, the International Association of Universities (IAU) had identified more than 17,000 degree-conferring higher education institutions around the world.[45] By comparison, AACSB has estimated as of June 30, 2010 that approximately 12,600 institutions offer at least one business degree program at the undergraduate level (or equivalent) or above. As Table 2.3 later demonstrates, these institutions are distributed across both developed and developing economies. They are found in urban and rural areas, and in some cases they offer courses and programs in multiple locations. Some offer only undergraduate programs, while others offer only graduate-level education, and still others offer a comprehensive array of program levels and orientations.

The starting point for our effort to characterize this landscape is, necessarily, a discussion of the numerous definitional and interpretive challenges to measuring the existence of business schools and management education globally. By acknowledging these challenges, we are able to identify the limitations of the numbers and analyses that follow. Still, the numbers do reveal significant characteristics of today's provider landscape. As mentioned above, the number and breadth of institutions offering business degrees is astonishing, yet their impact is even further augmented

---

[44]Chisholm, Alex, Courtney Defibaugh, and Hillary Taliaferro, Asian Geographic Trend Report for GMAT Examinees, 2005–2009, Graduate Management Admission Council, McLean, VA, 2010; Peyton, Johnette, Asian Geographic Trend Report for GMAT Examinees, 2001–2005, Graduate Management Admission Council, McLean, VA, 2005.
[45]International Association of Universities, IAU Online Databases, Higher Education Systems, 2010, electronic document, http://www.iau-aiu.net/onlinedatabases/index.html, accessed April 27, 2010.

Table 2.3: Number of Institutions Granting Business Degrees at the Undergraduate Level or Above, by Region.

Region/Subregion	Estimated Number of Institutions[46]
Africa	767
Northern Africa	211
Eastern Africa	151
Middle Africa	41
Southern Africa	46
Western Africa	318
Americas	3,695
Northern America	1,726
Caribbean	97
Latin (Central & South) America	1,872
Asia	6,087
Central Asia	138
Eastern Asia	1,725
South-Eastern Asia	1,978
Southern Asia	1,829
Western Asia (Middle & Near East)	417
Europe	1,975
Eastern Europe	685
Western Europe	1,290
Oceania	99
Australia and New Zealand	76
Mela-, Micro-, and Polynesia	23

Source: AACSB analysis, as of June 30, 2010.

through growing cross-border activity in the form of branch campuses, franchise programs, and the scale of online delivery. The distribution of institutions with international accreditation is notably uneven, however, relative to the global distribution of providers. This imbalance is likely due primarily to the initial location of those accreditation bodies, the largest of which have their roots in the U.S. and Western Europe.

Indicators also show a growing level of connectivity between management education providers globally, though much of this growth appears to be

---

[46]Estimates result from information collected from numerous sources, including but not limited to ministries of education and other government websites, higher-education organizations, school websites, and country-specific higher education profiles. For some countries, it was possible to identify by name and count every known institution granting business degrees; for others, an informed estimate is used.

incremental with an ever-increasing level of commitment. A basic level of cross-border connectivity comes through affiliation with regional or international management education organizations, yet often these networks serve as a foundation for deeper connections in the form of international partnerships, joint ventures, and strategic alliances. It is the development of this latter category of deeper connections that the Task Force believes will define the next phase of management education development.

2.3.1. Identifying Providers—Definitional Challenges

At the time of our analysis, not enough information was available regarding each management education provider to complete a detailed analysis of the global management education landscape. Challenges to understanding and measuring these providers are many. These challenges typically fall into two broad categories. First, differences in terminology within and across countries impede the gathering and reporting of comparable data. At times, data is available, and even comparable, but it is not specific to business degree programs.[47] Second, cross-national variations in educational systems and in the structures of the institutions that comprise them blur boundaries between types of providers and inhibit accurate segmentation. These challenges require us to begin this sub-section by exploring what is considered a business school and what is considered business/management education.

What is considered a "business school"? The AACSB estimate of approximately 12,600 business degree providers globally is based on an approach that counts each institution once, in its country of origin, regardless of the number of branch campuses or cross-border programs the school operates. Beyond an awareness that the institution offers business degrees, little information is known about the majority of identified institutions, thus it is difficult to determine what proportion of the approximately 12,600 institutions granting business degrees can acceptably be called "business schools." No single, generally accepted definition for a "business school" currently exists. A definition might include a minimum number of degrees awarded, a minimum number of faculty members supporting the business degree programs, a minimum number of degree programs, the existence of certain levels or types

---

[47]For example, though it collects enrollment and graduate data in the narrow field category of "business and administration," UNESCO only publicly reports students enrolled in the broader category of "social sciences, business, and law." Information in the narrow field category of "business and administration" is available for select countries via the Eurostat and OECD.Stat databases.

of degree programs, the existence of a clearly identifiable administrative unit for business programs, and/or other criteria.

The AACSB International Eligibility Criteria and Standards for Business Accreditation provide guidance regarding how the business school is defined for AACSB accreditation purposes, taking the general approach that the institution considered for accreditation review "is an organization through which business programs are authorized, resourced, and overseen."[48] Given substantial variation in the structures and regulation of higher education institutions around the world, the actual application of this definition for accreditation purposes can be complicated. The way disciplines are defined and organized within a higher education setting varies across national contexts, and may result in "business and administration" programs offered in multiple units and/or in a unit that also offers programs in other fields. While the eligibility criteria for AACSB accreditation outline a process and guidelines for reaching consensus on how each institution under review is defined, this process only applies to a small subset of the estimated 12,600 institutions known to grant business degrees.

What is considered "business" or "management" education? The AACSB International Eligibility Criteria and Standards for Business Accreditation include a comprehensive list of "traditional business subjects" generally considered to be included in accreditation reviews.[49] This list is used in the determination of the AACSB estimate of institutions granting business degrees. The International Standard Classification of Education (ISCED), used by the UNESCO Institute for Statistics as a framework for its higher education data collection efforts, employs a similar but not entirely congruous definition.[50]

---

[48]Factors considered in this determination include the degree of financial control, service provision, autonomy, and brand dependence. AACSB International, *Eligibility Procedures and Standards for Business Accreditation*, revised January 31, 2010.

[49]This list includes "Accounting, Business Law, Decision Sciences, Finance (including Insurance, Real Estate, and Banking), Human Resources, Management, Management Information Systems, Management Science, Marketing, Operations Management, Organizational Behavior, Organizational Development, Strategic Management, Supply Chain Management (including Transportation and Logistics), and Technology Management." AACSB International, *Eligibility Procedures and Standards for Business Accreditation*, revised January 31, 2010.

[50]The "business and administration" field of education in the ISCED 1997 scheme is defined as inclusive of the following: retailing, marketing, sales, public relations, real estate; finance, banking, insurance, investment analysis; accounting, auditing, bookkeeping; management, public administration, institutional administration, personnel administration; secretarial and office work. UNESCO, International Standard Classification of Education 1997, electronic document, http://www.unesco.org/education/information/nfsunesco/doc/isced_1997.htm, accessed October 28, 2010.

Further complicating efforts to isolate and identify business programs is the seemingly ever-growing presence of extensions of the "traditional business subjects" through interdisciplinary or integrated courses, majors, programs, concentrations, or areas of emphasis. Programs in fields as seemingly diverse as hospitality management, aviation management, engineering management, forestry management, and healthcare administration are delivered partially or in full by institutional units not traditionally considered "business schools," but these courses of study still might warrant classification as business programs based on their content. Some countries, particularly those with a high level of state-owned enterprises, consider public administration programs (which in the U.S., for example, are often considered distinct from business administration programs) to be business programs and classify them as such.

Despite these complexities and ambiguities, in the pages that follow we draw upon available information to characterize the global nature of management education in 2010. The focus of the analysis is on degree providers, as this focus provides the simplest basis for analysis given the information that is currently available.

2.3.2. Size and Distribution of Providers

A global analysis of management education degree providers shows us that degree-based management education is present in all regions of the world, and in nearly every country. Table 2.3 provides a breakdown of the estimated number of institutions granting business degrees by geographic region and subregion. Of the approximately 12,600 institutions granting business degrees, nearly half are found in Asia. In fact, three of the top five countries in terms of absolute numbers are in Asia (China, the Philippines, and India). Just under one-third of the institutions are located in the Americas, split almost evenly between Northern America (the U.S. and Canada) and the countries of Latin America and the Caribbean. Schools in Eastern and Western Europe together slightly outnumber those in Northern America. Available data for a sample of countries across all regions suggest that institutions granting undergraduate degree programs are more numerous than institutions granting graduate-level degrees.

Other than to affirm the global scope of management education, however, the meaning of these estimates is somewhat limited. The number of institutions granting business degrees gives no indication of degree program size, level(s), or quality—all of which undoubtedly vary substantially. Changes in the number of schools over time must also be interpreted cautiously; without corresponding information on changes in enrollments, tertiary education demographics, and the educational context of a given country, it is impossible to attribute shifts in the number of institutions to shifts in student interest or societal need.

The actual number of institutions is in a constant state of flux; each year new schools open their doors, existing schools cease operations, and mergers and acquisitions combine formerly independent institutions under one brand. In some markets, in response to a declining student population, national consolidation of higher education institutions is likely to result in a reduction of the number of business-degree granting institutions. For example, over the last two decades, government policies in Chinese Taipei resulted in a dramatic increase in higher education access. Now, as the country faces declines in the traditional student-age population, some of the institutions are expected to shut their doors or be acquired by others.[51] Similarly, the Japanese management education landscape is one in which the government's establishment, beginning in 2002, of "professional graduate schools" (including business schools) adds to the pool of providers even while a corresponding decline in the student population will likely result in the closing of many private institutions.[52]

Followers of AACSB publications will find that in recent years the association's estimate of the number of institutions granting business degrees has gradually increased. As recently as 2008, the Global Foundation for Management Education, a joint venture of AACSB International and the European Foundation for Management Development (EFMD), used information for a sample of countries to estimate that 8,000 institutions worldwide were granting business degrees. Since then, AACSB has continued efforts to refine that estimate by looking at all countries and synthesizing information from numerous sources. In some countries, initial estimates were found to have excluded private institutions or to be limited to only institutions with "university" status, despite the fact that institutions of other types also offered business degrees.

The exclusion of private institutions is particularly significant given UNESCO's estimate that private higher education providers now account for 30 percent of global enrollment in all fields,[53] though the impact of

---

[51]Taiwan Central News Agency, "Taiwan's Universities See Record High Vacancies," *Taiwan News*, August 7, 2009, electronic document, http://www.etaiwannews.com/etn/news_content. php?id=1025483&lang=eng_news, accessed July 22, 2010.

[52]McNeill, David, "Enrollment Crisis Threatens Japan's Private Colleges," *The Chronicle of Higher Education*, October 25, 2009, electronic document, http://chronicle.com/article/ Enrollment-Crisis-Threatens/48909/, accessed July 22, 2010.

[53]UNESCO, "UNESCO World Conference on Higher Education opens With Call to Address Global Challenges," press release, July 7, 2009, electronic document, http://www.unesco.org/new/ en/media-services/single-view/news/unesco_world_conference_on_higher_education_opens_with_ call_to_address_global_challenges/browse/6/back/18276/, accessed March 30, 2010.

private providers varies significantly across countries. For example, Brazil, Chile, and Mexico all have over 50 percent of their tertiary students enrolled in private higher education, while places such as Chinese Taipei, Indonesia, Japan, the Philippines, and South Korea all have greater than 70 percent enrollment in private higher education. Altbach et al. note that such countries have "coped with the funding dilemma by keeping the public sector relatively selective and elite, shifting the burden of mass enrollments to private higher education,"[54] a tactic that may see increasing use across the globe as countries deal with the fallout from the recent economic crisis.

2.3.3. *Branch and Networked Campuses, Franchise Programs, and Other Cross-Border Models*

Accounting for all management education providers is only the beginning of our process. Augmenting the global "map" of roughly 12,600 business degree providers is the presence of foreign education providers based in one country that deliver degree programs through a presence in another. Increasingly large numbers of institutions provide education to students across multiple locations, and such institutions follow a variety of models. International providers may reach their students through actual branch campuses or through rented space in other facilities. In some cases, one institutional brand may have campus locations in multiple countries, as is the case for the European University, with campuses in Austria, Chinese Taipei, Germany, Kazakhstan, Spain, Switzerland, Syria, and the U.K. In other cases, such as the network of providers owned by for-profit educational firm Laureate Education Inc., each is part of a global network of independently branded institutions. Some institutions reach their students through validated or franchise degree programs, which are actually delivered by independent local institutions. Still others, such as U.S.-based Nova Southeastern University, deliver online programs targeted at students located anywhere in the world. Hybrid models incorporating two or more of the above models are common.

Accounting for the cross-border provision of management education is complicated not only by differences in the models management education providers use to deliver education in countries outside their home nations, but also by differences in countries' regulatory environments. Many countries do not include foreign education providers under the purview of their local education ministries, and therefore comprehensive lists are difficult to obtain.

---

[54]Altbach, Philip, Liz Reisberg, and Laura E. Rumbley, "Tracking a Global Academic Revolution," *Change*, Vol. 42, No. 2 (2010), p. 36.

Still, enough information emerges to demonstrate the substantial added impact of foreign education providers on the global map of management education.

One of the most highly visible approaches taken by foreign providers is the establishment of branch campuses in other countries. (Some institutions prefer to refer to a "network" of campuses to avoid implications that one campus has less stature than another.) Although no universal definition of an international branch campus is agreed-upon, in a 2009 publication the Observatory on Borderless Higher Education (OBHE) defines it as an "off-shore entity of a higher education institution operated by the institution or through a joint venture in which the institution is a partner (some countries require foreign providers to partner with a local organization) in the name of the foreign institution."[55] Based on this definition,[56] the OBHE reports that the number of international branch campuses (offering degrees in any discipline) grew 43 percent in the three years from 2006 to 2009, to a total of 162.[57]

Table 2.4 indicates the top home and host countries of international branch campuses according to OBHE data. As indicated in its report, institutions from a total of 22 different countries had established international branch campuses by 2009, up from 17 in 2006.[58] Further OBHE analysis reveals that a slight majority (51 percent) of home-to-host country pairs are those in which a university in a developed country establishes a branch campus in a developing country. Thirty percent of the pairs were branch campuses established by schools from developed countries, in other developed countries, while those in which both campuses

---

[55]Becker, Rosa, "International Branch Campuses: New Trends and Directions," *International Higher Education*, Vol. 58, Winter 2010, electronic document, http://www.bc.edu/bc_org/avp/soe/cihe/newsletter/Number58/p3_Becker.htm, accessed July 22, 2010.

[56]OBHE's definition excludes the following schools: schools with franchise programs that are offered through a partner institution or that provide only joint/dual degrees; schools offering multiple foreign institutions' courses (such as the Singapore Institute of Management); foreign campuses that do not offer complete degree programs; study-abroad campuses for students of the home institution only (such as New York University's campus in Prague); schools modeled on a foreign country's higher education system but without ties to a specific institution (such as the American University of Cairo); and foreign-backed universities, which have been established within the host country's higher education system and jurisdiction but which have initial academic support from foreign providers (such as the Swiss-German University of Indonesia or the Pyongyang Business School in North Korea).

[57]Jaschik, Scott, "International Campuses on the Rise," *Inside Higher Ed*, September 9, 2009, electronic document, http://www.insidehighered.com/news/2009/09/03/branch, accessed July 22, 2010.

[58]Maslen, Geoff, "GLOBAL: Huge Expansion in Overseas Campuses," *University World News*, November 22, 2009, electronic document, http://www.universityworldnews.com/article.php?story=20091120103411843&mode=print, accessed July 23, 2010.

Table 2.4: Top Home and Host Countries of International Branch Campuses.

Top Home Countries	Total Foreign Branch Campuses Established by Institutions in Home Country	Top Hosting Countries	Total Foreign Branch Campuses in Host Country
United States	78	United Arab Emirates	40
Australia	14	China	15
United Kingdom	13	Singapore	12
France	11	Qatar	9
India	11	Canada	6
Others	35	Others	80
Total Worldwide	162	Total Worldwide	162

Source: 2009 OBHE report—"International Branch Campuses: Markets and Strategies," by Rosa Becker.[59]

in the pair were in developing countries had increased from previous years to comprise 16 percent of the set.

We caution that the number of campuses listed in Table 2.4 for each of the top home countries does not necessarily equate to the number of institutions in those countries with international branch campuses. As some examples of institutions that offer management education through multiple campuses that fit the OBHE definition above, U.S.-based Webster University maintains six international campuses in Austria, China, the Netherlands, Switzerland, Thailand, and the U.K., while Australia-based Monash University has two international campuses, one each in Malaysia and South Africa.

Some countries rely more heavily than others on foreign providers to create needed higher education capacity. For example, the inclusion of the United Arab Emirates at the top of the list of host countries is not surprising given recent government-led efforts in several of the emirates to build educational capacity by actively recruiting foreign education providers. In Dubai, for example, an "International Academic City" hosts more than 32 international universities from countries including Australia, Belgium, France, India, Iran, Pakistan, Russia, Sri Lanka, the U.K., and the U.S. Business degrees are offered by institutions based in Europe, India, and Australia. In nearby Qatar, an "Education City" hosts campuses of six

---

[59]Becker, Rosa, *International Branch Campuses: Markets and Strategies*, Report for the Observatory on Borderless Higher Education (OBHE), London, 2009.

U.S.-based schools (one of which, Carnegie Mellon University, offers undergraduate degrees in business administration), as well as a branch of the HEC School of Management, Paris, which offers its EMBA program in addition to non-degree executive education. In fact, in all the top hosting countries other than Canada and China, the number of branch campuses of foreign-based institutions exceeds the number of domestic higher education institutions.

Perhaps the largest supplemental impact on the global map of management education providers comes from cross-border delivery of degree programs through channels other than actual branch or networked campuses. Singapore and Hong Kong, for example, are regarded as world leaders in the number of franchise degree programs offered (across all disciplines).[60] Currently, four Singapore-based universities award their own business degrees within the country, as do several branch campuses of foreign-based institutions. However, *no fewer than* 70 institutions based outside Singapore also offer business degrees in the country through franchise agreements with private Singaporean education providers.[61] Similarly, Hong Kong's Education Bureau maintains lists[62] of hundreds of collaborative and franchise programs (all disciplines) with foreign providers, almost all of which are British, Australian, or American. Nearby, Malaysia is home to more than 800 transnational education programs, just under half of which involve collaboration with British institutions (again, all disciplines).[63] The map of management education providers in Southeast Asia, therefore, changes drastically when one takes into account these foreign degree providers.

---

[60]Gürüz, Kemal, *Higher Education and International Student Mobility in the Global Knowledge Economy*, State University of New York Press, Albany, NY, 2008.

[61]The vast majority of these Singaporean educational providers do not have authority from the Singaporean Ministry of Education to grant their own degrees, but they instead deliver an array of degree programs through franchise agreements with numerous partners, and often certificate/diploma-level courses of their own.

[62]Education Bureau of the Hong Kong SAR Government, Non-Local Higher and Professional Education (Regulation) Ordinance, List of Exempted Courses, 2010, electronic document, http://www.edb.gov.hk/index.aspx?langno=1&nodeID=1247, accessed July 23, 2010; Education Bureau of the Hong Kong SAR Government, Non-Local Higher and Professional Education (Regulation) Ordinance, List of Registered Courses, 2010, electronic document, http://www.edb.gov.hk/index.aspx?langno=1&nodeID=1438, accessed July 23, 2010.

[63]Gill, John, "Malaysia: Full of Western Promise," *Times Higher Education*, August 27, 2009, electronic document, http://www.timeshighereducation.co.uk/story.asp?sectioncode=26&storycode=407873&c=2, accessed July 22, 2010.

The full impact and scale of cross-border provision through online- and distance-delivery degree programs, delivered via Internet connection rather than through a physical classroom, is less completely understood. The U.S.-based University of Phoenix, for example, offers online courses through its Global Division, claiming to have "helped thousands of students from over 130 countries."[64] The Open University of the U.K., which virtually pioneered the concept of quality online and distance-based education, likewise claims to have served "nearly 30,000 students in 107 countries across the world" in 2009.[65] Many of the world's largest providers of online and distance education are those higher education institutions characterized as "open," although such institutions tend to be publicly funded and to have missions focused primarily on serving national populations.[66] Recently, however, the National Open and Distance Learning University of Mexico (Educación Superior Abierta y a Distancia or ESAD) took its local focus global by beginning to allow Mexican citizens living abroad to enroll in one of five online undergraduate degree programs (including international marketing as well as small and medium-size business administration).[67] As more schools look at ways to expand the reach of their online programs, this mode of delivery will be an area deserving of greater attention.

Finally, evidence suggests that business is a disproportionately popular field for cross-border degree programs, at least in some regions. In 2008, nearly half (48 percent) of all foreign students enrolled in Australian universities studied business and management.[68] Australian universities are also major players in offshore transnational education, with 26.5 percent of all international students in 2007 completing their degrees either entirely

---

[64]University of Phoenix, Global Division web page, electronic document, http://www.phoenix.edu/colleges_divisions/global.html, accessed January 5, 2011.

[65]The Open University Business School, History and Milestones web page, 2011, electronic document, http://www8.open.ac.uk/business-school/about/history-milestones, accessed January 5, 2011.

[66]Open universities are commonly defined as higher education institutions that have an open-door admissions policy; in other words, they are institutions that accept enrolling students with few or no requirements regarding previous education, experience, or references. They are an increasingly common phenomenon, particularly in developing areas where the higher education capacity or the ability to access higher education providers is low.

[67]Lloyd, Marion, "Mexico Will Offer Online-Degree Programs to Citizens Living Abroad," *The Chronicle of Higher Education*, August 8, 2010, electronic document, http://chronicle.com/article/Mexico-Will-Offer/123854/, accessed December 30, 2010.

[68]Universities Australia, "The Nature of International Education in Australian Universities and its Benefits," 2009, electronic document, http://www.universitiesaustralia.edu.au/resources/285/2009-09%20-%20Intl%20Educ%20Benefits_SPRE_FINAL.pdf, accessed August 18, 2010.

or partially through offshore Australian university degree programs (many of which are located in Singapore, Malaysia, Mainland China, Vietnam, and Hong Kong).[69] A 2009 issue brief from the American Council on Education (ACE) indicates that business was by far the most popular field of study at the overseas branch campuses of U.S. institutions, and the summary references an earlier (2006) ACE survey that found that 64 percent of all degree programs offered abroad by U.S. institutions were in the field of business.[70] The strong representation of business among cross-border degree programs may be due to a variety of possible factors, including a higher demand for or interest in business programs (and a corresponding lack of supply in a given region), the lack of a formal connection between management education and local licensing to practice (as often exists for medicine), or perhaps business schools are simply leading among disciplines in efforts to deliver cross-border programs.

2.3.4. *Quality of Providers*

Undoubtedly, the quality of management education providers varies substantially, though defining just how much and in what ways that quality varies remains elusive.[71] While all institutions accounted for in our estimate are subject to some form of regulation or quality assurance (i.e., the number does not include any known diploma mills, per se), the reality is that national accreditation, quality assurance, and/or regulatory programs are highly inconsistent, and comparisons of quality across schools reviewed within those schemes are difficult to draw.

Over the past few decades, numerous organizations that have focused specifically on the quality of management education have emerged or expanded the scope of their operations from a national to an international focus. This common purpose enables some level of comparison of quality across borders, yet collectively the schools with international accreditation for business programs represent only a small portion of management education providers, and we are careful not to imply that all indicate comparable quality.

---

[69]Australian Education International, "Transnational Education in the Higher Education Sector," Research Snapshot Series, 2009, electronic document, http://aei.gov.au/AEI/PublicationsAndResearch/Snapshots/2009073120_pdf.pdf, accessed August 18, 2010.

[70]Green, Madeleine F., and Kimberly Koch, U.S. Branch Campuses Abroad, Issue Brief Series, American Council on Education, September 2009.

[71]The information in this sub-section draws upon analysis undertaken by the Global Foundation for Management Education (GFME), a joint venture between AACSB International and EFMD.

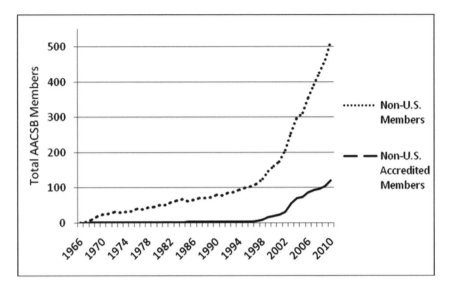

Figure 2.4: Growth in AACSB's Non-U.S. Representation.
Source: AACSB analysis, 2010.

The first cross-border accreditation of a business school was the accreditation of the University of Alberta in Canada by the U.S.-based AACSB International in 1968.[72] Nearly three decades later, in 1997, ESSEC in France became the first business school to be accredited by an organization based in another world region, again by AACSB International.[73] Soon after, in 1999, École des Hautes Études Commerciales de Montréal (HEC Montréal), in Canada, became the first non-European school to receive EQUIS accreditation from Belgium-based EFMD. The accreditation of schools in other regions by both organizations has expanded significantly since that time. For example, Figure 2.4 shows the growth in AACSB's members and accredited members located outside its home country of the U.S.

Today, approximately 10 percent of the roughly 12,600 institutions granting business degrees globally are accredited (or have programs accredited) by one or more of the nine management education organizations

---

[72]At the time, the organization was known as the American Association of Collegiate Schools of Business.

[73]At the time, the organization was known as AACSB International—the International Association for Management Education.

known to provide accreditation on a regional or international scale.[74] As shown in Table 2.5, the distribution of institutions accredited by one or more such organizations is highly uneven across the world. Most institutions with an international business accreditation are currently concentrated in Northern America and Western Europe; seven of the nine organizations included in our analysis (excluding only CEEMAN and AMDISA) were founded in and initially focused on these regions.

Our analysis of the global distribution of schools with an international accreditation is not meant to imply that all schools with an international accreditation are of equal quality, or are necessarily of better quality than other schools that have only national-level accreditation. Major differences exist among accreditation providers, both in the standards they enforce and in the ways in which they enforce them, that prevent us from making this generalization. Additionally, whether or not standards of one organization are appropriate for all regions or tailored (as is the case for AMDISA's SAQS accreditation) for schools in a specific geographic region is questionable. Here, we use this analysis to represent the schools that, by nature of their pursuit of international accreditation, imply some concern for international brand, reputation, and/or benchmarking.

Another way of looking at the distribution of international business school or program accreditations is shown in Figure 2.5. These maps show the countries of the world with their relative sizes adjusted for number of business degree-granting institutions (2.5.b), number of institutions with AACSB accreditation (2.5.c), and number of institutions with some form of internationally awarded business accreditation (2.5.d).

The shifts in country size from Figure 2.5.a (the standard map of the world) to Figure 2.5.b (map proportionate to the number of business-degree granting institutions) are notable, but for the most part they are not dramatic. The biggest shifts appear to be the expansion of European countries as well as of China, India, and Mexico, and the shrinkage of Africa. The next two maps, however, change dramatically. AACSB accreditation (Figure 2.5.c) is clearly

---

[74]The nine accrediting organizations include the Association to Advance Collegiate Schools of Business (AACSB), the Accreditation Council for Business Schools and Programs (ACBSP), the Association of MBAs (AMBA), the Association of Management Development Institutions in South Asia (AMDISA), the Central and East European Management Development Association (CEEMAN), the European Council for Business Education (ECBE), the European Foundation for Management Development (EFMD), the Foundation for International Business Administration Accreditation (FIBAA), and the International Assembly for Collegiate Business Education (IACBE). AMDISA offers the South Asia Quality Assurance System (SAQS). EFMD offers two separate accreditation products: the European Quality Improvement System (EQUIS) and the EFMD Programme Accreditation System (EPAS). All others offer accreditations that share the name of the organization.

Table 2.5: Global Distribution of International Accreditation, by Region*.

Region/Subregion	AACSB	EFMD EQUIS	EFMD EPAS	AMBA	ACBSP	IACBE	CEEMAN	FIBAA	AMDISA SAQS	ECBE
Africa	1	2	–	4	–	–	–	1	–	–
Asia	36	17	2	10	3	5	3	1	7	1
Eastern Europe	–	1	7	14	3	–	5	5	–	11
Western Europe	46	74	26	97	17	14	6	150	–	8
Latin America & Caribbean	10	10	–	28	11	2	–	–	–	1
North America	490	12	–	4	171	141	–	1	–	2
Oceania	10	12	–	8	–	1	–	–	–	–
WORLD	593	128	35	165	205	163	14	158	7	23
# Countries	37	35	18	40	17	11	10	13	2	10

*AMBA, EPAS, and FIBAA are programmatic accreditations and are counted if at least one of the school's programs holds the accreditation. This table does *not* take into account schools with multiple overlapping accreditations, nor the location of an accredited school's cross-border operations.
Source: AACSB analysis, as of July 1, 2010.

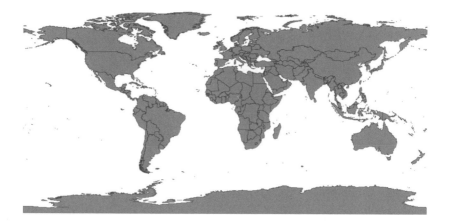

(a) Standard map of the world, Mercator projection

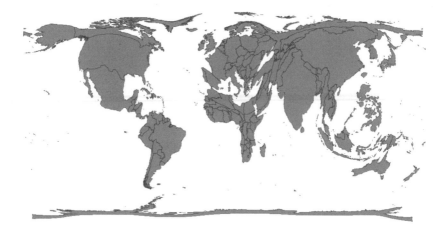

(b) The world proportionate to the number of business degree-granting institutions

Figure 2.5: The World According to Business School/Program Accreditation. (All maps are as of 2010.)

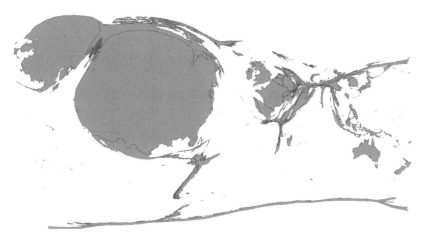

(c) The world proportionate to the number of AACSB-accredited business schools

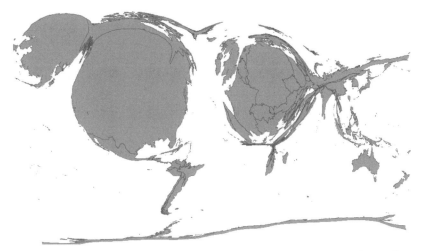

(d) The world proportionate to the number of institutions with some form of international business accreditation

Figure 2.5: (*Continued*)

concentrated in the U.S. and, to a lesser degree, Western Europe. When we bring in other forms of international accreditation (Figure 2.5.d), the primary added emphasis is in Europe, which expands substantially. Only barely noticeable growth occurs in some countries of Latin America, Africa, and Asia.

Of the accreditations offered by the nine organizations in our analysis, the three that are the most internationally represented are AACSB, EQUIS, and AMBA, which, as of July 1, 2010, have been awarded to schools or programs in 37, 35, and 40 countries and territories, respectively. Relative to other accreditations, these three programs also tend to include schools with more globally recognized reputations. Figure 2.6 shows the distribution of schools with one or more of these three business school/program accreditations. Together, these institutions represent approximately 6 percent of the estimated 12,600 institutions offering business degrees worldwide. The greatest amount of overlap between these three accrediting bodies is in Western Europe, where 51 percent of institutions with accreditation from one of the three organizations also hold an accreditation from at least one of the other two. The largest total number of schools accredited by any one or more of the three is found in Northern America (due primarily to the large number of AACSB-accredited schools in the U.S.).

International accreditation also tends to be unevenly distributed across levels of economic development—being much more prevalent in high-income, developed countries. As shown in Figure 2.7, more than 90 percent of institutions with AACSB, EQUIS, and/or AMBA accreditation are located in countries that the World Bank has classified as High-income

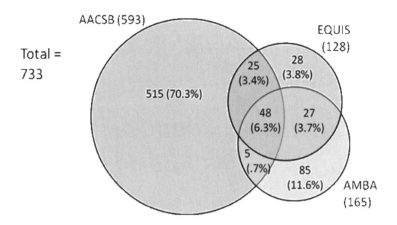

Figure 2.6: Distribution of Schools with AACSB, EQUIS, and/or AMBA Accreditation.

Source: AACSB analysis of publicly available data as of July 2010.

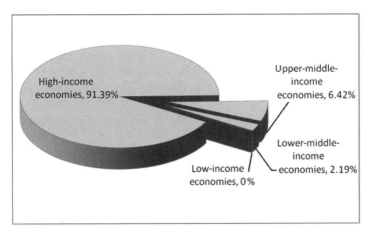

Figure 2.7: Distribution of Schools with AACSB, EQUIS, and/or AMBA Accreditation, by Country Economic Classification.*

Source: AACSB analysis of publicly available data as of July 2010.

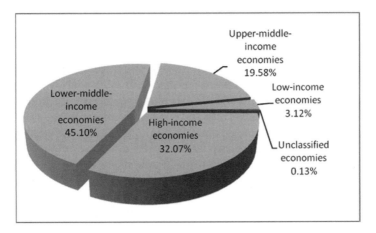

Figure 2.8: Distribution of Schools Offering Business Degrees, by Country Economic Classification.*

Source: AACSB analysis of publicly available data as of July 2010.

*As of July 1, 2010, the World Bank defines high-income as those countries with $12,196 or more 2009 GNI per capita, upper-middle-income as those with $3,946–$12,195 2009 GNI per capita, lower-middle-income as those with $996–$3,945 2009 GNI per capita, and low-income as those with $995 or less 2009 GNI per capita

(2009 GNI per capita of $12,196 or more). By contrast, those countries host only about one-third of all institutions that grant business degrees, as shown in Figure 2.8. Likely causes of this disparity are both the origins of the three accreditations (which have their roots in more well-developed countries), and the resource requirements for a school to offer management education in a way that conforms to their standards.

Even more interesting and relevant for our study of globalization is understanding what has been driving schools to seek international accreditation in increasing numbers. Most countries have local quality assurance or accreditation schemes, requiring institutions to undergo periodic assessment against a set of standards. These national accreditation frameworks are not always discipline-specific, may not apply to all higher education institutions (for example, in some cases they exclude private and/or foreign institutions), and may have relatively low thresholds of quality that must be met. But deficiencies in local accreditations are not always a reason, or the only reason, that international accreditation is sought.

Instead we see interest in international accreditation as evidence of an emerging global system of management education. Broadly speaking, accreditation generally serves two purposes. First, for the institution and the higher education system of which it is a part, accreditation serves as a process and framework that enable the institution to a) hold itself accountable for its commitment to maintain high quality, b) identify areas for improvement, and c) act to enhance the quality of the services it offers and the activities in which it engages. Second, for the institution's stakeholders (students, organizations, and the community), accreditation serves as an indicator of quality along a given dimension or set of dimensions that inform the development of future relationships between those stakeholders and the institution.

International accreditation frameworks serve similar purposes, but on a scale that transcends national borders, hence eliminating the need for multinational employers, international students, and potential collaborative partners in other countries to understand the differences between national accreditation schemes. International accreditation is as much about the pursuit of excellence (along globally recognized standards of quality) as it is about branding and positioning in the globalizing worlds of business and higher education.

Another dimension that may lend insights into the relative quality of management education providers is the positioning of various schools relative to one another in global business school rankings such as those published by *BusinessWeek*, the *Financial Times*, and the *Economist*, as well as by newcomers such as EdUniversal. As we will show in Chapter 3, despite the pressure among ranked institutions to increase their position in the tables, significant overlap within the rankings means that together they represent only a very narrow slice of business degree providers—between 2 and 9 percent of the estimated total, depending on the rankings included.

The relatively small number of business schools either with an international accreditation or included in a global ranking speaks to several gaps in quality assurance. At one level, it suggests that the vast majority of management education providers could benefit from access to incentives for strategic, continuous, and sustainable improvement aligned with an internationally recognized standard.

Furthermore, the finding highlights the need for greater availability and transparency of information on management education institutions and their quality—particularly for the stakeholders of those schools for which benchmarking on an international scale is currently not a reality. Transparency is important for our working definition of *quality*. If quality is about delivering on the promise of the school's mission and meeting expectations, then ensuring the public availability of accurate data and information about the institution is crucial. Appropriately so, accreditations have tended to focus on institutional improvement, while national systems are often regulatory or administrative in nature. Noteworthy, then, is the fact that few global structures currently exist primarily to inform and protect internationally mobile students and multi-national employers against the hazard of implausible claims.

2.3.5. *Institutional Connectivity*

For many reasons that were discussed earlier within this chapter, we believe the world will continue to see an increase in the number and diversity of management education providers. This growth will occur particularly in parts of the world where management education is currently under-developed, which in many cases happen to be the regions with the greatest expected growth in the traditional student age cohort.[75]

However, we believe that what will emerge as a unique characteristic of the next phase in the global development of management education will be a greater emphasis on the emergence of connections, collaborations, and even competition between providers in different regions of the world. The beginning of this phase is already underway.

Throughout much of the twentieth century, the groundwork for this phase was laid through the establishment of new management education providers in all regions of the world. We also saw, in the history recounted earlier, the development of cross-border linkages, some more subtle than others, resulting in the diffusion of management education models and pedagogical approaches across borders.

---

[75]Global Foundation for Management Education, "The Global Management Education Landscape: Shaping the future of business schools," 2008, electronic document, http://www.gfme.org/landscape/reportonlineversion.pdf, accessed January 31, 2010.

While these informal channels of influence can be described anecdotally, they are difficult to quantify and measure. Today, however, we see the emergence of various *formal* networks that are likely to increase the pace at which new ideas and approaches are exposed and then adapted and adopted across borders. Two types of such linkages are explored in depth in the pages that follow: institutional affiliation with regional or international management education organizations, and international partnerships, joint ventures, and strategic alliances.

Affiliation with Regional or International Management Education Organizations. AACSB estimates that 18 percent of the approximately 12,600 institutions granting business degrees worldwide are members (accredited or non-accredited) of the regional or international accrediting organizations referenced earlier. The largest is AACSB International, whose members as of July 1, 2010 included approximately 1,180 institutions, or slightly less than 10 percent of institutions granting business degrees worldwide. Geographically, the highest concentrations of management education providers with international affiliations (relative to the regional population of providers) are found in Northern America, Western Europe, and Oceania, as shown in Table 2.6. The table also shows, by the percent of institutions in each region affiliated with multiple associations, the inter-connectivity between each of the individual organizations' member networks. Members of other associations, such as the Consejo Latinamericano de Escuelas de Administración (CLADEA), the Association of Asia-Pacific Business Schools (AAPBS), and the Association of African Business Schools (AABS)—that offer services and international networking, but not accreditation, to members—augment this network.

While actual historical membership data was not collected from each of these organizations, recent years have seen a growth in the number of management education organizations operating with an international scale, as well as an expansion in the geographic scope of their operations. Such organizations offer opportunities for their members to network with other business schools, share effective practices, and promote quality improvement through professional development, benchmarking, and other activities. Often, these networks facilitate the connections that form the basis for future collaborative arrangements ranging from student exchanges to joint or dual-degree programs, or other initiatives.

Other, more specialized networks also connect schools with similar interests for the purpose of advancing a particular dimension of education or other outcomes. An example is the Principles for Responsible Management Education (PRME), a list of principles to which more than 300 schools in 59 countries have become signatories. In doing so, these institutions express their commitment to integrate corporate responsibility and sustainability throughout the school's education and research initiatives. Being a signatory institution

Table 2.6: Global Distribution of Membership in International
Management Education Associations, by Region*.

Region/Subregion	Regional Institutions that are members of multiple International Management Education Associations	Regional Institutions that are members of only one International Management Education Association
Africa	1.0%	2.5%
Asia	1.5%	5.1%
Eastern Europe	5.1%	7.3%
Western Europe	15.7%	24.5%
Latin America & Caribbean	1.9%	2.9%
Northern America	7.9%	52.6%
Oceania	26.3%	11.1%
WORLD	4.3%	13.3%

Note: Approximately 56 percent of total memberships in the nine organizations analyzed were held by institutions with membership in only one international management education association. This table does not take into account the location of a school's cross-border operations.
*Analysis includes members of AACSB International, ACBSP, AMBA, AMDISA, CEEMAN, ECBE, EFMD, FIBAA, and IACBE. Institutions are those offering business degrees.
Source: AACSB analysis, as of 1 July, 2010.

engages the school in a broader multinational, multi-stakeholder network by connecting the school with the worldwide network of corporate signatories to the United National Global Compact (UNGC), and by providing a framework for the public sharing of best practices and benchmarking data related to implementation of the principles.

International Partnerships, Joint Ventures, and Strategic Alliances.   Also tracing its way across the global map of management education providers is a growing web of connections formed through international partnerships, joint ventures, and strategic alliances. Often defined by formal contracts entered into by two or more "partners," these collaborative initiatives support a variety of activities, including student and faculty exchange, joint research, the sharing of resources or physical space, program development and delivery, and more.

While networks of influence such as those created by affiliations with international organizations are significant for the opportunities they create, partnerships are significant because they are the basis for undertaking specific initiatives that neither institution could do (or do as well) on its own.

International partnerships in particular have in recent years captured the attention and imagination of business school leaders.

An AACSB survey conducted in 2008-09 revealed that, among the participating sample of member business schools,[76] four out of five had at least one formal collaboration with another school. A "collaboration" was defined in the survey as an official partnership between two or more institutions, founded on an agreement delineating the terms of the partnership, and focused specifically on the students, faculty, programs, and services of the business school.

The 200 schools that provided information regarding their partnerships reported an astonishing number of collaborations (3,126) and together identified 1,212 unique institutional partners. Less than 10 percent of the identified partners (112) were also survey participants. Interestingly, nearly 60 percent of institutions identified by AACSB members as partners were not members of the association at the time of the survey, indicating that engagement in partnership activity is a much broader phenomenon than what is revealed among the limited number of schools surveyed.

Analysis further confirmed that business schools in all regions were engaged in some level of partnership activity. Schools that reported collaborations represented 34 countries and all major geographic regions except Africa, though some regions were represented to a much greater extent than others. Sixty-nine percent of the participating schools (and 65 percent of those reporting collaborations), for example, were based in the U.S., reflecting the fact that U.S. schools make up a majority of AACSB members. In all, there were 178 participants from Northern America (U.S. and Canada), 31 from Europe, and 19 from Asia. Another 16 were split evenly between Oceania and Latin America.

Survey participants in the U.S. were, generally, less active in international partnerships than participants from other world regions. One hundred percent of European schools and 95 percent of Asian schools had existing partnership agreements at the time of the survey, compared to only 76 percent of U.S. schools. Eighty-eight percent of U.S. schools without partnerships, however, expressed a desire to enter into them.

Schools identified as partners, on the other hand, represented 86 countries in all major geographic regions, including Africa. Their geographic locations also followed some interesting patterns, as shown in Table 2.7. Europe was the region most frequently reported by schools in all regions to be the location of their partner institutions, though schools in Oceania were nearly as likely to

---

[76]Two hundred forty-four member schools participated in the survey, representing 22 percent of AACSB's members at the time. Of these, 201 reported having existing collaborations, and 200 provided additional information about those collaborations.

Table 2.7: Location of Survey Participants and Existing Partner Schools*.

Location of Survey Participants	Total Reported Partnerships*	Location of Partner Schools					
		Asia	Europe	Oceania	N. America	L. Amer/ Carib.	Africa
Asia	270	24%	45%	3%	29%	0%	0%
Europe	1347	15%	54%	3%	18%	9%	1%
Oceania	268	34%	35%	3%	24%	4%	0%
Northern America	1239	25%	47%	2%	15%	11%	1%
Latin America	212	3%	45%	2%	32%	17%	1%

*Multiple partners/partnerships might correspond to each reported collaboration.
Source: AACSB Member Collaboration Survey 2008.

partner with schools in Asia. Latin American schools were slightly more likely to partner with other schools in the Americas than to venture across the ocean to Europe or Asia. More than half of the partnerships reported by European schools were with other schools in Europe.

Out of all the regional groups, European schools reported the highest level of partnership activity, both in terms of likelihood to have one or more partnerships and in the average number of partnership agreements per school. At the same time, the partnership activity also is highly concentrated within the European region. Fifty-four percent of partner schools also were located within Europe, which is more than twice the next highest percentage of intra-regional partners (Asia). We believe the high level of partnership activity within Europe is attributed to several factors, including the relative geographic proximity of its countries to one another, the presence of pan-European initiatives to encourage greater student mobility (e.g., the Bologna Accord and the Erasmus Programme), and incentives such as the emphasis on international partnerships included within the EFMD's EQUIS accreditation standards.

We also note, however, the generally lower rate of partnership activity by schools from all regions with schools in Africa, Oceania, and Latin America/ Caribbean. The low rate of activity in Africa is explained by the relatively low stage of higher education development across large swathes of the continent. Oceania hosts a relatively small number of schools, limiting the availability of potential partners. Yet Latin America has both an increasingly competitive higher education landscape and large numbers of business schools (more than in Northern America). We suspect that other factors might be to blame, such as the volatility of the political situation in many countries and the region's lagging economic development relative to Europe, Asia, and Northern America.

The survey was also revealing in other ways. First, the vast majority (95 percent) of collaborative agreements were bilateral agreements between two schools.[77] Yet 16 percent of schools that reported collaborations had at least one involving more than four additional partner schools. (Together, collaborations with more than four partners represented only 1.6 percent of the total collaborations reported.) Though no specific threshold for the number of institutions comprising a "consortium" exists, many of these collaborations likely would fall into such a category (See box "Consortia: International Organizations or Multilateral Partnerships?").

Consortia: International Organizations or Multilateral Partnerships?

International consortia or networks have proliferated in recent years and fill a gray area between large international organizations, such as those discussed in the preceding section, and multilateral partnerships. Some serve to bring together business schools with common characteristics, such as the International Association of Jesuit Business Schools (IAJBS) and the Association of BRICS Business Schools (ABBS), a consortium composed of business schools located in Brazil, Russia, India, China, and South Africa. Other consortia focus on a particular type of education. For example, the International University Consortium for Executive Education (UNICON) and the SUMAQ Alliance were established to focus on executive education, though the scope of the latter has since expanded. International business is a focus for both the Network of International Business Schools (NIBS) and the Transatlantic Business School Alliance (TABSA). Members of the Consortium of International Double Degree Programs (CIDD) all maintain dual degree programs with at least one other member, creating a network for the sharing of effective practices related to a very specific activity. Still others such as CEMS-The Global Alliance in Management Education and the Consortium of Universities for International Studies (CIMBA) offer actual degree programs.

Many business schools also benefit from or contribute to university-level consortia, such as the ASEAN University Network (AUN), the Association of Commonwealth Universities, the International Alliance of Research Universities (IARU), *Universitas 21* (U21), the Worldwide Universities Network (WUN), the International Forum of Public Universities, and others.

---

[77]Participating schools were given the opportunity to report the names of up to four schools participating in a given collaborative agreement, and to indicate the total number of partners if there were more than four.

Second, lest it be too easy to overemphasize the collaboration occurring between business schools, we should point out that a majority of collaborations reported in the survey (74 percent) were established to support only one specific type of activity (e.g., student exchange, faculty exchange, dual-degree program, etc.) rather than being comprehensive agreements to support a variety of collaborative activities. In three of four cases, that activity was student exchange. Additionally, no provision in the survey determined the level of activity supported by a given collaborative agreement—e.g., in the case of student exchange, the number of students (if any) who actually were "exchanged" in a given year. Likely, a review of all the linkages reported between business schools would reveal many that are quite tenuous.

At the same time, the survey suggests there is substantial opportunity for business schools to explore other potential avenues for collaboration with existing partners. Student exchange agreements are low-risk and allow partner schools to begin to build a foundation for further, deeper collaboration. Chapter 5 provides additional information regarding the types of activities supported by the collaborative agreements, and the ways in which business schools augment their capabilities through strategic partnerships.

2.4.   What Today's Landscape Means for Globalization of Management Education

In her book *Territory, Authority, Rights: From Medieval to Global Assemblages*, sociologist Saskia Sassen speaks of a "tipping point that launches a new organizing logic in the assemblage of state capabilities for international action and collaboration ... [meaning] that while particular older capabilities may still be there the larger assemblage within which they function has been foundationally transformed." She goes on to suggest that the transformation is not just "integration, harmonization, or convergence of national ... orders," but rather the creation, addition, and overlay of something new.[78]

At what point do we reach a tipping point toward the emergence of a global system of management education that transcends various national systems? A global system need not apply a common structure or approach across institutions in all countries, as the Bologna Accord is trying to do for its signatories; national boundaries will remain important, and rightly so. But a global system does imply a greater degree of interaction among institutions and individuals that once operated in somewhat isolated

---

[78]Sassen, Saskia, *Territory, Authority, Rights: From Medieval to Global Assemblages*, Princeton University Press, Princeton, NJ, 2006, pp. 229 and 268, respectively.

contexts. It also implies an increasing orientation toward global agendas (namely the needs of the ever-globalizing business environment being served) and systems.

The trends and other indicators discussed in this chapter suggest growing momentum in this direction and point to the emergence of a global higher education system around the corner. The cross-border diffusion of ideas that characterized the early global emergence of management education is likely to accelerate as individuals and institutions become more connected across borders. Those connections will be driven by supply and demand dynamics as well as the need for border-transcending systems that facilitate the exchange of individuals, institutions, information, and ideas. In the following chapter, we address whether further globalization is inevitable and whether forces are at play that may deflect business schools off that path.

Chapter 3

The Fault Lines of Management Education Globalization

As the last chapter indicated, management education is clearly becoming more global along many dimensions. This trend is something to be celebrated and encouraged. Yet it also presents many new challenges. Business schools are entering unfamiliar territory (literally and figuratively) as they pursue various globalization strategies. Moreover, the forces they encounter on this journey are hardly consistent or stable.

We begin this chapter by looking at what is driving business school globalization, then focus on some of dimensions along which debates about globalization tend to be most complex, and at times most polarized. Decisions along these dimensions—economics, culture and tradition, public policy, and strategic positioning—will determine how broadly and evenly the benefits of globalization are felt.

3.1. The Promise of Globalization

The perceived benefits of globalization are well-known: accelerated economic growth and employment, transfer of technology and new products, and alleviation of poverty. As Jagdish Bhagwati,[1] Martin Wolf,[2] Johan Norberg,[3] and others have argued, globalization of business is the best hope of the poor. In his focus on globalization in higher education, Ben Wildavsky writes, "The biggest factor driving continued growth in higher education world-wide, both within nations and across borders, is the mounting evidence of the economic benefits of postsecondary education for both individuals and societies. It may be a commonplace to say that the

[1]Bhagwati, Jagdish, *In Defense of Globalization,* Oxford University Press, Oxford, 2004.
[2]Wolf, Martin, *Why Globalization Works,* Yale University Press, New Haven, CT, 2004.
[3]Norberg, Johan, *In Defense of Global Capitalism,* Cato Institute, Washington, D.C., 2003.

world has moved from a manufacturing to a service to a knowledge economy, but sometimes truisms are just that—true."[4] It also appears true that these changes are not constrained within national borders; though the impacts are not likely to be even in all regions, few populations will be excluded from the promise of globalization.

The Task Force furthermore believes that globalization of management education supports responsible globalization. In other words, more responsible globalization in business is likely a function of more *and better* globalization in management education. Thus far, business has led higher education in globalization efforts. Business schools are in an important position to capture lessons and ideas from this experience and to use them to assist organizations with and improve the outcomes of globalization. AACSB, in *Business Schools on an Innovation Mission*, points to the important role of research to test, codify, organize, and diffuse innovation and suggests that "high quality management research can legitimize new ideas and facilitate adoption in organizations" and "can help people to decide what not to do and how not to do it."[5] These points imply strong complementarities between research and education and between theory and practice in high-quality management education. By expanding the capacity of business schools to achieve global learning and research outcomes, the globalization of management education holds the promise of improving globalization more generally.

3.1.1. What is Motivating Globalization of Management Education?

Among business schools, motivations for globalization vary substantially, and often they reflect the culture of the school and its leadership or the pressures applied by stakeholders. In many cases, multiple motivating factors originate from the school itself, the business community that it serves, and/or the country/region in which the school is located.

Most business schools would claim that the motivation for their globalization efforts is simply that the activity or strategy is an inherent part of their missions as education providers. These schools see globalization as a natural and necessary extension of their efforts to teach, conduct research, and reach out to the communities they serve. In a recent study of mission statements submitted to AACSB by 642 member schools, 65 percent of statements were found to have the terms "global," "international," and/or "world" (or some variation thereof). The most frequently used term was global, which was found in 69 percent of mission statements using variations

---

[4]Wildavsky, Ben, *The Great Brain Race: How Global Universities Are Reshaping the World*, Princeton University Press, Princeton, NJ, 2010, p. 196.
[5]AACSB International, *Business Schools on an Innovation Mission: Report of the AACSB International Task Force on Business Schools and Innovation*, 2010, p. 25.

of one or more of the three words (45 percent of the total sample). About one-third of the schools using at least one term also used another. We also note that some school names imply an "international" or "global" focus, such as the Brandeis University International Business School (U.S.), China Europe International Business School (China), Jönköping International Business School (Sweden), and Thunderbird School of Global Management (U.S.).

Among mission statements, in some cases the use of these terms is very general, e.g., "in the world" or "in a global context," while other uses are more direct (e.g., "global awareness" or "global leadership"). In both cases, references generally fall into one or more of four general categories. Table 3.1 shows some of the categories of globalization referenced within business school mission statements and the specific dimensions that were most often cited.

Certainly, even among not-for-profit schools, revenue generation opportunities may motivate—or at the least, help encourage—certain internationally oriented activities. The reality is that the relationship between educational objectives and financial objectives is complex. On the one hand, our research reveals that many strategies for achieving global learning outcomes are costly.

Table 3.1: AACSB Member School References to Globalization in Mission Statements.

Category	Specific Topics Referenced in Mission Statements
Global Nature of Business	• International trade of goods & services • Economic integration • Inherently "international" nature of various disciplines
Global Market for Talent	• International networks of business professionals • Labor mobility • Need for "global leaders" • Role of developing economies • Transition to knowledge economies
Need for Intercultural Awareness	• Social constructs • Values (personal and professional) • Leadership styles • Communication styles
Global Higher Education Landscape	• Institution's unique role/contribution in a global context • Global benchmarking & competition • Opportunities for international collaboration

Source: AACSB analysis.

Schools must find ways to fund investments and ongoing expenses to achieve these desirable outcomes. On the other hand, in a time when traditional sources of funding are being cut, business school leaders are exploring globalization as offering one of several possible sources of funding to subsidize other initiatives.

The relationship between reputation and other objectives is similarly clouded by the realities of the industry. Reputational investments, in rankings placement for example, are often an expensive part of a globalization strategy, but they hold the potential for a huge payoff in terms of mission achievement (e.g., by improving the partnership opportunities) and/or financial return (e.g., by increasing alumni support). In the end, it is impossible to separate any single motivation completely.

3.1.2. Global Asymmetries and Globalization Challenges

Despite its promises, globalization is highly complex and likely to be shaped by (and result in) asymmetries across schools and countries. Not all attempts at globalization have been successful. Overly optimistic or otherwise unrealistic expectations of the market size in a given region have led to the failure of some international branch campuses or programs. These experiences have shown that estimates of market size must be based on much more than the number of individuals of the relevant age who live in the region or the country's perceived economic potential, but also on an assessment of potential students' secondary education credentials, ability to pay tuition, ability to speak and write fluently in the language of program delivery, and more. Cultural differences and national regulations have brought well-intentioned efforts to develop collaborations or operations in other countries to frustrating delays and even halts.

The asymmetries on the outcomes side are most visible when globalization strengthens the position of some schools relative to others. Resource constraints seem aggravated, the need to differentiate becomes ever more important, and schools wrestle—perhaps more than ever before—with defining the set of stakeholders they intend to serve and upholding that definition. The next section provides a discussion of four dimensions of asymmetries likely to influence the pace and direction of globalization in management education.

3.2. The Fault Lines of Globalization

The Task Force views globalization as an inevitable process that all schools today must face, whether inclined to do so or not. Yet the process is not inexorable. Globalization is being driven and shaped by complex forces that may change in direction or intensity at any given time. Some of these forces facilitate business schools' globalization efforts; others present challenges or constraints that must be accommodated or overcome. Praise and criticism for globalization of management education tend to divide along the fault-lines of economics, culture and tradition, public policy, and strategic positioning.

- **Economics.** Does globalization alleviate resource constraints of schools of management or improve the quality of student experience? The answer could be neither or both. Regardless, the economics of globalization will have a tremendous impact on the future of globalization, and the answers may depend on specific characteristics of the school, such as its location (e.g., in developed versus emerging economies).
- **Culture and tradition.** Does globalization respect or diminish differences in norms, values, practices, and institutions? The answers, and opinions about the answers, may vary among local purists versus cosmopolitans, and internationalists versus nationalists. Even among developed economies, strong differences in attitudes exist among the Continental European, Japanese, and Anglo-American spheres. Will we, or should we, ever reach a state in which knowing when to *Kiss, Bow, or Shake Hands* is unnecessary?[6]
- **Public policy.** Are the benefits from globalization available to schools irrespective of the regulatory environment they face? The hand of government affects mobility for individuals and institutions as well as the degree to which knowledge and ideas are freely disseminated. Higher education institutions, including business schools, in the new knowledge economy are viewed increasingly as assets, worthy of protection and subsidization. But does this viewpoint limit the competitive benefits of globalization or enhance it?
- **Strategic positioning.** In what ways does globalization reshape how organizations, in this case business schools, are positioned relative to one another? How do schools differentiate themselves in this environment? Responses differ along lines that define strategy and the strategic position of an institution—reputation, mission, and resources—and among, for instance, elite schools versus mass-education schools.

Along these dimensions, opportunities and constraints—both for business schools and their constituents—tend to align. Academic leaders, government administrators, and policy makers view globalization as positive on some dimensions and threatening on others.

3.2.1. Economics

Countries and institutions differ greatly in their degrees of economic development. The great variation in GDP per capita across countries is generally understood and serves as a conventional indicator of a country's overall

---

[6]Morrison, Terry, and Wayne A. Conaway, *Kiss, Bow or Shake Hands, 2nd edition*, Adams Media, Avon, MA, 2006.

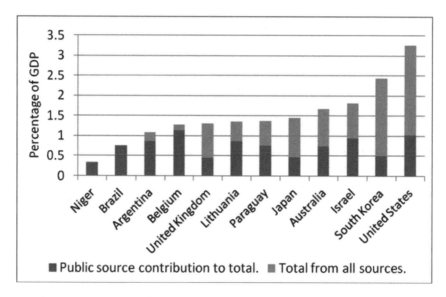

Figure 3.1: Total Expenditure on Tertiary Educational Institutions and Administration as a Percentage of GDP. Select Countries. Public Sources and All Sources. 2007.

Source: UNESCO Institute for Statistics. Finance Indicators by ISCED level.

economic well-being. However, variances in economic context also produce large differences in demand for higher education and in the support that educational institutions can expect to receive. These differences, in turn, influence the ability of institutions to recruit quality faculty and generally fulfill their missions.

Figure 3.1 shows that, as compared to GDP, great disparity exists across countries in terms of both total tertiary education spending and the proportion that comes from public and private sources. In some countries, such as Argentina, Belgium, Brazil, and Niger, the majority of spending on tertiary education is from public sources. In five of the countries shown (Australia, Japan, South Korea, the United Kingdom, and the United States), public sources comprise less than half of the overall spending.

The *UNESCO Global Education Digest 2009* gives some indication of just how disparity in GDP is reflected in resource constraints for higher education in developed versus developing countries:

> Broadening access to tertiary education has massive cost implications for governments, especially in developing countries. Despite low participation ratios, many developing countries already spend a similar share of their national wealth

on tertiary education as developed countries. This can be attributed to the extremely high expenditure per tertiary student compared to the expenditure per primary or secondary student or GDP per capita. When expenditure is compared in absolute terms, it becomes apparent that options to reduce expenditure are limited, which then raises the question of whether further expansion of tertiary education can be sustained by government funding or needs to rely increasingly on private expenditure.[7]

If lower participation ratios mean generally lower economies of scale and higher costs, does globalization of management education (or of higher education more broadly) present opportunities for the creation of economies of scale? Does it enable greater resource levels for countries to cope with an expanding tertiary education sector? The answers may lie in the significant (and often growing) role of private expenditure in sustaining higher education; compared to public funding, private funding is less constrained by national borders. Furthermore, private funding can come in the form of cross-border operations by foreign educational institutions, which (though they may receive public funding support in their home countries) are often considered private institutions in other nations.

Faculty Salaries and the Global Faculty Market. In its analysis of tertiary education financing, the *UNESCO Global Education Digest 2009* also notes that "tertiary education systems and their costs are more strongly tied to international markets than costs for primary or secondary education. While salaries for primary school teachers need to be competitive at the national level to attract qualified teachers, the competition for highly-skilled staff for universities is on a global scale. As such, the risk of academic 'brain drain' tends to deter the lowering of salaries for tertiary education staff."[8]

In fact, the international markets for some faculty members are extremely competitive and all but exclude some countries from recruiting internationally. This experience is particularly true for faculty members with doctoral education credentials and extensive publication records in respected journals. (See box "Shopping for Talent across Borders").

---

[7]UNESCO Institute for Statistics, *Global Education Digest 2009: Comparing Education Statistics Across the World*, Montreal, Quebec, Canada, 2009, electronic document, http://www. uis.unesco.org/template/pdf/ged/2009/GED_2009_EN.pdf, accessed January 31, 2010, p. 49.
[8]Ibid., p. 50.

Shopping for Talent across Borders

A Dean at an American business school recounted how globalization had intervened in her faculty relations.* Having worked hard over several years to increase the international diversity of the school's faculty, she was surprised by separate encounters with two of the brightest younger faculty members. Both had recently been recognized for strong research accomplishments. Both faculty members were compensated at the 80th percentile of their U.S. peer group, adjusted for rank and field of specialization.

Niraj, the full professor, had been raised in Mumbai, educated in the U.S., and risen to the top of his field specialty. He appeared one day to ask for a leave of absence to teach at a leading business school near London. His salary there would be 2.5 times his compensation in the U.S. Even adjusting for cost-of-living differences, this was an extraordinary jump.

Yee Cheng, a native of Shanghai, asked to revise her teaching assignment for the next year so that she could take a six-month unpaid leave of absence to teach at a major university there. Her salary would be comparable to what she was receiving in the U.S. She would also receive a very generous housing allowance, a car and driver, and tax exemption on earnings while there. She estimated that the total package of compensation was about twice her U.S. salary.

In separate meetings, the Dean counseled each faculty member to reflect seriously on his or her commitment to the future of the U.S. institution. Each person expressed sincere commitment. The Dean agreed to both requests.

Two years later, Niraj resigned from the U.S. school. Within six months of joining the school near London, he had been awarded a tenured full professorship and directorship of a center. Yee Cheng remained with the U.S. school, but had arranged to spend her spring semesters and the summers in Shanghai.

The Dean reflected that globalization was radically changing the market for faculty talent. Her mistake was in gauging faculty compensation against peers only in her country. But the market for top faculty talent was now a global market, characterized by aggressive entry by new global elite schools.

*Identities have been disguised by the Task Force at the request of the contributing institution.

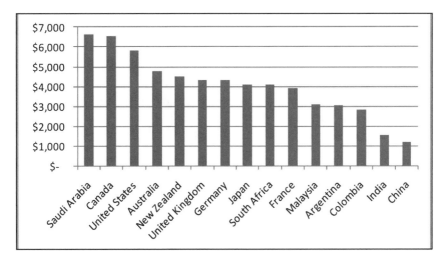

Figure 3.2: Average Monthly Salaries, Higher Education. U.S. Dollars, 2008, Adjusted for Purchasing Power Parity.

Source: Rumbley, et al. (2008).[9]

Figure 3.2 reveals the wide disparities in average salaries across countries, even when adjusted for purchasing power parity. Measuring these differences is complicated by the existence of different tax structures and the addition of non-monetary forms of compensation, such as housing, healthcare, and supplemental support for travel and professional development.

In several countries, including Israel, Saudi Arabia, Chinese Taipei, Thailand, and Malaysia, the salaries of faculty members are regulated at the national level, though in some cases such regulations apply only to national or public universities. In other countries (including Japan and Lebanon), salaries are commonly regulated at the university level according to faculty rank and/or other criteria, with the established salary ranges applying equitably across all disciplines. In such cases, business school administrators must align faculty salaries with a national or university structure rather than the market rates for faculty members with business doctorates. This practice makes the recruitment of international faculty for business positions difficult to nearly impossible for these schools because of higher salaries offered by schools in countries without such constraints. Some schools utilize bonus systems or other forms of supplemental compensation as a means of

[9]Rumbley, L.E., I.F. Pacheco, and P.G. Altbach, *International Comparison of Academic Salaries: An Exploratory Study*, Boston College Center for International Higher Education, Chestnut Hill, MA, 2008, p. 22.

increasing salaries beyond regulatory constraints, but not all schools have the resources or authority to implement these programs.

Of course, salary is not the only dimension governing international faculty markets, in the same way that tuition is far from the only basis for students' school selection. Language, culture, sociopolitical environments, geographic preferences, and many other factors often have strong influences on where faculty members seek employment. Business schools in countries such as China and India, for example, have had notable success luring native-born professors working or studying abroad to return to teaching positions back "home."

Contributing to the complexities of international faculty markets is the location where individuals receive doctoral training. Some countries and world regions have particularly low numbers of doctoral education providers (at least, providers perceived to be of high quality), causing individuals from those regions to seek training elsewhere, and making the hiring of faculty with doctoral training more difficult for institutions in those regions. According to data from the U.S. Survey of Earned Doctorates,[10] between 2001 and 2007, 36 percent of graduates from U.S. AACSB-accredited business doctoral programs studied in the U.S. on temporary visas. Yet, only approximately 15 percent of graduates who knew their post-graduation destination reported that they would leave the U.S. for work or further study.[11] Thus, approximately 21 percent of the new doctorates on the market for faculty positions at U.S. business schools during that seven-year timeframe represent a net "brain gain" for the U.S. and a "brain drain" for various other countries. This figure represents approximately 250 business doctoral program graduates per year.

Certainly, numerous complex factors influence the cross-border flows of human and financial capital. It is along this "fault line" of economics that the asymmetries in outcomes are likely to become most visible. Faculty salaries and institutional budgets are more easily quantified than many of the characteristics of fault lines discussed later in this section, resulting in easier identification and comparison of the "haves" and the "have nots." At the same time, too much emphasis on this dimension can distract attention from schools' true educational objectives, or from long-term investment (e.g., in faculty development) at the expense of short-term gain (e.g., faculty recruitment). The economics will require comprehensive and creative thinking about the most effective strategies for individual schools and the industry.

---

[10]NSF/NIH/USED/NEH/USDA/NASA, 2007 Survey of Earned Doctorates, custom report.

[11]Less than 10 percent of graduates indicated that their post-graduation location was unknown.

3.2.2. Culture

Vast differences in culture, tradition, and administrative practices produce a global playing field that is not "flat" in the sense of Thomas Friedman's definition, but rather, one that is characterized by a series of complexities that individuals must anticipate and navigate.[12] With the advent of electronic distribution of entertainment and news, and with the greater interactivity and social networking enabled by evolutions in communication technologies, some people fear the homogenization of cultures and the loss of local identities. At the same time, individual and organizational efforts to work across national and cultural "borders" often remain hampered by real and substantial differences. The notion that universal truths and global best practices exist in management is challenged by the belief that "business is done differently here."

Navigating these differences is often a challenge for schools, students, and the institutions that serve them. Even among the most developed countries, cultural differences can lead to material differences in institutional governance—such as the differences among Anglo-American, Continental European, and Japanese traditions—which complicate collaborative efforts between schools.

One reason for these complications is that cultures have different paradigms for determining a sense of authority or expertise. Across cultures, individuals of the same age, professional experience, academic experience, and even gender may be perceived very differently. These differences are reflected in faculty models as well as in organizational leadership and decision-making frameworks. Does an MBA student benefit more from a teacher who is an accomplished academic, or one who is a successful practitioner? How should faculty members split their time between teaching, research, and service activities? How are individuals selected for departmental or school leadership positions, and what kind of decision-making authority do they hold? Different cultures will likely answer each of these questions differently with varying implications for the ways in which business schools are structured and managed.

As schools endeavor to internationalize faculty and student bodies, differences in teaching and learning styles also present challenges in the classroom. Cultural differences in the acceptability of practices as diverse as expressing disagreement with professors, cheating, learning beyond the required scope, and forming gender-heterogeneous work groups all

---

[12]See Friedman, Thomas L., *The World is Flat: A Brief History of the 21st Century*, Picador Press, New York, 2007.

complicate classroom management, curriculum development, and teacher-student interactions.[13]

In some cases, individuals and organizations feel pressure to align with "foreign" values or practices in order to access opportunities in a global context. Whether these practices are actually *best* practices or simply *dominant* practices is the subject of much debate, as faculty members at the Korea Advanced Institute of Science and Technology (KAIST) can attest. The school's president, Nam Pyo Suh, recently instituted a series of controversial reforms that included changing the language of instruction to English and shifting tenure from an automatic entitlement to a merit-based award.[14] While embraced by many members of the school and its surrounding community, for others these changes represent an unnecessary rejection of tradition.

While a tension certainly exists between opportunities presented by alignment and the desire to preserve existing traditions and cultures, several examples of frameworks that unite different cultures and traditions exist as well. These examples emphasize common ground while still respecting cultures' unique characteristics.

One example is the Principles for Responsible Management Education (PRME), developed by an international task force of sixty deans, university presidents, and official representatives of business schools and academic institutions under the coordination of the United Nations Global Compact. The principles serve as a guiding framework designed for all business schools around the world to adopt. PRME signatory institutions commit to incorporate into their academic activities and curricula the values of global social responsibility as portrayed in international initiatives such as the United Nations Global Compact. As of July 2010, business schools in 59 countries had agreed to uphold these values. In his closing remarks at the Global Leaders Summit in Geneva 2007, U.N. Secretary-General Ban Ki-moon acknowledged the PRME by stating, "the Principles for Responsible Management Education have the capacity to take the case for universal values and business into classrooms on every continent."

Examples of alignment in higher education more generally are found in recent efforts to harmonize, or "tune," various educational systems so as to minimize (or minimize the obstacles resulting from) structural differences. The

---

[13]Gerhard, A., K. Hansen, S. Keuchel, M. Neubauer, S.H. Ong, N. Tapachai, and C. Mueller, "Cross-cultural Learning Styles in Higher Education," *International Journal of Learning*, Vol. 12, No. 5 (2005), pp. 247-56. (This study is one of many that focuses on cross-cultural learning styles. Its focus is on business students in Austria, Germany, Singapore, and Thailand.)

[14]McNeill, David, "No Looking Back: KAIST's President Fights for His Legacy of Change in South Korea," *The Chronicle of Higher Education*, June 20, 2010, electronic document, http://chronicle.com/article/No-Looking-Back-Kaists-Pr/65974/, accessed August 27, 2010.

Bologna Process, to which 47 European countries have become signatories, is an example of an attempt to strike a balance between respect for "the diversity of cultures, languages, national education systems and… University autonomy,"[15] and the creation of opportunities through development of a common approach to higher education across national borders. Other "tuning" initiatives have emerged in many regions of the world, such as the ALFA Tuning Latin America Project involving 19 countries across Central America, South America, and the Caribbean,[16] or the beginning discussions of an Asian-focused Bologna-style accord among the ASEAN nations.[17] These experiences show that harmonization and tuning of educational frameworks is possible, but these processes are extraordinarily complex and difficult to implement, and countries will continue to grapple with them for decades to come.

Other initiatives at the level of individual schools are intended to align certain aspects of their programs with those in other countries in order to facilitate cross-border collaborations. For example, a school's decision to offer courses on a semester, trimester, or quarter schedule may have implications for student and faculty exchange agreements. Schools may also try to enhance interest in incoming student exchange opportunities by adding a series of courses in the language of their exchange partner school or by catering to international student preferences along dimensions such as food, entertainment, and worship.

Still other shifts are motivated by a desire to perform better against a specific measure of quality that has come to dominate. Of all the motives for cultural shifts, this one should be regarded with the most caution. The existence in nearly every country of some form of quality assurance or controls related to higher education is evidence that quality is something valued across cultures. However, views about how quality should be defined and enforced differ widely and are often linked to cultural traditions. What one culture deems necessary or important is not always valued in other cultures. For example, in Asia test scores are relied upon as an indicator of the quality of individual students more than in other regions of the world. Quality frameworks—whether used to measure institutions or individuals—developed in one context may not always apply in all settings.

---

[15]European Ministers of Education, The Bologna Declaration of 19 June 1999, joint declaration of the European Ministers of Education, 1999, electronic document, http://www.ond.vlaanderen.be/hogeronderwijs/bologna/documents/MDC/BOLOGNA_DECLARATION1.pdf, accessed June 10, 2010, p. 4.

[16]ALFA Tuning Latin America, "Tuning Latin America Project" web page, electronic document, http://tuning.unideusto.org/tuningal/, accessed June 10, 2010.

[17]Maslen, Geoff, "SOUTHEAST ASIA: Bold plan to duplicate Bologna," *University World News*, November 23, 2008, electronic document, http://www.universityworldnews.com/article.php?story=20081120154941889, accessed December 31, 2010.

The AACSB's mission-linked approach to accreditation is intended to address this issue of diverse quality measures by enabling interpretation of a series of standards in the context of a school's mission and setting. Through this approach, the organization has come to accredit schools in nearly 40 countries using a single set of mission-based quality standards and by relying on the professional judgment of accreditation reviewers. Yet, even this procedure is not always easy, as individuals' own past experiences and biases, as well as their views about what constitutes equity, are likely to influence professional judgments.

3.2.3. Public Policy

Ironically, some of the most significant opportunities and obstacles for business school globalization are presented through national policies and regulations that impact individual mobility and higher education delivery. Such policies are designed both to control global "trade" in higher education and to develop higher education capacity (or a talent pool) aligned with a strategy for national competitiveness. The hand of government, motivated by values of protectionism versus free trade, has the power to enable, encourage, discourage, and prevent mobility for individuals, institutions, and ideas.

Since the adoption of the General Agreement on Trade in Services (GATS) by members of the World Trade Organization (WTO) in 1995, much has been written about the agreement's implications for cross-border education. The intent of the GATS is to provide WTO member countries with legally enforceable rights to trade in services, including education.[18] However, relative to other services covered by GATS, education has so far received only low levels of attention from the signatory countries. As of 2010, only 49 of 153 WTO members (32 percent) had made market access commitments in the education sector overall, and only 40 (26 percent) had made commitments in higher education specifically.[19]

---

[18]In particular, the GATS covers four "modes of supply" for trade in services, each relating (in the higher education sector) to different aspects of cross-border education. Mode 1 services are supplied in another country (for example, distance education and e-learning). Mode 2 services involve travel by the consumer (for example, students travel to study in another country). Mode 3 services require the service provider to establish a commercial presence in another country (for example, through branch/satellite campuses or franchise agreements). Mode 4 services are supplied by the movement of professionals from one country to another to provide the service (for example, visiting faculty from an institution in another country).

[19]World Trade Organization, Services Database web page, 2010, electronic document, http://tsdb.wto.org, accessed August 5, 2010.

The low level of commitments within the GATS framework for higher education does not, however, indicate of a lack of government interest or involvement in international higher education. On the contrary, around the world we find numerous examples of how national policies and regulations concerning higher education (as well as other sectors) enhance or constrain the globalization of management education. In recent years, numerous countries have enacted policy reforms, set target objectives, and/or invested in strategies designed to address a need for increased mutual understanding and collaboration with other countries, a more skilled labor force, enhanced higher education capacity, and revenue to sustain existing higher education infrastructure.[20] Other (not necessarily mutually exclusive) aims include consumer protection, insulation of the local higher education system against competition, and elevation of quality among local providers through foreign competition.

The resulting strategies create a complex system that business schools must navigate if they wish to globalize, especially because, in any given country, a change in political leadership can lead to sudden shifts in policy. These shifts have the potential to impact the globalization of management education by influencing mobility of individuals, institutions, and ideas.

Mobility of Individuals. Recognition of the value of cross-border educational opportunities by governmental authorities is hardly a modern-day phenomenon. With *Authentica Habita,* a proclamation declared by Holy Roman Emperor Frederick I in 1158, we find a precedent for today's national, state-sponsored initiatives to foster international student mobility. The edict exempted traveling students and scholars from tolls, taxes, and customs dues and provided general protection for them and their property, contributing to extensive student and scholar mobility.[21]

Today, national initiatives to attract foreign students are aimed at accumulating the human capital necessary to compete in a globally competitive marketplace. Approaches may include investments in marketing campaigns, reform of visa/immigration policies, and modifications to tuition and fee models—all aimed at enticing bright students who would otherwise study and work elsewhere to congregate in and contribute to the supporting country's intellectual capacity. These same efforts also lead to and sustain substantial wars for talent. Initiatives such as that in Singapore, which aims to attract 150,000 foreign students by 2015, may have an effect of draining talent from nearby countries.

---

[20]See Naidoo's four main national-level rationales behind growth in student, program, and institution mobility: Naidoo, Vikash, "International Education: A Tertiary-level Industry Update," *Journal of Research in International Education*, Vol. 5, No. 3 (2006), pp. 323–45.
[21]Gürüz, Kemal, *Higher Education and International Student Mobility in the Global Knowledge Economy*, State University of New York Press, Albany, NY, 2008.

Similarly, in 2001, China set a target to attract 120,000 students by 2007, and subsequently they exceeded the target by more than 60 percent. The government facilitated this effort in part through the development of a network of Confucius Institutes on six continents. These institutes engage in partnerships with foreign universities to promote Chinese language and culture and by extension to promote Chinese institutions of higher learning.[22] The government of Japan has set a target of increasing the number of incoming international students from approximately 100,000 in 2008 to 300,000 by 2020.[23] In Turkey, the Higher Education Board (YÖK) is considering measures such as encouraging private universities to lower tuition costs for foreign students, requesting that state universities consider boosting admissions of foreign students, and even making changes to the Foreign Student Exam (YÖS) that foreign students must pass before being admitted to a Turkish university.[24] The European Commission's Study in Europe web portal is part of a campaign to increase the number of non-European students studying in the EU by making information about study opportunities more accessible.[25]

The easing of employment restrictions has been an approach used by Canada as well as Hong Kong and the United Arab Emirates[26] as a means not only of attracting more foreign students, but also of enticing them to remain in the country upon graduation. In Canada, thanks in part to leadership by the Rotman School of Management at the University of Toronto, new government regulations now allow individuals studying in a degree program in Canada to remain in the country for three years after graduating in order to look for a job.[27] Similar legislation in France now guarantees foreign master's-level students a six-month timeframe post-graduation to secure in-country employment as well as a working visa if

---

[22]Hvistendahl, Mara, "China Moves up to Fifth as Importer of Students," *The Chronicle of Higher Education*, September 19, 2008, electronic document, http://chronicle.com/article/China-Moves-Up-to-Fifth-as/8224/, accessed February 2, 2010.

[23]Hazelkorn, Ellen, "Globalization, Internationalization, and Rankings," *International Higher Education*, No. 53 (Fall 2008), p. 8.

[24]Asalioğlu, Ibrahim, "YÖK seeks to attract foreign students to Turkish universities," *Today's Zaman*, October 7, 2008, electronic document, http://www.todayszaman.com/tz-web/detaylar.do?load=detay&link=155186&bolum=101, accessed August 27, 2010.

[25]w?>EuropeanCommission,StudyinEuropewebportal,electronicdocument,http://QJ;ec.europa.eu/education/study-in-europe/,accessedDecember30,2010.

[26]Krieger, Zvika, "Build It And They Will Learn," *Newsweek*, August 8, 2008, electronic document, http://www.newsweek.com/2008/08/08/build-it-and-they-will-learn.html, accessed June 12, 2010.

[27]Bradshaw, Della, "Canada eases work rules for graduates," *Financial Times*, July 28, 2008, electronic document, http://www.ft.com/cms/s/2/f65d3e04-5a80-11dd-bf96-000077b07658, dwp_uuid=02e16f4a-46f9-11da-b8e5-00000e2511c8.html, accessed June 12, 2010.

full-time employment meeting minimum skill and salary thresholds is obtained. As in Canada, the passing of the legislation in France resulted in part from advocacy from the higher education sector, in this case the Conférence des Grandes Ecoles.

By contrast, other countries have tightened their borders as a response to perceived threats to national labor markets or national security. In 2008, for example, the United Kingdom tightened visa regulations, requiring that individuals from outside the European Economic Area interested in studying in the U.K. be "sponsored" by an institution licensed by the U.K. Border Agency.[28] Such policies have the potential to impede the ability of business schools in these countries to recruit international students. A 2009 decline in international applicants to U.S. MBA programs is similarly attributed primarily to new visa restrictions and more stringent criteria to qualify for student loans.[29]

Employment regulations also affect mobility of faculty members or other institutional staff. In Brazil, for example, faculty members who have earned PhDs outside of Brazil must have their degrees first validated by a Brazilian institution—a process reported to be as short as 30 days or as long as two years. In other countries, differential treatment of citizen and non-citizen faculty may discourage or bar foreign faculty members from seeking positions at local institutions. In Indonesia, for example, government regulation restricts full-time faculty positions to only Indonesian citizens; all non-citizens are only eligible to teach in a part-time capacity.

Mobility of institutions. Business schools interested in establishing branch campuses abroad often find that relevant policies and regulations in other countries fall within a spectrum of relatively laissez-faire to very strict.[30] An analysis of the regulatory environments in OECD and several other countries with regard to cross-border education reveals just how significantly regulation impacts institutional mobility. Some countries have fairly simple requirements that branch campuses must meet for official recognition, such as the

---

[28]Alderman, Geoffrey, "Bordering on the bureaucratic," *The Guardian*, September 2, 2008, electronic document, http://www.guardian.co.uk/education/2008/sep/09/internationalstudents .visas, accessed August 27, 2010.

[29]Damast, Alison, "U.S. Business Schools: Why Foreign M.B.A.s are Disappearing," *BusinessWeek*, August 3, 2009, electronic document, http://www.businessweek.com/bschools/ content/aug2009/bs2009083_042666.htm?link_position=link1, accessed June 11, 2010.

[30]In 2005, the Observatory on Borderless Higher Education classified a selection of countries' regulatory models and implications for foreign higher education providers on a continuum of virtually impossible, restrictive, transitional (either direction), moderately liberal, liberal, and no regulations. See Verbik, Line, and Lisa Jokivirta, "National Regulatory Approaches to Transnational Higher Education," *International Higher Education*, No. 41 (Fall 2005), pp. 6–8.

requirement that programs offered on branch campuses are fully transferable to the parent institution and/or that the parent institution have authority to operate in its home nation. Examples of this level of regulation are found in Australia, Chinese Taipei, Israel, Japan, the Philippines, Singapore, and the U.A.E.

Slightly less lenient regulations may require that the branch campus itself become part of the local educational system, such as by establishing itself as a private higher education institution or as a local not-for-profit agency through which it offers the programs of the parent provider. Examples of this level of regulation are found in Austria, Chile, Hong Kong, South Africa, and South Korea. Countries with stricter requirements, such as China and India, mandate that any foreign educational provider must operate in conjunction with an approved local provider to offer transnational education of any type within their borders. Even when regulations do not appear to be strict, the processes for gaining approval often are heavily bureaucratic and take months to navigate. In recent months, many eyes have been turned on India in anticipation of the passage of a bill that could open the country up to foreign educational providers.[31] (See box "Liberalizing National Entry.")

Liberalizing National Entry

India has struggled to find the right balance between gaining mass access to higher education and establishing truly world-class institutions. The Indian Institutes of Management (IIMs) enroll a truly elite student body—these schools admit less than one-half percent of applicants. Yet, access to higher education in India is lower than in the other major emerging economies of the world: India educates about 11 percent of its age group in higher education versus 20 percent for China and 71 percent in North America and Western Europe.* Low rates of compensation for academics spur departures for business careers and/or defection to other schools across borders. A portion of faculty slots is reserved for employment of disadvantaged castes. Entry by foreign institutions is limited by tight restrictions. Consequently, government policymakers have concerns about whether India's rapid economic growth rate is sustainable under these circumstances.

---

[31]Neelakantan, Shailaja, "Indian Higher Education Minister to Court Top U.S. Universities," *The Chronicle of Higher Education*, October 24, 2009, electronic document, http://chronicle. com/article/Indian-Higher-Education/48926/?sid=at&utm_source=at&utm_medium=en, accessed June 11, 2010.

In early 2010, India's Cabinet and Prime Minister brought to parliament draft legislation to permit foreign institutions to enter India. The Foreign Educational Institutions (Regulation of Entry and Operations) Bill sought to lift restrictions somewhat on the entry of foreign educational providers and thereby improve access and raise the quality of university instruction. The legislation would allow institutions to enter the country on condition of maintaining a fund of not less than 500 million rupees ($11 million). And any surplus profits earned in these operations could not be invested in any business other than growth and development of the institution.

Some observers of the proposed legislation feared that the bill would result in little expansion of access to higher education and might attract relatively lower-quality service providers. Professor Philip Altbach states the following in his article on the subject:

> The decision to enact legislation to permit foreign universities to set up shop in India is likely to have negative consequences and unlikely to have a positive impact on the provision of quality education services. India's higher education bureaucracy, in coping with the complexity of dealing with foreign education service providers, will find itself distracted from the more important task of improving the quality of Indian universities. The foreign universities themselves may be interested in offering services where they can make a profit, or in setting up advanced post graduate centers. There is little likelihood of a significant expansion of access.**

The issue in this illustration is that government policy changes can lead to unexpected consequences for providers and consumers of management education services. India proposes to relax the barriers to entry by foreign institutions. But the partial relaxation proposed seems destined to induce entry by only the very wealthiest schools and by schools who are adept at generating a surplus through a mass education approach. Will this conditional effort satisfy the huge demand for education in India?

---

*UNESCO Institute for Statistics, *Global Education Digest 2009: Comparing Education Statistics Across the World*, Montreal, Quebec, Canada, 2009, electronic document, http://www.uis.unesco.org/template/pdf/ged/2009/GED_2009_EN.pdf, accessed January 31, 2010.

**Altbach, Philip, "Open Door in Higher Education: Unsustainable and Probably Ill-Advised," *Economic and Political Weekly*, Vol. 45, No. 13 (2010), p. 13.

Still other countries have no legal provisions for the existence of foreign branches at all. This situation results in various outcomes: foreign branches may operate, but with little to no local oversight (e.g., Mexico); or they may operate, but without local recognition of validity by educational authorities (e.g., Greece, Switzerland); or foreign branches may be forbidden entirely (e.g., Cyprus).

In several countries, national initiatives aimed at attracting foreign providers of higher education involve the offer of financial subsidies or tax incentives. In Singapore in 1997, for example, the government announced its target to attract 10 world-class universities to Singapore within a decade, an effort termed the "Global Schoolhouse Initiative." By November 2005, thanks in part to financial subsidies by the Economic Development Board, the country announced that it had surpassed its target by six universities. South Korea, on the other hand, is seeking to entice foreign schools to set up operations in new free economic zones where they will find lower taxes and fewer regulations than they would have otherwise encountered.[32] The Seoul Metropolitan Government has further announced plans to attract a European- or American-based business school to open a branch campus in Yeouido, an island in central Seoul that serves as one of the country's financial hubs.[33]

Similar initiatives have appeared recently in the Middle East. Dubai International Academic City (DIAC), for example, located in a 25-million-square-foot "free zone," now hosts more than 32 international universities from countries including the U.S., U.K., Belgium, Iran, Russia, Australia, Sri Lanka, France, Pakistan, and India. Schools operating in DIAC pay no taxes in Dubai and are able to repatriate 100 percent of their profits.

More than the other "fault lines" discussed in this section, there seems to be more alignment among business schools in support of free trade in higher education. Likewise, it is the view of this Task Force that free trade in higher education would promote student mobility and entry by foreign institutions into local markets. Protectionism, on the other hand, would restrict mobility and entry and very likely result in higher prices, underserved demand, and lower quality. As Ben Wildavsky writes, "Just as constraining traditional forms of trade hurts consumers and stymies economic creativity, closing doors to the free flow of people and ideas thwarts knowledge generation, which is the lifeblood of successful economies."[34]

---

[32]World Education Services, "University Deregulation Measures Welcome News for Potential Foreign Campuses," *Korea Herald*, September 16, 2008, electronic document, http://www.wes.org/ewenr/PF/08oct/pfasiapacific.htm, accessed June 11, 2010.

[33]Tae-gyu, Kim, "Seoul Aims to Attract Top Business School," *Korea Times*, January 22, 2009, electronic document, http://www.koreatimes.co.kr/www/news/biz/2010/07/123_38322.html, accessed June 12, 2010.

[34]Wildavsky, Ben, *The Great Brain Race: How Global Universities Are Reshaping the World*, Princeton University Press, Princeton, NJ, 2010, p. 197.

3.2.4. Positioning

The fourth "fault line" has more to do with the outcomes of globalization. Globalization is changing the relative positioning of business schools, bringing some into closer proximity to one another and adding greater distance between others. It is changing definitions of what constitutes a "peer" or "competitor" school—in many cases by decreasing the importance of national identity as a defining characteristic.

Schools of management come to the globalization process endowed with different strengths and weaknesses. Leading research universities enjoy world-class brand names, access to excellent talent, and advantages in funding. In comparison, schools that emphasize accessibility rely on financial models of large-volume attendance.

What constitutes a "peer" or "competitor" school? Business schools that seek accreditation through AACSB, an association that operates its accreditation through a peer-review process, are asked to identify other accredited schools that are similar in mission and resources—a so-called set of "peer" schools against which the school might benchmark, and from which the members of the accreditation review team are drawn. An analysis of peer school selection from 2006-2009 shows that U.S. schools selected other U.S. schools as "peers" in 97.2 percent of cases, whereas European schools chose peers from within the same region in only 52.9 percent of cases, and Asian schools chose others within the same region in 48.3 percent of cases. These patterns are likely due to the need for "peers" to represent AACSB-accredited institutions and the relatively lower proportion of accredited schools in Europe and Asia.

Yet the tendencies also suggest an area for ongoing attention and analysis. The years 2008 and 2009 saw an upsurge in the percent of schools choosing peers based outside their home region. The Task Force hypothesizes that growing awareness of institutions in other countries through international accreditation and rankings, as well as international collaborations, will encourage more business schools to position themselves against peers on a global rather than local or regional level.

There are many dimensions along which schools in very distant and different regions might find parallels. The Stanford Graduate School of Business and the Indian Institute of Management-Bangalore, for example, decided to capitalize on an important similarity by teaming up to offer students a collaborative, experiential learning opportunity. Though the U.S. and India are obviously dramatically different contexts, the partnership is based on the schools' respective locations in their countries' high-tech corridors. Opportunities to identify shared contexts across borders exist for other industries and stakeholder groups as well.

Globalization also changes how schools are positioned in a competitive sense. Recent years have seen increased attention to *global* business school rankings by incumbents such as *BusinessWeek*, the *Financial Times*, and the *Economist*, as well as newcomers such as EdUniversal. Leaders of business schools frequently are under intense pressure by potential students, advisory boards, and university-level administrators to attain, maintain, and improve position in rankings that transcend national boundaries.

Still, much of this jockeying for positions takes place within a very small set of schools that offer business degrees. The institutions included in the most recent publications of a wide range of business school rankings[35] include only 1,024 distinct schools, or less than 9 percent of all schools worldwide that are known to offer business degree programs. Without the EdUniversal ranking, which is the largest ranking in the set with 1,000 business schools, we find that the remaining lists together include only 267 distinct institutions, or slightly more than 2 percent of the estimated 12,600 institutions that grant business degrees worldwide. As noted in the last chapter, international accreditations are held by only a relatively small percent of business degree providers.

Many international business school accreditation schemes emerged with the primary mission to provide a framework against which schools might pursue higher quality and then assess progress and opportunities for improvement. In this sense, the accreditation schemes were intended primarily for internal purposes within the business school. But the needs of stakeholders to know more about the quality of business schools has enhanced the signaling role of such accreditations, with the seal of the accrediting bodies increasingly serving as a "mark" that helps to distinguish recipient schools from others that have not met the quality standards.

How do schools differentiate themselves in a marketplace with thousands of providers? Given the (relatively) elite nature of most business school rankings, it is interesting to question what constitutes a *top* or *elite* business school. Is it one of the 1,000 business schools that are included in a major international ranking, or one of the similarly sized (but different) set of business schools with some form of international accreditation (as discussed in the previous chapter)? Is it one of the less than 300 that are included in the more selective rankings? One of those in the top 50, 20, or 10 percent of that 300? Certainly competition among even the top ten ranked schools (however defined) is intense.

---

[35] 2009 Beyond Grey Pinstripes Report; 2009 EdUniversal Official Selection; 2009 EIU Full-Time MBA Rankings; 2009 *Financial Times* Global MBA Rankings; 2009 Forbes Best U.S. Business Schools, Top Non-U.S. One-Year Business Schools, and Top Non-U.S. Two-Year Business Schools lists; 2009 QS Global 200 Business Schools Report; and the 2007 *Wall Street Journal* MBA Recruiter's Scorecard. Note: some adjustments are made for differences in the ways the various rankings define the "unit" being ranked.

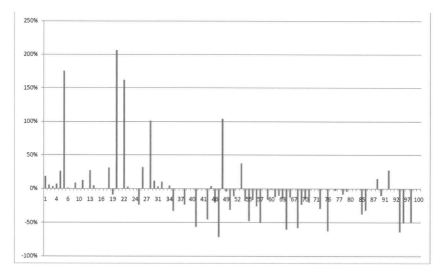

Figure 3.3: Percent Change in Full-Time MBA Enrollments of *Financial Times* Top 100 Schools 2000–2008.
Source: AACSB analysis.

Position in the rankings notably has little to do with market share, gross revenue, or other indicators of size. Based on analysis of information submitted for the 2009 *Financial Times'* Top 100 Global MBA Program Rankings, we find evidence that, aside from the top 30 or so schools, full-time MBA program enrollments at the vast majority of ranked schools have declined (see Figure 3.3 above). Similar findings exist when analyzing the 34 schools that have been included in *Business Week*'s ranking of top 30 U.S. full-time MBA programs in the years between 2000 and 2008. This finding suggests that incumbents in the management education landscape are focused on protecting or attaining a premium position in the ranking, rather than gaining market share. As Ted Snyder, dean of The University of Chicago, Booth School of Business, has observed, "top schools are not interested in share; they are interested in slice."[36]

In a global world in which individuals are increasingly mobile and information about a wide range of schools is readily available, finding the right "slice" of the population to serve is challenging. Not all business schools can be considered "elite." In an era of mass access to higher

---

[36]Snyder, Edward A., Globalization of Management Education: A Conversation with AACSB Deans, AACSB Deans Conference presentation, February 2010. See also Snyder, Edward A., "The Party's Over: The Coming B-School Shakeout," *BusinessWeek*, April 2, 2009, electronic document, http://www.businessweek.com/print/bschools/content/apr2009/bs2009042_773939.htm, accessed June 12, 2010.

education, the number of individuals seeking higher education is larger than ever before, and all are seeking the right "fit" with an education provider.

Yet, precisely for this reason, differentiation becomes increasingly important. Sociologist Saskia Sassen writes of how globalization lessens the importance of differentiation along national lines, instead highlighting and leading to classification along other differentiating characteristics that apply regardless of the school's national context.[37] Rankings, unfortunately, fail miserably at capturing differentiation along more than just a few dimensions, most notably falling short of differentiation according to differences in mission.

In an effort to differentiate themselves in a global context, an increasing number of schools have implemented strategies and branding designed to help the school let go of an association with any one national context. INSEAD (with campuses in France and Singapore), for example, brands itself as the "Business School for the World," whereas The Fuqua School of Business at Duke University promotes itself as "the world's first legitimately global business school."

And while some universities strive to become *global*, others find their niche in creating a brand that is more *local*. Recently, four business schools in Asia (China Europe International Business School, Hong Kong University of Science and Technology Business School, Indian School of Business, and Nanyang Business School) have joined forces as "Top Asia Business Schools," a tagline the schools hope will position them as an Ivy League of the East. Still others—a set likely consisting of hundreds if not thousands of schools globally—orient themselves to primarily serve students in a single country or even city.

But geographic boundaries (or the lack of them) are hardly enough to differentiate schools in a world in which comparisons transcend borders. Rankings and accreditations, as noted earlier, are additional dimensions that schools also call upon, but often these still are not enough to differentiate schools from close competitors. In this context, some schools have pursued other niches such as orientation toward a particular industry, excellence in a particular discipline, recognition for a particular style of delivery, access to corporate partners, and others. Overall, globalization has made focus and specialization more important.

3.3. Implications

From a macro perspective, globalization of management education seems likely to positively serve students, the business profession, and the creation

---

[37]Sassen, Saskia, *Territory, Authority, Rights.* Princeton University Press, Princeton, NJ, 2006, p. 268.

of new knowledge. Increases in cross-border institutional engagement, rising student mobility, and growing access to private funding for higher education are likely to produce "win-win" outcomes globally. Harvesting such outcomes would be well-served by government policies in support of freedom of speech, meritocratic access, and freedom of mobility for students, faculty members, and institutions.

Locally, however, the impact of globalization could be highly asymmetric. It may well accelerate a Darwinian scenario in which the strong institutions grow stronger, the weak grow weaker, and those in between jockey more intensively for resources and results. Globalization will not be an unalloyed blessing to all institutions, and it will mean a continued need for institutions to examine their mission and positioning in this context.

The responses of individual institutions will, as a result, vary widely. The divisions complicate the efforts of institutions seeking to go global. Nobel Laureate Joseph Stiglitz sums up this duality in his book *Globalization and its Discontents*: "I believe that globalization—the removal of barriers to free trade and the closer integration of national economies—can be a force for good and that it has the *potential* to enrich everyone in the world, particularly the poor. But I also believe that if this is to be the case, the way globalization has been managed … needs to be radically rethought."[38] Applied to the globalization of management education, the likelihood that a single canon of curricula or a single mode of global outreach will be appropriate for all schools of management is small. The central task of academic leaders as they contemplate their response to globalization is to consider the *varieties of approach*—this is the "radical rethinking," as Stiglitz might say.

Finally, the local asymmetries in the context of global benefit suggest that robust international frameworks for quality assurance will grow in importance as management education globalizes. Providers of management education will likely continue to proliferate and evolve to meet the burgeoning demand for trained administrative talent. Organizations, such as AACSB, will play a vital role in helping to set a global standard of excellence in management education, shape expectations of consumers of management education, and resolve the tensions that globalization creates.

---

[38]Stiglitz, Joseph E., *Globalization and Its Discontents*, W.W. Norton & Company, New York, 2002, pp. ix–x.

Chapter 4

Responses to Forces of Change: A Focus on Curricular Content

Pankaj Ghemawat

This chapter focuses on the content of what business schools teach their students about globalization. Content might seem to be *the* obvious response to the question of how business schools should deal with globalization: in an academic context, there is a natural attraction to the idea that if we want students to learn about something, we should teach or discuss it in the classroom. This is the reason Gordon and Howell, in their influential 1959 study of business education, devoted more than 40 percent of their report to detailed treatment of curricular issues, or more than one-half if one includes a prefatory chapter that conflates business schools' educational programs with their curricula. But in the context of globalization, curricular content has failed to command much attention—a state of affairs that cannot be allowed to continue. Or so this chapter argues.

This report, which is written for a diverse set of business schools, could not possibly prescribe exactly what should be taught and how that should be accomplished in each setting. The approaches that schools take to globalize their curricula will vary substantially across schools and also within schools across educational levels (undergraduate, master's, executive master's, doctoral) and programs.

Yet, the Task Force does aim to stress several points that all schools should take into consideration.

First, curricular efforts should be the primary area of emphasis for business schools that seek to globalize. If business schools are serious about ensuring that their graduates have the global awareness and competencies to succeed in a global business environment, the necessary place for each school to start is by paying attention to the curriculum. Other strategies that are discussed in Chapter 5 may supplement, and in fact may provide avenues for, curriculum development, but they are not, by themselves, sufficient for developing the global competencies so critical to management education today.

Second, successful globalization of students' learning experiences requires a comprehensive approach that involves attention to *both* individual courses and the overall program design. The global nature of today's business environment demands that international content be consciously included within the core curriculum of all business programs—and that it not be solely an optional elective or supplemental course, or a component of only those programs with a specifically "global" focus. The business environment further demands that such content be aligned with program objectives and learning goals in a way that truly complements the array of knowledge and skills that are imparted through the program.

In this chapter, we focus on the incorporation of global perspectives within the core curriculum as well as supplemental training and experiential learning. We draw upon existing research, a new survey of academic thought leaders, and several examples that involve the case-study schools (see Appendix) as well as other business schools in order to inform the discussion. In doing so, we aim to spark reflection and dialogue among faculty members, program directors, and business school administrators regarding the approaches most appropriate for various programs given their size, objectives, student profile, delivery format, resources, and other characteristics.

4.1. The Curricular Imperative

In their 1988 survey of the state of management education, Porter and McKibbin note that, with regard to globalization of management, "a beginning has been made, but much more remains to be done."[1] They conjectured that part of the lack of drive toward globalization in business schools might have stemmed from the fact that corporate America was not pressuring business schools to teach international business. At the same time, they felt that this was an area where business schools could have, and should have, led the business community.

Since then, significant progress has been made by many business schools. Indeed, individual schools and faculty members around the world have championed innovative curricular globalization initiatives at the course and program levels over the past several decades. In the U.S., the Centers for International Business Education and Research (CIBERs) hosted at more than 30 business schools have provided leadership in curriculum development, faculty training, and outreach to the business community and to other schools. Numerous models for globalizing business curricula have been proposed by scholars, and various versions of those models have been

---

[1]Porter, Lyman W., Lawrence E. McKibbin, and the American Assembly of Collegiate Schools of Business, *Management Education and Development: Drift or Thrust into the 21st Century?* McGraw-Hill Book Company, New York, 1988.

adopted and implemented by schools around the world; these are discussed in more depth in Section 4.3.

Schools' self-reports also seem to provide evidence of a fair amount of curricular changes that relate to globalization. Thus, the 2009 Curricular Innovation Study by the MBA Roundtable found that 69 percent of the 232 respondent programs reported that they had made a significant revision to their MBA curriculum within the previous four years. And 47 percent of all programs reported that they had provided more emphasis on global perspectives, which came in just behind that hardy perennial of leadership development offerings (49 percent).[2]

For AACSB-accredited business schools, attention to globalization of curricula aligns with new expectations within the AACSB accreditation standards. In 2009, the AACSB International Accreditation Quality Committee, which was charged with recommending changes in accreditation standards, provided additional guidelines for schools seeking to document their satisfaction of the AACSB accreditation standard concerning management of curricula. The new guidance stated that schools were expected to "show how the curriculum across the dimensions outlined in the standard demonstrates a global perspective."[3] The Accreditation Council (comprised of all schools that held AACSB accreditation) also voted that year to include "dynamics of the global economy" among the general knowledge and skill areas that were expected to be covered in an undergraduate business program, and to require that master's-level students have the capacity to understand management issues from a global perspective (or, in the case of specialized master's degree students, to understand the specified discipline from a global perspective). Each of these revisions reflected a broad acknowledgement by the members of the Accreditation Council that students should be able to apply their business knowledge and skills in a global context.

Yet more than 20 years after Porter and McKibbin's observation, the Task Force's perspective today is that business schools around the world still strive to figure out how to add appropriate globalization-related content to their curricula, with no clear agreement on how to proceed.[4] Often such

---

[2]MBA Roundtable, Insights into Curricular Innovation, electronic document, http://mbaroundtable.org/members_events.html, accessed March 17, 2010.

[3]AACSB International, *Eligibility Procedures and Accreditation Standards for Business Accreditation*, revised January 31, 2010, p. 71.

[4]For example, in their book *Rethinking the MBA*, Datar, Garvin, and Cullen note a great deal of heterogeneity in the strategies employed to globalize the MBA programs at the business schools they studied. The same is true of the schools that serve as the focus of the case studies in this report (see Appendix) and of many others reviewed during the course of researching this topic.

efforts have been fragmented or at best ad hoc. In other cases, schools have incorporated a substantial level of global content into their programs, but with insufficient attention to ensuring that the *right* content is incorporated rather than what happens to be most readily accessible. They also may overestimate how global their curricula are because of a tendency to conflate locality with topicality.

Furthermore, this Task Force believes that today's environment presents an imperative for business schools to improve. Even those schools that are currently leading the way still have numerous opportunities to make globalization of their curricula *more deliberate, less fragmented,* and *better aligned* with the intended student population and program objectives. For all schools, improvements in curriculum globalization need to be material and meaningful. Relabeling a course, e.g. renaming a "strategic management" course as one on "global strategic management," without many other changes hardly rises to this level. When globalization-related material is included at the end of the course, it is more likely to be compressed or cut if "core" material takes longer to cover than anticipated, and it might raise questions for students about the topic's perceived importance. And while elective courses can be valuable supplements, they also may present the problem of a "globalization ghetto": anecdotal evidence exists that international students are more likely than domestic students to enroll in courses with an explicitly international or global focus.

The imperative for more focused globalization of business schools' core curricula comes from many sources within the business community that business schools are positioned to serve, and is driven most strongly by the need to produce graduates with the knowledge and skills necessary for conducting business in a global environment. Datar, Garvin, and Cullen cite "a global perspective"[5] as first among a list of unmet needs that were identified through interviews with employers and business school deans. The interviewees in their study noted that meeting the need would require more than just providing students with "abstract, theoretical knowledge about the world's many different economic and political systems." Instead, they argued that students need to be able to have an operational understanding of different contexts that would enable effective decision-making and action.

Some of the unmet needs appear to be related to simple updating of curricular content to address evolutions in business practice that relate to globalization. For example, a recent survey by the American Accounting Association and KPMG, LLP, of 535 undergraduate accounting professors at

[5]Datar, Srikant M., David A. Garvin, and Patrick G. Cullen, *Rethinking the MBA: Business Education at a Crossroads*, Harvard Business School Press, Cambridge, MA, 2010.

U.S. schools found that 62 percent indicated that they had not taken any significant steps to integrate International Financial Reporting Standards (IFRS) into the undergraduate accounting curriculum. The gap is even larger when one considers that only 22 percent of professors reported that they could incorporate global financial reporting standards into the 2008-09 coursework in any meaningful way. And where business schools fall short, business is stepping in to fill the gap: the Big Four accounting firms all have launched IFRS curricular initiatives in recent years, and Pricewaterhouse Coopers has even gone so far as to specify IFRS-awareness levels for new recruits.[6]

This level of specificity from the business community about needed skills is rare; in most cases, business schools are tasked with assessing more general evidence of the business world's needs and interpreting the implications for their educational programs. For example, as noted in Chapter 2, many companies admit that they do not fully exploit their international business opportunities, and they cite that a key reason is insufficient personnel with international skills. The outcomes range from missed opportunities to failures in anticipating customer needs or in recognizing the distinctive policies that apply to foreign-owned corporations. The challenge for business schools is that to bridge the "knowing-doing gap" often means that the must address needs that, like the "global perspective" identified above, tend to be abstract and void of concrete, actionable dimensions for response. We explore some suggestions for how schools might respond later in this chapter.

In addition to relevant knowledge and skills, a second dimension of this curricular imperative concerns students' attitudes and values—or the cultivation of a "global mindset." As was argued in Chapter 3, globalization offers numerous benefits for the world at large, but can meet with antagonistic responses at a local level. Surveys[7] suggest that, while the opinions of individuals within business schools and leaders within the business community tend to converge around support for globalization, the general

---

[6]Jones, Christopher G., Rishma Vedd, and Sung Wook Yoon, "Employer Expectations of Accounting Undergraduates' Entry-Level Knowledge and Skills in Global Financial Reporting," *Journal of Business Education*, Vol. 2, No. 8 (2009), pp. 85–102.

[7]This statement is based on Ghemawat's surveys of groups of deans, business executives, and business students as to whether the effects of globalization have been basically good, bad, or mixed. Less than 1 percent of each of the three groups characterized globalization as basically bad or mixed. Business undergraduate and graduate students tend to feel a bit less gung-ho about globalization than business school deans, but they remain significantly more so than the general population (overwhelming majorities of students end up believing that globalization is basically good). Other student surveys have reported similar findings. See, for example, Peng, Mike W., and Hyung-Deok Shin, "How Do Future Business Leaders View Globalization?", *Thunderbird International Business Review*, Vol. 50, No. 3 (May/June 2008), pp. 175–82.

population tends to be significantly more skeptical about globalization. Such skepticism has clearly swelled in recent years as economic downturns and high unemployment have fanned the flames of protectionism.

Business school deans and faculty need to ask themselves whether they are adequately equipping their students to preserve the power of their convictions—let alone proselytize for further opening up—in a world that generally is much more hostile to globalization, particularly in developed economies. To avoid spending time in the curriculum on anti-globalization ideas that most business school professors believe are nonsense frees up time for other, more "constructive" pursuits, but it also leaves business school graduates ill-equipped for real-world interactions that they are likely to encounter. This, too, is a globalization-related curricular gap, albeit one of a more specific kind than the sort discussed previously. This gap further reinforces the broader sense that the curriculum deserves urgent attention.

4.1.1. The Social Multiplier Effect of Curricular Change

Several important points are worth noting that reinforce the need for globalization of the curriculum to be a greater priority. First, for schools with relatively limited resources, the curriculum may be even more critical to the achievement of the globalization-related objectives they set for themselves since they may be unable to employ other levers relied on by schools with more resources. Course syllabi, pedagogical tools, textbooks, and other curricular aids can more easily be shared and replicated—in full or in part, and in original or modified form—than strategies for branch campuses, collaborative cross-border partnerships, international student recruitment, etc. As long as such resources are carefully selected for their relevance to learning goals and the student population, an expansion in the volume and breadth of available course materials can have an impact that is much more far-reaching than in the classroom or school in which they were initially developed.

The same point applies *a fortiori* to business schools (and education) in emerging countries, which already represent 64 percent of today's universe of business schools and which are likely to account for most if not all of the growth in demand over the next several decades. Cross-border program delivery, branch campuses, and franchise programs can go a long way toward helping to build management education capacity in underserved regions of the world. However, we are concerned that content adaptations are insufficient and not specifically relevant to their student populations and business communities. For example, one study of the success of an "exported" U.S. curriculum to Chinese students, through a joint-degree program staffed in both locations by faculty members from the U.S. partner school, has shown that the Chinese students tended to be less satisfied than their U.S. student counterparts, and they tended to perceive program emphases differently.[8]

Finally, we come back to the earlier point that business schools tend to be much more pro-globalization than society at large. To equip students to operate in such a world requires getting them to think through and ideally be able to be persuasive about the costs and benefits of globalization.[9] Schools that dedicate explicit attention to this goal in the curriculum ultimately will help their students to be knowledgeable advocates within their companies and within other networks—of friends, family, and community members—where they will have influence.

Taken together, these three points suggest that developing and deploying better globalization-related content would, in addition to benefiting the schools that play a leading role in such development, have a large social multiplier. In other words, curricular tools developed for one school or program also are likely to be useful in another. Furthermore, the impact of curricular initiatives is likely to extend beyond the students in the classroom through their interactions with the surrounding community.

4.2. Barriers to Globalizing Curricula

If globalization of the curricula is so important, why have curricular changes been slow to achieve a meaningful level? The most obvious set of explanations focus on *motivational and structural barriers* that create *action disconnects*, that is, they prevent what needs to be done from getting done. But we also should look at *cognitive barriers* that create *knowledge disconnects*, or a failure to translate what we already know about globalization into actionable curricular specifications. In addition to being discernible in the present context, cognitive barriers can be addressed without the sort of political rebalancing that dealing with motivational and structural barriers often requires; moreover, addressing cognitive barriers can help break down other barriers to change as well.

4.2.1. Motivational Barriers

In regard to the motivations among business school leadership, based on various surveys of deans, schools' websites, etc., the lack of interest in

---

[8]Van Auken, Stuart, Ludmilla G. Wells, and Daniel Borgia, "A Comparison of Western Business Instruction in China With U.S. Instruction: A Case Study of Perceived Program Emphases and Satisfaction Levels," *Journal of Teaching in International Business*, Vol. 20, No. 3 (2009), pp. 208–29.
[9]For a comprehensive discussion, see Ghemawat, Pankaj, *World 3.0: Global Prosperity and How to Achieve It*, Harvard Business School Press, Cambridge, MA, 2011.

globalization among business school deans discerned by Porter and McKibbin in 1988 seems no longer to be a fair characterization more than 20 years later. The emphasis on globalization does in fact seem significant. And while motivations for globalization include corporate pressures and signaling considerations, most deans *would* seem favorably disposed, *a priori*, to proposals to enrich the globalization-related content of curricula.

Motivational problems seem more plausible in regard to (some) faculty and the way that they are organized. Thus, the deans of at least some well-regarded schools acknowledge that their globalization efforts to date often have worked better for students than for faculty—typically in the sense that the efforts seem not to have passed the cost-benefit tests of personal involvement on the part of enough of their faculty.[10] Since faculty must develop and deliver educational content, this situation does not bode well for the globalization of content.

What might account for indifference, if not resistance, among faculty in this regard? The lack of drive, in part, may reflect research preferences: faculty members typically prefer to teach what they research, rather than the other way around, and there are some structural impediments to getting more of them to internationalize their research. One such hindrance—the tendency of most researchers to, other things being equal, look for insights that are universal rather than clearly local or national—is particularly pertinent, given the recommendation (developed later in this chapter) that additional globalization-related content in the curriculum focus on the differences between countries. A further related concern is whether anything distinctively stimulating or new exists about the international dimension—this will be discussed further in Section 4.3. And finally, faculty values such as status and collegiality may be obstacles, particularly to the physical expansion of schools' footprints, which raises issues around the dilution of status as a result of the implied expansion of faculty size and the creation of a split faculty, not to mention the wear-and-tear implied by the likelihood of increased travel.

4.2.2. Structural Barriers

Such motivational problems at the individual level are compounded by the way business schools are organized. Thus, according to a survey reported on by Kwok and Arpan,[11] only 6 percent of the business schools that responded had international business (IB) departments: "IB specialists were

---

[10]One example is provided by remarks by Ted Snyder in the course of his keynote address at the 2009 AACSB Deans' Conference in San Francisco on February 5, 2009.

[11]Kwok, Chuck C.Y., and Jeffrey S. Arpan, "Internationalizing the Business School: A Global Survey in 2000," *Journal of International Business Studies*, Vol. 33, No. 3 (2002), p. 572.

mostly located in functional fields with no international title (54 percent) and in functional fields with the title of IB specialist (33 percent)." As John Daniels once observed, "In retrospect, it seems inevitable that once IB was in a functional department, it would be viewed as a branch or subset of that function rather than as a separate discipline."[12] And of course, it is at the inter-departmental level that zero-sum competition for class sessions, particularly in the first-year core (which is often critical to departmental status), comes to the fore.

In addition to the impact of these relatively recent changes—apparently, a wave of dissolution of IB departments occurred in the 1990s—the longer-run conditioning effect of business schools' heritage also factors in. Business schools, particularly in the U.S., were late to look across national borders: more than 100 years after the first collegiate school of business was founded in the United States (Wharton, in 1881), Porter and McKibbin could still conclude that little interest or enthusiasm for globalization efforts existed among business school deans.[13] The routines that such institutions have developed over the decades are significant obstacles to change; so, probably, is hubris. Particularly in the U.S., there is (or was) a sense of being at the cutting edge of management and management education that reinforces a domestic focus: as the former dean of a top U.S. school put it, "Why does the world come to our door? Part of the answer lies in the fact that ... since this school's founding, the American economy has been a remarkable engine of growth."[14]

Motivational and structural barriers to the globalization of business curricula and, more generally, management education, clearly require attention. The next chapter discusses some mechanisms for dealing with them. But such barriers do not seem—on the basis of evidence already cited, plus considerations discussed next—to be a complete explanation for the lack of progress observed. Cognitive barriers seem to be significant impediments as well.

4.2.3. *Cognitive Barriers*

Cognitive barriers relate to knowledge disconnects rather than action disconnects, or what might be called a knowledge gap—a gap in plugging

---

[12]Daniels, John D., "Specialization to infusion: IB studies in the 1990s," in Alan M. Rugman (ed.), *Leadership in international business education and research*, Elsevier Ltd, Oxford, 2003.

[13]Porter, Lyman W., Lawrence E. McKibbin, and the American Assembly of Collegiate Schools of Business, *Management Education and Development: Drift or Thrust into the 21st Century?* McGraw-Hill Book Company, New York, 1988.

[14]Khanna, Tarun, Rakesh Khurana, and David Lane, "The Globalization of HBS," HBS Case 9-703-432, p. 13.

existing knowledge about globalization into actionable specifications of what to teach students—rather than the more familiar knowing-doing gap. Two related knowledge disconnects must be considered: business schools may not fully register the extent of international differences, and, even if they do, they may have trouble devising adequately creative responses to deal with them.

Evidence of business sector biases toward overestimating various measures of cross-border integration, such as international flows of information, people, capital, and products as fractions of the (international plus intra-national) total, is readily available.[15] Surveys of MBA students have shown that they too seem prone to overestimate levels of cross-border integration and to agree with strategic propositions that make sense only in a (close to) borderless world. Even business school administrators seem to easily adopt this bias. As the dean of a well-regarded (European) business school described, his institution is focused on "[t]raining the next generation of transcultural leaders who can step off a plane straight into effective management anywhere in the world." This objective is probably, according to various scholars of cross-cultural management, unrealistic no matter how clever the means deployed to achieve it are.

Under-adaptation to international differences is most obviously a problem for schools that have expanded their scope internationally—most frequently through diversity or partnerships—but also for schools that have stayed at home, given the general increases in most measures of the globalization of markets and firms in recent decades. Under-adaptation also applies—at the level of ideas rather than instructional materials—to numerous schools that recognize and try to react to differences but have responded like one senior strategy professor who had recently become involved in his school's programs in emerging markets: "Here are the ideas what we want to teach; now let us find local cases, examples and accents."

Perhaps more interestingly, there are schools that run campuses in more than one country or have developed a global technology platform—that is, they are highly globalized in structural terms—that nevertheless standardize their curricula across delivery locations. This strategy of "universalization," which focuses attention on phenomena that are invariant across space, makes sense in inverse proportion to one's assessed significance of cross-country differences. Such an approach is usually accomplished by propagating curricula that are developed domestically across national borders rather than on the basis of a thorough redesign rooted in the

---

[15]See, for instance, Ghemawat, Pankaj, *Redefining Global Strategy: Crossing Borders in a World Where Differences Still Matter*, Harvard Business School Press, Cambridge, MA, 2007; and Ghemawat, Pankaj, "The globalization of business education: through the lens of semiglobalization," *Journal of Management Development*, Vol. 27, No. 4 (2008), pp. 391–414.

identification of globally invariant common factors—with the implicit rationalization that, if international differences are small, these two approaches should converge on the same outcomes. But if differences are large, this is a recipe for stretching domestic content past its point of applicability, hence, under-adaptation.

Such under-adaptation likely has some motivational and structural roots of the sort that have already been discussed. But there seems to be a cognitive component as well, in the sense of a failure of imagination constraining action—a failure made more plausible by the novelty of the globalization challenge for long-established business schools, poor priming on international differences, the possibility that schools may have been pushed to globalize by employers or pulled into it by the allure of large student pools without being prepared and so are still operating in catch-up mode, and the observed divergence in (and dissatisfaction with) how top schools' curricula handle globalization. Such cognitive barriers should be dealt with differently than motivational and structural barriers by articulating a specific vision of what might be done. If the vision is persuasive, it can help with motivational/structural barriers as well.

This last point is worth emphasizing because many business-school professors who do not work on globalization-related issues profess willingness to make room for them in the curriculum as long as they are convinced of the existence of some distinctive content around such issues. This requirement is not unreasonable: without such distinctiveness, wasteful duplication of efforts would occur. This chapter goes on to discuss *what* globalization-related content will help meet this requirement and *how* it might be introduced into the curriculum.

4.3. Globalizing Curricular Content

Questions within business schools about the level of international content to include in a given degree program and how to include it are hardly new.[16] We see through the emergence of the world's early business schools that

---

[16]This chapter focuses primarily on curricula for undergraduate and master's level programs. Doctoral programs are very different from other kinds of educational programs in terms of their relationship to research and to faculty development and so would require a separate, very different treatment, stretching the scope of this chapter to a breaking point if included. Discussions on how, if at all, to globalize research and knowledge development are available elsewhere, and, in any case, the research agenda is typically driven by the "invisible colleges" of top researchers in specific disciplines or functional areas in ways that a report such as this one probably has little hope of influencing. For some insights into what the Task Force believes doctoral education might include, consider the discussion in Chapter 5 regarding faculty resources.

Table 4.1: Suggested Approaches to Teaching Global Perspectives.

Source[17]	Summary
Pyramid Model—Toyne (1992)	Levels: global awareness, understanding, competency
Gregersen, Morrison, and Black (1998)	Categories: inquisitiveness, personal character, duality, savvy
A Field Guide to Inter-nationalizing Business Education—Scherer et al. (2000)[*]	Categories: international business skills, fluency in a second modern language, understanding of another culture
Edwards et al. (2003)[*]	Levels: international awareness, international competence, international expertise
Thunderbird Global Mindset® Inventory—Javidan (2010)	Categories: intellectual capital, psychological capital, social capital
Datar, Garvin, and Cullen (2010)	Categories: knowing, doing, being

*Undergraduate focus.

international trade (and specifically the need for related knowledge and skills) was a driver for the development of many early business programs. Today, the effects of globalization are even more pervasive, strengthening the imperative for *all* business schools to identify effective means of preparing students for the business environment in which they will play a role.

Many attempts have been made to answer the question about what should be taught in business schools with regard to globalization. A few of the more prominent proposals are summarized in Table 4.1.

Each of these summaries suggests a multidimensional approach to teaching global perspectives, though the actual dimensions presented differ

---

[17]Toyne, Brian, "Internationalizing Business Education," *Business and Economics Review*, Jan.-Mar. (1992) pp. 23–27; Gregersen, H.B., A.J. Morrison, and J.S. Black, *Global Explorers: The Next Generation of Leaders*, Routledge, New York, 1999; Scherer, R., S. Beaton, M. Ainina, and J. Meyer (eds.), *A Field Guide to Internationalizing Business Education: Changing Perspectives and Growing Opportunities*, Center for International Business Education and Research, Austin, TX, 2000; Edwards, R., G. Crosling, S. Petrovic-Lazarovic, and P. O'Neill, "Internationalisation of Business Education: Meaning and implementation," *Higher Education Research and Development*, Vol. 22, No. 2 (2003), pp. 183-92; Javidan, M., "Global Mindset: Why is it important for Global Leaders?" 2010, electronic document, http://www. tobiascenter.iu.edu/conferences/documents/GlobalMindset-presentation3609.ppt, accessed on June 6, 2010; Datar, Srikant M., David A. Garvin, and Patrick G. Cullen, *Rethinking the MBA: Business Education at a Crossroads*, Harvard Business School Press, Cambridge, MA, 2010.

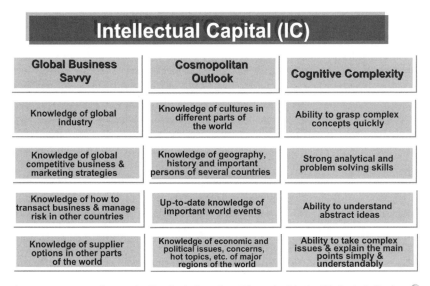

Figure 4.1: Intellectual Capital in the Thunderbird Global Mindset®
Inventory.
Source: Javidan (2010).

and in some cases might be better referred to as levels. More important,
perhaps, is that the summaries also suggest—and more detailed readings of
the original source materials confirm—that specificity about what to teach in
the classroom about globalization tends to be in short supply.

The one apparent exception to the rule is Thunderbird's impressively detailed
Global Mindset® Inventory, which highlights intellectual capital as one of its
three key categories (the other two are psychological capital and social capital)
and unbundles it into three components—global business savvy, cosmopolitan outlook, and cognitive complexity—and into 12 subcomponents (see
Figure 4.1). This approach appears to lack specificity in another sense, however:
the subcomponents listed under global business savvy and cosmopolitan
outlook, in particular, basically add up to general knowledge about the world at
large. Given the lively debate about whether people can develop, for example,
usefully detailed knowledge of cultures in different parts of the world[18]—just
one of the 12 subcomponents—the presumption of seeking mastery of *all* 12
subcomponents is of little help in developing curricular priorities.

---

[18]See, for example, Earley and Mosakowski's skepticism about the strategy—or actually, brute
force approach—of simply learning enough details about the cultures of enough places: Earley,
P.C., and E. Mosakowski, "Cultural intelligence," *Harvard Business Review*, Oct. (2004),
pp. 139–46.

Similarly, the general approach of each of the models mentioned above presents limitations when actually determining how to incorporate the various components (however named or defined) into an existing curriculum. While useful as overarching objectives across an educational program, these models provide little guidance as to how the components might be relevant to courses or course sections that are devoted to particular functional areas, or to how faculty with expertise in various functional areas might be well-positioned to contribute. This lack of implementation specificity contributes to one of the biggest obstacles in implementing a strategy to globalize curricula: the belief by individual faculty members that "some other course" is the best home for these concepts.

In an effort to further the understanding of what business schools should teach their students to prepare them for a globalizing business world, the Task Force collaborated with Pankaj Ghemawat and Bernard Yeung to survey academic thought leaders about the globalization-related content that schools *should* put into their educational programs. In order to encourage more specificity, participants were asked to respond in the context of MBA programs, but we believe that many of the findings can, with some adaptation, also be applied to undergraduate education and other types of master's level education.

Survey participants were individuals who represented a cross-section of business fields and who might be considered thought leaders in their respective fields of focus. Though some variation existed in the number of respondents from different fields, each field generally yielded individually respectable levels of respondents. Furthermore, while geographic representation was skewed slightly toward the U.S., significant representation was obtained from participants in Europe and Asia/Oceania as well. In any case, sample selection was driven by the desire to come up with a distinguished roster rather than to meet preset geographic or field quotas.

With regard to curricular content, survey participants were asked the following question: "What international elements of [your field] do you believe are important for functional/general managers with expertise in the international dimension of business to master? (The expectation is that graduates' knowledge in the areas you identify should exceed simple awareness and be sufficient to support application of the concepts in a global context.)."[19] Each participant's question was tailored to his/her

---

[19]Actually, two variants of this question were asked in hopes of flushing out differences in recommendations for MBAs with and without specialization in a given field. The results from this exercise were not particularly conclusive, although in several instances respondents seemed to suggest that the depth of understanding of a particular topic might differ optimally between the two types of programs.

primary field of expertise (e.g., accounting, finance, etc.). In an open-ended format, most participants identified multiple topics in their responses to each question. These topics were separated so that, for analytical purposes, each topic within a given response appeared as a unique response (i.e., the result was a one-to-many relationship between the participant and the topics deemed relevant for each question.)

An analysis of identified topics revealed the presence of numerous similar themes across responses and fields. Specifically, many of the responses referred to various dimensions and effects of cross-country differences that figure distinctively in the international context. Six categories of environmental/contextual differences emerged naturally from the data, relating to many of the individual topics that were cited: cultural, legal/regulatory, political, economic, financial, and a miscellaneous "other" category.[20] This, in turn, led to the creation of a matrix that arrayed these six categories of cross-country environmental differences against ten business fields. For each field or row, topics that correspond to each environmental/contextual category or column (if any) were inserted into the relevant matrix cell as a summary of the managerial (education) implications of the broad aspects of a country's context (e.g. its political environment) across the various fields.[21] The results from this process are summarized in Table 4.2 below.

Undoubtedly, if various faculty groups were to engage in an exercise in which they sought to fill in cells on a blank version of Table 4.2, the contents of the resulting matrix from each group would differ to some degree. Further, the contents likely would be broadened, particularly in fields such as economics and operations for which there were fewer respondents to our survey. As is mentioned in the footnote to the table, the cell contents reflect responses to an open-ended survey question, and are not necessarily exhaustive. Blank cells should not be interpreted to indicate the absence of any relevant content, nor should the list in any given cell be considered indicative of *the* set or the *full* set of relevant content.

Yet, several cross-cutting insights do emerge from the matrix. The first is the breadth and the depth of the sense that an understanding of cultural, legal/regulatory, political, economic, etc. differences across countries and their implications should be a key component—perhaps the central one—of what we teach our students about globalization. In addition, if one combines Human Resources and Organizational Behavior, each of the fields

---

[20] An AACSB staff member based the grouping decisions on the utilization of similar terms and on her knowledge of the topics identified.

[21] Of course, presentation in terms of differences does run the risk of underemphasizing the extent to which the respondents had firms' responses to such differences in mind as well as the differences themselves.

Table 4.2: Relevance of Country-Specific Environmental Conditions to Understanding/Applying Various Business Disciplines in a Global Context*.

	Cultural Environment	Legal/Regulatory Environment	Political Environment
Accounting		■ National tax systems	
Economics	■ Cultural and ideological conditions	■ Impact of laws and policies on trade; Strategies by firms to "get around trade hindrances"	■ Effects on trade, business systems
Finance		■ National tax systems (influence on subsidiary capital structure, dividend policies)	■ Political risk management (as related to international investments)
Information Systems	■ Influence on management of information resources	■ Influence on management of information resources; ■ Influence on availability of suppliers; ■ Regulations on open-source systems	■ Influence on management of information resources
Marketing	■ Impact on: – Customer demand, preference, and behavior (including B2B and B2C) – Marketing strategy; – Reporting norms (metric variance across countries on international surveys)	■ Impact on customer demand and preference) ■ Reporting norms (e.g. on surveys, data collection) ■ Impact on export marketing, gray/parallel marketing	■ Impact on marketing function

Management	■ Influence on management strategy ■ Influence on human resources ■ Gender division of labor	■ Governance of business activity	■ Political system

Management–Human Resources	■ Influence on:
	  – Work values
	  – Motivation
	  – Performance management
	  – Compensation
	  – Perceptions of equity
	  – Succession planning
	  – Management development
		■ Employment regulations: Who can be employed and how
		■ Motivation
		■ Performance management
		■ Compensation
		■ Existence of labor management policies, unions	

Management–Organizational Behavior	■ Influence on:
	  – Interactions (communication, negotiation)
	  – Values, assumptions, perceptions
	  – Leadership styles
	  – Existence & acceptance of corruption		

Management–Strategy	■ Implications for human behavior; management, HR; strategy and competitive advantage	■ Implications for managing human capital	■ Implications for human behavior ■ Government-business relationships

(Continued)

Table 4.2: (*Continued*)

	Economic Environment	Financial Environment	Other Environment
Accounting		■ Financial reporting standards & expectations ■ Approaches to evaluating financial performance ■ Currency valuation	
Economics	■ Economic conditions ■ Trade regimes		
Finance		■ Financial markets ■ Currency valuation ■ Interest rates ■ Foreign exchange risk	
Information Systems	■ Influence on management of information resources		■ Electronic markets

Marketing	■ Impact on:
	  – Marketing management decisions
	  – Execution of marketing strategy
	  – Customer demand & preference
			■ Technological environment (effect on customer demand & preference)

Management	■ Economic conditions	■ Foreign exchange rates	■ Impact of national business structure/systems on MNC strategy
Management–Human Resources	■ Impact of economic development level on degree to which foreign HRM practices are welcome, appropriate or understood		
Management–Organizational Behavior			
Management–Strategy	■ Business/Economic context (planned vs. free market, socialist vs. capitalist) ■ Implications for human behavior ■ Implications for strategy and competitive advantage	■ Currency valuation	■ Role of government (including business ownership, relationships to business) ■ Structure of business environment, including public markets ■ Role of location-specific resources ■ Implications for strategy and competitive advantageImpact of national business structure/systems on MNC strategy

*The table reflects a categorization of responses to an open-ended survey question, and is not intended to be prescriptive or exhaustive. Blank cells should not be interpreted to indicate the absence of any relevant content, nor should the list in any given cell be considered indicative of *the* set or the *full* set of relevant content. Operations was also included as a surveyed discipline but is excluded from the table because of a low response rate.

surfaced more than one contextual dimension in a way that spans the differences emphasized, often to the exclusion of all else, by culturalists (cultural differences), institutionalists (legal/regulatory and political differences), economists (economic and financial differences), and others (e.g., geographers and geographic differences). This basic six-fold classification of differences, or some schema like it, therefore seems to be potentially of cross-functional use (compared, for example, to a one-to-one mapping between types of cross-country differences and different subject fields).

The recommendation of focusing on cultural, legal, political, and other differences between countries is narrower than the general knowledge required for intellectual mastery according to the inventory in Figure 4.1. This concept also permits a different approach to learning: instead of simply stressing recognition of differences from one country to the next, it calls attention to metrics—admittedly incomplete as well as overlapping—of *distance* or *degrees of difference* along various dimensions that can be used as a meta-cognitive frame for organizing observations about individual countries. In other words, the idea presented by this matrix is not to learn about the specific differences between particular countries; its intention instead is to develop a way of thinking about differences that can be applied to any pair (or group) of countries.

Second, an approach that focuses on differences between countries *can* fit with the traditional functional approach to courses currently utilized by many business schools. While some schools experiment with curricular models that blend two or more functional areas within the same course, many still isolate the various functions (e.g., marketing, management, finance, etc.) in separate courses and develop majors or concentrations that also fall along functional lines. The identification of function-specific dimensions of differences suggests that this approach can work with either model.

Third, the matrix also draws attention to the cross-disciplinary nature of several of the topics that were identified. Nearly all of the nine disciplinary rows, for example, incorporate some aspect of broad business topics such as financial management (currency, pricing, tax), personal interactions (collaboration, negotiation, motivation), and sourcing (financial capital, human capital, supply chain) in a global environment. This reinforces both the need for concepts to be integrated across courses, and the possibilities for a course that creates a foundation for connecting the concepts across disciplines.

Finally, though responses in the matrix came in reply to a question about general MBA program content, many respondents suggested that graduates of MBA programs with an emphasis in a particular discipline should have a greater level of competency along the dimensions that were identified than graduates of a program without such a disciplinary emphasis. Similar principles would also allow for the matrix to be applied at the undergraduate and specialized master's degree levels.

The models presented by Toyne and by Edwards et al., each of which focuses on different *levels* of outcomes, may provide some guidance in this regard. Certainly, even among programs of the same level and type, adaptations should be made for the relevant student population (e.g., mid-career executives versus recent undergraduates) and available majors or areas of emphasis (whether disciplinary or focused on a particular country/ region). As stressed earlier, the point is to use a focus on cross-country differences as a framework for designing a curriculum that aligns with the specific program's objectives. At the master's level, for example, for a given functional area, one might expect the greatest levels of related knowledge and skills among students of specialized master's programs in that field, followed by graduates of an MBA program with an emphasis in that field, followed by graduates of general MBA programs.

4.4. Structuring Global Content: Insertion, Infusion, and Interlock

The previous section addresses the question of "what" global content a business curriculum should include and suggests that cross-country differences and their business implications should be highlighted in the core of business degree programs. This section addresses the question of "how" the material should be included by focusing on approaches to incorporating international content into curriculum design. A historical perspective provides an opportunity to introduce two broad and, in a sense, polar design approaches: *insertion* of a stand-alone global course (e.g. a general/survey course, a specialized functional course, or an internationally-oriented non-business course such as world politics or comparative economic systems) and *infusion* of global content into functional courses or other existing business courses to the point of pervasiveness. Consideration of their pros and cons suggests a third model, *interlock,* in which a required course or module provides a cross-functional platform for discussing globalization and business that the functional courses then explicitly build on to at least some extent.

Drawing upon examples from several schools, we then offer a number of other recommendations in order to facilitate the implementation of this curricular design. Given the previously mentioned divergence in how business schools globalize, looking across them does not necessarily serve to identify a set of best practices; instead, the idea is to look within this small group of schools to identify what the late C.K. Prahalad used to refer to as "next practices" that schools might consider in moving forward.

4.4.1.   A Historical Perspective

One of the first known initiatives to globalize business school curricula was Raymond Vernon's influential experiment several decades ago at the Harvard Business School. According to Vernon,

> [w]hen the School decided in the early 1960s to adopt a formal structure based on functional areas, international business was designated one such area. I could teach what I liked; but at the same time I could exert little or no influence over the content of other courses at the School. ... When in the late 1960s, the Dean of the Business School proposed to me the abolition of the international business area, it seemed to me a reasonable and logical step. Thenceforth, according to the proposed plan, the various functional areas would internatio-nalize their respective curricula. And to ensure that the shift occurred, the handful of faculty members associated with the international business area would be distributed strategically among the various functional areas. With hindsight, it seems evident to me that the shift came too early.[22]

Vernon's recollections span the two polar approaches that business schools have employed in their attempts to globalize their curricula: *insertion* of a stand-alone globalization-related course into the curriculum and *infusion* of global content into functional courses or other existing business courses to the point of pervasiveness. They also highlight the potential problems with both approaches: insertion is a recipe for isolation and infusion can potentially result in invisibility.

These problems have been independently discovered and rediscovered by many schools. Thus, in 1999, the Stanford Graduate School of Business first decided to insert a required course on global management in the first year of its MBA program, as a follow-on to its required strategy course. Over the next few years, issues with overlapping content and student acceptance led to the decision to infuse the content of the global management course into the strategy course, which was lengthened as a result. But problems with staffing this new format led to scaling back the course, and much of the international content was eliminated. Several years later, in 2006, an overhaul of the MBA program curriculum brought international content

---

[22]Vernon, R., "Contributing to an international business curriculum," *Journal of International Business Studies*, Vol. 25, No. 2 (1994), pp. 215–28.

back to a prominent role with the inclusion of a course titled The Global Context of Management as a required first-quarter course—and one of only a few required courses in a highly customizable program.

More broadly, fluctuations appear to occur in the general popularity of these two polar approaches. The 1990s, in particular, saw an emphasis on infusion that was not unrelated to the wave of dissolution of International Business departments during that decade. In recent years, there seems to have been a revival of interest in insertion. The question that this historical perspective poses for the present is: why should we expect insertion to work any better this time around, as opposed to being just the latest in a series of oscillations between extremes?

4.4.2. The Interlock Model: Insertion Plus Infusion

The limitations of both insertion and infusion as models for curricular globalization suggest a third model, *interlock*, in which a globalization course provides a cross-functional platform for talking about the phenomenon that is used, to at least some degree, by the functional courses (see Figure 4.2). Note that insertion and infusion can be seen as degenerate versions of interlock: insertion involves zero interlock between the globalization course and functional courses, and infusion can be thought of as involving such a high degree of interlock that no room is left for a distinct focus on globalization: it is supposedly everywhere in the curriculum. Given the problems with the two endpoints of this continuum that were highlighted by Vernon, it seems reasonable to look for an interior solution.

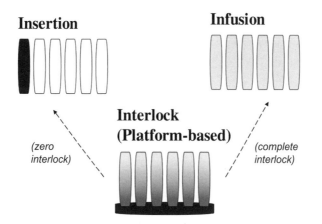

Figure 4.2: Models of Curricular Globalization.

Having said that, the thesis behind the interlock model is not that it is necessary to find a middle-of-the-road solution; rather, it suggests that both insertion of a required course on globalization and infusion of globalization-related content into other required courses are necessary to break down barriers to the globalization of curricular content that have historically proven paralyzing.

A recent MBA program revision at IESE Business School demonstrates how an interlock model might be used to incorporate the content areas that are discussed in the previous sections. The new model envisages two components that are related to globalization. The first, insertion of a platform course relatively early in the MBA program, is intended to provide visibility and focus for globalization-related issues and to serve as a feeder for globalization in other courses.[23] This Globalization of Business Enterprise (GLOBE) course centers on a module that focuses on exploring cross-country differences systematically as well as discussing levels of cross-border integration and the costs and benefits of globalization from a social perspective. The second component involves infusion in the form of a requirement that follow-on functional courses have a 10 to 20 percent cross-border component that focuses on covering at least some of the topics listed in the relevant row of Table 4.2—and monitoring to prevent this infusion from becoming invisible over time.[24] This approach accepts the fact that schools and curricula generally are partitioned by function; rather than requiring them to reorganize, this approach can be used to connect globalization-related content directly to core functional courses—or to other ways of structuring the rest of the curriculum.

Some limited coordination between the GLOBE course and the functional courses *was* achieved in the pilot offering of GLOBE in the 2010 winter term: the results of a cultural intelligence questionnaire administered earlier by colleagues in organizational behavior were reused, and GLOBE was explicitly leveraged to add more of an international perspective to the required course on strategy that is offered slightly later in the year. But the teaching experience and follow-up with students did

---

[23]While interlock could, in principle, be achieved at the end through a capstone course rather than toward the beginning, through a cornerstone course, Ghemawat's experience—admittedly, back in the 1990s—running the integrative exercise that was then the capstone to the first year of the MBA program at HBS suggests that the really powerful role for that slot, given the predominantly functional organization of most MBA programs, is one of cross-functional rather than cross-border integration.

[24]At Stanford, the follow-up course that is emphasized is a Global Experience requirement that, as its name suggests, involves travel; specific attention to interlocks with other courses does not seem to be given. The Wharton design is still being developed.

suggest that achieving more interlock with functional courses is the single most important determinant of the long-term success or failure of an initiative that aims, ultimately, to broaden and deepen the discussion of globalization-related issues throughout the curriculum. As a result, the plans for the medium term concentrate on moving further to implement the second component of the interlock design: ensuring that globalization-related content is infused into functional courses as well.

An example of the multidimensional interlock approach at the undergraduate level is seen at the University of South Carolina, Moore School of Business. All International Business majors are expected to complete a "Globalization and Business" course that focuses on "the business opportunities and threats for individuals, companies, and countries created by the growth of globalization, and how companies must operate in diverse foreign environments and engage in specialized transactions."[25] The course is divided into major-specific sections in order to allow customization toward the students' chosen areas of focus. Students then complete additional functional courses that focus on the international components of a specific managerial function, such as finance or marketing, thematic courses that take a multidisciplinary perspective on an international business issue (such as foreign market entry), and a regionally focused course.

All undergraduate business students (including those who are not International Business majors) at the Moore School of Business are required to extend their exposure to international topics and perspectives by completing at least nine credit-hours of courses, of their choosing, with an international orientation. At least one course toward this requirement must be offered by the Moore School of Business, but the students may otherwise complete courses that are offered by other colleges and departments at the university, thereby simultaneously fulfilling general education requirements. Furthermore, faculty members who teach various functional courses within the business school (e.g., finance, marketing, etc.) are expected to infuse their courses with international content so that students graduate with an understanding of the international dimension of that functional field.

4.4.3. Implementation Recommendations

A review of these and several other similar recent initiatives (see Box 4A) suggests a few basic themes that administrators who are interested in

---

[25]University of South Carolina, Darla Moore School of Business, International Business Courses web page, 2010, electronic document, http://mooreschool.sc.edu/facultyandresearch/departments/internationalbusiness/internationalbusinesscourses.aspx, accessed January 3, 2011.

Box 4A.   Comparisons of Globalization-Related Required MBA Courses at Three Schools

The table below compares key features of recent efforts, still unfolding, to add globalization-related content to the required MBA program curriculum at Stanford Graduate School of Business, IESE Business School, and the Wharton School. The Stanford and, particularly, IESE courses are broadly consistent withthe interlock approach recommended in this section; the Wharton course is planned, for now, as a compressed insertion initiative. All three courses are broadly consistent with the recommendations from this section, and they offer some insight into the design and implementation choices that likely will arise.

School	Stanford	IESE	Wharton
Course	Global Context of Management	Globalization of Business Enterprise (GLOBE)	Wharton Global Summit (Planned)
Focus on Differences/ Distance	Cultural Distance	Cultural Distance	Institutional Differences
	_____	Administrative Distance	
	Institutional Distance	_____	
	_____	Geographic Distance	
	Technological Distance	_____	
	_____	Economic distance	
	Market Distance		
First Offering*	2009–2010	2009–2010	2012–2013
Number of Sessions**	18	12	12
Duration	11 weeks	5 weeks	4 days
Start Time	Beginning of 1st Year	Halfway through 1st Year	Beginning of 2nd Year
% Business Cases	72%	33%	25%
Project Component	Yes	Yes	No
Staffing	Strategy/IB	Strategy/IB	IB
Structural Difference vs. Other Courses	Relatively Low	Relatively Low	Very High

*Stanford's course on the Global Context of Management was first offered in 2007 under a slightly different model: the first model did not focus on cross-country differences as does the current model; contained a lesser emphasis on the use of business cases; included more economics faculty in the staffing of the program; and had a high degree of structural difference from other courses (with content offered in plenary sessions rather than sections). **The calculated number of sessions excludes exams.

strengthening a program's international emphasis should consider. Under-lying each of these points is the philosophy that an "interlock" strategy essentially calls for a blend of both infusion and insertion approaches in which they deliberately complement one another. In fact, interlock might better be described as less of an approach than an outcome or "state." And insertion is possibly—although not necessarily—an initial step in moving toward interlock.

First, given the intent to interlock, the staffing of an insertion initiative should, at least over time, become more cross-functional. Initially, staffing should be driven by who is able and willing to lead or participate in such an effort. Ideally, however, this would be the first step of a process of informing, interesting, and involving a broader group of faculty than just international business or strategy scholars in a school's globalization efforts, which seems critical to institutionalizing rather than simply instigating such initiatives.

Second, the model must balance the needs to both conform to program structural constraints and not sacrifice necessary intensity or benefits from proper timing. The intensity (e.g., number of sessions per week) must not be so high as to squeeze out time for reflection nor so low as to fail to sustain attention. It must also be able to withstand pressures that will naturally emerge to cede time to other courses; the need to do so is likely inversely proportional to the degree of complementarity between the insertion and infusion approaches.

Start time (beginning, middle, or end of the program) will vary greatly, due in part to superordinate constraints (e.g., Stanford Graduate School of Business has a policy of confining required courses to the first quarter of its MBA program). A slot at the beginning of a program helps set a global (or semi-global) framing but is less geared toward following through on the business implications, as "business basics" have yet to be covered. A slot in the middle of the first year can look backward as well as forward but does imply that discussions in courses offered earlier are uninformed by a global perspective (at least at the time). And a slot after a year of required courses allows one to look across all the functional areas–but *is* subject to questioning about why all the discussions in the required curriculum were allowed to unfold prior to the discussion of a global perspective.

Specific designs for an interlock approach will also vary substantially according to program structural constraints. Undergraduate programs with substantial course requirements outside the discipline (e.g., those with a strong liberal arts focus) may find that opportunities to incorporate additional globalization-related courses are limited, or the programs may need to more rigidly adhere to a traditional calendar schedule. Master's programs may have more flexibility to incorporate more structural differentiation, for example, short-term courses, but they often have binding time constraints (particularly one-year programs) that may require even tighter engineering. Online programs at any level present their own distinctive challenges and opportunities.

It is also important for course designers to be deliberate when deciding how much structural differentiation from other required courses to allow—especially if a "dominant design" exists. Structural differences from other required courses provide helpful flexibility but do raise the issue of potentially limited student absorption of material structured in unfamiliar ways, for reasons ranging from routinization of learning modes (e.g., difficulties reading and discussing conceptual material in a case-based context) to the difficulty of grading unconventional course structures with mechanisms that are developed for conventional courses.[26] Both Stanford and IESE, for example, are shifting from plenary-style sessions for the "insertion" course to a more conventional design with the course offered in smaller sections to enable case discussions. In other words, schools would be advised not to overdo the scale of the change. The structural differentiation of the Wharton summit is likely, however, to continue to be high, at least in the early going.

Third, a shift toward an infusion approach can be accomplished as part of a broader curricular review—or on its own, if the need is clear. And the approach should be expected to evolve over time. First offerings of both the Stanford course and the (planned) Wharton course were parts of broader curricular reviews. The GLOBE course at IESE, in contrast, was started prior to such a review, given the clear sense that globalization would be a major emphasis in the revised program. So insertion of global content into the required curriculum does not necessarily require a full-blown curricular review.

Additionally, the inherent complexities and ambiguity in pursuing a new direction suggest that any plans for insertion of such a course into the required curriculum should be accompanied by plans for iteration. Both the transformation of Stanford's Global Context of Management course from its debut model in 2007 to its current model and, less dramatically, the changes planned for the second offering of GLOBE at IESE suggest that such evolution will likely be necessary and beneficial. For related reasons, a sequenced introduction of new material is generally preferable to introducing it all at once. Stanford's Global Context of Management course, while introduced without an official pilot, drew to some extent on earlier work at the school that began in 1999. GLOBE drew on a global strategy elective

---

[26]These problems are particularly likely at business schools with a "dominant design" for their required courses.

that was developed over a decade by Ghemawat at Harvard Business School and IESE as well as a pilot four-session seminar for first-year MBA students at IESE in the Spring 2009 term. Wharton plans pilots in existing electives and in the executive MBA before rolling out the Summit to regular MBA students—in what can itself be seen as an insertion effort that, if successful at building awareness, should pave the way for the infusion of more global content into the rest of the curriculum.

Fourth, with regard to content, the real design challenge is to get a handle on cross-country heterogeneity, as recommended in Section 4.3, without proliferating variety to the extent that every country that is considered ends up being treated as *sui generis*. The perspective that underlies the designs elaborated in this section does more than emphasize the differences between countries as important; as noted earlier, it goes "meta" by providing a framework for organizing observations about cross-country differences, in terms of the distance between them. We note the structural similarity in this approach to an approach often used in business (e.g., the automobile industry) to adapt to cross-country heterogeneity: the designing a common *platform* that, relatively easily, can be customized to varied country contexts.

Both Stanford's Global Context of Management course and the IESE GLOBE course, for example, explore cross-country differences systematically using similar frameworks. The frameworks focus on four related if not parallel types of distance that cover, in a somewhat more aggregated way, the categories of differences that are highlighted by the thought leader survey. The similarity between the two treatments is no accident: Stanford's current model is, according to its current course head, "obviously inspired" by Ghemawat's 2001 presentation of the CAGE distance framework—an acronym for cultural, administrative, geographic and economic distances across countries—that is also used, without modification, in the IESE GLOBE course.[27] The Wharton Global Summit, based on its preliminary design—it will be offered broadly in 2012–13—is rather different from the other two: it focuses on institutional differences and their implications for economic and financial governance. In addition, a required Foundations of Teamwork and Leadership course, offered at the beginning of the first year of the Wharton MBA program, raises issues related to national cultural differences. The GLOBE course also includes discussion of levels of cross-border integration and the costs and benefits of globalization from a social perspective.

---

[27]Ghemawat, Pankaj, "Distance Still Matters: The Hard Reality of Global Expansion," *Harvard Business Review,* Sept. (2001), pp. 137–47.

Finally, consideration should be given to the ways in which cases, textbooks, and other pedagogical tools are used to align with course and program learning objectives. Business cases, for example, are used in all three of the courses shown in Box 4A, but in different ways. For example, the IESE course concentrates on full-length cases and case discussions: on case days, no additional readings are assigned for class. The Stanford course, on the other hand, supplements traditional case sessions with sessions that feature caselets or videos that are read or viewed in class; such snippets can help introduce issues and illustrate principles for dealing with them but are generally reserved for topics for which a deeper evaluation is less important. Despite the importance of the appropriate selection, adaptation, and use of pedagogical tools to the successful implementation of a curricular globalization initiative, we are concerned that the best intentions for curriculum globalization are often challenged by a lack of appropriate pedagogical tools. In the following sub-section, we offer some observations about the globalization gap in classroom tools/content.

4.4.4.   Cases and Other Pedagogical Tools/Content for the Classroom

Case studies, textbooks, and other supplemental materials play a key role in business courses, and should be considered an integral component of a curriculum globalization strategy. If business schools are to enhance their ability to globalize their courses and curricula, a shift in the quantity, type, and focus of pedagogical tools is needed. Overall, there seems to be a need for more truly "international" material—not just cases involving, for example, a U.S. firm in another country setting—and for textbooks that pay particular attention to the international dimensions of the topic of focus. Second, there is a critical need for proportionately more material that focuses on different world contexts and populations, particularly those of emerging markets.

These points will be illustrated by an in-depth examination of the case studies that are taught at business schools. The point is not that instruction about globalization should entirely or even largely be based on the case method, although we point to the value of using *some* cases in this particular context. Rather, we have finer-grained information about case-study usage, so some of what follows can simply be read as a (vivid) illustration of problems that appear to affect other kinds of content for the classroom as well.

In addition to resonating with what seem to be broader (but less well-documented) patterns, a focus in this chapter on cases is important for two other reasons. One set of reasons is related to what are arguably the special attractions of the case method in the context of globalization. Given the challenge of making decisions that cut across multiple, partially integrated markets, discussions of globalization and business are likely to involve a particular emphasis on the higher-order cognitive/thinking skills in Benjamin Bloom's classic hierarchy of knowledge-comprehension-application-analysis-synthesis-evaluation. These are precisely the areas in which advantage has traditionally been claimed for the case method: thus, according to Wallace P. Donham, the Harvard Business School dean who imported the case method into business from law in the 1920s, "[p]rimarily, it appears to be applicable only where the principal effort is to develop the students' power of analysis and synthesis."[28] Second, the case method also helps with reasoning by analogy,[29] which could be improved in the context of globalization if the common stereotypes of global monopolists/oligopolists that operate the same way all around the world are any indication. Finally, cases seem to lend themselves, unlike lectures, to an egalitarian, participant-centered mode of learning with cross-cultural appeal. Thus, data on international exchanges suggest that business school students prefer a participative learning culture to a more directive one, even if the latter coincides more closely with the national culture in their country of origin.[30] This style of learning can presumably be helpful in dealing with some of the challenges of classroom diversity that are discussed in the next section.

A second, specific reason for focusing on cases relates to the fact that many business schools draw from sets of cases that are developed and disseminated by a small set of schools; thus, biases in the original set likely will be reflected in the sets of cases that are adopted at other schools. The small-numbers aspect of this situation, which is directly tied to the resources that are required for case development and distribution, provides another reason for raising concerns instead of simply relying on decentralized processes ("the marketplace of cases") to attain the best outcomes.

Truly "international" cases and other content. While the need for more truly "international" cases and other content is well-documented, we rely on several partially complete samples to reinforce this point. The first is of a well-regarded, U.S.-based school that actually emphasizes the globalization of its curriculum on its website by asserting that about one-third of the cases developed each year by its faculty are international in scope. Ghemawat analyzed the work of a research assistant who had graduated from that school in 2006 and who had maintained a contemporaneous log of all the

---

[28]Donham, W. B., "Business Teaching by the Case System," *American Economic Review*, Vol. 12, No. 1 (1922), pp. 53–65.

[29]Gavetti, Giovanni, and Jan W. Rivkin, "How Strategists Really Think: Tapping the Power of Analogy," *Harvard Business Review* Vol. 83, Apr. (2005), pp. 54–63.

[30]See, for instance, Kragh, Simon U., and Sven Bislev, "Political Culture And Business School Teaching," Academy of Management "Best Conference Paper," 2005.

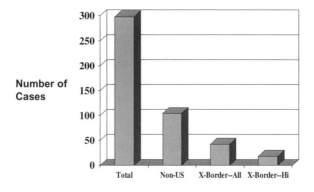

Figure 4.3: First-Year MBA Program of a Top U.S. Business School.
Source: Ghemawat, Pankaj, analysis.

cases he had studied in his first year (2004–05) in that school's MBA program. The results of a reconstruction of the global content of all the cases in the core first-year curriculum—except the country/macroeconomic cases from the international economy course—appear in Figure 4.3.

In this sample, about 35 percent of the cases did indeed have significant content that was related to activities outside the United States, as the school proudly pointed out. But if cases without cross-border content (in other words, domestic cases set in countries outside of the United States) are excluded, the percentage falls to 15 percent. Even more subjectively, cross-border issues seem to be highly important in only 6 percent of the cases.

Of course, this procedure excludes cases that are set outside the U.S. without an explicit cross-border component that nonetheless might provide useful insights into comparative management. However, many of the single-country "international" cases in this school's case banks seemed context-free in the sense that it did not really matter whether a particular business situation was set in, say, Georgia, the former Soviet Union, or Georgia, the former Confederacy. And in any case, a recent recalculation at the same business school that attempts to fix this omission concludes that only about 10 percent of the cases in the first year of the MBA program have significant globalization-related content. Clearly, locality should not be confused with topicality.

Though the above example highlights the situation at just one school, we believe that many readers of this report will find similar situations in their own business schools.

Another way of deepening insight is to narrow the scope by looking at globalization-related content in a particular area across a broad range of schools as opposed to across a broad range of areas at one or a handful of schools. In this vein, Ghemawat and Jordan Siegel conducted a 2007 study of curricula in strategy (an area in which globalization has attracted above-average attention).[31] The researchers compiled a list of faculty members who taught core strategy courses, with a focus on business schools that were ranked in *BusinessWeek*'s 2006 Top 30 U.S. full-time MBA programs or included among the top 50 ranked schools in *Financial Times*' 2006 Top 100 Global MBA Program Rankings. They sought core strategy MBA syllabi from 56 schools from this list, leaving aside Harvard Business School, with which both authors were affiliated at the time. They also contacted 21 schools that did not make the above lists but that were still well-recognized, for a total of 77 total contacts. The solicitation yielded 58 core strategy MBA syllabi from 51 business schools for 2007.[32] Of these, 43 syllabi came from 38 schools that were ranked in the *BusinessWeek* or *Financial Times* lists and 17 came from outside the U.S. A total of nine of those last 17 came from Europe.

Based on the researchers' analysis, 33 percent of the courses in this sample did not have a single case set outside of the U.S. For the average course, the non-U.S. percentage came to only 34 percent. The most common non-U.S. settings were Europe or Israel, which accounted for 21 percent of the cases. About 7 percent were set in Asia or Australia, and very few cases covered Latin America or Africa. Even in the relatively globalized European subsample, the two regions of North America and Europe/Israel together comprised 85 percent of case settings.[33] Few courses seemed to teach global strategy concepts or tools, and when they did, they tended to focus on market entry issues.[34] Discussions of global strategy issues such as locational advantages, scope decisions, adaptation, and arbitrage seemed very rare, as did specification of any particular world-structural/historical view of globalization.

---

[31]See, for example, Arain, F.M., and S.A.A. Tipu, "Emerging Trends in Management Education in International Business Schools," *Educational Research and Review*, Vol. 2, No. 12 (2007), pp. 325–31. These authors actually only report courses that are offered at two or more of the eight schools in their sample. As a result, the globalization-related share of elective offerings is calculated by dividing the number of globalization-related elective offerings by the total number of offerings of electives courses offered at two or more of the eight schools.

[32]Some business schools had more than one approach to teaching core strategy, and hence the unit of analysis is the course and not the school.

[33]It is interesting to contrast this focus with projections that these two regions will account for one-quarter to one-third of total global economic growth through 2030.

[34]In their preliminary analysis of the European subsample, they found that 45 percent of the cases were set in Europe or Israel, 39 percent in the United States, and 2 percent in Asia and Australia, with 6 percent focused on multi-location global firms.

The issue is not reserved for case studies; it is also relevant to other class or group exercises, simulations, textbooks, and other sources of content (including sources of news and analysis on current events) that help create a multidimensional learning experience. As just one additional example, economics textbooks are reported to have gone from a situation in which they had very little globalization-related content to one in which substantial progress has been made at incorporating some such content into how macroeconomics is taught, but much less so in the teaching of microeconomics—apparently because of the extent to which basic notions of static efficiency are complicated by some of the correlates of globalization. This picture is not reassuring from the perspective of business schools, which have a primarily micro- rather than macro- focus.

Pedagogical tools focused on emerging markets.   The scarcity of pedagogical tools that focus on business contexts and practices outside of Europe and North America is especially alarming given the rapid growth of management education in many emerging markets. Here, we veer from our discussion of the need for more materials that focus on *foreign* contexts and practices to the need for more *domestically* focused materials. Just as a student in the U.S. would likely be dismayed to find that an entire course or program revolved around Chinese firms, so would students in China be dismayed by courses and programs devoid of such examples.

Sheer numbers help illustrate the need for more materials that focus on emerging markets: China and India, for example, now possess roughly 2,700 institutions between them that award business degrees at the undergraduate level or above—nearly as many as the U.S. and the European Union combined. Even more remarkable is the recent explosion of business programs in these markets: less than 10 percent of the MBA programs in China, for example, are estimated to have been in existence back in 1990. Since then, both China and India have managed to raise the number of such institutions per million inhabitants from about 0.1 to 1. Given the U.S. "density" of more than 5 schools per million inhabitants, and the rapid increases in per capita income forecast for China and India, these decades possibly will see a doubling or tripling of volume of activity in what are already big emerging markets.[35]

---

[35]Preferably the analysis would be conducted in terms of student enrollments rather than the number of business schools, but systematic cross-country data on the former are unavailable.

This explosion of quantity ideally will be accompanied by investments in deepening quality, which is an issue for many nascent schools. And all of this progress will have to be accomplished without too many experienced faculty, who are subject to particularly long development lags and therefore tend to be particularly scarce in such markets. Meeting the globalization-related component of this challenge—which surfaces in all subject areas—is likely to hinge on curricular development for most of these schools to an even greater extent than for schools in developed markets.

Given that this task represents, once again, one of the biggest challenges in the globalization of management education, it probably is not a process that the top international schools should simply observe from the sidelines. Note, however, that the usual "marriage games" that involve establishing links with the best local schools may not suffice. While reasons to form such tie-ups exist, these linkages will not, by themselves, do much to address the broader social challenge of ensuring an adequate quantity and quality of management education. For top schools to really play a leadership role in this regard, newer, broader forms of involvement are required.

4.5. Structuring Global Experiences: Immersion and Interlock

In addition to course content, international student and faculty recruitment, the availability (or requirement) of an "international experience," and even foreign language training can, given program objectives, provide valuable experiences to supplement and reinforce classroom learning. The categories are not mutually exclusive, and substantial opportunity exists for synergy when two or more are used together or when they are combined with other initiatives that are not mentioned within this chapter. Thus, collaborative partnerships and global footprint strategies, which are discussed in greater detail in Chapter 5, can serve as structural enablers of many of these approaches. Exchange agreements, for example, often target increases in student diversity, and joint- and dual-degree programs include opportunities for travel, language training, and even exposure to course materials and educational methods other than those available at the home institution. The biggest opportunity for synergy, however, is when these mechanisms are aligned with a broader focus on curriculum development, as discussed earlier.

That last point deserves particular emphasis because of the Task Force's concern that business schools too often pursue these and other "experiential" activities for reasons such as accessibility or visibility, without considering if and how the activity aligns with the overall curriculum and supports achievement of specified learning objectives. Too often, classroom diversity, treks abroad, special projects, and similar elements are relied upon in lieu of attention to course or program content along the lines discussed in Section 4.3. Furthermore, the survey of academic thought leaders that is discussed earlier in this chapter suggests a perception that business schools may rely excessively on certain types of activities at the expense of others, and that schools may need to think more creatively about the types of initiatives they use.

In the survey of thought leaders, of 13 mechanisms for reinforcing "global" concepts and perspectives within management education, respondents cited national diversity of student body, joint ventures with foreign institutions, treks, and student exchanges (in decreasing order) most frequently as overdone, naming cross-border collaborative projects most frequently as underdone. European respondents seemed particularly jaded in regard to student diversity and excited about cross-border collaborative projects. For activities that were reported as overdone, perhaps the sentiments are reflective of a sense that they simply are used as auxiliary activities rather than as integral components of the overall educational strategy.

In order to think more systematically through the possibilities for enhancing the effectiveness of these mechanisms, it is useful to adopt a unifying frame for what business schools typically try to accomplish when they emphasize recruiting international students, international exchanges, etc. Such tools generally are meant to emphasize personal exposure to and experience of peers from different countries ("diversity") or different countries themselves ("mobility"), that is, to be largely experiential. How one thinks of the relationship between these tools and the content described in the previous sections depends, then, on how one thinks of the link between academic knowledge and experience. Gordon and Howell saw a clear hierarchy:

> Knowledge is the chief product of education, although it can be acquired in other ways also—for example, through reflective observation and experience.[36]

---

[36]Gordon, Robert Aaron, and James Edwin Howell, *Higher Education for Business*, Columbia University Press, New York, 1959, p. 103.

Augier and March provide a more even-handed characterization:

> Experiential knowledge and academic knowledge are in many ways better seen as intertwined than as in opposition. Experience is interpreted within frames of reference that reflect academic sensibilities, and the research on which academic knowledge is based is deeply affected by the observations and understandings of experience.[37]

But note that these differences in perspective revolve around the extent to which content is sufficient—both characterizations imply that it is necessary.

Another way of reaching the same conclusion is by applying the criterion of distinctive competence. A focus on diversity and mobility as key globalization-related value propositions to students would risk turning business schools into a specialized segment of the travel and hospitality industry. Most schools presumably aspire to be more than that.

Experiential initiatives can be usefully arrayed in terms of the degree of immersion, which, from a student perspective—the one adopted in the rest of this section—might be said to range from aspersion or sprinkling (e.g., a trek) to submersion (e.g., attending a full-time MBA program in a foreign location). Similarly, the degree of immersion implied by classroom diversity is a function of levels of exposure to and interaction with individuals from other cultures. The resource-intensity of both types of initiatives appears to vary directly with the degree of immersion. So while one can, in line with Augier and March, think of immersion as the third leg of the interlock model, in addition to insertion and infusion, it is best thought of as a telescoping leg that can and should be adjusted , depending on a school's resources and strategy—unlike the other two legs, which are deemed generally necessary. The caveat is that this third leg may need to be at least of a minimum intensity measure to add value: several types of experiential initiatives seem subject to threshold effects, in the sense that, to be worth pursuing, they must be pursued to more than a token extent. To elaborate on these points, consider several types of initiatives for globalizing students' learning experiences—classroom diversity, international travel, international project work, and language training—one by one.

---

[37]Augier, Mie, and James G. March, "The Pursuit of Relevance in Management Education," *California Management Review*, Vol. 49, No. 3 (2007), p. 130.

4.5.1. Classroom Diversity

Statistics on the national diversity of students and faculty abound on business school websites, and can be a popular mechanism emphasized by schools that seek to convey an "international" focus. But what, really, is the relationship between classroom diversity and globalization of the learning experience?[38]

To start with some data, undergraduate education in business is, from the standpoint of student composition, significantly less globalized than graduate education. According to the AACSB membership survey for 2009–10, international students accounted for 5 percent of enrollment in U.S. undergraduate programs in business and 23 percent for programs outside the U.S.[39] By contrast, international students are 14 percent of the total MBA program enrollments at U.S. schools that responded to the AACSB's most recent survey and 29 percent elsewhere.[40] At the MBA program level, The *Financial Times*' list of top 100 MBA programs permits extension of this analysis to a somewhat smaller set of top ranked schools. An analysis of U.S. and European business schools, which are the two geographies that dominate the list, shows that the top European schools, with more than 80 percent non-nationals, exhibit much greater student diversity than their U.S. counterparts, with less than 40 percent non-nationals. The analysis further shows that this diversity is positively (but weakly) associated with status or, in other words, that it is negatively associated with numerical rank.[41]

Attempts to build and maintain a student body that comprises many nationalities often simply assume that student diversity will lead to greater mutual understanding. In addition, work in cognitive science suggests that cognitive diversity in the form of the different perspectives, frameworks, and

---

[38]Though the discussion in this sub-section focuses on classroom diversity, similar principles apply to individuals who are affiliated with international student networks. A growing number of supranational student organizations are being established or have expanded their scope beyond their original borders. These organizations include special interest groups (e.g., Net Impact and SIFE), professional associations (e.g., the Society for Human Resource Management), disciplinary associations (e.g., the Academy of Management), and honor societies (e.g., Beta Gamma Sigma). The Task Force encourages these institutions to also consider ways to leverage the international diversity of their members to enhance the learning opportunities for those involved.

[39]AACSB International, Business School Questionnaire, 2009–10.

[40]Ibid.

[41]Ghemawat, Pankaj, "Bridging the Globalization Gap at Top Business Schools: Curricular Challenges and a Response," Chapter 2.3 in Canals, Jordi (ed.), *The Future of Leadership Development*, Palgrave Macmillan, Houndmills, Basingstoke, Hampshire, UK, 2011.

so on that are likely to be associated with national cultural diversity *can* improve problem solving if people of different backgrounds are able to work together effectively.[42] However, this last caveat is a nontrivial one, as research on business organizations shows. Consider Williams and O'Reilly's summary of 40 years of research on this topic:

> Consistent with social categorization and similarity/attraction theories, the preponderance of empirical evidence suggests that diversity is most likely to impede group functioning. Unless steps are taken to actively counteract these effects, the evidence suggests that, by itself, diversity is more likely to have negative than positive effects on group performance.[43]

What kinds of steps might be taken to ensure positive rather than negative effects? First, appropriate curricular content is clearly a requisite: there is no point assembling a very global group, in terms of nationalities, and then subjecting them to a curriculum that essentially is entirely domestic in its content. Even if foreign students are encouraged to speak up in such a context, it is hard to imagine that a chain of classroom interventions along the lines of "that's not the way it works in my country" would be as fruitful as curricular content that explicitly addresses cross-country differences.

Second, to the extent that the diverse national backgrounds of students is supposed to complement such a curriculum, it is plausible that a certain minimum representation of foreign students and/or a minimum breadth of representation is necessary—a manifestation of the threshold effects for experiential learning initiatives that were discussed previously. While from the perspective of foreign students who study at a particular school, the immersion experience is intense and extensive compared to some of the other types of initiatives aimed at fostering mobility discussed in the next sub-section, from the perspective of domestic students, the immersion experience from classroom diversity is very limited if only a handful of foreign students are in the classroom.

Third, business schools and their faculty must pay explicit attention to managing diversity so as to exploit its potential while minimizing its pitfalls. A frequent expedient in this regard is deliberate diversification of study groups by nationality, which is certainly helpful. But this kind of "billiard ball" model of nationalities does not, for instance, attend to the possibilities

---

[42]Page, Scott E., *The Difference: How the Power of Diversity Creates Better Groups, Firms, Schools, and Societies*, Princeton University Press, Princeton, NJ, 2008, pp. 131–73.

[43]Williams, K.Y., and C.A. O'Reilly, "Demography and diversity in organizations: A review of 40 years of research," *Research in Organizational Behavior*, Vol. 20 (1998), pp. 77–140.

unlocked by "biculturals" who have deeply internalized more than one cultural profile[44]—or to other important dimensions of diversity (e.g., gender or socioeconomic status). And then, there is the problem we already know: increasing student diversity—whether through shorter-run exchanges or on a longer-run basis—complicates what goes on in business school classrooms by, among other things, requiring more attention to varying national expectations about class participation, etc.[45] Seemingly, outcomes could be improved by the inclusion and discussion of some content about these and other international differences, as argued on broader grounds in earlier sections of this chapter.

4.5.2. International Treks, Field Study, and Study Abroad

Similar points also apply to student mobility through international treks, field study projects, study abroad, and other mechanisms through which students travel to another country for a portion of their degree program. The actual models that are employed by business schools can be quite varied, from optional to required programs, from short-term treks to long-term residencies, and from course or project-based experiences to consulting or internship-based experiences.

Threshold effects seem particularly salient for trips abroad. Treks with low degrees of immersion likely will do little more than serve as catalysts for later voluntary engagement with another culture or context. Thus, for treks of low immersion intensity, it is particularly important that the experience be a supplement to considerable attention to international content within the curriculum. This can be achieved by preceding and following the trek with course content along the lines described earlier as well as other supplemental activities such as guest lectures, writing assignments, and/or research projects. In this way, the international experience serves to reinforce lessons from other aspects of the degree program, but it is not expected to be the primary vehicle for learning.

Longer-term study abroad experiences are more likely to serve as opportunities for a higher degree of immersion in another culture or context and thus as vehicles for acquiring greater knowledge and/or understanding

---

[44]Brannen, Mary Yoko, and David C. Thomas, "Bicultural Individuals in Organizations: Implications and Opportunity," introduction to special issue, *International Journal of Cross-Cultural Management*, Vol. 10, No. 1 (April 2010), pp. 5–16.

[45]Kragh, Simon U., and Sven Bislev, "Business School Teaching and Democratic Culture: An International and Comparative Analysis," *Research in Comparative International Education*, Vol. 3, No. 2 (2008), pp. 211–21.

of the environment. Gail Naughton, dean of the San Diego State University's College of Business and Administration, notes in a 2007 *BizEd* article that "Global executives have told us that it takes at least three months to become immersed in a geographical location and appreciate how the culture, politics, and history of a region affect business there."[46] A 2006 survey of students who had participated in the ERASMUS study-abroad program in Europe, which generally involves a semester or year abroad, resulted in the assessment that "[t]he ERASMUS period also shaped the attitudes and values of ERASMUS students substantially, particularly in personal values but also in career aspirations or educational competences, with between 65 percent and 95 percent of students reporting large changes or changes to some extent in their career-related attitudes and aspirations, the broadening of their general education, their personal values and their understanding of people from another cultural or ethnic background."[47]

But length alone is far from the only factor that contributes to a greater degree of immersion. Likely, readers are all too familiar with individuals who travel abroad only to socialize with the same type of people, engage in the same types of entertainment, eat the same food, etc., as they would at home—hardly an immersion within another way of life. Careful thought to the design of the experience (will the students be enrolled in courses with local students, live with a local family or in accommodations typical of a local student, be exposed to local businesses or only multinationals, and be expected to engage in and report on certain cultural activities?) can influence the actual level of immersion experienced during time spent abroad.

The AACSB survey of member schools' collaborative partnerships suggests a high prevalence of student exchange agreements (78.9 percent of all collaborations involved this dimension), which, because of their alignment with academic terms, tend to require at least several months in another location. However, anecdotal evidence gathered through many discussions with business school deans suggests that most student exchange agreements are optional in nature rather than required, and that not all are active in a given year. Furthermore, even when required, students more frequently have the freedom to select from an array of course and location options than follow a predetermined course that is tied very tightly with program objectives. The reasons for this

---

[46]Bisoux, Tricia, "Global Immersion," *BizEd,* Vol. 6, No.4 (July/August 2007), pp. 46–47.
[47]Otero, Manuel Souto, and Andrew Mc Coshan, 2006 Survey of the Socio-Economic Background of ERASMUS Students, ECOTEC Research and Consulting, Ltd., Birmingham, U.K., August 2006, electronic document, http://ec.europa.eu/education/erasmus/doc922_en.htm, accessed August 31, 2010.

noncompulsory approach are clear: both deeper immersion and stronger connections to the core curriculum require greater investment on the part of the home school in choosing the partner school, working collabora- tively with the partner to ensure the opportunity aligns closely with program objectives, and actively monitoring the learning outcomes from the experience.

Furthermore, even longer-term programs of this sort generally do not offer much of a framework, if any, for thinking about the locations that are visited. Nor do they seem to have assimilated modern approaches to building cultural and emotional intelligence, which stress the limits of in-depth learning about one or two "foreign" countries/ cultures[48] and the need to go "meta" instead.[49] In addition, basic questions exist about whether time spent traveling as opposed to living abroad actually has the stimulative effects that it is supposed to have on anything more fundamental than student ratings.[50] Either way, some broader content on international differences would once again seem to be useful preparation.

4.5.3. *Collaborative Projects and Other Experiences*

Not all students are in a position to travel, even for short timeframes, because of work and/or family obligations, or financial constraints. Students who *can* travel often find that their mobility is restricted by time, resources, or program structural constraints—they can only visit a certain number of locations for a certain amount of time. Furthermore, as discussed above, even opportunities for travel may not be accompanied by the depth of immersion that is necessary to actually create a significant learning experience. Projects, particularly those that leverage technology, therefore also frequently play an important role as curricular supplements.

With decreasing costs and enhanced capabilities, some technological applications support virtual cross-border connections between students as a

---

[48]For example, see Earley, P.C., and E. Mosakowski, "Cultural intelligence," *Harvard Business Review*, Oct. (2004), pp. 139–46.

[49]See, for instance, Smith, Peter B., Mark F. Peterson, and David C. Thomas, *The Handbook of Cross-Cultural Management Research*, Sage Publications, Inc., Thousand Oaks, California, 2008.

[50]For evidence that creativity is stimulated by living abroad but not by traveling abroad, see Maddux, W.W., and A.D. Galinsky, "Cultural Borders and Mental Barriers: The Relationship between Living Abroad and Creativity," *Journal of Personality and Social Psychology*, Vol. 96, No. 5 (2009), pp. 1047–61.

component of courses that are taken on their home campus. In addition to learning about working with colleagues of a different culture (i.e., by creating virtual classroom and/or project team diversity as discussed earlier), these collaborative projects also provide students with an opportunity to hone their skills in using technology to communicate virtually across distances and time zones. Students at East Carolina University in the United States, for example, videoconference with counterparts in 17 countries using an Internet connection and an inexpensive and basic, yet functional, camera/software package.[51] Ongoing technological advances are likely to make more high-tech endeavors even more accessible and robust, particularly as enhanced bandwidth brings increased quality of interactions.

Further along the resource intensity scale might be projects that incorporate both a virtual and an on-site component. For example, the Global Business Project, hosted by CIBERs at a consortium of 14 U.S. universities in collaboration with foreign partners, brings together students with prior business experience and foreign language skills to work on virtual teams to address a challenge that is identified by a company in another world region. After eight weeks of virtual collaboration, the students come together in the destination country for two weeks that include a few days of final mentoring at a partner business school and several days of work with the company in-country before presenting their findings.[52] Similarly, two programs offered by the Stanford Graduate School of Business with partner schools in India (Indian Institute of Management-Bangalore) and China (Tsinghua University, School of Economics and Management) require student teams that consist of two individuals from each school to work collaboratively on a research project prior to completing reciprocal one-week visits.

Other project components might be intended to supplement a curricular focus on cross-country differences, as discussed in Section 4.3. Stanford, for example, makes a Country Navigator tool available to its students and IESE facilitates the GLOBE project and broader application of the course's CAGE distance framework by distributing a detailed cross-country dataset and a CAGE Comparator™ software package built around it that uses industry-level estimates of the effects of distance along cultural, administrative,

---

[51]Fischer, Karin, "East Carolina U. Uses Simple Technology to Link Its Students With Peers Overseas," *The Chronicle of Higher Education,* May 7, 2009, electronic document, http://chronicle.com/free/v55/i35/35a02302.htm, accessed May 7, 2009.

[52]University of North Carolina at Chapel Hill, Kenan-Flagler Business School, Global Business Project Web page, 2010, electronic document, http://www.kenan-flagler.unc.edu/ki/ciber/GBP/, accessed December 30, 2010.

geographic, and economic dimensions on trade flows to, among other applications, adjust market size in a foreign country for distance.

Other, less formal means exist by which students may gain experience in and exposure to another country and interact with students from other world regions. MBA case competitions, such as those offered by the Concordia University John Molson School of Business, the University of Southern California Marshall School of Business, National University of Singapore Business School, and IESE, offer opportunities for small teams of students from (often) a select group of invited schools to compete to analyze cases on international firms. Other international competitions have been established around stock trading (e.g., Rotman International Trading Competition at the University of Toronto) and business plan development (e.g., the Hong Kong University of Science and Technology MBA International Business Plan Competition).

As noted by participants in the survey of academic thought leaders, cross-border collaborative projects may yet prove to be the most underutilized mechanism with the greatest potential. Particularly given today's technological advances, the opportunities that are presented by these projects seem relatively unexploited, and they suggest a new area for increased attention and experimentation.

4.5.4. Language Training

Before moving on, it is important to touch briefly on the inclusion of foreign language training into business programs. The ability to converse in another language and to understand another culture in the context of its language can contribute substantially to the ability of individuals to engage in smooth cross-border communications and interactions. At the same time, to achieve a level of fluency, or even proficiency, in another language requires many years of study and immersion.

Opinions about the value of foreign language training as a component of business degree programs therefore vary widely. In our survey of thought leaders, 79 percent of respondents indicated that they believed language requirements were ignored or underdone in business/management education (second only to cross-border collaborative projects, at 86 percent). The survey did, however, show some differences by region. None of the European respondents classified language requirements as overdone or exaggerated compared to 8 percent of North American and 9 percent of Asian respondents. Those who felt that current levels of language requirements were "about right" comprised 13 percent of North American respondents and 9 percent of Asian respondents, but a significant 27 percent of European respondents.

Some business schools have embraced foreign language skills as a critical competency for their graduates; these schools tend to be located in countries where English is not the native language. At ESSEC Business School in France/Singapore, for example, MBA students are expected to demonstrate proficiency in three languages, and undergraduate students to demonstrate proficiency in four languages by the time they graduate (of which one may be French). The China Europe International Business School (CEIBS) in Shanghai, China, offers its full-time MBA program in English. Given, however, its focus on providing talent to Chinese firms, the school has begun to emphasize the need for all students (many of whom are not Chinese citizens) to have a basic level of proficiency in Mandarin Chinese upon entry to the program and to provide students with ongoing opportunities to strengthen their language skills while in the program.

Still, foreign language requirements seem to be the exception rather than the rule among business programs, particularly those offered in North America. A study by Saiz and Zoido found that, though U.S. college graduates who speak a foreign language earn more than those who do not, the actual earnings gain (controlling for factors such as regional differences, quality of college, major, etc.) was minimal—between 2 and 3 percent depending on the language—and lower than the earnings premium for an extra year of schooling.[53]

To again reference the threshold effects that are introduced at the beginning of this section, the level of immersion in language training (and often, resources invested) likely is an important factor in its overall value. Thus, in order for foreign language skills to be useful in a business environment, the speaker should be able to engage in deeper levels of communication beyond discussion about the weather and ordering a meal in a restaurant, which are common themes of introductory language courses. To attain the level of fluency required for business negotiations in a foreign language requires a substantial investment on the part of the school—both in the acquisition of additional faculty resources and in the willingness to dedicate time in the program toward this training.

Practically, the condensed timeframe of master's-level programs makes language training at this level difficult. Thus, while INSEAD, for example, considers foreign language ability to be an integral skill of its graduates, the school invests relatively little in actually providing this training as a part of its MBA program. Instead the school requires incoming students to be fluent

---

[53]Saiz, Albert, and Elena Zoido, "Listening to What the World Says: Bilingualism and Earnings in the United States," *Review of Economics & Statistics*, Vol. 87, No. 3 (2005), pp. 523–38.

in English, to have a practical knowledge of another language before starting the program, and to work within the program to acquire basic knowledge of a third language before graduating.

Undergraduate programs can be more accommodating of students who wish to double major or minor in another language, and a few business schools have made substantial investments to facilitate stronger connections between business and foreign language study. The University of South Carolina's Moore School of Business, for example, recently instituted a track within the Bachelor of Science in Business Administration degree program called International Business and Chinese Enterprise that emphasizes language training through both classroom learning and immersion. Students in the cohort program take two full years of classes in Mandarin Chinese, including intensive summer programs—the first year at the Moore School and the second at the Chinese University of Hong Kong (CUHK). Before graduating from the program, students will spend a second year at CUHK and participate in an internship in Hong Kong where they will put their language skills to use in a business environment.

As with classroom diversity, trips abroad, cross-border collaborative projects, and other mechanisms for experiential learning, the value of language training as a curriculum supplement depends heavily on its integrality to program objectives. Business schools have a finite set of resources—including financial and human capital—and often a finite amount of time for delivery of the degree program. Thus, the first priority for resource allocation must be an investment in the curricular frameworks that will support appropriate global learning objectives, followed by selection of appropriate mechanisms for reinforcing those objectives and curricular content.

4.6. Assessment of Learning Outcomes

Finally, we come to the closing of the loop. If a business school succeeds at motivating efforts to globalize curricula, identifying or developing new content, and incorporating it into a program's design and delivery model, how does the school know that its significant investment has the intended effect? Checking or assessing the effectiveness of educational interventions is a generic area of weakness for business schools.[54] But perhaps because of

---

[54]See, for example, Pfeffer, Jeffrey, and Christina R. Fong, "The end of business schools? Less success than meets the eye," *Academy of Management Learning and Education*, Vol. 1, No. 1 (2002), pp. 78–95.

uncertainty and consequent fuzziness about basic objectives, globalization seems to present particular assessment challenges.

For example, anecdotal and survey data compiled by AACSB assessment seminar facilitators indicate that learning goals related to international competencies are considerably less common than those related to other skills. This deficiency makes analysis of the effectiveness of existing curricular models and approaches particularly difficult. One such facilitator notes that, from her experience, assessment of global perspectives tends "to relate to international trade and to be found in the form of questions on economics exams, with occasional exceptions where the incorporation of global perspectives in strategy development is assessed through a case-study."[55]

Even the comprehensive Certified MBA assessment schema retreats to a mostly macroeconomic plane in trying to specify what students should have learned by the end of their MBA programs (see Table 4.3A). If one were to restrict oneself to 10 knowledge-related but broadly managerial questions about globalization out of a total of more than 200—probably a suboptimal percentage—and take seriously the thrust of the arguments in this chapter, one might come up with a 10-point list like the one in Table 4.3B instead.

Readers can and inevitably will take issues with some of the items included as well as excluded from the list in Table 4.3B. But the broader point is that more clarity is needed about the implications of having a truly globally-educated business student. Even if such clarity did not yield measurable indicators—although, seemingly, some measurement should be possible—it would be helpful in refining what to do with the content-related and experiential components of educational programs.

Furthermore, assessments of knowledge that relate to globalization need to be supplemented with assessments of attitudes and values. Structured, research-based efforts to make such assessments—global mindset is a common rubric and the Thunderbird Global Mindset Inventory introduced in Section 4.3 is a leading example—help in this regard but also arguably are subject to some significant limitations. In addition, the vagueness with which the term "global mindset" is often used also sounds a caution. Thus, when a CEO argues that a global mindset is a high priority, what s/he may be saying is that everybody in the field should take a headquarters-perspective on decisions—from which it is a short step to decree that headquarters should take all decisions and end up with a standardized strategy that is not respectful of national differences. That a systematic managerial bias may exist in this regard is suggested by an exploratory study aimed at

---

[55]Martell, Kathryn, e-mail correspondence, April 1, 2010.

Table 4.3: Sample Areas of Globalization-Related Knowledge.

A. Certified MBA Sample Assessment Questions on Internationalization/ Globalization*

Macroeconomics

1. Explain how international translation and transaction risk may affect firm balance sheet and income statement.
2. Justify a decision to hedge international risk.
3. Explain the various tools for hedging international risk (e.g., currency options, futures, and forward contracts).
4. Recognize the special risks firms may face in operating in countries that use flexible exchange rates, pegged exchange rates, exchange controls, or currency boards to determine exchange rates.
5. Evaluate changes in national protectionist policies.
6. Show the connection between inflation rate and exchange rate.

Organizational Behavior

7. Analyze the factors that differentiate national cultures.

Strategy

8. Describe forces driving globalization.
9. Distinguish between multinational, global and transnational strategies.
10. Describe key organizational challenges in globalization

---

*All relevant questions out of a total of 229 in 10 functional areas.

Source: CertifiedMBA.com, CMBA_Exam_Overview_and_Objectives, 2010, electronic document, http://www.certifiedmba.com/exam/CMBA_Exam_Overview_and_Objectives.pdf, accessed May 19, 2010.

B. Potential Areas of Required Knowledge**

1. Levels of cross-border integration of markets of different types: products, capital, people, and information (semi-globalization)
2. Levels of internationalization/globalization of firms (firms as the visible hand of cross-border integration)
3. Changes in cross-border integration over time (the two waves of globalization, the current crisis in historical perspective)
4. Drivers of changes in cross-border integration over time (technological changes, particularly in transport and communications, and policy changes)
5. Net impact of differences of various types on cross-border interactions (estimates from gravity models of the effects of CAGE variables)
6. Differences in national cultures and implications for business (objective indicators and Hofstede's five—subjective—dimensions of cultural values and implications)

Table 4.3: (*Continued*)

7. Differences in business ownership and governance around the world and implications ("varieties of capitalism")
8. Distance and other geographic barriers and implications (regionalization—at international and intranational levels)
9. Economic differences and implications (wages and other factor costs; impact on arbitrage/vertical vs. aggregation/horizontal strategies)
10. Benefits and costs of increased cross-border integration (in the presence of market failures)

**Partial list, to be expanded and also supplemented with a) function-specific knowledge requirements, and b) attitudinal/value assessments.

---

deriving bases for measuring the globalization of mindset. The researchers themselves had to add dimensions related to national responsiveness because the managers whom they were surveying were apt to overlook these dimensions.[56]

4.6.1. Closing the Loop

The last element of the assessment cycle is the one that seems to draw the most current interest in at least one sense: most schools do not or at least should not need to check how they are performing against their globalization-related objectives to figure out that they need to act differently in this area (although assessment would, as noted previously, help calibrate the problem and identify specific countermeasures). If knowledge of what to do is not the binding constraint, the knowing-doing gap assumes that role.

As noted earlier in this chapter, many schools have, instead of forcing the globalization of curricular content, tended to focus on initiatives—such as classroom diversity, travel, and partnerships—that fall within their comfort zones, or at least do not require radical changes to what they are accustomed to doing. Thus, the emphasis on recruiting students from many different

---

[56]Murtha, Thomas P., Stefanie Ann Lenway, Richard P. Bagozzi, "Global Mind-sets and Cognitive Shift in a Complex Multinational Corporation," *Strategic Management Journal*, Vol. 19, No. 2 (1998), pp. 97–114.

countries fits with the traditional business school model of delivering residential programs at one location (while also helping to fill available seats). And partnerships are ways of achieving mobility without committing to physical locations overseas. Given all the motivation and behavioral obstacles to change that are discussed in Section 4.2, a reliance on purely bottom-up processes to eliminate the globalization gap is likely to yield results very slowly, if at all. Business school rankings that assess "globalization" by measuring student and/or faculty diversity, or the number of a school's partner institutions, reinforce this approach.

The good news is that improvements do seem possible. Business schools' current positions, not to mention their educational missions, suggest that instead of focusing on such bottom-up processes, they should invest their resources in the development and deployment of better globalization-related content as their distinctive competence in this arena. Thus, Jeffrey Pfeffer and Christina Fong's otherwise scathing critique of business schools concludes with the following hopeful remarks that characterize the kind of content development and deployment envisioned here:

> The rigorous thinking and theoretical grounding that characterizes business school scholars and their research, actually offer an advantage over the casual empiricism and hyping of the latest fad that characterizes much, although not all, of the research that comes out of nonacademic sources. And business school faculty have spent years honing the craft of preparing and delivering educational material in ways that are at once accessible and intellectually sound. There is no reason that, in a world seeking both knowledge and training, business schools can't succeed in doing both well."[57]

A final point that must be made about taking action is that this challenge is not just for business schools. The influential Gordon and Howell study of business from more than half a century ago that this chapter cites in its opening actually concludes with five pages on the role of AACSB that includes, among other things, the following observation:

> Perhaps most important of all, the Association should become more of an active force for improvement than it now is. Not only should it have minimum standards which all member

---

[57]Pfeffer, Jeffrey, and Christina R. Fong, "The end of business schools? Less success than meets the eye," *Academy of Management Learning and Education*, Vol. 1, No. 1 (2002), p. 93.

schools are expected to meet fully but it should engage in an active educational program that has as its purpose stimulating schools to raise the quality of their programs much beyond the minimum levels which all schools are now expected to achieve.[58]

But given the salience of globalization and the problems as well as possibilities that it presents for management education, Gordon and Howell's recommendation would seem to fit this area that they did not foresee.[59]

4.7. Summary

This chapter suggests that to think of more globalized content as just another mechanism for globalizing business schools would be a serious mistake: such content is a strategic factor because it is the critical constraint on business schools' ability to address the gap that has developed between the globalization of their reach and the globalization of their offerings. A survey of academic thought leaders suggests that content that is aimed at bridging this globalization gap should focus on cross-country differences and their business implications. The chapter presents a specific proposal for structuring global content within the curriculum, advocating an interlock approach that uses a course that focuses on globalization as a platform for globalization-related discussions that continue in follow-on functional courses. Mechanisms that reinforce global learning objectives, such as classroom diversity, international experiences, project work, and language training, when carefully selected and deployed, can be valuable supplements to course content. Assessment of learning objectives is an area that is just beginning to attract attention but that is clearly very important.

---

[58]Gordon and Howell entirely failed to discuss globalization/internationalization: levels of cross-border integration *were* significantly lower then and the mood pessimistic about whether they would resume the upward sweep of the "long nineteenth century." Gordon, Robert Aaron, and James Edwin Howell, *Higher Education for Business*, Columbia University Press, New York, 1959.

[59]Thus, Polanyi et al. (1957) and Deutsch and Eckstein (1961) emphasized that various measures of globalization had declined significantly since the period before World War I, and they asserted that this trend was unlikely to be reversed any time soon. See Polanyi, Karl, Conrad M. Arensberg, and Harry W. Pearson (eds.), *Trade and Market in the Early Empires; Economies in History and Theory*, Free Press, Glencoe, IL, 1957, and Deutsch, Karl W., and Alexander Eckstein, "National Industrialization and the Declining Share of the International Economic Sector, 1890–1959," *World Politics*, Vol. 13 (1961), pp. 267–99.

That last point is a reminder that many insights into effective curricular strategies and their correlates remain to be developed. The links between the globalization of the curricula on one hand, and faculty development and research on the other have yet to be understood thoroughly. The impact of technological improvements in areas such as telepresence, online educational platforms, and more is likely to be substantial but these mechanisms are still at an early stage of development. Interactions between business schools and members of the profession they serve will, one hopes, continue to increase clarity and specificity about the knowledge and skills required of business graduates in a globalizing world, as well as to enhance business schools' success in achieving those outcomes. More broadly, the study of business organizations suggests that the globalization of business schools is likely to prove to be a sequential process as well.

Acknowledgments

I am grateful to AACSB International's Globalization of Management Education Task Force and particularly its chair, Dean Robert Bruner, for many helpful discussions and encouragement, to Juliane Iannarelli and Dan LeClair of AACSB International for extensive help in assembling and interpreting some of the data that I rely on, to Dean Jordi Canals and IESE Business School for providing multiple forms of support for my work on this topic, and to Dean Bernard Yeung of the National University of Singapore Business School for his collaboration on the AACSB-supported survey of academic thought leaders reported on herein as well as for many helpful discussions on this broad topic. I have also benefited from discussions with Mary Brannen, Thomas Hout, Yih-teen Lee, Gerald McDermott, Riel Miller, Jeffrey Pfeffer, Carlos Sanchez-Runde and Jordan Siegel and the comments of seminar audiences at IESE, Darden, INSEAD, and Wharton. Steven Altman provided research assistance and Seth Schulman editorial assistance. However, the views expressed here should not be assumed to coincide with the perspectives of any of the individuals or institutions listed above.

Chapter 5

Responses to Forces of Change: A Focus on Structures and Processes

As we argued in the last chapter, business school globalization must begin in the curriculum. At the same time, the creation and transfer of meaningful, relevant knowledge involves many dimensions—educational experiences, intellectual capital, and external engagement—that integrate with and influence one another. Rarely do changes in curricula occur without consideration given to other areas of a school's activities. Fortunately, business schools today have more opportunities than ever before to infuse their teaching, research, and outreach activities with international, inter-cultural, local, and global dimensions—all of which are perspectives necessary for conducting business in the global economy.

Schools will globalize in a variety of ways; no single approach must be adopted by all schools. Methods will and should be as varied as the missions, resources, locations, leadership, regulatory environments, lan-guages, cultures, and even academic calendars of the numerous providers of management education that exist around the world today. The Task Force has deliberately avoided a classification of various activities as either effective or ineffective, though some approaches do seem to be more effective than others. Globalization strategies employed by business schools will, and should, evolve over time as each school learns from previous experiences and assesses its ongoing needs.

More important, the development of any strategy will involve trade-offs. Resources—of funding, time, energy, and expertise—are often limited, and must be managed carefully. The Task Force thus encourages business schools to think beyond the number of different types of international activities in which they engage. Such a check-list approach risks a movement toward "ill-considered follow the leader globalization of management education [that] may lead many schools into expensive adventures, with little or no return," to quote Rolf Cremer, dean of China Europe International Business School (CEIBS).[1]

Instead, schools should first identify the activities most likely to yield the institution's strategic objectives, given available resources, and then implement those activities with a plan for monitoring results. The schools that are most effective will be those that find ways for various activities to complement one another, creating synergies and therefore new capabilities and opportunities. A diversified strategy will also provide options to help "bridge the gap" when unexpected circumstances or disruptions (e.g., currency fluctuations, political disruptions, natural disasters, etc.) make an existing strategy less effective or no longer an option.

This chapter aims to help business school leaders think critically about globalization objectives and the broad range of ways in which they might be achieved. Section 5.1 takes a closer look at collaborative agreements, focusing on data that indicate current activity levels and areas of focus as well as on the strategies employed by schools to implement them successfully. Section 5.2 provides an overview of collaborative degree program models and strategies. The strategies used by schools to develop facilities, or "footprints" in other countries, are explored in Section 5.3. Section 5.4 looks at faculty strategies for globalization, including faculty recruitment, development, and management. Finally, Section 5.5 concludes the chapter by presenting a few observations that may help schools that seek to align various activities in support of an overall strategy. Throughout the chapter, the discussion is supplemented by specific examples of actual approaches taken by business schools around the world, including insights gleaned from in-depth case studies (see Appendix) of how some schools have approached globalization across their array of activities.

We do not pretend to exhaust all possibilities in the pages that follow; nor do we intend to provide a comprehensive study of all the potential risks and benefits associated with each activity, as an emerging body of literature on globalization of higher education is better oriented for this purpose. Yet, we do hope that this chapter helps broaden the thinking of program and school administrators regarding the array of dimensions a comprehensive globalization strategy might entail.

5.1.   Augmenting Capabilities through Strategic Partnerships

We earlier predicted that the next phase of development for management education will be characterized by the emergence of connections,

---

[1]Cremer, Rolf, personal interview, 2009; see case study in Appendix.

collaborations, and greater competition among business schools globally. Such a shift will also bring with it the emergence of new models for management education—with organizational and hierarchical structures built upon alliances and joint ventures rather than isolated within distinct, independently operating institutions. Strategic partnerships have the potential to be a key enabler of efficiencies leading to comparative and competitive advantages for the institutions that engage in them.

Much collaborative activity—or at least a growing web of contracts and agreements intended to foster collaborative activity—exists among business schools already. With some notable exceptions, however, much of this connectedness remains at a foundational level with substantial room for deeper, more meaningful collaborations.

5.1.1. Current State of Business School Collaborations

Results from a recent survey of AACSB member schools' collaborations reveal a few key insights into the current state of collaboration among business schools:

- **Large numbers of business schools already maintain collaborative agreements with other schools, and those that do not overwhelmingly report a desire to do so.**

Four out of five participating schools (201/244) reported having at least one collaborative agreement with another school; 88 percent of schools without existing collaborations indicated a desire to establish one or more collaborations with other schools. While schools with an interest in collaborations were probably more likely to respond to the survey, we also note that nearly 60 percent of institutions identified by AACSB members as partners were not members of the association at the time of the survey and therefore had not received survey invitations. This fact suggests that the survey results have implications for a broader set of schools beyond the roughly 1,100 that are AACSB members.

- **Existing collaborations tend to be based on bilateral agreements between two partner institutions.**

In fact, 95 percent of all collaborative agreements reported in the survey existed between only two schools. This statistic is not surprising considering that alliances with fewer partners are likely to be more manageable. At the same time, 16 percent of schools that reported collaborations were part of one or more collaborations involving more than four additional partner schools. (Together, collaborations with more than four partners represented only 1.6 percent of the total collaborations reported.) Though no specific threshold for the number of institutions comprising a "consortium" exists, many of these collaborations would likely fall into the consortium category.

- **Overall, the most common activity supported by collaborative agreement is student exchange.**

As shown in Table 5.1, student exchange was considered a cause for 79 percent of the reported collaborations, which makes it by far the most frequent cause for entering into an agreement with another school. The next most prevalent reasons for collaboration were faculty exchange (21 percent of collaborative agreements), joint programs (9 percent), and dual-credit arrangements (7 percent).

Schools that classified a collaboration in the "other" category were asked to provide a brief description of the collaboration. In these descriptions, we found evidence of collaborations that involve research publications, graduate teaching, internship and career services, program (conference/ seminar) development, degree program design and/or development, curriculum development, academic material exchange, and even a joint venture to connect Canadian companies with investors and strategic partners in the Middle East.

Table 5.1: Frequency of Collaboration Type.

Collaboration Type	Total Reported Collaborations*	Percent of Total (3,126) Collaborations
Student Exchange	2466	79%
Faculty Exchange	662	21%
Other	352	11%
Joint Program	278	9%
Dual Credit	234	7%
Joint Research	195	6%
Non-Degree	107	3%
Shared Resources	80	3%
Shared Location	39	1%

*These figures do not sum to 100, as each collaboration could be classified as more than one type.
Source: AACSB Member Collaboration Survey 2008.[2]

---

[2]AACSB International, AACSB Member Collaboration Survey 2008, Internal survey data, 2008.

- **Existing collaborative agreements tend to be one-dimensional in purpose, supporting just one type of activity. This activity is most often student exchange.**

Of the 3,126 collaborations reported, nearly three-quarters (74 percent) were identified as one type, and another 17 percent were identified as only two types. The type of collaboration most likely to appear alone was student exchange; in fact, in 70 percent of the collaborations designated as student exchange, no other collaboration type was designated. Other types likely to have a single purpose were collaborations designated as "other" (58 percent), followed by those involving programs or courses: awarding of dual credits for coursework (55 percent), joint programs (41 percent), and non-degree education (37 percent). Collaborations that involved faculty exchange, on the other hand, were most likely to also involve other types of activities, with 97 percent of the 1,059 collaborations designated as "faculty exchange" also involving other types of activities.

As we look across the collaborations reported by any given school, of the 200 schools that reported data on their collaborations, nearly 25 percent reported having only one type of collaboration, with a similar percentage of schools engaging in two types of collaboration (see Table 5.2). Only one school reported engagement in all eight types and more (represented by "other"). Schools engaged in only one type of collaboration (across all collaborations reported) were most likely to be engaged in student exchange (48 percent of such schools), followed by joint programs (26 percent).

- **Collaborative agreements focused on the master's level are most common, followed by those focused on multiple levels and those focused on the undergraduate level; doctoral-level collaborations are rare.**

As shown in Table 5.3, the largest set of collaborations corresponded to master's-level education (35 percent of all collaborations), followed by those

Table 5.2: Distribution of Participation in More than One Type of Collaboration.

# of Types of Collaboration per Participating School	1	2	3	4	5	6	7	8	9
# of Schools (200)	46	43	35	30	22	12	5	6	1

Source: AACSB Member Collaboration Survey 2008.[3]

---

[3]Ibid.

Table 5.3: Distribution of Collaborations by Educational Level.

Level	Number of Reported Collaborations	Percent of Collaborations
Undergraduate	962	31%
Master's	1108	35%
Doctoral	26	1%
Multiple	904	29%
Non-Degree	54	2%
Not Applicable	72	2%

Source: AACSB Member Collaboration Survey 2008.[4]

that corresponded to undergraduate education (31 percent). Another 29 percent reportedly corresponded to multiple levels. Given the high prevalence of master's and undergraduate-level collaborations, these two levels likely are highly represented within the "multiple" category as well. Seventy-eight percent of master's level and 83 percent of undergraduate-level collaborations involved student exchange, as did 86 percent of agreements that corresponded to "multiple" levels. In all three cases, the second most common collaboration type was faculty exchange, at 17 percent, 14 percent, and 32 percent, respectively.

A very small number of collaborations corresponded to doctoral-level education. Among collaborations at the doctoral level, faculty exchange agreements were the most common (46 percent), followed by those for student exchange (31 percent), joint research (23 percent), and joint programs (also 23 percent).

The case studies provide an opportunity to review how a sample of schools has approached the tasks of entering into and managing an array of partnerships. All of the case-study schools, with the notable exception of the Stanford Graduate School of Business, maintain a web of partnership agreements with business schools in many different countries and world regions. They do not, however, maintain the same level of commitment to, or involvement with, each of their partners.

In fact, we found that schools commonly provided long lists of partner institutions on their websites (in one case, more than 100 schools were identified), but closer exploration revealed a significant difference between partnerships intended as a foundation for potential activity and those with actual ongoing activities of a high level. Many schools we spoke to acknowledged that they already had many basic-level partnerships and were now looking to strengthen existing relationships (rather than add new ones).

---

[4]Ibid.

This strategy was articulated well by the University of Minnesota's Carlson School of Management, which in the early 1990s set out to develop a "constellation of partnerships" that would involve a widespread set of relationships with institutions around the world yet sustain a focus on developing and maintaining deep relationships with only a small set of schools. Thus, the vast majority of partnerships at the Carlson School of Management were initially founded on the basis of facilitating student exchange opportunities between the schools—a common pattern among many of the schools we studied.

This practice was not unusual among the schools we examined; exchange agreements are generally low-risk, enable schools to begin exploring connections in different regions of the world simultaneously with little up-front investment, and provide a foundation for further development. A wide variety of partners for student exchange programs (particularly those based on non-reciprocal exchange agreements) also serve as a hedge against shifting interests among students in different regions of the world. Generally, however, the schools in the case studies balanced a broad scope of partners with a few select partners with which the school engaged in higher intensity partnerships, along with the incremental growth of these partnerships.

5.1.2. Selecting Strategic Partners

In a 2004-05 AACSB survey, partner selection was cited as one of the most important "success" factors for achieving success in program alliances with foreign business schools (see Table 5.4). The other most important success factor had to do with the objectives and terms of the agreement.[5] Both of these factors suggest that high up-front investments in the selection of partners and design of the partnership reap rewards down the line. Among schools in the case studies, commonly cited characteristics of deeper partnership relationships were a high level of trust between the schools, a clearly articulated focus for the agreement, and a commitment to long-term success as opposed to short-term financial results.

In many cases, the sense of mutual trust and reliance is something that evolved over time. Four of the dual-degree programs operated by Fundação Getulio Vargas-São Paulo, Escola de Administração de Empresas de São Paulo (FGV-EAESP), for example, are offered in partnership with other

---

[5]AACSB International, Canadian Federation of Business School Deans, and European Foundation for Management Development, 2004–05 Alliances Survey Results, 2005, internal communication to survey participants.

Table 5.4: Program alliance success factors.

	Factors	Percent of all responses
1	Partner Selection	25.9%
2	Agreement Objectives and Terms	25.9%
3	Management of Alliance	18.4%
4	Interest, Commitment, and Involvement	11.3%
5	Quality	9.9%
6	Resources	6.1%
7	Environmental Factors	2.4%

In an open-ended question, respondents were asked to indicate the most important factors to achieving success in "program alliances" with foreign business schools. Responses were coded into the categories listed in the table.
Source: AACSB International, 2004–05 Alliances Survey Results (AACSB, EFMD, CFBSD).[6]

members of the Partnership in International Management (PIM), a network the school joined in 1975. The PIM network provided a platform on which the member schools could learn more about one another and gradually develop a sense of trust. Similarly, through participation in another network, the Sumaq Alliance, FGV-EAESP, and another member, the Instituto de Empresa (IE) Business School, established a relationship that evolved into the development of a dual PhD program.

A sense of reliance and mutual commitment to an agreed-upon set of objectives is especially critical for new programs that may take several years to become fully established. The agreement between the Hong Kong University of Science and Technology, School of Business and Management and the Northwestern University, Kellogg School of Management to jointly offer an EMBA program, outlined in a simple, half-page memorandum of understanding, relies heavily on the level of trust between the two schools and a shared interest in seeing the program succeed. Therefore, although the program did not reach capacity until eight years after its launch, the schools remained committed to the founding vision and the program's long-term potential. Rolf Cremer, dean at CEIBS, similarly notes that the school's deepest relationships with other schools are those based on a general attitude of mutual support toward shared objectives rather than a "quid pro quo" accounting of who has provided what to whom.

---

[6]Ibid.

Relationships of this type are not possible with every partner school. ESSEC president Pierre Tapie, whose school maintains numerous basic-level partnership agreements with other business schools, notes that not all schools have the shared values, objectives, and complementary capabilities that would support "strategic alliances" at the level of ESSEC's relationships with the University of Mannheim, the Indian Institute of Management-Ahmedabad, and Keio University. Relative to other partners, the relationships with these schools involve a variety of activities and the "highest level" of commitment. Tapie adds that relationships of this level can in fact be self-limiting because of the substantial commitment involved.

Another common characteristic of many partnerships was that the institutions in the relationship shared common contexts or core strengths. The partnership between the Stanford Graduate School of Business and the Indian Institute of Management-Bangalore to offer a project-oriented exchange program, for example, was seen as a good fit for each school given their locations in the technology and entrepreneurship centers of their respective countries. By contrast, other partnerships were begun specifically because one school had access to a resource that another lacked. FGV-EAESP, with its strong corporate connections in Brazil, has noted that an area of future focus for its partnerships will be on those that will facilitate internships with Brazilian firms for foreign students and, in turn, internships for the school's own students with firms abroad. CEIBS' has recognized the ability of its Case Development Center to be a valuable partner for schools interested in collaborating to develop cases specific to China and the Chinese business environment.

The degree of "likeness" between two institutions is difficult to measure because "likeness" can apply to a variety of dimensions. Evidence suggests, however, that measuring likeness in terms of reputation is an important dimension for partner selection. The 2004-05 survey of AACSB, EFMD, and CFBSD member schools asked participants about the importance of various factors in considering potential partners for international student exchange and program alliances. Presumably, a school's status as accredited (in the case of the survey question by AACSB or EFMD) serves as a signal of the school's quality and thus as a contributor to overall reputation. As shown in Figure 5.1, roughly 40 percent of schools said that accreditation was a "very" important or "extremely" important factor in partner selection for student exchange alliances, compared to 50 percent of schools for program alliances.

A school's reputation, however, also commonly incorporates other factors, such as its ranking in one or more league tables. Survey participants were more likely to rate the partner's reputation/rank than the partner's accreditation status as a "very" important or "extremely" important factor.

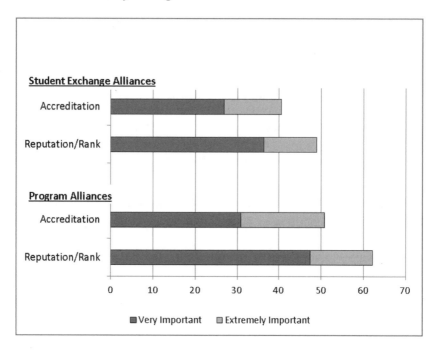

Figure 5.1: Percent of Respondents that Rank Accreditation and Reputation/Rank as Very or Extremely Important Factors in Partner Selection.
Source: 2004–05 Alliances Survey Results (AACSB, EFMD, CFBSD).[7]

Not surprisingly—given that program alliances require greater investment to develop and maintain—schools placed greater importance on both accreditation *and* rank/reputation in selection of program alliance partners versus student exchange partners.

In an effort to determine the extent of associations between schools with similar reputations, the Task Force analyzed data from the AACSB Member Collaboration Survey 2008 for 25 participating schools that were included in the *Financial Times* (*FT*) 2009 Global MBA Rankings and had reported collaborations at the master's level. Specifically, the Task Force looked at the percent of partnerships these schools reported with other schools in the same ranking, as well as with AACSB-accredited schools.

---

[7]Ibid.

The first striking pattern that emerged showed that the more highly ranked schools were more likely to partner with other highly ranked schools, while lower-ranked schools tended to collaborate with lower-ranked schools. In fact, for every 10 points down the rankings a school is positioned, it could expect 4 percent fewer collaborations with other ranked schools. Viewed another way, the number-one ranked school could expect to have 40 percent more ranked partners than the school ending the list of the *FT* top 100.

Another relationship that the Task Force discovered relates to the *FT* rankings and the percent of accredited schools that are collaborative partners. Running a similar analysis to the one above, we discovered a 3-percent increase in accredited partners for every 10 spots higher in the rankings. Eighty-six percent of schools ranked in the top 50 had more than 40 percent accredited partners, while only 50 percent of the lower-ranked group met this criterion. While the correlation is not as strong as that between partners' ranks, a stark difference still exists between the two groups of schools.

The results from this analysis are telling. They suggest that business schools that are ranked highly and accredited tend to partner with similar schools. Doing so allows these schools to ensure that the collaborative partners' curricula, professors, and students meet a standard of quality or, in the case of rankings, reputation. Rankings and other measures of reputation also may create a barrier inhibiting efforts by schools that are not included to establish partnerships with schools that are included.

5.1.3. Capacity-Building Partnerships

Before moving on from a discussion of partner selection, we note that partnerships between two institutions that are arguably unlike in terms of reputation have had substantial impacts on building management education capacity in some regions of the world. Numerous business schools around the world, some of which were mentioned in the Chapter 2 discussion of the global emergence of business schools, were developed through the direct assistance of other, more established business schools in other countries. We reference these types of partnerships here in case schools are inclined to disregard the potential mutual benefits of such relationships.

Specifically, these capacity-building collaborations are those in which faculty, staff, and administrators at one school (or multiple schools) provide guidance, expertise, and resources to establish new schools, develop new programs, or enhance existing educational offerings. Often, the partnerships are between schools in a developed country and a school, government, business, or nongovernmental organization in the developing world.

Many of these partnerships have resulted in the establishment of entirely new business schools. While Chapter 2 noted several examples that took place during the 1950s and '60 s, this activity continues even today. In 1998, the J. Mack Robinson College of Business at Georgia State University (U.S.) partnered with USAID and three institutions from the nation of Georgia to establish the Caucasus School of Business (now a part of Caucasus University). The Indian School of Business, established through the support of Kellogg School of Management, the Wharton School, and the London Business School, welcomed its first students in 2001. The Sarajevo Graduate School of Business was established in 2004 as a joint venture between the University of Delaware (U.S.) and the University of Sarajevo. In 2009, the Judge Business School at the University of Cambridge announced its involvement in the establishment of the Karachi School for Business and Leadership in Pakistan.

Other capacity-building collaborations are aimed at program development and/or teaching enhancement, with a focus on meeting the local management education needs in the less developed school. For example, the business school at the University of Nebraska-Lincoln in the U.S., funded through a USAID grant program, helped develop the MBA program at the University of Tirana in Albania.[8] Faculty of the Robert W. Plaster School of Business Administration at Missouri Southern State University (also funded through a USAID grant) are working with the University of Quisqueya (UniQ) in Haiti to strengthen the teaching of business at UniQ, with a focus on accounting and finance.[9] The Thunderbird School of Global Management in the U.S. and Zayed University in the U.A.E. have teamed up on a Curriculum and Skills Enrichment (CASE) Partnership intended to develop a Master of Science program in international business at Zayed University to prepare women in the U.A.E. to acquire real-world business administration skills and knowledge.

Many initiatives to develop faculty capacity are underway as well. The Tulane University Freeman School of Business, for example, has worked for years with schools in Latin America to provide their existing faculty members with doctoral education, graduating nearly 70 PhD students in the past 16 years.[10] Taking a different approach to faculty development,

---

[8]Lee, Sang M., and Silvana Trimi, "Transforming Albanian Business Education," *International Journal of Entrepreneurship and Small Business*, Vol. 2, No. 1 (2005), pp. 27–33.

[9]Higher Education for Development, "Missouri Southern State University to Provide Accounting and Finance Expertise in Haiti," *HED Articles*, June 2, 2008, electronic document, http://www.hedprogram.org/tabid/225/itemid/164/Missouri-Southern-State-University-To-Provide-Acco.aspx, accessed June 20, 2010.

[10]AACSB International, Spotlight: Business Schools and Doctoral Education, Featured School: Tulane University, 2010, electronic document, http://www.aacsb.edu/resources/doctoral/spotlights/TulaneLatinAmerican.pdf, accessed November 1, 2010.

the Massachusetts Institute of Technology's Sloan School of Management, which is involved in numerous developmental initiatives, has partnered with three Chinese universities on an MIT-China Management Education Project that puts the Chinese faculty alongside MIT faculty and researchers for training in teaching, course development, and research. Like the leaders of other successful developmental partnerships, MIT president Susan Hockfield recognizes that capacity building is not about replication, noting that "[r]ather than produce a 'cookie-cutter' replica of MIT Sloan, ...[the project] encourages Chinese management faculty to develop MIT Sloan's knowledge base responsively to local context and opportunity.[11]

A different collaborative, capacity-building model is the 10,000 Women project sponsored by Goldman Sachs, which involves more than 70 academic and not-for-profit partners, many of which are business schools. The initiative's two goals are: to increase the number of underserved women receiving a business and management education and to improve the quality and capacity of business and management education around the world. In accomplishing the latter, Goldman Sachs supports, "new partnerships between business schools and universities in the United States and Europe and business schools in developing and emerging economies," with a focus on partnerships that aim to "train professors, exchange faculty, develop curricula, and create local case study materials."[12] The Global Business School Network (GBSN) has aided the development of the initiative since 2007 through support in identifying academic partners globally to participate in 10,000 Women. For example, Pan African University in Nigeria[13] established, with the assistance of GBSN, a short term training program for small and medium enterprises, which has served as a model for the 10,000 Women initiative.[14] GBSN also advises the Goldman Sachs Foundation (which funds the initiative) on international best practice in

---

[11]Massachusetts Institute of Technology, Sloan School of Management, Global MIT Sloan website, 2011, electronic document, http://mitsloan.mit.edu/globalmitsloan/initiatives.php, accessed January 5, 2011.

[12]Goldman Sachs, 10,000 Women press release, electronic document, http://www2. goldmansachs.com/china/citizenship/10000women/press-releases/332.pdf, accessed on January 5, 2011.

[13]Pan African University Enterprise Development Services, Women's Enterprise & Leadership Program web page, 2011, electronic document, http://www.pau.edu.ng/eds/index.php?option= com_content&view=article&id=49&Itemid=124, accessed on January 5, 2011.

[14]Global Business School Network, Entrepreneurship web page, 2011, electronic document, http://www.gbsnonline.org/component/option,com_fjrelated/Itemid,76/id,80/layout,blog/view, fjrelated/, accessed January 5, 2011.

enhancing and supporting management education in developing countries and establishing short-term entrepreneurship education programs.[15]

Such capacity-building collaborations are important because, whereas at one time only national systems of higher education existed, business schools today are components of a global system, producing graduates who may one day work together as colleagues or clients on different sides of the globe. As members of this system, business schools have a collective responsibility to help elevate the quality of management education around the world. International partnerships that support synergies between schools, benchmarking, and institutional development have the potential to contribute to the global growth of quality management education.

5.2. Collaborative Degree Program Models

In the AACSB survey of business school collaborations, 80 percent of European schools, compared to only 43 percent of schools in the U.S. and Canada, reported involvement in one or more partnerships whose mission is to deliver collaborative degree programs.[16] Despite the significant difference in sample size between the two regions (30 schools from Europe versus 138 in the U.S. and Canada), the findings parallel those of the U.S.-based Institute for International Education (IIE). The organization found that European campuses currently offer twice as many collaborative degrees (across all disciplines) as their U.S. counterparts, and that U.S. students are less likely than European students to participate in collaborative degree programs. Additionally, the IIE study found that although most survey participants reported plans at their institutions to develop more international joint- and dual-degree programs, U.S. and European schools alike found the potential cost to be a significant challenge.[17]

According to data published by the U.S.-based Council of Graduate Schools (CGS), a growing number of American graduate schools are moving to establish joint-degree or dual-degree programs with international

---

[15]Global Business School Network, Goldman Sachs' 10,000 Women Initiative web page, 2011, electronic document, http://www.gbsnonline.org/programs/current/goldman-sachs-10000-women-initiative.html, accessed January 5, 2011.

[16]AACSB International, AACSB Member Collaboration Survey 2008, Internal survey data, 2008.

[17]Institute of International Education and Freie Universität Berlin, Joint and Double Degree Programs in the Transatlantic Context: A Survey Report, 2009, electronic document, http://www.iienetwork.org/file_depot/0-10000000/0-10000/1710/folder/80205/TDP+Report_2009_Final21.pdf, accessed June 30, 2010.

universities. From August 2007 to August 2008, the percentage of all graduate schools (not discipline-specific) that reported at least one such degree or certificate program rose from 29 percent to 38 percent, while 31 percent reported plans to start a program in the following two years. Among all fields offered, business was the field in which joint- and dual-degree programs were most common, with 39 percent of CGS member schools reporting collaborative programs at the master's level in business (followed by engineering at 26 percent). At the same time, no graduate schools reported collaborative business degree programs at the doctoral level; programs at that level were most likely to be found in the physical sciences and engineering (at 19 percent and 11 percent of member schools, respectively).[18]

Collaborative degree programs take many different forms, and involve varying levels of collaboration intensity. Within this extensive and very diverse space, however, there are some general categories into which collaborative degree programs fall. In this sub-section we aim to provide a brief overview of the differences between these categories, as well as their common opportunities and challenges.

Joint-degree programs are operated and administered through a collaborative agreement between two or more partner institutions and result in the awarding of a single degree. In some cases, the diploma received by the student carries the names and seals of both (or all) institutions, while in others the degree is awarded by one institution but with the participation of the other institution(s) noted. In other cases, the student receives a degree from one institution and a certificate from the other(s).

Dual-degree programs (also known as double-degree programs) are also formed through a collaborative agreement between two or more institutions, yet the courses taken by the student count toward fulfillment of the requirements for two (or more) distinct degrees. Often, some (or all) of the credits taken at one institution also count toward the requirements for a degree from the other institution, and vice versa, meaning that such programs may only be slightly longer in length than a traditional, single-degree program.

In business fields, joint- and dual-degree programs are most common at the master's level, with a smaller number at the undergraduate level and even fewer at the doctoral level. Both are resource-intensive endeavors for the partner institutions and may be costly and time-consuming. Therefore,

---

[18]Council of Graduate Schools, Findings from the 2008 CGS International Graduate Admissions Survey: Phase II: Final Applications and Initial Offers of Admission, CGS Research Report, August 2008, electronic document, http://www.cgsnet.org/portals/0/pdf/ R_IntlAdm08_II.pdf, accessed August 27, 2010, pp. 9–11.

schools that engage in such endeavors must be committed to the initiative and have well-defined objectives. Numerous factors may lead schools to choose one form over the other.

First, the regulatory systems in some countries do not permit joint degrees, and business schools that operate as a unit of a larger university may find institutional policies and processes unaccommodating to jointly administered degrees. Dual-degree programs often face fewer legal and institution constraints than do joint degrees, as each institution awards its own degree.

Different educational structures within the countries where the partners are located also may mean that one partner requires a certain type or number of courses not considered necessary by the other. An example of this is if only one of the two partner institutions requires an undergraduate curriculum to include a substantial liberal arts component.

Regulatory and structural issues aside, the development and administration of collaborative degree programs require substantial but varying levels of coordination between partners. Partners that offer joint-degree programs must collaborate to develop a complete curriculum, while partners that deliver dual-degree programs must agree on only the portion of the curriculum that will count toward fulfillment of both schools' degree requirements (though often this is substantial). It is typical for a student in either type of collaborative degree program to take courses at both schools, meaning that challenges may arise if the two schools have different approaches to course grading or different academic calendars. In both joint- and dual-degree programs, the assessment of program learning goals must be coordinated across courses delivered in (often) two or more locations, often by faculty or administrators in multiple locations. Furthermore, the partner schools must determine how tuition will be assessed and how tuition revenue will be allocated between partners.

Due to the numerous factors that require coordination, these programs often involve significant transactional costs. Faculty and staff who represent each partner involved in administering the program often report spending a large amount of time in coordination with each other. If the locations of the schools are separated by multiple time zones, an extension of those activities outside of traditional working hours, or delays, may occur. Staffing the program also involves many dimensions of coordination. Partner schools must ensure that faculty in both locations have the necessary qualifications for the courses they deliver. In some cases, each school provides its own faculty for the courses it is responsible for administering. In other cases, particularly if one institution has a different set of expectations for faculty qualifications than the other, one institution may send its own faculty on a temporary basis to administer courses at the other location, or its faculty may oversee delivery of the course by the other school's resident faculty.

The actual delivery models for dual- and joint-degree programs also vary substantially. In AACSB's recent collaboration survey, of the collaborative agreements that involve jointly administered degrees, the vast majority (90 percent) involved only two partner schools. Some, on the other hand, involve three or four partners, or several institutions as members of a consortium. Students may be expected to spend equal time at each institution, or may complete only a small part of the program at the "partner" institution.

At the undergraduate level, for example, the University of South Carolina's Moore School of Business and the Chinese University of Hong Kong's Faculty of Business Administration collaborate to offer an International Business and Chinese Enterprise degree program, which involves alternating years of study at the two institutions and completing internships in each country. Each institution follows its own policies and procedures concerning student admissions, matriculation, and academic progress, and students ultimately receive a degree from the institution to which they were originally admitted. Undergraduate students in the TransAtlantic Business School Alliance (TABSA) program, on the other hand, spend their first two years at their home institution and the following two years at one of the six other schools in the alliance, ultimately earning a degree from each of the two institutions.

At the graduate level, models are also varied. The OneMBA program, for example, is a joint executive MBA delivered by a partnership of five schools.[19] All five partners collaborate to market and brand the program, in which students take the majority of a pre-defined, common set of courses at their home institution but come together with other program participants for one-week residencies in each of the other locations. More common are joint- or dual-degree programs between two partner institutions, such as the series of joint-executive MBA programs offered by the University of Minnesota's Carlson School of Management with schools in China, Poland, and Vienna. By structuring the programs to run simultaneously and follow similar curricula, however, the Carlson School of Management is able to bring students from each program together for an "integrated residency" period.

Collaborative degrees offer numerous opportunities for schools to create synergies between their own strengths and those of their partners. A school

---

[19]Faculty of Business Administration at The Chinese University of Hong Kong, Rotterdam School of Management at Erasmus University in the Netherlands, Tecnológico de Monterrey Graduate School of Business Administration and Leadership in Mexico, The University of North Carolina at Chapel Hill's Kenan-Flagler Business School in the United States, and Escola de Administração de Empresas de São Paulo da Fundação Getulio Vargas in Brazil.

with a particular strength in one discipline (for example, marketing) may partner with a school with a strong focus on entrepreneurship, the combination of which enhances the strength of the education beyond what one school could deliver on its own. In an international setting, such programs also provide opportunities for students to learn more about the business environment in another country as well as to actually be immersed in life in that country during the time spent there. In this way, collaborative degree programs are taking "student exchange" to the next level. By predetermining or regulating the courses in students of which joint/dual-degree programs may enroll (according to degree requirements), schools ensure that the courses taken abroad are directly relevant to the degree pursued.

Other collaborative program delivery models may take the form of twinning programs. Often based on articulation agreements between schools, twinning programs are based on one institution's agreement to accept students who are completing a substantial number of course credits (in many cases, about half) at another institution into its own degree program as mid-program transfer students. Other articulation agreements may provide students who are completing a certain set of credits at the first institution with advanced standing at the second institution, or they may eliminate the need for certain prerequisite courses that would otherwise be required for entry or transfer into a program. In all cases, the student ultimately earns a single degree from the institution at which he/she completes the program.

Twinning and articulation agreements are more common among undergraduate-level than graduate-level programs and are frequently referred to by the number of years spent at each partner school (e.g., 2 + 2, 1 + 2, 1 + 1, etc., programs). Compared to joint- and dual-degree programs, twinning programs often require less of an ongoing commitment by the degree-granting institution to collaborate with, or provide oversight of, the partner institution. The degree-awarding institution may, however, provide oversight of or assistance with the design and delivery of the portion of credits taken at the initial admitting institution. Tuition is typically paid separately to each institution according to the number of courses taken.

In some cases, students who are completing the first part of the degree program at one school are given a conditional guarantee of admission to the degree-granting partner institution. Conditions may be as simple as satisfactory completion of the initial courses, or also may include a certain score on an entrance exam or demonstrated proficiency in the language of instruction. Some agreements, on the other hand, require students to apply for a place at the second institution, with no guarantee of selection.

When twinning and articulation agreements involve schools in different countries, students are generally responsible for securing their own visas to travel to the second country for degree completion. This stipulation poses a problem if, at the time the student prepares to move, his or her visa application is rejected. As a safeguard, some institutions in the position of offering the first part of the degree program enter into similar agreements with universities in more than one country. If a student's visa application to one country is rejected, the student may instead apply for a visa to complete his/her education at another partner institution in a different country.

In the previous section, we discussed evidence that a school's reputation was a factor in partner selection, particularly for program alliances. Joint- and dual-degree programs and twinning programs each are mechanisms through which management education by a reputable institution is made more accessible in underserved regions of the world. At the same time, the complexities of administering such programs, the segregation of operations across multiple locations, and the (often) accompanying pressures for such endeavors to generate a profit call for particular oversight by program administrators and their accreditors to ensure that the program quality is consistent with expectations.

Though the standards and processes of accrediting bodies vary, most accreditation schemes expect the institution awarding the degree to ensure that collaborative degree programs are of an equivalent quality to those delivered at the home campus (in other words, that the programs satisfy the same set of standards to which degree programs delivered entirely "at home" are subject). To use AACSB accreditation standards as an example, these standards include policies for student admission and retention, access to student services, appropriate financial strategies, a sufficient number of courses delivered by "participating" faculty, a commitment to academically and professionally qualified faculty, and a rigorous assessment process for measuring attainment of learning objectives.

5.3.   Establishing a Presence Abroad

A quest for a "global footprint" at some business schools goes beyond simply having connections with schools in other parts of the world to include the establishment of an actual physical presence in other countries. Approaches to achieving this goal, however, vary. Some schools have opted to "franchise" a presence in another market through arrangements with local institutions. Others seek to maintain a presence themselves, by building or renting physical space designed in some cases to support a wide range of campus activities and in other cases to support a single, specific function.

5.3.1.   Franchise Degrees and Validations

Our discussion of franchise and validated degree programs is intentionally separated from the discussion of collaborative degree models described above. Although these program arrangements are similar collaborative degree programs in that their models involve multiple institutions, franchise and validation programs are utilized more often as a means of gaining a presence in a different country/region rather than as a way to benefit from the education each institution has the capacity to deliver.

Franchise degree programs and validated degree programs are delivered by one institution on behalf of another. Typically, the parent (or franchisor/ validator) institution is located in one country, while the program provider is located in another. This provider may be another degree-granting institution, but in some cases it may be an independent educational provider that does not have authority to grant its own degrees. A franchise degree program is one that is also offered by the parent institution on its home campus, while a validated degree program is unique to the location of the independent provider. In both cases, the degree carries the name of the parent institution.

In a recent study by Kingston University, franchise agreements were reported to be the most common type of international partnership among the set of U.K. universities studied.[20] Universities in Australia, Canada, and the U.S. also contribute substantially to the provision of franchise degree programs in existence today. On the delivery end, notable concentrations of franchise degree programs exist in regions such as Southeast Asia (particularly Hong Kong, Malaysia, and Singapore) and the Middle East Gulf States. Often, the provider institutions offer an array of degrees from multiple institutions.

Actual agreements between the parent institution and the provider vary, but typically the provider assumes responsibility for advertising the program to local students, recruiting them into the program, hiring faculty to deliver the courses, providing a facility in which the courses are delivered, and handling other logistical and student services. The parent institution normally provides a brand that is valued or recognized in the provider's location, a curriculum for the program, and oversight of the program's quality in accordance with its own national accreditation standards and any additional accreditations it may hold. As in corporate franchise agreements,

---

[20]Middlehurst, Robin, Steve Woodfield, John Fielden, and Heather Forland, *Universities and international higher education partnerships: making a difference*, project report, Million + , London, 2009, electronic document, http://www.millionplus.ac.uk/file_download/7/ INT_PARTNERSHIPS_summaryReportfinal_003.pdf, accessed August 30, 2010.

the provider institution (franchisee) supplies the parent institution (franchisor) with an agreed-upon percentage of program revenue.

Franchise degree programs are a means of quickly accommodating an increasing demand for higher education in locations where the local educational infrastructure is underdeveloped. In many cases, franchise programs are available to students at a much lower cost than at the parent institution's home campus. Thus, these agreements enable the parent institution to access a student population that might not otherwise be able to travel to another country or afford the tuition for the program delivered at the home institution.

More so than dual- or joint-degree programs, however, franchise degree programs tend to raise concerns regarding educational quality and to provoke charges of financial opportunism among the institutions involved. Providers that are obligated by contract to transfer a portion of program revenue to the parent institution have a financial incentive to cut costs in order to maximize profit—a move that may result in cutting corners and thus lower quality. Therefore, the responsibility of the parent institution to ensure the quality of the education delivered and the parent institution's right to annul the contract with the provider if specified standards are not met are both critical.

5.3.2. Branch Campuses/Facilities Abroad

Talk of a global footprint most often conjures images of facilities in one country that are developed, connected to, and maintained by an institution based in another. Among the schools included in the set of case studies, five have established some type of facility outside the school's original national borders. These facilities, however, vary by scope, size, and range of functions, as well as in their relationship to the main campus. Those designed to support the widest range of functions are the campuses established by The Fuqua School of Business and ESSEC Business School.

The Fuqua School of Business's new "global campus" consists of campuses in six different locations: China, India, Russia, the U.A.E., the U.K., and the U.S. Each campus is intended to provide classroom facilities to be used for the school's degree programs and to also serve as a home base for a set of faculty. Together, the campuses are intended to operate as a network rather than as separate entities; while each location host a unique set of staff, the staff at each location maintain a strong connection to a core set of staff at the main campus in the U.S. (Durham, NC). Space for each campus was acquired through different approaches; in some regions the school is constructing new facilities (e.g., China), while in others (e.g., Russia) the school has acquired shared space in facilities owned by a partner institution.

ESSEC's Singapore campus, located in the Singapore National Library building, is similarly designed to support a range of activities. The campus hosts students who are enrolled in the "Asian" track of various degree programs or who are on campus for two-week residencies as part of the ESSEC-Mannheim EMBA program. The campus also provides facilities for custom executive education courses and for seminars and conferences on special topics. A team of "core" faculty and staff living in Singapore provide a permanent presence at the campus, which also serves as a base for faculty members who travel to the region for shorter-term teaching assignments or research projects.

The cross-border facilities of the Booth School of Business, HKUST School of Business and Management, and CEIBS (in London and Singapore, mainland China, and Ghana, respectively) are intended primarily to support delivery of executive MBA and non-degree executive education programs. Faculty members rotate between the schools' main campus and cross-border facilities for short periods aligned with course schedules. The Booth School of Business and CEIBS have both noted the possibility of expanding the functions of their facilities to support other activities at a future date.

In several of the above cases, the locations of the cross-border facilities were chosen because of their roles as business centers in their respective regions and for their accessibility by students and faculty traveling from other regions of the world. The Booth School of Business realized the impact of a location in a major regional business center when comparing the ease with which it attracted guest speakers and media attention in Singapore and Barcelona and subsequently decided to relocate its Barcelona campus to London. Accessibility was also particularly important in all cases, as this would ease the burden of travel for those faculty members spending time at multiple campuses. Singapore's connectivity (and proximity, relative to Paris) to other parts of Asia made the city appealing to ESSEC, as the campus could serve as a launching point for other initiatives within the region.

As noted in Chapter 2, the establishment of branch campuses abroad is a strategy that a growing but still relatively small number of schools have undertaken. This fact is likely due to the substantial resource requirements and risk inherent in such an approach. In addition to the substantial cost involved, schools that operate branch campuses also often find themselves in the position of being an employer abroad, with a resulting need to navigate the hiring laws and salary markets of multiple countries. Staffing issues can be challenging; many schools struggle to hire the same caliber of faculty members that they command at home, or to find faculty willing to relocate for short-term assignments. Still, the OBHE reports that while a few notable closures of branch campuses have occurred, such as George Mason University's withdrawal from the United Arab Emirates, over time, it has only found 11 instances in which branch campuses were subsequently closed.[21]

More common than full-scale campuses abroad are more modest facilities designed to support a single function. Often, such facilities operate out of rented space in office buildings or may even be located on the campus of an accommodating university. In other cases, the school has purchased the facility outright. Facilities intended to provide classroom space used during student trips abroad or for local delivery of executive education courses often have a multipurpose nature that enables variable use for orientations, on-site courses, meetings between student groups, presentations, and other functions as needs arise. Schools that maintain single-function facilities enjoy several benefits in that the facilities, in most cases, are easy to shut-down if services are no longer needed, or they can be expanded over time as the school's need for a presence in the region expands.

In some cases, these facilities function primarily as administrative offices for staff that support student recruitment, alumni relations, and other auxiliary functions in other countries. For example, the Schulich School of Business at York University has recently opened satellite facilities in Beijing, China; Mumbai, India; and Seoul, South Korea. These centers each serve four main functions: 1) student recruitment, 2) career planning and placement assistance for students and alumni, 3) executive and leadership development courses for local executives, and 4) support for international alumni chapters.[22]

In other cases, these facilities may be opened primarily to support research activities. For example, under its current dean, Nitin Nohria, Harvard Business School is pursuing a strategy designed to create "a small physical footprint" but a "very large intellectual footprint," through the establishment of research centers abroad.[23] Similarly, Cambridge Judge

---

[21]Jaschik, Scott, "International Campuses on the Rise," *Inside Higher Ed*, September 9, 2009, electronic document, http://www.insidehighered.com/news/2009/09/03/branch, accessed July 22, 2010.

[22]Schulich School of Business, Creating Canada's Global Business School, 2010, electronic document, http://www.schulich.yorku.ca/ssb-extra/ssb.nsf/docs/Transnational, accessed August 30, 2010.

[23]Mavin, Duncan, "Harvard Business School Won't Open Asia Campuses," *The Wall Street Journal*, August 2, 2010, electronic document, http://online.wsj.com/article/SB100014240 52748704905004575404960728487290.html?KEYWORDS=management+education, accessed August 2, 2010.

Business School recently launched a Centre for India & Global Business in New Delhi, which is a research center that will focus on Indian firms and broader issues such as the role of emerging markets and issues related to the "bottom of the pyramid."[24] The Stanford University Graduate School of Business extends its "intellectual footprint" to China by using space in the university's Shorenstein Asia-Pacific Research Center for teaching and research purposes, as well as through collaboration with Fudan University to support the Cisco Supply Chain Leadership Institute in China.

5.4. Faculty Strategies

A school's most important asset that supports its globalization efforts is its human capital—namely its faculty members, staff, and administrators. Aligning its human resources with the school's globalization goals and objectives involves attention to the qualifications sought among faculty and staff recruits, investments in their ongoing development, and attention to their effective deployment. Table 5.5 provides a framework of non-mutually exclusive dimensions along which business schools might help develop their faculty in support of the school's globalization strategy.

First, faculty recruitment strategies that support globalization objectives generally involve pursuit of one or more of three types of individuals: faculty members who value globalization of management education and see contributions to it as a priority; faculty members with international or intercultural knowledge, perspectives, and/or past experiences; and faculty

Table 5.5: Framework: Three Dimensions of Faculty Strategies for Globalization.

Recruit	Develop	Manage
Interests/Values	Pedagogical Training	Faculty Interactions
Knowledge/Perspectives	Immersion/Experience	Incentives
Connections	Research Support	Deployment

---

[24]University of Cambridge, "Cambridge Launches Centre for India & Global Business," press release, March 10, 2009, electronic document, http://www.admin.cam.ac.uk/news/dp/2009030903, accessed March 11, 2009.

members with connections to institutions, organizations, and communities abroad.

Second, while many schools focus on how to globalize the learning experiences of students, they often neglect to place the same priority on ensuring similar ongoing development of faculty members who design courses, conduct research, and instruct students. Business schools can actively support this kind of development among their faculty in several ways, including training on pedagogical methods, support for international immersion or other experiences, and support for internationally focused research.

Third, faculty management involves assuring that the individual motivations and capabilities of the faculty members are complemented by opportunities for faculty interaction that facilitate the sharing of ideas, incentives that encourage faculty to engage in internationally focused research, and effective management of (often) limited faculty resources across programs and locations.

5.4.1. Faculty Qualifications

The opening or addition of faculty positions is a good opportunity for a school to incrementally align its human capital with the school's globalization goals and objectives. While many factors are important in the selection and hiring of a new faculty member, for purposes of globalization schools generally look at the applicant's characteristics along one or more of three dimensions: global values; global knowledge or perspectives; and global connections.

International Values. The first characteristic that a school might seek in a faculty member is that of international values. Faculty members who are interested in how business is conducted across borders or in different world regions are critical to a school's efforts to globalize curricula or pursue other international strategies. Without these faculty, grand visions for curricular change, cross-border partnerships, or new areas of focus for research are likely to remain unfulfilled. At a minimum, therefore, business schools should seek to clearly articulate their values and plans related to globalization and to look for alignment among the interests and values of potential new faculty hires.

Knowledge/Perspectives. A growing number of schools seek to recruit faculty members with international or intercultural knowledge, perspectives, and/or past experiences. One approach is to recruit faculty who have lived, worked, or have been educated in other countries as a means of "importing" a diverse set of perspectives and experiences among faculty members. For example, a recent analysis by AACSB of business schools included in the *Financial Times* Global MBA Rankings between 2002 and 2008 revealed that in that timeframe, 71 percent of the schools studied increased the proportion of faculty classified as "international," and 38 percent increased that proportion by at least 10 percentage points.[25]

This trend is supported by data collected through AACSB's annual survey of its member schools, though limitations to the data make comparisons across regions difficult. U.S. schools, for example, report the number of faculty members who are in the country on temporary visas and thus do not identify individuals with other countries of origin who have become permanent residents or naturalized citizens, resulting in figures that understate the presence of "international" faculty. Using this measure, in 2008 5.7 percent of full-time faculty members at U.S.-based AACSB member schools were reportedly on temporary visas—a substantial increase from only 2.9 percent in 2001. Slightly more than 50 percent of U.S. survey respondents in 2008 reported having at least one full-time faculty member from outside the U.S., up from 42.7 percent in 2001. Non-U.S. schools, on the other hand, identify faculty according to country of origin. Member schools outside the U.S. reported in 2008 a total of 41.1 percent of full-time faculty members with a country of origin other than the school's location, with 92 percent of schools reporting at least one faculty member with an origin outside the host country.

Business schools today have many mechanisms for recruiting faculty internationally, particularly by advertising positions through various online job boards that are accessible globally. Examples include the *BizSchoolJobs* site hosted by AACSB, sites hosted by higher education publications such as the Chronicle of Higher Education, and those hosted by international disciplinary associations, such as the Academy of Management. Growing involvement by individuals and schools in international associations also facilitates networking that may lead to the identification of potential candidates located in other countries.

A recent study of U.S. faculty members by Walker Finkelstein and Rong Chen found a positive correlation between the likelihood that a faculty member would incorporate international issues into his/her teaching and the amount of time the faculty member had spent abroad after earning an undergraduate degree. In fact, faculty members who spent one or two years

---

[25]AACSB International, Business School Faculty Trends 2008, Report from AACSB International Knowledge Services, 2008, p. 21.

abroad as adults were twice as likely to work international issues into their teaching than faculty members with little experience abroad.[26]

Recruitment of international faculty members is a common activity among schools in our set of case studies, and it has generally been determined to have positive outcomes for the schools. According to ESSEC president Pierre Tapie, for example, efforts to increase the international diversity of ESSEC's faculty have accelerated the intercultural dimensions of the school's research and have created new opportunities for connections to other universities (and their faculty) that otherwise likely would not have existed. Another, likely even more important, dimension of global knowledge and perspectives is that gained through research on international business practices, an area we discuss in the next subsection on faculty development.

Connections. The third characteristic—that of international connections—is a rationale that repeatedly emerges from business schools speaking of their cross-border recruitment efforts. A series of interviews between AACSB staff and business school deans who represent more than thirty countries revealed that a common motivation for recruiting faculty internationally was the hope that the school might be able to build upon the relationship between the faculty member and his/her former institution(s). Thus, for schools that wish to become more "networked" internationally, faculty recruitment is a means of forming bridges that otherwise might be more difficult to build.

At the same time, significant barriers to international recruitment exist. The costs to recruit internationally are prohibitive for some schools. At times, this limitation results from competition between well-resourced schools for certain individuals, though in theory, international competition along this dimension is no different from competition among schools in the same country. In some countries (particularly among public institutions), salaries are regulated by a central ministry of education or a similar governing body, which gives schools in these contexts little flexibility to compete with salaries offered in more market-based environments. Schools in large cities with nearby access to international airports may have an easier time recruiting internationally than schools in more rural locations.

---

[26]Finkelstein, M.J., E. Walker, and Rong Chen, "The internationalization of the American faculty: Where are we? What drives or deters us?" unpublished manuscript, College of Education and Human Services, Seton Hall University, South Orange, NJ, 2009. See also Fischer, Karin, "U.S. Academics Lag in Internationalization, New Paper Says," *The Chronicle of Higher Education*, February 2, 2009, electronic document, http://chronicle.com/daily/2009/02/10660n.htm, accessed June 30, 2010.

Language barriers and the country's socio-political or geographical environment may also limit success.

Schools that seek to globalize through the recruitment of international faculty also must answer a broader set of questions. These questions concern a school's desired mix of knowledge, skills, and perspectives among its faculty members as well as a close examination of the best way to achieve this mix. Is the school's intent solely to seek individuals with foreign citizenship, or is it to also factor in foreign education credentials or work experience? While country of origin or citizenship may serve as a simple indicator of the international composition of a school's faculty (and thus be an attractive measure for inclusion in school rankings), these dimensions potentially ignore the different contributions of local citizens with foreign experiences, or they overstate the different perspectives of someone who has foreign citizenship but has spent much of his/her life in the local context.

5.4.2. *Ongoing Faculty Development*

A common theme that emerges among the case-study schools is that globalization of faculty is measured not simply in terms of the diversity of faculty members' country of origin, but rather, it is measured in the competence and self-confidence with which faculty continually engage the world beyond their home school's borders. In other words, if business schools emphasize and encourage opportunities for their faculty members to expand their own international and cross-cultural awareness, the schools are better equipped to succeed in producing students with these same aptitudes. Ongoing faculty development related to globalization generally involves three areas of focus: pedagogical training; immersion/experiential learning; and research.

Pedagogical Training. The first way that schools can contribute to faculty development in support of a globalization strategy is through pedagogical training. Often, failed efforts to infuse international content across the curriculum are attributed to professors' lack of comfort with incorporating international perspectives or their lack of self-confidence in their ability to teach international content effectively. With this in mind, Elon University's Martha and Spencer Love School of Business launched a major effort to infuse international content into its curricula, taking initiative to invest in faculty development. Faculty members were asked to attend a series of seminars designed to cover the importance of incorporating international perspectives into the curriculum, to provide guidance on incorporating these perspectives into the curriculum and adjusting the course syllabi accordingly, and to expose faculty members to resources that were available.

A curriculum committee was appointed to monitor changes to the content of individual courses and to provide guidance where needed.[27]

Pedagogical training might also focus on how to teach students who are accustomed to different learning environments—a challenge that is increasingly relevant as both student and faculty mobility lead to classroom settings with a blend of learning and teaching styles. Senior associate dean of the HKUST Business School, Steve DeKrey, notes, for example, that the school's professors adapt their teaching methods across the multiple locations in which programs are delivered in order to align with the dominant culture within the classroom.[28] With an educational delivery model that is entirely online, U21Global requires that prospective faculty members participate in (and pass) a special training program that provides instruction on how to communicate with students in an online teaching environment.

Faculty members who are interested in enhancing their ability to incorporate aspects of international business into the curriculum also have some options for formal training programs. The CIBER at the University of South Carolina Moore School of Business, for example, offers a six-day workshop, Faculty Development in International Business, through which the Moore faculty share their expertise with faculty members at other schools that are preparing to teach international business or that are seeking to enhance their capabilities. The workshop includes tracks focused on the international dimensions of various functional areas.

Immersion/Experience. A second type of development focuses on opportunities to gain contextual knowledge through immersion and/or interactions in another setting. While some schools may claim to account for this experience through international recruitment efforts (i.e., "importing" faculty, as mentioned earlier), The Fuqua School of Business at Duke University, for example, specifically rejects the notion that bringing faculty members with different ethnic, national, and cultural backgrounds together on one campus is, by itself, a sufficient means of creating a "global" cadre of faculty members. Rather, the school's approach reflects a philosophy that the continued engagement of faculty members with other parts of the world is a necessary supplement to their unique individual backgrounds. Faculty are expected to have a "heavy foot" in one of the school's several campus locations and to establish a "light foot" in other locations through

---

[27]Cort, Kathryn T., Jayoti Das, and Wonhi J. Synn, "Cross-Functional Globalization Modules: A Learning Experience," *Journal of Teaching in International Business*, Vol. 15, No. 3 (2004), pp. 77–97.

[28]DeKrey, Steve, personal interview, 2009; see case study in Appendix.

opportunities for mobility to other campuses and through collaboration with faculty based elsewhere.

ESSEC similarly takes advantage of its two campuses to complement international faculty recruitment efforts with a priority on faculty members' international mobility. "Learning expeditions" financed by the business school enable approximately 25 faculty and staff members from the Paris campus to travel to Asia each year. The trips provide the individuals with opportunities to incorporate international perspectives into their research and course development, and they also provide members with an enhanced understanding of the complementary roles played by the school's Singapore and Paris campuses.

Opportunities for international teaching and learning experiences are not, however, limited to only faculty members of schools with multiple campuses. At the University of Minnesota's Carlson School of Management, the International Programs Office, which oversees international experiences for students, also seeks to provide a variety of means for faculty and staff members to expand their international perspectives and competencies. These opportunities include teaching opportunities in the school's global enrichment programs or the Global Executive MBA programs, faculty exchanges, and research grants for projects of an international scope. Notably, at both ESSEC and the Carlson School, staff members as well as faculty members are encouraged to broaden their perspectives internationally—an approach that emphasizes the role of staff members contributing to the schools' overall globalization efforts.

Similarly, a belief in the importance of international experiences for faculty led the president of Rollins College, in the U.S., to recently pledge that every faculty and staff member with teaching duties will go abroad every three years. The college provides $3,000 grants to support faculty members for research trips abroad or to lead student groups to other countries.[29]

The use of international visiting faculty is particularly common among executive education programs, which are more likely to be offered in a modular format that does not require faculty members to relocate on a permanent or semi-permanent basis. This kind of faculty mobility also helps facilitate or strengthen connections between schools and helps faculty gain experiences that will help them incorporate more international perspectives into their teaching and research. In its early years, for example, CEIBS relied

---

[29]Fischer, Karin, "Professors Get Their Own Study-Abroad Programs," *The Chronicle of Higher Education*, October 31, 2008, electronic document, http://chronicle.com/article/Professors-Get-Their-Own-St/21290/, accessed August 30, 2010.

heavily on visiting faculty with permanent appointments at reputable business schools abroad to serve their global education needs. The approach, according to Cremer, helped the new business school establish its own reputation while it gradually built its own set of permanent faculty, and it helped the school establish connections with the institutions in which those faculty members were based.

Collaborative agreements with schools in other countries also provide opportunities for faculty development. In the AACSB's recent survey of member business schools' collaborations, 33.8 percent of collaborations identified included opportunities for faculty exchange. Interestingly, 97 percent of the 1,059 collaborations that were reported to involve faculty exchange were also identified as having other dimensions (e.g., student exchange, joint programs, etc.), making faculty exchange the least likely type of collaboration to exist alone. The most common additional activities included in the collaborative agreements were student exchange (in 57 percent of agreements involving faculty exchange), joint research (in 14 percent of the cases), and joint programs (in 9 percent of the cases). Of course, we note that an agreement to support faculty exchange between two institutions does not always mean that it is acted upon, and we should be cautious in drawing assumptions about the level of cross-border mobility among faculty members that is actually taking place. Some faculty members may also coordinate such opportunities independently, meaning that any resulting mobility would not be captured by our survey.

All of these approaches provide opportunities for the sharing of ideas, for exposure to new cultures and ways of doing business, and for training or competency interchange. At the same time, efforts to encourage or support faculty mobility present several management challenges for schools.

As noted by Associate Dean Roberts at Stanford GSB, not all faculty members are willing or able to travel abroad for long periods of time due to family or other personal obligations. Thus, some schools have sought to provide opportunities for faculty members from partner institutions to come for shorter-term modules. FGV-EAESP, for example, frequently hosts visiting professors from partner institutions to teach elective courses during the school's short winter term each July. The school has made increased opportunities for faculty exchange with its partner institutions one of its priorities for future development.

Other avenues may include engagement in international networks or consortia. Disciplinary and professional associations, such as the Academy of Management, Association of Information Technology Professionals, Society for Human Resource Management, Strategic Management Society, and countless others have increasingly international networks of faculty members and practitioners, as well as forums for the exchange of ideas and best practices. Management education associations also provide numerous opportunities for the exchange of ideas between individuals affiliated with their member schools, such as through participation in professional development activities, engagement with one or more special interest groups, and connection through online networking platforms.

Research. A third form of faculty development is that which takes place through research opportunities—which may or may not involve actual travel to another country or region. Much evidence suggests that, globally, substantial needs exist for additional research focused on business in an international context. As Ghemawat has noted, only a very small percentage (about 6.2 percent) of articles published in the top 20 management journals between 2002 and 2006 appear to have specifically cross-border content. The portion drops to less than 4 percent if the *Journal of International Business Studies*, home to more than 40 percent of those articles, is excluded.[30]

In the recent survey of AACSB member schools' collaborations, joint research was identified as a purpose for only 6 percent of collaborations reported by AACSB member schools. This figure may under-represent the actual amount of collaborative research that takes place, as many faculty members will independently identify research partners without a formal agreement between their respective schools. Still, the question arises as to whether business schools have incentives or processes to encourage or enable faculty to develop cross-border collaborative relationships for research purposes.

The recently published SCImago Rankings of research institutions includes "international collaboration" as one of five measures that determine the institution's rank. An institution's position is determined based on the ratio of outputs in the Elsevier SCOPUS database that have authors affiliated with more than one country address. While not specific to either higher education institutions (the ranking also includes government, health, corporate, and other institutions) or to the business discipline, the approach hints at a measure that may emerge among individuals who seek to assess business schools' research output in new ways.[31]

---

[30]Ghemawat, Pankaj, "Bridging the Globalization Gap at Top Business Schools: Curricular Challenges and a Response," Chapter 2.3 in Canals, Jordi (ed.), *The Future of Leadership Development*. Houndmills, Hampshire: Palgrave Macmillan, 2011. Ghemawat's conclusion is based on Pisani, N., "International Management Research: Investigating its Recent Diffusion in Top Management Journals," *Journal of Management*, Vol. 35, No. 2 (2009), pp. 199–218. For a similar study covering the period between 1996 and 2000, see Werner, S., "Recent developments in international management research: A review of 20 top management journals," *Journal of Management*, Vol. 28, No. 3 (2002), pp. 277–305.

[31]SCImago Research Group, SCImago Institutions Rankings (SIR): 2009 World Report, Report Number 2009-003, 2009, electronic document, http://www.scimagoir.com/pdf/sir_2009_world_report.pdf, accessed June 20, 2010.

Collaborative efforts are especially fruitful for research efforts focused on comparisons across world regions or on global issues. The 10 member schools in the Social Enterprise Knowledge Network, for example, which are located in the U.S., Spain, and eight Latin American countries, collectively select a research topic and design a common set of questions to guide research in their respective locations. This research results in the development of analytical cases set in each country that in turn serve as a foundation for cross-country comparative analyses.[32] Similarly, the Global Entrepreneurship Monitor brings together more than 120 scholars and researchers to focus on entrepreneurial activity in 52 countries, producing both national reports and global comparisons.

In other cases, research centers are developed to support the activities of a group of faculty members at one school. At the University of South Carolina Moore School, research on global topics is funded by the school's Center for International Business Education and Research—one of 33 such centers at U.S. business schools funded through the national government. At The University of Chicago, business partners fund an Initiative on Global Markets, which supports research by the university's Booth School of Business faculty and visiting fellows and sponsors numerous forums and conferences. On the other hand, some business schools, such as INSEAD and Harvard Business School, have gone so far as to establish facilities abroad that are solely or primarily designed to support research efforts.

Finally, while in many of the above examples the schools strive to provide opportunities for faculty members to broaden their perspectives globally, we note that at times, schools are challenged to help their faculty members apply global perspectives more locally. A majority of faculty members at CEIBS, for example, are ethnically Chinese, but most of them previously held positions at foreign (primarily Western) institutions. The school therefore strives to help those faculty members apply their international perspectives to the local environment by encouraging them to engage in research projects that are of interest to the Chinese businesses and that are relevant to the Chinese economic environment. This effort is facilitated in part by numerous research centers, including the CEIBS Lujiazui International Finance Research Centre, the Centre of Chinese Private Enterprises, the China Centre for Financial Research, and the CEIBS Case Development

---

[32]Social Enterprise Knowledge Network, SEKN Home web page, 2010, electronic document, http://www.sekn.org/en/index.html, accessed June 20, 2010.

Centre (established in 2001 with the vision to become "the most influential knowledge center of China-specific teaching cases in the world").[33] The University of Evansville's Schroeder Family School of Business Administration takes a different approach, using the school's Institute for Global Enterprise in Indiana to connect global research with the local southwestern Indiana (U.S.) business community.[34]

5.4.3. Faculty Management

Of course, having motivated faculty with the knowledge and skill development to successfully lead a school's globalization strategy is only as useful as the structures and processes in which the faculty operate. Opportunities for faculty interaction that facilitate the sharing of ideas, incentives that encourage faculty to engage in globally focused research, and effective management of (often) limited faculty resources across programs and locations are each critical complements to the individual capabilities of the faculty.

Interaction. Faculty structures determine whether faculty members who are focused on international research interact with other faculty members or whether they are clustered together in isolation from other academics. For institutions with multiple locations, faculty management processes determine the degree to which faculty at different campuses identify themselves as part of the larger institution or as isolated in another location.

Several of the 10 case-study schools have faculty departments that house individuals focused primarily on international business research. By providing a formal framework within which faculty focused on international business issues work together and interact, these schools say they can better provide opportunities and incentives for cultivating international research. William R. Folks, Associate Dean of International Activities at the University of South Carolina Moore School of Business, characterizes the school's Sonoco Department of International Business, for example, as "a home for cross-disciplinary scholars [that] allows the creation of cross-disciplinary teams."[35] Faculty in other departments commonly share similar areas of focus and influence course and program development.

---

[33]China Europe International Business School, CEIBS Case Development Centre web page, 2010, electronic document, http://www.ceibs.edu/cases/centre/index.shtml, accessed December 29, 2010.

[34]University of Evansville, Institute for Global Enterprise in India website, 2010, electronic document, http://www.globalindiana.com/about/, accessed December 30, 2010.

[35]Folks, William R., personal interview, 2010; see case study in Appendix.

Incentives. Incentives may include incorporation of certain policies to guide promotion and tenure reviews, staff support focused on grant acquisition to fund global research, or flex-time for international travel to conduct research. We again reference the Moore School, where each faculty department has its own promotion and tenure policies, and thus the Sonoco Department of International Business is able to set up policies that encourage output focused on international business, either in publications such as the *Journal of International Business Studies* or other discipline-specific journals.

At the same time, other schools opt against having a department or division of "international business" faculty, with the reasoning that such a framework might limit the diffusion of international research and perspectives across the faculty. The University of Minnesota Carlson School of Management, for example, does not have an international business department but still strives to offer incentives for faculty to engage in international research. A small Research Grant Program provides funding to support faculty research activities that address global business issues and reflect an international or cross-national scope.

Deployment. Yet another aspect of faculty management that becomes increasingly complex as schools globalize is that of deployment, particularly when faculty members must be assigned to teach courses across multiple locations. Unlike schools with campuses in downtown and suburban locations, schools with campuses in multiple countries must take into account substantial travel time, accommodations, and other factors when managing faculty across locations.

Several of the case-study schools with campuses abroad relied on a model in which faculty based at the original campus travel for short-term assignments at other campus locations. At the Booth School of Business, all faculty members are based at the Chicago campus but travel to London and Singapore for course delivery—an approach that is meant to ensure that, despite having numerous campuses, all faculty members maintain a high level of "collegiality and collaboration," according to former associate dean Bill Kooser.[36] Similarly, courses at CEIBS' Ghana campus will be staffed by full-time faculty members who travel to Ghana for short periods, complemented by visiting faculty.

The HKUST Business School also uses the same pool of faculty to support its programs across all locations, yet, because all locations are within a four-hour flight of Hong Kong, faculty mobility across locations is relatively easy to facilitate, according to Kate Chan, associate dean and

---

[36]Kooser, Bill, personal interview, 2009; see case study in Appendix.

director of the school's Bilingual EMBA Program. More difficult, she says, is just managing faculty resources across the numerous programs offered—a challenge for any school balancing a variety of programs, regardless of the programs' locations. DeKrey affirms that position, adding that the faculty management challenges faced by the school have little to do with its international diversity or the geographic spread of programs offered. Rather, the school places an emphasis on both quality research and capable instruction, which are sometimes competing qualities; "some of our best researchers are not a good fit for the MBA program," he says.[37] The challenge they face, like many other schools, is thus to balance faculty talents with the program needs.

By contrast, The Fuqua School of Business' three-phase plan for staffing its global network of campuses will ultimately lead to a different model. The first phase resembles the approach taken by the schools noted above, with the faculty network projected primarily from Fuqua's "home base" in Durham, North Carolina. In the second phase, the school intends to hire faculty members in more permanent roles at each of the campus locations, in order to form a sustainable core in each region. Finally, in the third phase, the school's dean, Blair Sheppard envisions more integration between campuses, with individual faculty members having a "heavy foot" in one region, and a "light foot" in either Durham or one of the other host regions.[38]

For other schools, deployment of visiting faculty plays a significant role. When first begun, CEIBS relied heavily on visiting faculty members to help rapidly build the intellectual capacity of the institution. A heavier reliance on residential faculty has brought more stability and direction to the school's development and to its research output. At the same time, the use of visiting faculty played a substantial role in enabling CEIBS to establish relationships with an international network of business schools. Today, Cremer says that striking the right balance between residential and visiting faculty is something the school continues to question, particularly in light of international accreditation expectations (the school holds both EQUIS and AACSB accreditation) and the school's mission.

5.4.4. *Administrative/Staff Services*

Before concluding the section on faculty strategies, we must note that similar considerations for administrators and other staff members are often just as crucial for a school's globalization strategy, though these considerations are

---

[37]DeKrey, Steve, personal interview, 2009; see case study in Appendix.
[38]Sheppard, Blair, personal interview, 2009; see case study in Appendix.

perhaps more likely to be overlooked. Are individuals in the school's admissions office prepared to make good judgments regarding the qualifications of individuals educated in other countries? Does the marketing and communications staff have a good grasp of how to develop and implement a strategy that involves multiple countries and cultures? If the school has an international programs office, how do its staff members maintain currency in best practices for student and faculty exchange, collaborative programs, experiential learning, and other international activities? Is the career services office capable of assisting students interested in internships or careers with multinationals and foreign firms? Schools that take a comprehensive approach to recruiting, developing, and managing faculty *and* staff will greatly enhance their capacity to globalize.

5.5. Pulling It All Together/Building a Strategy

Clearly, the options presented to schools for globalizing aspects of their teaching, research, and outreach activities are numerous, and the possibilities for variation and customization are endless. While the abundance of options creates many opportunities for schools, some institutions find the process to be an overwhelming and paralyzing array of decisions and trade-offs.

As with any strategy development, schools are advised to begin by first identifying their own priorities, objectives, and existing resources/ capabilities. The Task Force recommends the Business School Conceptual Framework developed by an earlier AACSB task force as one resource that can serve as a useful tool for this exercise; the framework guides a school through an analysis of its context, stakeholders, and array of activities to assess how they relate to one another and the school's overall mission.[39] This analysis then provides a foundation for determining the types of activities the school is interested in, whether it will go alone or seek a partner, and the attributes it will seek within a partner.

As further guidance for schools in this process, this section offers a few general observations from case-study schools that should help schools develop strategies and implement them over the long term. While the sections above present guidance for specific types of activities (e.g., partner selection, footprint strategies, collaborative degree models, etc.), this section focuses on guidance to help schools pull those activities together into a broader, comprehensive strategy.

---

[39]This tool is available for download at http://www.aacsb.edu/resources/administrator/ framework.asp.

5.5.1. Blending Standardization, Adaptation, and Customization Strategies

Do business schools have a tendency to standardize their operations across borders, to adapt them slightly to conform to unique environments, or to provide entirely customized and unique operations across borders? Among the set of schools included in the case studies, we see evidence of all three approaches, sometimes in conjunction with one another.

First, we note numerous examples of product line extensions among the schools studied. Many global programs are manifest adaptations of domestic programs to a joint-venture or international sphere. ESSEC's Advanced Master's degree in Strategy and Management of International Business, for example, offers students the option to choose from among seven program "tracks," several of which are offered in partnership with other universities. Course options vary according to the track chosen. By establishing similar agreements with schools in numerous regions, ESSEC is able to provide "custom" variations of an existing program to meet varied student interests for study in a particular world region. Similarly, students in FGV-EAESP's Master's in International Management program have options to complete between six and 12 months of study through the CEMS alliance or one of five other partner schools.

The Kellogg-HKUST joint EMBA program, similarly, is one of several joint-EMBA programs offered by the Northwestern University Kellogg School of Management with various partner schools, all following the same general model.[40] This degree program in turn served as a model for development of HKUST's International Executive MBA program (IEMBA). Given the different audience for the IEMBA program, HKUST made a few practical adaptations, including the program's location and language of delivery, as well as content adaptations to include a greater focus on the legal, political, and economic environment in China. HKUST's Shenzhen MBA is similarly modeled after the school's part-time MBA in Hong Kong. Chan notes that the school's approach to the curricula of these programs is one of consistency and adaptation, with adaptations in the curriculum content and delivery techniques.

The University of Minnesota Carlson School of Management offers four variations of an EMBA program in Minneapolis, Minnesota (EMBA); Vienna, Austria (VEMBA); Warsaw, Poland (WEMBA); and Guangzhou, China (CEMBA). The four programs run simultaneously and follow similar

---

[40]In addition to HKUST, other EMBA joint-degree partner schools include Recanati Graduate School of Management at Tel Aviv University in Israel; WHU-Otto Beisheim Graduate School of Management in Vallendar, Germany; and the Schulich School of Management at York University in Toronto.

curricula, though the actual course structure varies among programs, as do course materials, discussions, and guest speakers.

In contrast, though The University of Chicago Booth School of Business offers its EMBA program in three locations (Chicago, London, and Singapore), it considers each location to be a separate delivery point for the same program. Students who pursue the program at each location follow the same set of classes in the same order, and access the same core faculty. Any variations across locations are slight; for example, professors might adjust the examples used in class or use cases that involve local firms, and guest speakers may frame their discussions in the local context.

Similarly, the One MBA Global Executive MBA program offered by FGV-EAESP in collaboration with four other schools[41] is also a single program delivered in multiple locations, though with some variation of courses across locations. The five partner institutions collaborated to develop a standard curriculum that is delivered on each campus. In total, 160 of the 624 teaching hours in the program are spent in "coordinated courses" (courses that are the same at all campuses), and 192 teaching hours are spent in global residencies that bring together the participants from the five locations. The remaining 272 teaching hours are spent in "regional courses" that are developed by and unique to the host school.

As we see in the examples above, a degree of consistency in partnership agreements and degree program structures may in fact provide opportunities for students to "customize" their degree programs by choosing the location in which to pursue a portion of the program or an entire program.

Such consistency also yields opportunities for students in different programs, tracks, or locations to come together for short timeframes at the beginning, end, or throughout the program. Students in the Kellogg-HKUST EMBA program participate in a "live-in week" at the Kellogg Campus, as do students in Kellogg's other joint EMBA programs. Students who follow the Booth EMBA program at its various locations spend a total of four weeks together at each of the three locations during the course of the program. Students in the Carlson School's various EMBA programs collaborate during the program on a virtual team project and conclude the program with an "integrated residency" at the Minneapolis campus. Finally, as noted by Bill Kooser while at the Booth School of Business, schools that rotate faculty between campuses for brief periods benefit from

---

[41]The OneMBA Global Executive MBA program is offered by FGV-EAESP, Tecnológico de Monterrey Graduate School of Business Administration and Leadership (EGADE), The University of North Carolina at Chapel Hill's Kenan-Flagler Business School, the Faculty of Business Administration at The Chinese University of Hong Kong (CUHK), and the Rotterdam School of Management at Erasmus University.

consistency in technology and facilities that require little on-the-spot adaptation.

Additionally, schools evidently find benefit in sticking to a model that "works," replicating it with perhaps some slight alterations in other contexts. The exchange program between the Stanford Graduate School of Business and Tsinghua University's School of Economics and Management (Stanford-Tsinghua Exchange Program, or STEP), which was developed as an alternative to the traditional model of student exchange, yielded positive outcomes for students and faculty and led each school to subsequently develop similar programs with other partners.

In all of the above examples, however, the challenge is to be consistent across programs and yet adapt to the special mission of the program. The six campuses of The Fuqua School of Business each serve multiple missions: that of Fuqua, those of the school's degree programs, and those of the respective campuses in their local contexts. In addition to supporting delivery of the MBA programs, each campus also has a set of objectives that are unique to the needs of the local region. When developing plans for each campus, according to Sheppard, rather than ask whether there was a market in each country for the school's existing products, the school engaged in conversations with numerous groups of local stakeholders in order to explore how it could best provide value in the local context.

Consequently, in Dubai, The Fuqua School of Business will work with the Duke University Sanford School of Public Policy to offer a Master of Management Studies in Government degree through the locally based Mohammed Bin Rashid Programme for Leadership Development. The program is specifically designed to meet the educational needs of government officials in the Middle East. During the school's exploration process in India, a recurring theme in conversations with local citizens was a need for better-trained human capital at entry level positions, which led Fuqua to consider a role for pre-experience programs in the country.

5.5.2. Balancing the "Local" and the "Global"

As the schools in the case studies globalize, they manage the contradiction that they are at once local and global, seeking to strike an appropriate balance between the two. This balance and the methods by which schools attain it vary between schools; no two schools have exactly the same approach.

Some of the schools we studied work to infuse students and faculty with global perspectives but maintain a focus on a particular world region. For example, HKUST seeks to develop business leaders in Asia for the world.

Its EMBA with Kellogg seeks "to foster a new network of leaders with global insights and local sensitivities."[42] HKUST has a strong focus on Asia, yet it asserts that global perspectives are important. Similarly, the CEIBS mission articulates its objective "to support China's economic development and to further China's integration into the world economy by preparing highly competent, internationally-oriented business leaders capable of working within the Chinese economic environment."[43] Among the principles that guide the globalization strategy at FGV-EAESP are that the school will "preserve its local, national, and regional identity," and that it will establish joint projects with other international business schools "that include a Brazilian, a Latin American, and a BRICS component."[44]

Yet another approach is the one pursued by The Fuqua School of Business at Duke University, with facilities and operations in six cities across the globe. The first principle on which the school's new approach is based is one of both embedding within and connecting across multiple regions, or in other worlds, striving to meet the unique needs of each region while also facilitating connections and transferability between regions. To embed within each region requires the school to determine how it can be a good "citizen" of the host country in such a way that the surrounding community sees the value in its presence, rather than simply asking if there is a market in that country for the school's existing products. In many cases, to accomplish this goal the school needed to be open to the substantial modification of existing products or the development of new products, policies, or approaches. Connections between regions are facilitated through faculty and student mobility, but also through collaborative cross-border projects among faculty.

ESSEC Business School, which has striven to globalize its programs and curricula, offers students the option to focus on a particular world region. Courses offered at the Singapore campus are a combination of those from the standard ESSEC catalog as well as those distinctly oriented to focus on the Asian business, economic, and cultural environment.

---

[42]Northwestern University Kellogg School of Management, Kellogg-HKUST Executive MBA Program web page, 2009, electronic document, http://www.kellogg.northwestern.edu/Programs/EMBA/Global_Partner_Programs/HKUST.aspx, accessed November 4, 2009.

[43]China Europe International Business School, About CEIBS web page, 2010, electronic document, http://www.ceibs.edu/africa/aboutceibs/index.shtml, accessed December 29, 2010.

[44]Fleury, Maria Tereza, personal interview, 2009; see case study in Appendix. The "BRICS component" refers to the school's participation in the Association of BRICS Business Schools (ABBS), which includes select business schools in the emerging BRICs economies as well as South Africa.

The University of Chicago Booth School of Business, on the other hand, greets visitors to its EMBA program's website with the following mantra: "One Program. One Faculty. Three Campuses. The same distinctive approach. Where you learn how to think, not what to think. In or out of the box. In any situation."[45] The school's objective is to maintain a global brand for its product that is consistent across various contexts and that strives to build a curriculum that gives students the tools to adapt their knowledge and skills to any new context.

5.5.3.   Using Exploration and Experimentation as a Foundation for Building

Finally, a common theme across all of the schools we reviewed is the step-by-step process each has taken toward globalization. The array of programs, activities, and processes in place today are the result of experimentation and learning by doing. As a reminder and reassurance to schools, we underscore the fact that globalization is not an objective to be pursued overnight, but rather it is an incremental process of building upon past successes and lessons learned.

A common example of this experimentation is found in various school policies and processes, particularly those that are initially provided in an optional capacity and then later made mandatory. Schools that require students to engage in international experiences as a part of one or more degree programs—such as the Carlson School of Management, the Booth School of Business, and the Stanford Graduate School of Business—made these experiences mandatory after having first offered them on an optional basis. In this way, the schools had opportunities to gain familiarity with the logistical needs of running such a program before implementing it on a large scale. The Carlson School of Management, furthermore, first made such programs mandatory for undergraduate students (beginning with its 2008 freshman class) and then followed with a similar requirement for MBA students (beginning with the class entering in 2009).

The curriculum at the Stanford Graduate School of Business has undergone a series of evolutions, trying a range of different approaches to incorporating global perspectives into its MBA program curriculum. What began as an optional elective series evolved to a required course for all students and then shifted to an "infusion" approach with international

---

[45]The University of Chicago, Booth School of Business, Executive MBA Program web page, 2010, electronic document, http://www.chicagobooth.edu/execmba/, accessed December 29, 2010.

content across the curriculum. The school's current model involves a mandatory first-quarter Global Context of Management course as well as additional channels to support faculty members in efforts to incorporate global knowledge and perspectives in other courses.

Other examples include cross-border initiatives that schools later decided to discontinue or change. The Booth School of Business, as mentioned earlier, relocated its Barcelona campus to London after determining that it preferred its European campus to be in a city more recognized as a "business center" for the continent. Through its early attempt at offering an MBA program in Frankfurt, Germany, and through the initial years of the school's Global Executive MBA program, The Fuqua School of Business learned several lessons that would shape its future cross-border initiatives. Among these lessons were the value of connecting with local firms or other organizations to benefit from their expertise on the legal and regulatory environments of the country and the benefits of having a permanent infrastructure in other cities to support international student recruitment and job placement.

Chapter 6

Summary and Implications

The field of management education is amid the third great wave of development. The first wave stretched over decades, even centuries, as institutions sought to identify and develop a body of knowledge that would serve to elevate the practice of business. This wave was one of entrepreneurship and innovation, in which business schools experimented with the form and content of education.

The second wave, which began after World War II, marked the intellectualization of management education and was characterized by the advent of rigorous research, a canon of broadly accepted ideas, the professional development of educators in doctoral programs, and standards of quality that were reflected in accreditation programs. In some respects, the second wave reflected the growing professionalization of management itself.

This third wave promises to be no less transformational: it is the wave of globalization. This wave is characterized by surging demand, engagement of institutions across borders, widening access to higher education, rising acceptance of the value of business degrees worldwide, the reach for global brands in education, and the use of totally new educational formats that experiment with new technology, travel, and local experiences. Rarely, if ever, have the world's business schools experienced change as far-reaching and powerful as the current wave of globalization. Little about business schools and their environment has been unaffected by this evolution. The sources and composition of students and faculty have changed, as have the concepts they study and skills they must develop. In response to the changing environment, business schools have altered their missions and strategies and the way in which strategic initiatives are financed. Reputation has taken on additional importance, especially in the area of international collaborations. The globalization of management education, as a process of change, is in many respects already deeply rooted.

However, globalization is still in its formative years. Globalization, many would argue, is at once the most visible opportunity and the most persistent challenge faced by business schools. A frustratingly-wide curriculum gap remains alongside large risks of misdirected and incoherent strategies. Globalization has obviously been difficult for business schools and, unquestionably, they must do more to deepen our understanding of global business and to extend the reach of educational engagement across borders.

The globalization of management education is being shaped by a complex web of forces we have only just begun to understand. The field's outcomes have not been predetermined and will depend enormously on the actions, individually and collectively, taken by business schools and a wide range of stakeholders today.

The main purpose of this chapter is to apply what we have learned about globalization toward implications for various constituents and the actions they should take. We first describe the potential benefits of globalization and assess the industry's performance in achieving these benefits. Then we discuss various impediments to the globalization of management education in order to draw attention to opportunities for proactive, industry-level leadership that will accelerate and improve the globalization of management education. We then bring together various pieces of our study to discuss the implications of globalization for management educators and for industry-wide initiatives they could lead. Finally, we present a set of overarching principles to guide policy makers in ways they can support the responsible globalization of management education.

6.1. Globalization of Management Education: Benefits to Global Society

More than 50 years ago, the path-changing research of Gordon and Howell was motivated by an overarching concern for America's competitiveness. Leaders in business believed that high-quality management education was essential to economic performance, but they viewed the vast majority of business schools at the time as too vocational and not scientific enough. Though change had already begun, the Gordon and Howell report moved many more schools to action and guided the whole business school sector toward more rigorous research and theory-based education that was aligned with the social sciences model. The report helped American management educators lift their heads from the sand and see that they shared a common objective and operated within the same larger system, and it helped them understand that they must work together to attract investments that could enable a transformation of the whole sector. Over time, the industry and almost everything about it—including the faculty, students, curricula, and reputation—changed accordingly.[1]

Likewise, the work of this Task Force has been motivated by the economic and social potential of a more globalized society. The globalization of management education is not an end in itself. It matters because the potential benefits to humankind from the globalization of business are enormous. These benefits include accelerated economic growth and employment, faster transfer of technology and new products, and the alleviation of poverty. Globalization has the potential to improve health, safety, and human rights. It is not just about the efficient utilization of resources; globalization is also necessary to achieve workable solutions for environmental sustainability.

Successful globalization of management education results in greater competence and confidence among graduates who hope to do business with global impact; it provides more research insights into the global complexity of the managers, enterprises, and markets; and it ultimately facilitates better service of the global business profession. Successful globalization also means that business schools turn out more graduates who are capable of succeeding and leading in an increasingly global environment. By illuminating the strategies, practices, and social impacts of business globalization, management educators not only can accelerate it, they also can help ameliorate its costs and disruptions. Better international management education promotes more responsible globalization in business and society.

Globalization does not mean that differences are stripped away. As we have emphasized throughout this report, cross-border differences matter deeply in the practice of management, as the field is heavily influenced by contextual factors such as culture, social norms, and national regulations or policy. The contextual nature of management magnifies the benefits of an education in which international differences and, more importantly, how we organize and think about differences are central. People who have the ability to span a contextually complex society are a critical resource for both businesses and governments; they are future leaders who are more capable of advancing international peace as well as economic prosperity.

More direct economic benefits are also derived from the globalization of management education. As students, employers, and providers become

---

[1]The fact that the scope of the Gordon and Howell study published in 1959 was limited to the United States while its influence has been broader presents an interesting contrast to our study, which encounters a much more complex, global industry and argues that structures and processes should not carry over easily across borders.

Gordon, Robert Aaron, and James Edwin Howell, *Higher Education for Business*, Columbia University Press, New York, 1959.

more mobile, the number and variety of choices they have expands. Today, for example, we see that increasing numbers of American and European citizens opt for degree programs in Asia because they hope to launch a career or business in the region and because, more and more, they believe the quality is comparable to their next-best Western alternative. A similar expansion has occurred in recruitment and continuing education options for businesses around the world, and the number of prospective foreign partners for high-quality business schools has increased. These types of international comparisons intensify rivalries and elevate overall quality. Further, they drive schools to identify and strengthen unique centers of excellence. More choices, increased quality, and specialization in management education signify a healthy, efficient industry.

Competition is not the only aspect of globalization that elevates quality and performance in management education. Globalization also opens management educators' eyes to new models and expands benchmarking opportunities. When different educational and research processes, cultures, and experiences meet, more innovation is likely to occur. Business schools also augment and improve capabilities through partnerships and use them as a platform to launch capacity-building initiatives. When faculties generate and share educational content relevant to local communities, "social multiplier" impacts result. Successful initiatives of one school help countless others globalize.

The globalization of management education is also important because globalization itself is fragile. It can be slowed, or worse, it can be brought to an abrupt halt. Critical debates along the fault lines that we defined in Chapter 3—economics, culture and tradition, public policy, and strategic positioning—have the potential to fuse or fracture our future as it relates to globalization. The benefits and costs of globalization are asymmetric, and these asymmetries are a source of inspiration for political activists. The true economic and social impacts of globalization are easy to distort, and, because of Internet and social media advances, armies of discontents are easy to mobilize. Strong and natural economic forces have always been around to encourage globalization; only politically-guided protectionist policies have limited it.

In *The Great Brain Race*, Ben Wildavsky writes that the largest barrier to the "flourishing of global higher education" is the "widespread notion that a nation whose education system is on the rise poses a threat to its economic competitors."[2] However, managers with a global mindset do not support this flawed notion. They are credible and capable advocates for globalization. They understand and clearly articulate the benefits and risks of

---

[2]Wildavsky, Ben, *The Great Brain Race: How Global Universities Are Reshaping the World*, Princeton University Press, Princeton, NJ, 2010, p. 7.

globalization to society, inside and beyond higher education. To them, the pitfalls of academic protectionism and nationalistic competitiveness are transparent, and, as Wildavsky reminds us, "increasing knowledge is not a zero-sum game."[3] Global business schools do not just accommodate and respond to globalization; they help shape its future by preparing globally educated citizens.

6.2. Performance

Our comprehensive study leaves no doubt that the globalization of management education already is an established process. As enterprising providers have established operations in other countries and reached out to connect with other foreign institutions, growing numbers of curious and ambitious students are crossing borders to study. Many schools have attempted to globalize learning experiences by increasing the international diversity of student bodies, introducing international travel courses or modules, and creating international projects and simulations. Business schools have set up research programs and centers in foreign countries, entered into franchise agreements, and negotiated international degree program partnerships to extend their international presence and capability. We could go on and on—a wide range of activities fit under the broad umbrella of globalization.

The fact that progress has been made in the globalization of management education is not surprising; it reflects the tighter integration of our economies, the globalization of business, and the interconnectedness of our governments. Some business schools see their international efforts as an extension of their commitment to providing high-quality, relevant education, while others view it as a way to exploit new sources of revenue and to invest in their brands. For yet others, their actions are preemptive or reactive, as they view globalization as a threat to their position in the market or to their existence.

What is surprising is that, given the importance of management education globalization to business and society, *more* progress has not been made. Overall, our view is that the globalization of management education has not achieved its full potential. The explanations and evidence to support this sweeping conclusion were discussed throughout this report and are summarized below in three overlapping areas. These areas reflect the Task Force's definition of a global business school, which is an institution that 1)

---

[3]Ibid.

prepares students to perform competently and confidently in a world of global business competition and inherently global issues (learning outcomes), 2) generates research insights about trends and best practices in global management (intellectual capital), and 3) leverages diverse cultures and practices in pursuit of innovation and continuous improvement (industry performance).

6.2.1.   Learning Outcomes: Unmet Expectations and the Curricular Content Gap

A gap has opened between expected educational outcomes and actual achievements in globalization. This conclusion, which is described in more detail in Chapter 4, is shared by business leaders, academic thought leaders, and deans alike. Datar, Garvin, and Cullen list "a global perspective" as one of 10 "unmet needs and opportunities," which were revealed in interviews with executives and deans worldwide.[4] Though little specificity is expressed in what business leaders say they expect, they mostly agree that not enough preparation for international management has occurred in business degree programs. Similarly, in the global survey by Ghemawat, Yeung, and AACSB reported on in Chapter 4, only 4 percent of academic thought leaders said that the attention business schools pay to globalizing their educational programs should stay the same, while 96 percent believe that it should increase or increase significantly.

The fact that expectations could go unsatisfied for so long is difficult to comprehend—more than 20 years have passed since Porter and McKibbin said with regard to globalization of management education, "a beginning has been made, but much more remains to be done."[5] Since then, expectations have risen and many sources have contributed to increasing pressure for business schools to globalize: business leaders, university administrators, students, accrediting bodies, and rankings. The voices have been loud, but they have not always been consistent or beneficial. For example, even while company leaders touted the need for managers with a global mindset, their recruiters often looked for graduates who used their credits mostly to gain functional competence. Similarly, ranking formulas tend to rely on measures of diversity without drilling down to determine the

---

[4]Datar, Srikant M., David A. Garvin, and Patrick G. Cullen, *Rethinking the MBA: Business Education at a Crossroads*, Harvard Business School Press, Cambridge, MA, 2010.

[5]Porter, Lyman W., Lawrence E. McKibbin, and the American Assembly of Collegiate Schools of Business, *Management Education and Development: Drift or Thrust into the 21st Century?* McGraw-Hill Book Company, New York, 1988.

true extent of international education. Although more work clearly must be done, what is not clear is exactly what should be done to advance globalization.

Calls for globalization have not necessarily been ignored. Rather, school responses have been incomplete and sometimes misdirected or misaligned. Our analysis of a sample of business schools suggests that, with some exceptions, schools place a greater emphasis on the incorporation of global experiential learning opportunities than on the development and integration of global content within the curriculum. Business school websites are more likely to contain references to international partnerships than to reference efforts to globalize curricular content. These concerns are not restricted to North American institutions. At a 2007 colloquium at IESE Business School, deans and faculty ranked "utilizing courses and methods to successfully deliver key material on international business/management" as last among 13 globalization-related dimensions of school performance.[6]

In Chapter 4 of this report, Task Force member Pankaj Ghemawat argues that business schools have not included enough international content in their curricula, delivered that content effectively, or supplemented it adequately with appropriate pedagogical tools and structures. In a world best characterized as semi-global, to attempt to reduce international management education content to a global "canon" makes little sense. Instead, the cultural, legal/regulatory, political, economic, and financial differences across countries and their implications should be a central component of what we teach about globalization. Interestingly, this characterization of the content is exactly what makes international education difficult, and it may explain why the approach has not been more readily adopted in business schools. Most people, including business faculty, tend to overestimate the degree of cross-border integration. That is, we consistently understate the contextual nature of management and the importance of international differences.

6.2.2. Intellectual Capital: Is the Foundation Adequate?

Progress in the globalization of management education also can be measured by the amount of relevant intellectual capital. The stock of collected knowledge about globalization is important because it is a foundation for global education. Learning from the experiences of

---

[6]IESE Business School, Colloquium on the Globalization of Business Education, Barcelona, Spain, October 4-6, 2007.

globalization is essential to achieving its benefits. Globalization is work in process, and improvements are generated through experience and reflection. To be useful, the creation and dissemination of intellectual contributions should keep pace with the globalization of business. As we state in Chapter 1:

> [t]he relationship between the business profession and the business academy is largely symbiotic: they support each other in various ways that advance the welfare of society. When one gets materially ahead of the other, it is a moment for reflection, action, and realignment. The Task Force judges that globalization has created such a moment in the relationship between business and business schools.

Given the importance of globalization in business, the global content of academic management journals is relatively small. Excluding the *Journal of International Business*, the percentage of articles with "cross-border" content in a top-20 group of management journals is less than 4 percent.[7] The percentage appears to be even smaller in other disciplines. To some, such low percentages are not surprising because many of these journals seek basic contributions—insights that are universal rather than local or national. And the small percentage does not imply that growth in the amount of cross-border research has stagnated, especially since there has been an expansion in many other areas of management research. Nonetheless a disconcerting fact remains that globalization, arguably the most dominant force in business, has not earned more journal space.

Even if one argues that discipline-based scholarship ought to focus on "science" that transcends international differences, for management practice, as we have consistently conveyed, the most valuable knowledge about globalization is contextual. We are concerned that not enough emphasis in applied and pedagogical contributions has been placed on country and regional context in research; content adaptations have been insufficient and not particularly relevant to most student populations and

---

[7]Ghemawat, Pankaj, "Bridging the Globalization Gap at Top Business Schools: Curricular Challenges and a Response," Chapter 2.3 in Canals, Jordi (ed.), *The Future of Leadership Development*. Houndmills, Hampshire: Palgrave Macmillan, 2011. Ghemawat's conclusion is based on Pisani, N., "International Management Research: Investigating its Recent Diffusion in Top Management Journals," *Journal of Management*, Vol. 35, No. 2 (2009), pp. 199–218. For a similar study covering the period between 1996 and 2000, see Werner, S., "Recent developments in international management research: A review of 20 top management journals," *Journal of Management*, Vol. 28, No. 3 (2002), pp. 277–305.

business communities. Management education institutions lack truly international cases and pedagogical tools, especially those focused on developing and emerging economies. Several regional business school networks, such as the Association of African Business Schools (AABS) and Association of Asia Pacific Business Schools (AAPBS), have stepped up to establish case databases and journals, and several schools have expanded their case-writing efforts globally, especially to Asia. But the number of borders is vast, and we have only begun to scratch the surface.

Intellectual capital is more than the tangible outcomes of scholarly activity; it is also embedded in the relationships among management education participants, students and faculty in particular. More internationally diverse student populations, for example, contribute to the global intellectual capital of a school. Many schools have been purposeful and successful in increasing student diversity. But, as we noted in Chapter 4, globalization efforts have worked far better thus far for students than for faculty. To compound existing difficulties of hiring, retaining, and developing qualified academic faculty, the numbers of new and incumbent faculty who are "globally ready" remains relatively small, and school budgets are strained. Critical globalization issues are left unexplored in our research agendas as a consequence. Because faculty are responsible for developing educational content, this deficiency can be a significant barrier to achieving better learning outcomes.

The intellectual capital gap calls attention to the fact that the globalization of management education is not strictly a matter for individual schools; it is an industry matter that is impacted by the relationships between schools and the institutions that support these relationships. Let us look at doctoral education in North America, for example. In the model, a business school spends money and intellectual resources to educate doctorates, future scholars and teachers and then works diligently to place them in competing schools. We also see new faculty-sharing or visiting-faculty models emerge across borders. These trends, and other observations discussed below, compel us to examine schools as a whole rather than in isolation.

6.2.3. Industry Performance: Have the Benefits to Management Education Been Realized?

As predicted, globalization already has presented students with more—and more diverse—alternatives across schools and programs. Students, alumni, and businesses have surely benefited from burgeoning global networks of business schools. Although schools in the U.S. and Western Europe have historically led the field in research, curriculum design, innovation in programs, and ultimately in global reputation, countries such as China and India have witnessed a few remarkably fast entries into the top echelon of business schools.

But the globalization of management education has only just begun. It is too early to tell whether it will deliver fully the benefits described above. We have not been able to validate our intuition that competition drives quality improvement in management education. Many complicating factors prevail. The industry is vast. It includes more than 12,600 institutions that award business bachelor's degrees or higher. It is a wide umbrella that covers institutions of vastly different missions and ambitions. The most visible, internationally recognized schools represent only a miniscule share of an industry that is still growing larger and more diverse. Rather than maximize enrollments or financial contribution, these schools appear to focus on maintaining their small "slice" of market share while they invest heavily in their reputation. The most familiar instruments for reputational investments are media rankings, which are highly influential, although they are fabricated on surface-level data that could not possibly provide the depth required to assess quality.

We have also shown that, for a variety of reasons, the global structures and processes of schools often are fragmented, inefficient, inconsistent, and unsustainable. Our study reveals that globalization has not yet produced the anticipated and much needed sharing of best practices in higher education, management education more specifically, and, perhaps most important, with business schools in emerging markets. We still see more wholesale exporting, rather than creative blending and innovating, of education models.

The present day is a pivotal time in the globalization of management education. We will not in the relevant future find common structures or approaches across institutions in all countries. Even so, we are witnessing nothing less than the emergence of a global system of management education that transcends national systems. The connections and depth of interaction among institutions and individuals around the globe will become the most important defining characteristic of the new system.

The quality and the reputation of management education are at risk. Only about one in 10 institutions that award business degrees is involved in the most established international networks that facilitate benchmarking and continuous improvement. Only half of that 10 percent of schools participate in global accreditation systems designed to improve and validate quality. Others might be subject to local and regional quality assurance and authorization schemes, but these systems are highly uneven in terms of rigor and relevance. Combined with growing numbers of mobile students, a shortage of credible data and information is likely to mean that unfulfilled promises will become more common. The risks from unfulfilled promises are not evenly distributed. They are more pronounced in the fastest growing, low- and middle-income regions—partly because nearly all of the institutions that participate in international networks are located in countries that the World Bank classifies as high-income.

6.3. Challenges to the Globalization of Management Education

This section explores why business schools have not kept pace with expectations and been more effective in their globalization efforts. But we suggest that current barriers are not insurmountable. Several of these challenges already have begun to fall and will eventually be reduced to "speed bumps" or "frictions." What is more important is that we begin to reveal what is necessary to accelerate and improve the globalization of management education. As such, this discussion of challenges is more appropriate as a foundation for the sections that follow.

Today, not even the most isolated of campuses and faculties can be easily impervious to escalating calls for more global education and research. The globalization of society and business has led to a huge derived demand for global management education. Business deans would be remiss to ignore these calls in a world of increasing transparency, engagement, and accountability in higher education. We would rightly expect a steady erosion of support and commitment by students, employers, and benefactors of unresponsive institutions.

In addition to pressures related to the focus of education and research, globalization also can be a disruptive force of change in the industry of management education. It is changing assumptions, practices, and strategies. For example, previously in this report we have predicted that management education's "next phase of development will be characterized less by the proliferation of providers than by the development of strategic connections between them." These connections do not just happen; they require proactive and strategic action by schools to position themselves in this new environment. The branches in the future network map are being drawn today and will forever alter the strategic opportunities and competitive landscape faced by many business schools. As we wrote in Chapter 1, "business schools that fail to adapt to the realities of globalization do so at their own peril."

Schools that disregard the pressures will still be faced with the numerous opportunities that globalization brings to expand programs, build brand, and generate revenues. These pressures have been great—sometimes so great that they have led to missteps and misfortunes. Sometimes pressures have come on too hard and fast for business schools to accommodate. For example, we saw a number of instances in which institutional officials set out financial goals that were impossible to meet. Overzealous responses have not been difficult to find. Well-intentioned entrepreneurial professors have created kingdoms of unfit and unsustainable programs and examples of "get rich quick" schemes that have permanently damaged established educational brands.

We cannot ignore the possibility that some schools are simply not responsive to the mounting pressures. However, we believe several other obstacles have challenged and will continue to challenge the globalization of management education.

6.3.1. Novelty and Complexity

The stories we heard about globalization usually came in one of two versions. In the first version, the current wave of globalization arrived abruptly in the normally quiet and insulated world of higher education. It produced windfall opportunities that called for immediate decisions as well as created surprising and difficult challenges. Mistakes happened. In the second version, globalization swept in quietly over time on the backs of enterprising faculty and ambitious students. In either version, we easily see how business schools, even those based in mature and connected economies, could be caught off guard and respond hastily and how globalization initiatives could appear incomplete or inconsistent.

Even as the novelty began to wear off, we could hardly expect anyone to fully comprehend management education in all of its new-found complexity. Each of us on the Task Force can confess to moments of surprise when confronted by new data or different perspectives, and we were chosen partially because of our knowledge and experience in the area. We were shocked, for example, by the sheer numbers of providers, franchising operations, and mobile students. We were stunned by the remarkable diversity that still exists across business schools in (and within) different countries. We were caught off guard and uniformly disappointed by the widespread agreement that international content is "underdone" in curricula.

Now, we clearly see that we should not have been surprised. Our study merely confirmed that the international environment is much more diverse than the domestic environment and that decisions in a global environment are not merely extensions of decisions in a domestic environment. We have highlighted the significance of cross-border differences throughout this report, and we have noted that most people tend to underestimate the amount and importance of cross-border difference. Difference, after all, is the reason that global education is so important and why it is significantly difficult to achieve. No global best practice exists that can be shared with business schools around the globe. And business and management dynamics force learning to be continuous; what is relevant tomorrow may not be relevant today.

Finally, about structures and processes, we state in Chapter 5 that "the options presented to schools for globalizing aspects of their teaching, research, and outreach activities are numerous, and the possibilities for variation and customization are endless. While the abundance of options creates many opportunities for schools, some institutions find the process to be an overwhelming and paralyzing array of decisions and trade-offs." To evaluate these alternatives, management educators must gather data, forecast the future, and anticipate emerging demands in countries and regions in which they have little experience.

6.3.2. *Finances and Risk*

The financial demands of globalization often are severe. Education costs can rise sharply as a consequence of globalization. The cross-border provision of management education is a service that requires mobility and is expensive. Academic faculty members need heightened financial support to pursue international research agendas and professional development. And the most significant costs are not always explicit. Globalization involves trade-offs, and the value of forgone opportunities mount, sometimes unexpectedly. For example, many schools in our interviews were surprised to discover how much time is consumed to manage collaborations.

Globally, rankings unfortunately exacerbate these costs. We observe an "arms race" of sorts in expensive advertising programs, the construction of new facilities, competition for prominent faculty, and the like. The net effect may be a homogenization of programs and zero-sum competition for resources and stature; unfortunately, the most innovative responses by schools are not likely to move a program to a higher position in the rankings. The Task Force encourages a non-zero-sum outlook in the face of robust demand for management education and seeks to acknowledge and legitimize a diversity of strategies.

Meanwhile, traditional public sources of funding have been diminishing, millions of students have been struggling to make ends meet and qualify for financial aid to gain access, and the prospects of other sources of financial support, such as corporations, are highly uncertain. The financing of higher education is indeed a worldwide conundrum. The predominant financial models of today are not sustainable in the global environment of the future, especially since a culture of philanthropy in support of higher education is largely confined to a few countries. The needs today are inevitably greater than they used to be because schools anticipate the future. As Canadian hockey player Wayne Gretzky once said, "skate to where the puck is going to be, not to where it has been."

Operating in a global environment is also inherently much more risky than in a domestic environment. This increased risk is in part due to pressures for financial gain as well as difficulties in fully understanding the complex global environment. But these pressures can be managed. Globalization also brings risk from unpredictable events, such as fluctuations in exchange rates, political disruptions, and natural disasters. Abrupt regime changes in partner institutions, changes in property right protections, and security and health concerns all can potentially occur. These and other risks from uncertainty are less manageable.

6.3.3. *Norms and Regulations*

The importance of regulations and norms (traditions, conventions) in a global environment cannot be overstated. Both reflect and define shared expectations about behaviors in a community. Significant differences in higher education regulations and norms across borders are still the rule. These differences constitute significant barriers to globalization, the extent of which varies by region depending on many factors. For example, globalization often is less difficult for Europeans than for Americans, because the "norm" is multinational and multilingual.

However, important differences exist between regulations and norms. Regulations are explicit. They are written down and, as a consequence, can be torn up, rewritten, and redistributed. Norms are implicit. They are intangible and, as a result, cannot easily be changed. To change a tradition requires much more leadership, communication, and time. On the other hand, regulations cannot usually be violated without repercussions; norms can.

Thus, norms and traditions often are lower but more persistent barriers to the globalization of management education. To use one example, the motivation of faculty to globalize content potentially can be muted by the "norms" of research cultures. In some places, faculty want to teach the specialty areas that they research, yet the current "norm" in research tends to value results that can be generalized.

Regulations can be removed or lowered to encourage or facilitate globalization, but global higher education is not and will never be a "free market." We do not expect adjustments and investments to lack distortions.

Directly and indirectly, governments are a material source of support for management education. Government policies change, sometimes quite quickly, which heightens uncertainties in areas such as funding, institutional entry or exit from markets, mobility of students and faculty, pricing of programs, and even freedom of expression. The visible hands of governments around the world will be significant shapers of the future of globalization in management education.

6.3.4. Positive Externalities

A positive externality exists when there are benefits to others when a product or service is consumed. Although not technically an impediment, the existence of such externalities still might explain why less globalization has occurred than is optimal. We generally accept the notion that a more educated population carries substantial benefits to society, such as improved governance and health, beyond what is received by the students. The existence of such "externalities" explains why education in many countries has been supported by public funds.

Earlier in this chapter, we argued that similar societal benefits to global management education exist. But more obvious, tangible examples of externalities also abound. Throughout this report, we have discussed the external benefits of capacity-building, developing cases and other pedagogical tools that are relevant to local communities, and sharing best practices. Each of these types of activities improve the globalization performance of many other schools, but not enough schools will initiate them because they do not factor the extra benefits into their decisions.

We close the discussion of impediments by continuing the story we started at the beginning of this chapter. Looking back 50 years, we can easily see that the Gordon and Howell report made a tremendous difference in management education. It confirmed the suspicion that the field was too vocational to serve American business. It enabled management educators to envision the future, and it provided guidance about how that vision could be achieved. The report showed that the change would involve every aspect of the industry.

But the Gordon and Howell report came at a much simpler time. Business schools were more homogeneous then, and, after all, the scope was confined to the United States. As far as we can tell, no real or organized resistance stood in the way of the agenda that the report advanced. Looking ahead, the challenge of change presented by globalization will carry much higher stakes, and its achievement will be much more difficult. The gaps are wide and the obstacles are significant. Business schools are more diverse and they no longer play by just one set of rules. We are now consumed by a more challenging set of issues.

Undoubtedly, regardless of what is done, the change that is sweeping through management education will seem no less profound a half-century from today than it does now when we look back to 1960. But more purposeful and proactive leadership and action today will have a huge impact on the benefits of globalization in the future and on the swiftness with which those benefits are realized. With this in mind, we now consider the implications of globalization for management educators, the role of industry-level initiatives, and the influence of policy makers.

6.4.   Implications for Management Educators

The most powerful force in the globalization of management education is the collected actions of individual business schools. In this section, we discuss the implications of globalization for business schools and the people—faculty and administrative staff—who lead them. The section serves as a high-level summary of concepts and ideas raised throughout this report—especially those raised in Chapters 4 and 5, which address curricular content, supplemental tools and activities, and structures and processes for global education.

However, we aim to go beyond summarizing what has already been stated. First, we try to draw a stronger connection between the challenges brought on by globalization and the possible responses from business schools, and the outcomes and performance that can be achieved. Second, we elevate the level of analysis beyond individual schools to view them in relation to each other, and we consider the shared benefits of individual action. By rising above the complexity of individual schools, we are able to imagine much greater possibilities for change. Business schools are part of a larger system and have a responsibility to take a leadership role in the globalization of business and society—to move from change taker to change maker. The main objective of this section is to synthesize what we have learned to help management educators envision, and ultimately achieve, the type of change we are advocating.

6.4.1. Mission and Purpose

Globalization has a tendency to make us believe that business schools ought to be more things to more people. Business schools are asked to embrace increasing numbers of students that come from all over the world. They are invited by foreign institutions to develop and deliver new programs in other countries. Their students and faculty insist on traveling to emerging economies or developing ones, while more companies ask for research and training about how to compete and manage internationally. Meanwhile, the pressure of additional competition forces schools to offer new program options, spend more on marketing, and add more student services.

Similarly, one of the most difficult aspects of globalization for management educators is that there are so many alternatives to consider, factors to weigh, and risks to assess. How should international topics be included in our curricula? In which countries should we have exchange partners and at what levels? What are the risks of accepting an offer to franchise our degrees? Should more foreign students be accepted if they are unable to find jobs in our economy? How should we divide and manage responsibilities for joint-degree programs? Whenever change presents so many options and issues, the potential to be overwhelmed and immobilized or to make inconsistent decisions emerges.

The global environment also encourages distraction. Schools commonly tie strategic objectives to easy-to-measure indicators, such as the international diversity of students and faculty. But these indicators are not the end game; they do not imply that international learning objectives have been met, and they may actually detract from the globalization objectives of the program. The potential for financial gain also can be a significant motivating force, especially as business schools are increasingly left to their own devices to acquire the resources to achieve their missions. Yet, schools that take a purely financial, deal-driven approach to globalization, especially collaboration, usually do not succeed. Globalization also can be viewed as a way to increase and expand a school's reputation. Regrettably, doing so often requires that schools conform to the narrow and sometimes dysfunctional criteria of media rankings.

For all of the reasons above, the significance has never been greater for business schools to have a well-defined mission and to stick to it. Thoughtful, well-articulated missions help business schools to envision what globalization compels them to do. Missions also set boundaries; they help schools decide what not to do. In the opportunity-rich global environment, one might easily view the availability of resources as a binding constraint. Trade-offs are expected, and, as a consequence, missions bear a larger burden in a global environment.

Missions are shaped in large part by context—including the cultural, historical, economic, and political circumstances of the region in which the school is based as well as, in most cases, the larger institution to which it is connected. Thus, globalization has called attention to a wider array of mission possibilities than ever before, and what it means to a particular school is in many ways unique. This point is especially important in business and management. Whether we are talking about family business in India, Mittelstand in Germany, state capitalism in China, or maquiladoras in Mexico, the local context of business matters deeply. What works in one place may not work well in another, and this reality has important implications for the way business schools view their missions. As Clara Lovett writes, "the chaebol curriculum [at Yonsei University] reflects the work of American researchers, but the program works only where it reflects indigenous value systems."[8]

Cross-border differences in our society suggest that business schools ought to have larger distinctiveness in their missions than what we actually observed. Our review of mission statements has not uncovered the contextual richness we expected to see. Even when mission statements clarify the balance of activities, they tend not to specify the role of a business school in the communities they serve. As a result, incoming INSEAD dean Dipak Jain concluded that business schools have focused more on "performance" than on "purpose."[9] Missions of business schools should not be restricted to weighing the relative emphasis on education and research or to describing the ideal graduate. They should define the overarching purpose of the business school—its reason for being or the societal needs it intends to serve. Whether its aim is to reduce poverty or improve health in a region, to foster sustainable business practices, or to fuel information technology innovation, a clearly defined purpose will distinguish a business school more effectively in an increasingly competitive environment, and it will offer more useful guidance for globalization initiatives.

Globalization is a two-edged sword. At the same time it requires missions to be clear and more judicious, globalization is the most powerful force driving business schools to change. Missions should endure; after all, much of their value stems from their stability. But in a world as dynamic as ours, missions should not be static. Globalization has been altering the landscape of management education and missions should be reconsidered as a consequence. In doing so, business school leaders should think beyond what globalization means to their school and reconsider its purpose in an increasingly global context. Only then can business schools move beyond "catch up or keep up" and begin to lead, advocate, and influence the direction of globalization.

---

[8]Lovett, Clara M., "American Business Schools in the Post-American World," *The Chronicle of Higher Education*, September 10, 2010, p. A22.
[9]Jain, Dipak, keynote speech, Annual Conference of CLADEA, Cartagena, Colombia, November 4, 2010.

One example of how the changing environment has altered the way some business schools think about their purpose is in the responsibility for "capacity-building." Many schools now view their purpose in developing countries not as educators but primarily as a developer of the education capacity. For some, this role means taking on an "educate the educators" approach. By jointly developing innovative doctoral education to support a region, schools can increase the supply of qualified faculty. Others intend to fill the gap in contextual information about business in a region by establishing research centers to prepare cases on emerging economy businesses. In either case, business schools are investing in the future capacity of global management education.

Our emphasis on the distinctiveness in business school missions should not be misinterpreted. Although diversity is and should be a part of what business schools do, the Task Force emphasizes that today's environment presents an imperative for business schools to improve the curriculum. This obligatory part of any business school mission cannot be "traded off" or "avoided," even by schools that carry the most globally recognized brands, suffer the most severe resource constraints, or operate in the most remote corners. As we state in Chapter 4, "even schools that are currently leading the way still have numerous opportunities to make globalization of their curricula *more deliberate, less fragmented,* and *better aligned* with the intended student population and program objectives." In the end, the biggest opportunity to seize is to align everything around a stronger focus on the curriculum.

6.4.2. Complementarities

Our study has highlighted the importance of complementarities in the globalization of management education. Two products, services, or processes are complements when both are more valuable, attractive, or efficient together than separately. When the benefits of a pairing are asymmetric, we might describe one as a supplement to the other. In either case, globalization calls for management educators to accurately assess themselves and potential partners in order to understand, manage, and exploit these complementarities.

In no other place are complementarities more obvious than in the curriculum. The previous section reminded us that every school can and should incorporate more international content into their curricula. In Chapter 4, Ghemawat discusses the contextual nature of this content and various approaches to adding it to degree program curricula. One approach is to create a new required course (insertion); another is to weave international content in existing courses (infusion). Separately, each approach has benefits, costs, and limitations. However, insertion and infusion must be thought of as complements rather than substitutes. Business schools should consider using both not only to compensate for the limitations of each, but they should structure the curriculum to make each approach more effective and beneficial—to exploit the complementarities. Also in Chapter 4, Ghemawat proposes an "interlock" strategy for how to do exactly that.

Two related concerns about business curricula have been raised. First, not enough truly international cases and other pedagogical tools exist to complement the necessary cross-border content required of business schools. Second, steps to increase international diversity and student travel have gone ahead without sufficient grounding in curricular content. The problem is not only that content has fallen behind but that it is unrealistic to believe that international learning objectives can be achieved on these tools alone. In Chapter 4, Ghemawat argues for strengthening the alignment between these supplemental tools and curricular content.

We similarly have been concerned with how other structures and processes complement the curriculum. In Chapter 5, we show that faculty-related structures should be more supportive of curricular content and pedagogies. Faculty departmental structures, evaluation systems, research incentives, and service opportunities should motivate and enable the development and maintenance of a globalized curriculum. Instead, current structures seem to mire the agenda for international content in the politics of core curriculum development and foster narrower research agendas rather than the interdisciplinary scholarship necessary to support global education.

So many elements comprise a business school that describing how they all fit together is impossible. The whole operation involves curriculum design; faculty recruitment, development, and deployment; staffing and facilities; financing alternatives; student recruitment and support; and more. Our main point is that present efforts to globalize too often include a series of independent and fragmented activities. Put another way, the Task Force is concerned that business schools have not been responding to globalization in a complete and coherent way, not only by putting insufficient emphasis on learning experiences, but also by paying too little attention to how the vast array of global activities relate to each other. At the very least, every business school should ensure that various structures and processes do not conflict with each other. However, the most successful global business schools will go further and view all activities as potentially powerful complements.

Complementarities are also the source of value across business schools and other organizations. As we state in the introduction to Chapter 5 that "the schools that are most effective will be those that find ways for various activities to complement one another, creating synergies and therefore new capabilities and opportunities." This statement calls attention not only to the strategic importance of collaboration[10] but also to the need for accurately assessing strengths and capabilities across organizations, whether they are foreign business schools, domestic counterparts, or nonacademic organizations. These assessments have important implications for the nature and types of collaboration that will be most beneficial. Also quite clear is the fact that, as with the curriculum, the full benefits of complementarities cannot be achieved without sufficient attention to coordination—this time with the added difficulties of working across organizations and borders; international partnerships involve significant transaction costs.

Finally, we encourage management educators to consider the social benefits of complementarities and collaboration. Partnerships are our most effective way to build management education capacity and to elevate the quality of management education, especially in developing countries. Partnerships allow schools to share the costs as well as to create stronger results. We discuss capacity-building in more detail below.

6.4.3. Capabilities

Just as it has done for business leaders and managers, globalization also has been forcing faculty members, staff, and administrative leaders of business schools to acquire new knowledge and skills. We already have given considerable attention to the capacity of faculty. Judging from their lack of preparation for international education, the low levels of cross-border emphasis in scholarly activities, and the resulting underdeveloped international content of curricula, sizeable room appears to exist for developing the capacity of faculty to globalize management education. Chapter 5 discusses strategies for faculty recruitment, development, and management. We have not focused as much on the capabilities of administrative staff—deans, directors, managers, and associates. Although we have not attempted a formal assessment of staff capabilities, we would find difficulty in concluding that they are adequately prepared for globalization given the observed fragmentation in business school strategies and structures.

The globalization of management education has pressured administrative staff to expand their knowledge of cross-border differences in structures,

---

[10]To exploit complementarities does not require taking on partners; it is also a vital consideration for setting up facility/footprint strategies. Each campus should create value for the others.

definitions, regulations, and business models. Participants in the AACSB collaborations survey have partner schools in an average of eight other countries. Although the extent of differences might vary, an average business school could therefore be exposed to eight different educational structures, faculty models, and management systems, as well as eight different economic, cultural, political, and legal contexts. And the number of international collaborations is expected to grow; nearly 90 percent of schools without existing collaborations indicated a desire to establish one or more with other schools.

Every staff member does not need to know everything about the differences across various systems relevant to the business school, but our discussion of complementarities in the previous sub-section shows that nobody is immune to some impact. When it is done well, the globalization of management education involves almost every aspect of and position in a business school. Take the "simple" example of creating an internationally-diverse student body. Recruiting for international diversity means traveling internationally to meet prospects, evaluating transcripts from different systems, and interpreting recommendation letters that are influenced by a variety of cultures. It requires being able to manage diversity in the classroom in a way that maximizes learning potential rather than detracting from it. Then the difficult task arises of assisting students with various citizenships to find internships and jobs. Increasing international diversity also gives way to challenges for the development staff as alumni are more internationally dispersed. For deans, the commitment to diversity could impact the program's rank by a number of publications, and that figure could have striking career implications.

We cannot possibly be precise about the attributes, knowledge, and skills that are most relevant to a "global" business school. Indeed, we have stumbled on a major reason why so little useful information exists from business leaders about what they expect from business school graduates. Expectations depend in part on the positions and on the types of international activities pursued as well as on the mission and context of the school. Like their counterparts in other organizations, business school leaders and managers are more likely to face unfamiliar problems and encounter additional complexity from existing ones in a more global environment. General leadership, communication, teamwork, and relation-ship development skills have always been important, but globalization has made them critical.

Two changes brought on by the globalization will likely have a larger impact. First, risk must be interpreted and managed in a global setting. In most national settings, higher education is characterized as stable and predictable in comparison to business and government. However, the global environment is by definition less insular and presents greater uncertainty and risk than that which is encountered in a strictly domestic setting. Exchange rates, regulations, and reputations can change quickly, so deans and directors must be more tolerant of ambiguity and able to manage risk.

Second, the globalization of management education will often require more creativity and innovation. Regardless of where they are based, universities and business schools have not normally required leaders to so consistently create new products, processes, and marketing methods. Little incentive has been offered to be innovative. In more competitive and collaborative global environments, we see more pressures and opportunities to invent and implement new ideas.

Business school leaders can invest in the global capability of administrative staff in many ways. For example, they might review and revise recruitment criteria to weigh more heavily international experience or cultural awareness. They might introduce international staff development programs. For example, the Carlson School of Management at the University of Minnesota encourages staff members from across the university to volunteer as travel coordinators for their international programs.

We recommend that schools begin by cultivating a global mindset among faculty, staff, and students. Having a global mindset enables individuals and their schools to leverage broader trends for the school's own advantage and to identify existing opportunities that are underutilized. Resources that are easily leveraged at little to no incremental cost include the increasingly international coverage of various news outlets, the internationally integrative nature of online social networking platforms, and the growing international membership of various disciplinary and professional associations. Consider, for example, two faculty or two staff members attending a disciplinary association meeting at the same cost for their host school. One tends to associate with individuals from other schools in the same country. The other proactively engages with individuals from other countries to discuss similarities and differences in their contexts—enhancing his/her understanding in a way that will likely impact teaching/research or the management process and also forming a potential foundation for future cross-border collaborative activities. Increased international mobility means that many cities have significant local immigrant populations that maintain political, economic, and cultural ties with their home countries, and these citizens would be happy to engage with the business school.

6.5. Role of Industry-Wide Initiatives

The globalization of management education is not just about business schools individually responding to powerful forces of change. It is also a matter for the industry as a whole. This chapter has already revealed several reasons why concerted, collective efforts at the industry-level can be advantageous. Business schools could use additional information, resources, and education to support globalization efforts. They could be stimulated and supported to collaborate in capacity-building initiatives, write international cases, and share best practices.

Industry-wide initiatives can accelerate and improve globalization. They can magnify the benefits and lessen the costs, as well as alter the distribution of each. But industry-wide initiatives are difficult to initiate and sustain without an organizing structure. A wide range of organizations can provide the needed structure and support for business schools to succeed with globalization. They could be suppliers, service providers, intermediaries, or regulators.

6.5.1. Data, Information, and Education

As this report has described, large data and information gaps exist in the global management education industry. We know little about the individual institutions that offer business degrees or the educational environments in which they operate. Few, if any, ongoing research projects aim to improve the success of business schools in globalization, and, to our knowledge, no industry-wide effort is underway to collect and share information about the globalization experiences of business schools.

Public information is available for only a tiny fraction of the institutions known to offer bachelor's degrees or higher in business and management. Basic data, such as the business degree program levels offered, how the institutions are organized to deliver these programs, and the number of business students, faculty, and staff, are not available or structured in a way that is useful. The absence of consistent, comparable, and high-quality data and information remains an impediment to deeper analysis of the globalization of management education and hinders the progress of globalization itself.

The lack of transparency about schools and their programs has become especially important due to the increased mobility of students and faculty, growing interest in international collaboration among business schools, and increasing cross-border recruitment by companies. In its 2008 report, the Global Foundation for Management Education described the core issue concisely:

> If quality is about delivering on the promise of the school's mission and meeting expectations, then it is important to ensure that accurate data and information about the

institution are available to the public. Appropriately so, accreditations have tended to focus on institutional improvement, while national systems are often regulatory or administrative in nature. It is thus noteworthy that few global structures currently exist primarily to inform and protect students and employers against the hazard of implausible claims.[11]

One industry-wide response might be to develop a global registry for institutions that award business degrees. This type of registry could achieve two objectives. First, it could assist individuals or entities interested in developing a relationship with a management education provider (as a student, partner, etc.) to validate the existence of providers and consider their claimed sources of legitimacy (e.g., a national Ministry of Education, an international business accreditation, etc.). In doing so, the registry would serve as a reference for students and a facilitator of collaboration and benchmarking among institutions. Second, it could enhance understanding of the global management education landscape by providing a set of institutional contacts for survey research.

Even without a global registry, the development of data definitions and naming conventions for institutions and degree programs would be helpful. Differences in terminology within and across countries impede the gathering and reporting of comparable data at the international level. At times, data are available, and even comparable, but are not specific to business degree programs.[12] Cross-national variations in educational systems and in the structures of the institutions that comprise them blur the boundaries between the types of providers and inhibit accurate segmentation. Common data definitions could alleviate some of these problems and reduce schools' costs for completing increasing numbers of surveys.

More qualitative information is also needed. Globalization is a process of change that improves and adapts based on experience and reflection. Yet, little effort has been made to study the globalization experiences of business schools and share what has been learned with other management educators. Business schools should collectively invest more to study globalization practices, develop case studies of global business schools, and synthesize lessons into best practices reports and white papers.

---

[11]Global Foundation for Management Education, "The Global Management Education Landscape: Shaping the future of business schools," 2008, electronic document, http://www.gfme.org/landscape/reportonlineversion.pdf, accessed January 31, 2010, p. 49.

[12]For example, the UNESCO Institute for Statistics reports students enrolled in the broad category of "social sciences, business, and law."

The vast majority of business schools around the world still serve a predominantly local set of stakeholders, and those schools that venture across national borders face an array of economic, cultural, political, and legal environments in the markets they enter. We expect much of the information about the experiences of business schools to be contextual, rather than generic. However, a vast abyss exists in what we know about management education structures around the globe. The Global Foundation for Management Education website has snapshots of management education in nearly 50 countries and territories, but they were posted nearly five years ago and cover only 25 percent of the countries in the world.[13]

While we benefit from the collection, preparation, and dissemination of information about globalization experiences, to actually learn from the experience of others usually requires more engagement. Faculty and staff can be educated and developed in many different ways. Seminars animate case studies and create additional knowledge through interaction among internationally diverse peers with a wide range of experiences. They provide valuable information about country and regional educational environments or address curricular content and supplemental tools. Experiential learning activities such as travel and immersion programs are often effective but generally involve longer time commitments and are more costly to design and operate than seminars are. Learning also comes from benchmarking activities, which bring together groups of people to learn about and discuss best practices.

The cooperation of business schools to educate and develop faculty and staff is particularly beneficial. They spread the costs, bring together a more diverse group, and build it into other activities. For example, faculty discipline association meetings offer an excellent opportunity to hold joint seminars on international curricula and research. Peer assessments through accreditation systems create benchmarking opportunities for management educators. Networks that span borders also are an especially important mechanism for sharing ideas and information about globalization through electronic formats.

6.5.2. Quality Assurance and Improvement

Two primary objectives are found in most quality assurance systems. One is the internal dimension in which accreditation standards provide a

---

[13]Global Foundation for Management Education, "A Global Guide to Management Education 2006," 2006, electronic document, http://www.gfme.org/global_guide/index.htm, accessed January 31, 2010.

framework and process that guide the school's efforts to ensure quality and make consistent efforts toward improvement. The second is the external dimension in which accreditation serves as a validation to the school's stakeholders that it has achieved widely accepted standards for quality. Data presented in Chapter 2 show that only a small fraction of the institutions that award business degrees participate in one or more accrediting bodies that are international in scope. More than 90 percent of the institutions are subject to highly uneven, country-specific programs that might be designed more to legitimize or regulate operations than to improve quality, or they are not subject to any quality-related processes at all. Three industry-level implications have emerged from our study.

First, a need is evident for quality improvement systems that consistently and reliably apply to a large and growing number of schools. Quality improvement has been mostly left to accrediting bodies, but as noted previously, these organizations cover only a small fraction of the institutions that award business degrees. Room is available for new quality improvement services as long as they are well-managed and clearly designed to create value for schools that are not already served by existing international accreditation programs. Our belief is that all-or-nothing accreditation systems that are designed to target only the top echelon are easily rejected by schools that perceive certain standards to be impossible to achieve (or misaligned with the school's objectives). Such schools should have opportunities to align with alternative criteria and processes that are consistent with their longer-term developmental goals.

Second, the need to ensure that schools actually deliver on the promises they make to students, employers, faculty, and partner institutions is increasingly evident. This need has become more important because of increasing mobility of management education participants. According to UNESCO, 23 percent of the three million internationally mobile students study business and management.[14] The absence of credible and easily understood data about increasingly complex organizational arrangements (e.g., franchising, etc.) has made international signals of quality much more important today than ever before. Our interviews also reveal that management educators also are looking for indicators of quality commitments from potential partners. In the AACSB collaborations survey, however, 57 percent of the joint program partners identified by AACSB-accredited institutions were not also accredited by AACSB at the time of the survey.

---

[14]UNESCO Institute for Statistics, "New Trends in International Student Mobility," electronic document, http://www.uis.unesco.org/template/pdf/ged/2009/UIS_press_conference_presentation .pdf, accessed March 30, 2010.

Media rankings have been expanding in response to demands for external validation. They have important impacts on the choices of students, employers, and schools, and they are scalable. However, the rankings are only deliverable because their formulae and criteria are superficial, simplistic, and incomplete. With richer, more in-depth peer-review processes, accreditation systems offer deeper assessments and better protection; but they are less scalable and not as visible externally. The longer this dilemma is unresolved, the greater is the risk that pressures for external validation could produce additional "accreditation mills" that do nothing more than provide a logo to schools that pay to use it.

Third, some individuals are concerned that quality assurance/accreditation systems stifle globalization. Globalization demands innovation, which is sometimes difficult for accreditations to embrace. Accreditation standards can extend the life of outdated norms that are inconsistent with globalization. On the other hand, one could reason that accreditation enables globalization through quality improvement and by signaling high quality to external constitutions. Regardless, we suggest that standards (on paper and in practice) be regularly reviewed to determine whether they discourage innovation in globalization.

6.5.3. Coordination, Collaboration, and Capacity-Building

For an industry like management education to transform requires sustained industry-wide leadership that coordinates change across a wide range of business schools and the organizations that support them. As we noted earlier in this chapter, industry norms and traditions, as well as international differences among them, can be difficult to change because they are implicit agreements about shared expectations that have been ingrained in the culture of a community over time. Consider, for example, what it would take for the U.K. to change from driving on the left side to the right side of the road. In management education, emphases in top scholarly journals on universality and specialization can slow globalization, but near-term increases in the focus on contextual differences and inter-disciplinary problems will require some degree of coordinated effort across a wide range of organizations, such as doctoral-granting schools and faculty disciplinary associations.

We have emphasized the importance of collaboration in the globalization of management education. Our research has revealed an industry-wide opportunity to assist business schools in identifying and reaching out to potential partners. In a 2004–05 AACSB survey, partner selection was placed at the top of the list of success factors for program alliances.[15] In the recent collaborations survey, nearly all participants either have sought or are seeking to establish international partnership agreements, or both.

A search service might be modeled on the process implemented by the U.S. Agency for International Development (USAID) Higher Education for Development (HED) program, which facilitates the posting of one school's formal "request for assistance" and the submission of proposals by interested potential partners. Other initiatives that were described previously, such as an international registry and expanded reach of quality improvement systems and validation schemes, can supplement the service.

We believe that such a search tool will facilitate efforts to develop management education capacity and quality in lower-income countries (i.e., capacity-building). The outcomes of capacity-building activities take many forms, including much-needed local case studies and pedagogical tools, increased numbers of qualified faculty, more relevant curricula, and new programs. Sometimes they involve the creation of entirely new business schools.

Nothing prevents a school from going solo into capacity-building. However, we found that capacity-building partnerships often are between schools in a developed country and a school, government, business, or nongovernmental organization in a developing country. In each case, significant benefits extend to the developing country that go well beyond the value created to participating partners. If, for example, a school creates instructional material relevant to a developing country, other schools benefit from the material when it is shared. This is one of the most important reasons that we conclude our discussion of industry-wide initiatives with a reminder that, to achieve the full potential of globalization in management education, field leaders must think beyond individual schools and consider the benefits of industry-wide collective leadership. As we state in Chapter 5:

> Whereas at one time only national systems of higher education existed, business schools today are components of a global system, producing graduates who may one day work together as colleagues or clients on different sides of the globe. As members of this system, business schools have a collective

---

[15]AACSB International, Canadian Federation of Business School Deans, and European Foundation for Management Development, 2004–05 Alliances Survey Results, 2005, internal communication to survey participants.

responsibility to help elevate the quality of management education around the world. International partnerships that support synergies between schools, benchmarking, and institutional development have the potential to contribute to the global growth of quality management education.

6.6.   Our Appeal to Governments and Policy Makers

Our study has necessarily focused on the management education "industry" and its participants, the individual institutions and their leaders. But our research shows that governments (national, regional, and local) and supranational organizations (such as the World Bank and United Nations) will have enormous influence on shaping the forward path of globalization of management education. The evolution of this path is of great significance to governments because the benefits from globalization may be accelerated or delayed by the policies they adopt in relation to higher education. Thus, for the sake of completeness, we offer the following comments to government leaders and their constituents.

As we discuss in Chapter 3, national policies are shaped by local contexts including traditions, histories, and systems of governance, and they are the subject of endless debate among the constituents they intend to serve. Based on our research and understanding about globalization, we recommend that government entities embrace underlying principles that both safeguard their constituents and entertain—if not encourage the development of—new opportunities related to quality management education.

Article 1 of the Universal Declaration of Human Rights adopted by the United Nations in 1948 states that "[a]ll human beings are born free and equal in dignity and rights. They are endowed with reason and conscience and should act toward one another in a spirit of brotherhood." This important principle is consistent with the advancement of quality management education around the world. We recommend that government entities implement policies that promote access and opportunity for all of their constituents and that they adhere to the following three principles critical to achieving the benefits of globalization of quality management education:

- **Mobility for individuals.** The movement across borders of students, faculty, and professional staff will hasten the dissemination of "best practices" and discovery of new knowledge. Yet, visa restrictions, entry and exit taxes, residency requirements, and other barriers that limit the mobility of individuals also inhibit the opportunities for the interactions upon which this dissemination and discovery depends.

- **Mobility of institutions.** Some countries erect high barriers to entry by foreign educational institutions—such barriers include requirements for large capital investments, personnel policies, and even admission standards. Often, these barriers are supported by the best of intentions, for example, to discourage the influx of low-quality institutions. But governments must recognize that such barriers may also have the unintended effect of enshrining local institutions and practices to the exclusion of the global best practices that quality entrants can bring.
- **Freedom of information and ideas.** The benefits of individual and institutional mobility depend on the freedom to express and access information and ideas. The sharing and development of best practices can only occur if opportunities are available for interaction among individuals and institutions. This free-flow of information and ideas, and the ability to freely explore alternate viewpoints, supports advances in educational delivery as well as in the knowledge on which that education is based. Additionally, transparency of information about the quality of management education providers is critical to exposing low-quality institutions, encouraging needed investments in quality improvement, and generally advancing students and the society they will serve.

6.7. Recommendations for Additional Research

In addition to serving as a launch pad for action by business schools and the organizations that serve them, as this chapter has described, we hope that this report will also encourage additional research related to this increasingly important and rapidly evolving dimension of management education. The space of globalization is vast, and within that space this report could not possibly have covered all relevant issues, trends, and strategies. The Task Force was often faced with the need to make trade-offs between bringing closure to a topic and pursuing the desired depth of research and analysis. In many cases, we were forced to present generalizations rather than expound upon the myriad variations of mission, structure, and context present among the array of business schools likely to be represented among report readers.

Already, the opportunities for continued research are great and will only continue to grow as we seek to understand how globalization of management education evolves. Underlying our recommendations is a reminder that those who lead or study business school globalization ought to look for opportunities to both contribute to and learn from the rapidly growing body of literature on higher education globalization. Schools of business have many unique qualities that differentiate them from schools in other disciplines. At the same time, they are closely linked with other parts of the academic community and share many common challenges. Though not meant to be all-inclusive, a list of some recommendations for additional research follows.

1. Will management education globalize like business? Our introductory chapter highlighted many fascinating questions about if and how business school globalization (or higher education globalization, for that matter) will resemble globalization by firms and other types of organizations. Business schools house many scholars of multinational enterprise who are intimately familiar with the issues, trends, and strategies of businesses seeking influence, resources, market share, and efficiencies across borders. Such individuals are in a unique position to use their expertise toward a shifted focus on the cross-border activities of academic institutions.

2. What global skills and competencies should educators aim to build? Chapter 4 notes that specificity from the business community (and particularly of segments within the business community) about needed skills among business school graduates is rare; in most cases, business schools are tasked with assessing more general evidence of the business world's needs and interpreting the implications for their educational programs. For business schools to develop the most appropriate educational responses, future research must enable these needs to be more clearly defined and articulated. As part of a broader effort by members of the academic community to develop and implement effective measures of learning outcomes, an enhanced understanding of the particular challenges posed by assessment of "global" competencies and capabilities is increasingly important.

3. How will innovations in technology and learning approaches advance the globalization of management education? Technological advances and the corresponding transformation of learning have implications for educational delivery far beyond the scope of globalization. But such advances play a major role in many globalization-related topics—including the cross-border provision of management education, the formation of international academic and professional networks, the facilitation of communication and collaboration between students and academics in remote locations, and the availability of enhanced learning tools and educational platforms. Much remains to be understood about the impact of technological change on the organization and delivery of higher education, and of business school globalization efforts as a piece of that puzzle.

4. How can the "haves" help the "have-nots"? The report references the important role of developmental relationships between established

business schools and those schools seeking to improve. Additional research on successful capacity-building efforts can yield insights that would be useful in helping to support these kinds of developmental relationships.

6.8. Concluding Remarks

This is the third great wave of development in management education. The Task Force believes that, given the trends we observed, we are relatively *early* in the wave. A history of the relationship between business academia and the business profession suggests that business practices drive academic research; research stimulates changes in practice; and revised practice drives more research. Given the rapid and monumental developments in practice associated with the globalization of business, this report is necessarily more of a prologue than a definitive exposition of the situation, more of a call for further research than a settling of mature questions, and more of an appeal to action than a satisfied endorsement of the status quo. This is a historic inflection point in the field of management education—we urge the reader to respond accordingly.

Case Studies of Business School Globalization Strategies

Global management education has evolved rapidly in over the past several decades and seems likely to continue to do so. In contemplating developments in the field, the AACSB Globalization of Management Education Task Force decided to complement survey findings and other research with case studies that might yield some additional insights. Case studies are especially useful in illustrating variations in motives, strategies, and tactics of management practice and in considering the range of possible outcomes.

Given our focused mission and limitations of time and money, we were not able to study all interesting cases; indeed, many schools and strategies came to our attention. Our selection of these particular schools does not constitute an endorsement of these schools' approaches (or, implicitly, a rejection of the approaches other schools are taking).

Furthermore, the Task Force recommends against any school trying to model its own approach too closely with any of those described in the case studies. The set of case studies illuminates how a set of business schools with very different missions, objectives, and resources have customized their strategies accordingly. Other schools would do well to consider the tactics most aligned with their own unique circumstances.

The Task Force chose nine business schools—all accredited by AACSB International—for the variety of approaches they represent. The documented approaches include undergraduate, specialized master's, MBA, and doctoral degree education, as well as non-degree executive or continuing education. They involve "at home" methods that require no cross-border mobility of faculty or students, as well as approaches that require a substantial level of mobility to partners or campuses abroad. Some approaches are resource-intensive on an ongoing basis; others involve substantial start-up investments but are relatively lower-cost to maintain; and still others may be implemented with little to no incremental cost.

CHINA EUROPE INTERNATIONAL BUSINESS SCHOOL

The very name of the China Europe International Business School (CEIBS) indicates the school's simultaneously domestic and international orientation.[1] Chinese and European in its roots, the business school is focused on the integration of the burgeoning Chinese economic powerhouse within the larger international community, and it is a driver of reform in the country's management training. The opening of China to the greater world market is one of the most significant recent developments for the modern business world; CEIBS was founded to support developments in China through the education and preparation of business leaders with a thorough understanding of the Chinese market context and its relationship to the global market. In this way, CEIBS seeks a niche for itself as a gatekeeper of understanding between China and the rest of the world.

A Foundation is Developed

The first international joint venture to provide management training in China, the China Dalian Training Centre for Industry and Science Management, was established in 1980.[2] The center, which was a joint venture between China's State Economic Commission (SEC) and the U.S. Department of Commerce, provided executive education courses. Cooperative training centers soon followed in partnership with several European countries as well as Canada and Japan.

In 1984, the SEC reached an agreement with the European Commission to establish the China Europe Management Program (later called the China Europe Management Institute, or CEMI) in Beijing. Negotiations, which took place over a three-year period, revealed China's interest in providing management training that went beyond short-term courses and was more aligned with the Western-style MBA. Thus, the CEMI (CEIBS' official predecessor) became the first institution in China to offer the MBA

---

[1]Each case study was prepared with the purpose of illustrating an interesting variation in approach to the globalization of management education. Inclusion in this report does not constitute an endorsement of this approach for all schools.

This case study was developed through conversations and email correspondence with Rolf D. Cremer (dean and vice-president, CEIBS), review of a presentation by Cremer at the AACSB World Class Practices Conference in Shanghai (2009), review of the CEIBS website, and review of accounts of the school's activities in press releases, periodicals, etc. Errors and omissions are the sole responsibility of the authors.

[2]China Europe International Business School, CEIBS Comes of Age web page, 2009, electronic document, http://www.ceibs.edu/link/latest/36702.shtml, accessed October 5, 2009.

program. The Dalian center had also been designated to offer the MBA, but was later discontinued.

The CEMI was, in some ways, a prototype of what would later emerge as the China Europe International Business School. Many of its early challenges served as learning experiences that would inform the mission and strategy of its successor school. These challenges included the identification and enrollment of students with sufficient English language skills. However, a more significant challenge faced by CEMI was the fact that, while China's SEC was a supporter of the school, the MBA degree that was offered was not officially recognized in China. Consequently, the school secured the agreement of five European business schools (London Business School, INSEAD, IESE, SDA Bocconi, and IMEDE) to participate in the program and, in doing so, to help lend credibility to the degrees. The degree also involved a practicum/internship in Europe as part of the degree requirements. What soon became evident, however, was the reality that this structure threatened the institute's mission to provide managers for the Chinese economy because several of the Chinese students chose not to return to China for employment upon completion of the program.

As the time neared for the second renewal of the institute's five-year contract, the European Foundation for Management Development (EFMD) worked with the European Commission to develop plans for a second stage of the program. This undertaking would entail transitioning the institute into a more formal "business school" that would offer not only its own MBA program, but also an EMBA program and executive education. The project—the China Europe International Business School (CEIBS)—was approved in November 1994 with a long-term, twenty-year contract. The school is a not-for-profit joint venture between the European Commission and the Chinese Ministry of Foreign Trade and Economic Cooperation (MOFTEC). Its partners are EFMD and Shanghai Jiao Tong University, and financial support was provided for the first ten years of operations by the European Union and the Municipal Government of Shanghai. The Degree Committee of the State Council, through the Ministry of Education of the People's Republic of China, provided CEIBS with degree-granting authority in 2002, and thus the MBA gained the official recognition that had been lacking with its predecessor organization.

Mission

In many ways, according to Rolf Cremer, CEIBS Dean and Vice-President, CEIBS is similar to any other internationally oriented business school in its programs, services, and faculty. However, he notes that CEIBS serves a more specific role as a pathway into the Chinese business environment for non-Chinese citizens and as a driver of reform in the area of management training (and, consequently, of economic reform) in China. This distinction is evident in the mission of the school as articulated in its founding documents, which state that the school's mission is:

> [t]o support China's economic development and to further China's integration into the world economy by preparing highly competent, internationally-oriented business leaders capable of working within the Chinese economic environment, while adapting to the driving forces of business globalization, international competition, and international co-operation.[3]

Given the school's location in China, most international students who enroll in its programs do so with the specific intent of seeking a career in China, says Cremer. He believes that CEIBS therefore serves a unique role as a pathway for foreign students to learn more about life and work in China and about the Chinese way of doing business.

Governance

The management committee at CEIBS is comprised of four positions: an executive president, a president, a dean, and a co-dean. The executive president and president are each appointed for five-year terms, with one appointed by the European Union and the other appointed by the People's Republic of China. Responsibility for the appointment of the two positions rotates at the end of each five-year term. The dean is appointed by the EU and serves as the academic head of the institution. The Chinese co-dean is appointed by the PRC and is primarily responsible for the day-to-day operations of the school.

The four members of the management committee meet approximately once per month at a meeting chaired by the executive president and report annually to a 10-member board of directors that consists of equal numbers of Chinese and European directors. Shanghai Jiao Tong University is responsible for appointing the chairman of the board, and EFMD is responsible for appointing the vice-chairman. The remaining eight directors are appointed

---

[3]China Europe International Business School, About CEIBS web page, 2010, electronic document, http://www.ceibs.edu/africa/aboutceibs/index.shtml, accessed December 29, 2010.

in equal number by the European Community and the PRC. A separate academic committee, comprised of scholars affiliated with distinguished schools in Europe, the United States, and China, provides guidance on academic matters, including quality oversight and faculty recruitment.

Likely established as a means of incorporating checks and balances into the governance of a very new model for a Chinese business school, says Cremer, the structure is unusual among business schools in that it has no single "CEO" and the dean and co-dean have no clear delineation of authority. Still, he notes that, particularly in a multicultural setting, the structure enables the strengths and weaknesses of each member of the management committee to complement those of the others. For example, Cremer notes that his Chinese co-dean, Zhang Weijiong, has a very strong connection with the approximately 300 nonacademic staff at the university, the vast majority of whom are also Chinese. Cremer believes that his ability to work well together with his co-dean is critical to the successful administration of day-to-day operations. Cremer, who is of European descent, believes he was chosen for his role in part because of the academic and international clout he would bring to the university. Despite an affinity for different areas of the school's operations, however, both the co-dean and he together oversee the entire business of the university.

A critical factor in the successful operation of this governance structure, notes Cremer, is a high level of communication among the four members of the management council. Additionally, a strong commitment by each of the members to "holding the team together" and a respect for the varying experiences and abilities of the other members are significant components to success.

MBA and EMBA Programs Blend Students and Languages, with a Focus on China

CEIBS offers MBA and EMBA programs, with a combined annual enrollment of approximately 900 students, as well as a variety of non-degree executive education programs.

Approximately 40 percent of students enrolled in the full-time MBA program came from abroad in 2009—a substantial increase from only 10 percent in 2002.[4] The MBA program is taught entirely in the English language,

---

[4]Schwertfeger, Bärbel, "CEIBS: MBA in Ghana," *MBA-channel.com*, April 16, 2009, electronic document, http://www.mba-channel.com/channel/article/ceibs-mba-in-ghana/, accessed December 28, 2009.

and English language proficiency is thus a qualification for admission to the program. At the same time, a lack of Chinese language proficiency is a frequent obstacle for international students who seek employment in China. Consequently, Cremer notes, the school is considering a requirement that students be proficient in Chinese upon graduation. In the meantime, he says, the school is working to align its student profile with the needs of the Chinese business environment by seeking students who demonstrate "tolerance, patience, and openness to bilingualism."[5] Increasingly, this tactic has resulted in an incoming class of students who have already received some Chinese language training, as this training is often a signal of the individual's interest in later seeking a career in China. As a reflection of this trend, students in the 2009 entering class were required, for the first time, to demonstrate a basic level of Chinese language ability. For students with little or no Chinese language training at the time of admission, the school offers a Chinese language pre-course over the summer that precedes the first semester.

In addition to compulsory courses on traditional management topics such as financial accounting, strategic management, organizational behavior, etc., students must also take a series of courses that are focused more specifically on the Chinese business environment. Included in these courses is a course on "Chinese economic reform," in which students use tools of modern economics to better understand the changes that have taken place in China's economy since 1979 and to predict what future trends might occur. Beginning in 2009, two new compulsory courses were added, one with a focus on human resource management in China, and the other, titled "China Within the World," focuses on the issues that individuals doing business with or within China might encounter. Students are also expected to participate in a lecture series that explores contemporary issues in the Chinese business environment.

The EMBA is offered at three locations in China: the school's main campus in Shanghai, in Beijing, and in Shenzhen—and as of March 2009, in Accra, Ghana.[6] Targeting a demographic with generally lower levels of English language proficiency, the EMBA programs in China are taught with Chinese language translation. Students also have the option to join the EMBA's English-language "International Class," which has instruction in English and also requires completion of a "global management module" at one of the school's three partner institutions (The Wharton School of the University of Pennsylvania, IESE Business School in Spain, and IMD in Switzerland).

---

[5]Cremer, Rolf, "Effective Practices: Asian Management Education Pedagogy," presentation at AACSB International World Class Practices Conference, Shanghai, China, June 2, 2009.
[6]China Europe International Business School, "CEIBS Holds Africa Programme Inauguration Ceremony," CEIBS press release, May 19, 2009, electronic document, http://www.ceibs.edu/media/archive/40160.shtml, accessed August 23, 2009.

These modules enable students to take courses at the other schools, to network with EMBA students at the host schools, and to visit with senior representatives of multinational companies headquartered in the host school location. The newly established EMBA program in Ghana is also taught in English.

Key to the school's ability to bridge the Chinese and English languages in its programs is a department of translation and interpretation. The department's 20 staff members, several of whom have U.N. certification in interpretation, are responsible for simultaneous and sequential interpretation of courses, enabling professors with varying levels of proficiency in English and Chinese to reach students across the various programs.

CEIBS also places a high priority on providing support for foreign students. MBA elective courses are offered in six-to-seven-week blocks so as to better facilitate student exchanges, and approximately 40 percent of MBA students participate in an international exchange at some time during the program. Accordingly, many students at the CEIBS campus are there for only a short timeframe. Cremer notes that the school takes pains to ensure that these foreign students see themselves as students of CEIBS during their time at the school and that they are not treated as "second-class" in terms of services and responsiveness of faculty and staff.[7] The school also offers an optional "China acculturation" seminar and includes both expat- and domestic-specific modules in the school's new student orientation.

Faculty Profile

For several years after CEIBS was first established, the school relied heavily on visiting faculty, essentially "borrowing" faculty from reputable institutions abroad in order to help establish the school's reputation. Gradually, however, the profile of the faculty has changed, and today between 75 and 80 percent of faculty resources, depending on the program, are CEIBS' own resident faculty. Non-degree executive education programs are more likely than degree programs to rely on visiting faculty members, while the MBA program has the greatest reliance on resident faculty.

The school continues its pursuit of the right balance between residential and visiting faculty, says Cremer, particularly in light of international accreditation expectations (the school holds both EQUIS and AACSB accreditation) and the school's mission. A heavier reliance on residential faculty has brought more stability and direction to the school's development

[7]Cremer, Rolf, "Effective Practices: Asian Management Education Pedagogy," presentation at AACSB International World Class Practices Conference, Shanghai, China, June 2, 2009.

and to its research output. At the same time, the use of visiting faculty played a substantial role in enabling CEIBS to establish relationships with an international network of business schools.

Cremer believes that, while in the school's early years foreign faculty enjoyed a presumption of possessing more "modern" knowledge, faculty members of foreign origin today must fight a perception that they will not know what is relevant in the fast-growing and rapidly evolving Chinese business environment of today. Between 70 and 75 percent of faculty recruited to join CEIBS are ethnically Chinese, though most come from positions at foreign (primarily Western) institutions. Many have work experience in China, though often not in the contemporary business environment. Thus, while seeking to recruit international faculty, the school also seeks to encourage its faculty members to engage in research projects of interest to Chinese businesses and that are relevant to the Chinese economic environment. These efforts are facilitated in part by numerous research centers, including the CEIBS Lujiazui International Finance Research Centre, the Centre of Chinese Private Enterprises, the China Centre for Financial Research, and the CEIBS Case Development Centre (established in 2001 with the vision to become "the most influential knowledge center of China-specific teaching cases in the world").[8]

Partnerships

CEIBS, like many other business schools, maintains several partnerships with other schools at varying levels of intensity. The school runs international exchange programs with universities in 19 countries. According to Cremer, the school selects exchange partners that will provide a "reasonable geographic spread" of options for students, as well as partners that align with students' values and interests. For example, an indication of growing student interest in studying at other Asian institutions has led CEIBS to begin evaluating additional options for student exchange within other Asian countries. International exchange programs are managed by an MBA International Affairs Manager.

Deeper collaborations, such as those that CEIBS maintains with Harvard Business School, IESE, and the Wharton School of the University of Pennsylvania, often have grown from relationships that were established

---

[8]China Europe International Business School, CEIBS Case Development Centre web page, 2010, electronic document, http://www.ceibs.edu/cases/centre/index.shtml, accessed December 29, 2010.

between faculty members with mutual research interests. These relationships often involve multiple levels of involvement and numerous individuals from the two schools, notes Cremer, such as faculty exchange, collaborative program delivery, and joint research efforts. Additionally, he notes that the deepest relationships are distinguished by an understanding between the schools that "quid pro quo is not a problem." In other words, he says, the schools exhibit a general attitude of support for each other's needs rather than keeping a detailed accounting of who has provided what to whom.

CEIBS co-develops and co-teaches executive education programs with Harvard Business School, IESE Business School, The Wharton School of the University of Pennsylvania, Tsinghua SEM, INSEAD, and Columbia Business School. Additionally, CEIBS jointly sponsors the CEO Learning Consortium, a series of roundtable conferences for graduates of the Global CEO Program for China, with the University of Michigan Ross School of Business. The CEIBS Case Development Center collaborates with numerous other business schools, including INSEAD, IMD, Wharton, and the University of Virginia's Darden Graduate School of Business Administration, to jointly develop cases specific to China and the Chinese business environment.

An Extension in Ghana

In April 2008, CEIBS announced plans to offer an EMBA program in Accra, Ghana.[9] One year later, the school admitted its first cohort of students into the program, which initially is hosting courses and administrative offices in rented space. A CEIBS professor native to Ghana, Kwaku Atuahene-Gima, was appointed to oversee the campus' development and has reported that plans for the campus include an expansion in the number of programs offered, as well as the establishment of a case-writing center to develop cases focused on the local African business context.[10] Courses will be taught by CEIBS' full-time faculty members, who will travel to Ghana for short periods, complemented by visiting faculty.

Cremer notes the parallels between the establishment of the Ghana program and the initial development of CEIBS, which was established by

---

[9]Bradshaw, Della, "Chinese school expands into African campus" *Financial Times,* April 6, 2008, electronic document, http://www.ft.com/cms/s/2/eaaedbb2-024c-11dd-9388-000077b07658. html, accessed August 23, 2009.

[10]Bradshaw, Della, "CEIBS inaugurates Ghana programme, *Financial Times,* May 19, 2009, electronic document, http://www.ft.com/cms/s/0/22f5d4e0-449f-11de-82d6-00144feabdc0, dwp_uuid = 87c504f8-2b20-11dc-85f9-000b5df10621.html, accessed August 23, 2009.

the Europeans in collaboration with the Chinese to support China's economic development and integration into the world's economy. Cremer says that this same process "has to happen in Africa as well," and that, given CEIBS' own beginnings, the school is particularly well-experienced in such an endeavor. At the same time, he also notes his own skepticism of foreign schools' abilities to deliver China-relevant management education in China, and he notes the irony that CEIBS is attempting to do the same in Ghana, though he sees CEIBS' role in Ghana more as one of development assistance. Cremer further notes that the experience has been valuable in that it has demonstrated that CEIBS can successfully manage development and delivery of its EMBA program in another country.

Outcomes

"Initially, CEIBS was set up as an international business school in China, with a clear, almost exclusive focus on the domestic market," notes Cremer. However, as the country in which the school is located has taken steps to become more integrated in the global economy, CEIBS has also changed its orientation. It has increased its recruitment of non-Chinese MBA students and established partnerships with universities in many parts of the world.

One might argue that globalization should be second nature to the school, given the unique circumstances of its establishment and the "international" nature of its governing bodies, faculty, and even funding. Cremer, however, credits the school's management committee with providing ongoing support for the globalization strategy and for maintaining a strategic focus on engaging in the most value-added activities. "I have some doubts as to whether all initiatives that carry the label 'global' are worth doing," he notes. "The costs of these activities are often underestimated, and the management distraction can be huge."

The school's globalization efforts so far, says Cremer, have had positive effects on the school's global reputation and day-to-day operations as well as on learning opportunities for both faculty and staff. He notes that CEIBS will need to continue to review whether its mission—with its strong domestic focus—is the right one for the school to serve. He also notes the strong regulatory environment of China, and the potential for the school to encounter legal constraints to the scope of its operations, for example, the introduction of new degree programs. Faculty constraints (such as limited resources and accreditation-related expectations) may also challenge the school's globalization efforts. At the same time, Cremer notes that CEIBS' autonomy and its international governance structure make the school well positioned to continue to evolve with the world around it.

DUKE UNIVERSITY, THE FUQUA SCHOOL OF BUSINESS

The Fuqua School of Business at Duke University has been working for the past 20 years to increase its international scope in terms of the knowledge created and transferred as well as the locations in which programs are delivered.[11] As aspects of the school's overall strategy have evolved, so has the school's array of degree programs and globally-oriented activities. Most recently, The Fuqua School of Business has begun a bold new initiative to become, in its own words, "the world's first legitimately global business school, based in the economic and cultural hubs of world regions."[12] Building on the lessons learned through the school's earlier activities, the "global campus" initiative involves campuses in five cities beyond the school's home campus in Durham, North Carolina (U.S.). Each campus is designed to support delivery of the school's degree programs, provide opportunities for faculty development, and serve some of the unique needs of the world region in which it is located.

Early Strategy Takes a Turn

Over its first eighteen years, The Fuqua School of Business gradually established itself by following what current dean Blair Sheppard terms a "resource-acquisition" strategy. As a new school, efforts were focused on bringing together the funding and the faculty members that would enable the school to compete with more established, reputable business schools. Strategy and decisions were based largely on what individual funders and faculty members wanted. The result, as noted during a strategic planning exercise conducted in 1988, was that the school had become a coherent and competitive deliverer of management education, but that its reputation was not as well-placed as it could or should have been.

---

[11]Each case study was prepared with the purpose of illustrating an interesting variation in approach to the globalization of management education. Inclusion in this report does not constitute an endorsement of this approach for all schools.

This case study was developed through conversations with Blair Sheppard (dean, The Fuqua School of Business, Duke University), review of a presentation by Sheppard at the AACSB 2009 Deans Conference, review of The Fuqua School of Business website, and review of accounts of the school's activities in press releases, periodicals, etc. Errors and omissions are the sole responsibility of the authors.

[12]Duke University, The Fuqua School of Business, International Locations web page, 2009, electronic document, http://www.fuqua.duke.edu/about/locations/, accessed June 29, 2009.

That strategic planning exercise marked a substantial turning point for The Fuqua School of Business. The goals of the exercise had been to examine three questions: where the world was going, the strengths and weaknesses of Fuqua, and the implications of these strengths and weaknesses on what the business school should do. From the corresponding analyses, three themes emerged that have served as the foundation for strategy development ever since:

1. The school's location in Durham, North Carolina, would continue to limit the school's efforts to enhance its international reputation; thus, the school necessarily needed to engage in efforts that would extend the campus borders beyond Durham.
2. Technology would continuously redefine how learning and research would be conducted.
3. The world itself was becoming increasingly international.

Launch of The Duke MBA—Global Executive Program

In the early 1990s, faculty and staff at the Fuqua School conceptualized a new MBA program model that would be branded as "the world's first global MBA program for senior executives."[13] Two main factors motivated the program development: a respect for existing executive education programs such as the Advanced Management Program offered at Harvard Business School, and awareness that merely replicating existing approaches could mean missed opportunities to tailor the program to the school's own strengths and to emerging trends such as technological advancements (e.g., the Internet) and globalization.

The Duke MBA—Global Executive program that emerged blended existing models for MBA and executive education and was launched in 1996. At the time, the school's faculty members had recently begun to undertake more proactive efforts to address research questions that were international in scope and to add more international content to the curriculum. The program model thus emphasized giving students the opportunities needed to a) understand cultural differences across regions, and b) to compare and contrast developed and developing parts of the world. To support the former, the program required students to attend

---

[13]Duke University, The Fuqua School of Business, Global Executive MBA web page, 2010, electronic document, http://www.fuqua.duke.edu/programs/duke_mba/global_executive/, accessed December 29, 2010.

short, residential classroom sessions on multiple continents. To support the latter, within each region, students would spend time in cities of varying stages of development. For example, students might have sessions in city pairs such as Tokyo and Shanghai, Moscow and Prague, or London and Frankfurt.

The choice of locations for these residential sessions often changed from year to year, originally for intellectual reasons as certain cities became more or less interesting, and then later based on the preferences of the program management staff according to both interest and ease of administration. Today, the program model has evolved to require students to complete a two-week residential classroom session in Asia, Europe, the Middle East and North America, though the actual locations within each region can vary slightly from year to year.

Lessons Learned

The Duke MBA—Global Executive Program. The school learned several lessons through the program's early years that influenced the strategy behind its recently launched efforts to develop a "global campus network."

First, the school learned that the program itself could not make the school more global or give it a more global brand. Over time, the school attracted more foreign faculty members, and faculty members conducted more research with an international focus. Greater numbers of foreign students began to enroll. The program was now being conveyed as a global program.

However, according to Sheppard, in many ways Fuqua remained a "southeastern U.S." school. The school discovered that, despite having faculty members with highly diverse ethnic, national, and cultural backgrounds, after some time at Fuqua, their perspectives and actions would begin to align with those of the traditional "southeastern American" population in Durham, North Carolina. Consequently, the mere fact that the school's faculty members had diverse backgrounds was not sufficient enough a qualification to create a faculty that would be "global" in the long term. Rather, the school believed that the faculty members would need to engage with other parts of the world on a more ongoing basis.

Second, while the often-annual changes in location for the various sessions of the program provided flexibility to the staff and the excitement of exploring different host cities, the changes also prevented the faculty and staff from maximizing the potential value of a given location. "You can't create a compelling experience on the ground if you don't know the place well enough," says Sheppard. The location changes discouraged faculty members from incorporating regional content into their courses because the lack of stability prevented that content from remaining a relevant component of the curriculum from year to year.

The location changes presented additional challenges for student recruitment and job placement, which relied heavily on the establishment of relationships within a community. The temporary nature of the school's presence in each location did not create the conditions necessary to develop those relationships. These challenges extended beyond the Global Executive MBA to the school's Daytime MBA, in which international student participation had grown tremendously. As the school sought more effective ways to support international student recruitment and job placement, the need was evident for a more permanent infrastructure that would enable the development of deeper relationships.

Frankfurt. The early years of Fuqua's international activities included another initiative to offer an MBA program in Frankfurt, Germany. The program, initiated in the late 1990s, had been started through an agreement with a major German firm. The firm had agreed to underwrite the risk of the program, assist in locating students, and find individuals to serve on a program advisory board.

The program, which had relatively steady enrollments of just over 30 students, did not grow as expected, though the student profile did change substantially—from nearly all students sponsored by corporations to almost none. Sheppard interprets this decline as a sign that the program had become self-sufficient, as it no longer relied on the German firm to recruit corporate-sponsored students, and he believes that student numbers would have continued to remain steady or grown.

At the same time, the contributions and influence of the German firm partner were viewed as both positive and negative by the school. In addition to underwriting the risk of the program, the firm also provided substantial assistance to Fuqua in dealing with immigration and tax issues related to the cross-border program delivery. Sheppard notes that one lesson learned from this experience was that the school would need thoughtful people from corporations to help the school succeed in diverse regions. At the same time, the two parties' aspirations for the program began to diverge. Fuqua wished the program to be viewed as a European program, located in the center of Europe. To program administrators, however, the heavy influence of the German firm was making the program a distinctly German offering, more in line with the German model of education.

In the end, program administrators decided that the program did not merit continuing investment, in part because of the lack of growth, but also because of a growing sense that Frankfurt would not in the long term be an ideal base for the school's future activities in Europe.

Looking to London as an alternative, and with a thought to Fuqua's emphasis on corporate education, the school aimed to repackage its European program. In 2003, Duke Corporate Education (CE) entered into a joint venture with the London School of Economics and Political Science's commercial subsidiary, LSE Enterprise, the second largest corporate education provider in Europe. The agreement now supports delivery of corporate education to Duke CE's European corporate clients.

A Portfolio of International Programs

Over time, The Fuqua School of Business has built a portfolio of programs and courses with an international dimension, some of which are outlined below.

The Duke MBA—Global Executive MBA Program: Duke's Global Executive MBA was launched in 1996 and is oriented toward senior executives with a minimum of 10 years of work experience. Beginning with the class entering in the summer of 2010, students begin and end the program in Durham, North Carolina and complete two-week residential sessions in each of three pairs of cities: London and St. Petersburg, New Delhi and Dubai, and Shanghai/Kunshan & Singapore.

The Duke MBA—Cross Continent Program: The Cross Continent MBA program was launched in 2000, intending to build on the strengths of the Global Executive MBA program but targeted at a younger demographic of junior and middle managers rather than senior executives. Beginning with the class admitted in the fall of 2009, students complete a two-week residency in China and four nine-day residencies in India, Russia, the U.A.E., and the U.K. – taking advantage of space established through the school's newly established global campus network. Students then finish their program with a two-week residency in Durham, North Carolina where they take their elective courses.

Opportunities for both Daytime MBA and Weekend Executive MBA students include the following:

Global Institute: The Global Institute is a three-week intensive program that takes place at the beginning of the Daytime and Weekend Executive MBA programs. It is designed to significantly increase students' global awareness and understanding as they enter the MBA program through two core courses: Leadership, Ethics and Organizations; and Global Institutions and Environments.

Global Academic Travel Experience (GATE): GATE courses are three-credit elective courses in which students study the business, culture, economy, and politics of a country or region for six weeks before traveling to the area studied. The travel portion of the course is typically 12 days in length and involves visits to multinational corporations, local enterprises, government agencies, exchange program partner schools, alumni, and/or others in the region.

Opportunities limited to Daytime MBA students include the following:

Global Consulting Practicum (GCP): GCP is a three-credit elective course in which students, working in teams under faculty supervision, learn about, visit, and engage in a consulting role with social entrepreneurs and businesses serving base-of-the-pyramid markets in developing countries.

Global Independent Study (GIS): GIS is any independent study which involves travel outside the United States. Projects are designed and initiated by Daytime MBA students who may take up to six credits of independent study as part of his/her program.

Focused Industry Topic (FIT): FIT courses are elective courses similar to GATE courses (see above). Students study and travel to a specific region, but they focus on a particular industry sector such as Energy and the Environment.

Student Exchange: Daytime MBA students have opportunities to take courses toward degree completion at one of over 40 partner institutions.

Duke CE also has offices for the delivery of customized executive education programs in Durham, North Carolina; Johannesburg, South Africa; London, England; New York, New York; San Diego, California; and Ahmedabad, India. Sheppard was the founder and first CEO of Duke CE, and he remains its Chairman of the Board.

Forming a New Approach: The Foundations of the Global Campus Network

As described above, Fuqua had for many years been building its international involvement, a global network of relationships, and an orientation of faculty research toward the international landscape. Under the leadership of Sheppard (who became dean in 2007), Fuqua adopted a new strategy intended to not only tie together the school's international activities, but to provide a broader, permanent, international infrastructure to support all aspects of the school's operations and to fulfill a vision of making Fuqua "the world's first legitimately global business school."[14]

According to Sheppard, the school's strategy also reflects a belief that globalization reflects the trend that the world is becoming not only increasingly interdependent but also increasingly multi-plex. The strategy

---

[14]Duke University, The Fuqua School of Business, About Fuqua web page, 2009, electronic document, http://www.fuqua.duke.edu/about/, accessed June 29, 2009.

does not assume that globalization will lead all countries of the world to adopt the same set of rules. Related to this assumption are three principles that, according to Sheppard, form a foundation for the school's new strategy: 1) embed and connect; 2) recognize diversity/interdependence; and 3) try, learn quickly from mistakes, and adapt.

The first principle on which the school's new approach is based is one of both embedding within and connecting multiple regions. The idea is that the school will strive to meet the unique needs of each region while also facilitating connections and transferability between regions.

Related to the first principle is the second principle, recognition of the juxtaposition of diversity and interdependence. This principle, says Sheppard, is based on a Jeffersonian notion that significant nuances or differences are unique to various parts of the world, and these require adaptation that truly acknowledges the diversity across countries and regions. According to Sheppard, this principle is based in part on the lessons learned from the early years of the Global Executive MBA program, which he says were "too closely tied to home."

The third principle is one of continuous, strategic experimentation and improvement. According to Sheppard, the program in Frankfurt and the Global Executive MBA program were both "adaptation stories," or programs that were modified to varying extents as circumstances required.

Applying the principle of embeddedness within regions required investigation to determine what types of activities and approaches were necessary and important. Rather than ask whether a market existed in the country for the school's current products, the principle instead required that administrators ask how the school could be a good "citizen" of a given country in such a way that the surrounding community would see the value in its presence. This inquiry meant that the school needed to be open to the substantial modification of existing products or to the development of new products, policies, and approaches. It also required that program leaders ask how the school's engagement in that community would have a lasting, positive impact on faculty and staff.

Fuqua has approached this analysis by repeatedly asking small, diverse sets of citizens in each country how the school could be a helpful presence. In India, for example, one of the themes that emerged from these conversations was a need for better-trained human capital at entry-level positions. This finding has led the school to consider a focus on pre-experience programs as well as possibilities for extending its Talent Identification Program that is aimed at students of primary and secondary education programs.

To apply the principle of connecting across regions, the school had to consider the ways in which areas of focus in one region (for teaching, research, and service) are transferable or complementary to others. For example, research that is focused on how to scale small businesses in South Africa, in order to build a sustainable middle class, might also be applied in other similar contexts such as Russia, the Middle East, and India. These connections would require structures and processes that enable the transfer of ideas from one region to another and the comparison and contrast of experiences as well as the subsequent adaptation of approaches based on what is learned.

One way that the school intends to facilitate these connections is through the new models for its Cross-Continent MBA and Global Executive MBA programs. For example, as faculty in each of the functional areas (marketing, finance, management, etc.) work to increase the global content of their courses, each group of faculty members will bring a particular focus on one or two world regions. As a result, students may take marketing courses in one of two locations, financial courses in one of two other locations, etc. These curricular enhancements will also be incorporated into the Daytime MBA and Weekend Executive MBA programs.

Several strategies and priorities of Duke University, encompassing all of the university's colleges and schools, also form a foundation for the approaches described above. First, globalization is a university priority, so Fuqua benefits from university support for undertaking initiatives that increase the international nature of education and research. Second, Duke University has placed an emphasis on multi-scholasticism, or the merging of two different disciplinary areas. In each region where Fuqua establishes one of its global campuses, it will collaborate with at least two other schools from the university (for example, offering a dual Master's degree in Management and in Public Policy, in collaboration with Duke's Sanford School of Public Policy). Often these collaborations are a direct response to local feedback regarding the specific needs to address in each country.

Building the Global Campus Network

Fuqua formally announced plans for its new "global campus" in September 2008. The plan initially called for development of six new campuses—in China, India, Russia, South Africa, the U.A.E., and the U.K.—to support the school's MBA programs, corporate education, executive education, research, and community outreach.

Market Selection.   According to Sheppard, the decisions to establish other campuses in Dubai, London, New Delhi, Shanghai, and St. Petersburg were made because they are the places "where you have to be to become part of the future in a significant way."[15] He classifies the approach as very deliberate and intellectual as opposed to opportunistic (which, in Sheppard's opinion, may work in the short term but is often an inadequate basis for long-term endeavors).

Based on the school's analysis, a focus on these five countries as the regions in which it was interested in establishing campuses came rather easily, but little determination at that point had been given to where and how the school would establish campuses within each country. Instead, the school took the risk of declaring its intention to operate in each country with the hope that it would be in a better position to locate the right partner(s). In fact, when the partnership with St. Petersburg State University's Graduate School of Management was announced in August 2008, school officials indicated that one of the remaining four partnerships would be revealed in each following month. However, the attention generated by the announcement revealed new possibilities for partnerships that had not been previously known, and the school substantially scaled back its timeline for announcing the additional partnerships while it considered other options.[16]

Market Entry. When Duke first contemplated the global campus network, its original plan was to partner with leading institutions in each of the key geographic areas identified. However, that strategy evolved to a more hybrid approach that would be open to partnerships not just with leading educational institutions, but also with individuals, municipalities, and organizations. In particular, according to Sheppard, these non-educational partners would be considered if the partner had greater assets than potential university partners, specifically assets "including large amounts of money, political connections and general ability to facilitate entry."[17]

When the school began to explore entry strategies, its awareness of local regulations and social/cultural norms was essential, so as to avoid an approach that would be illegal or considered inappropriate by the local community. Thus, in India, the school learned it would be most effective to work through alumni, whereas in China, the school developed its strategy

---

[15]Damast, Alison, "Duke Rethinks Idea of a Global Campus," *BusinessWeek*, September 15, 2008, electronic document, http://www.businessweek.com/bschools/content/sep2008/bs20080914_756410.htm?chan = bschools_bschool + index + page_the + education + business, accessed June 29, 2009.

[16]Love, Julia, "Globetrotting: Fuqua's Global Journey," *The Duke University Chronicle*, January 28, 2009, electronic document, http://dukechronicle.com/node/148142, accessed June 29, 2009.

[17]Sheppard, Blair, Santiago Iniguez de Onzono, and James W. Dean Jr., "Alliances and Global Collaboration," presentation at AACSB International Deans Conference, San Francisco, California, February 5, 2009.

through numerous interactions with municipal/provincial leaders. In Russia, collaboration with a partner school proved most effective.

In each region, a set of regional advisory boards and an overarching and overlapping board of visitors helps guide the school's entry and strategy. According to Sheppard, these advisory boards have been very helpful, especially in regions such as India and East Asia. Many advisory board members are representatives of corporations with a major regional or international presence. Sheppard believes that corporate support is essential to the success of the global campus network, but the support must be broader than that of a single firm, and it must be oriented toward the needs of the campus' host city/region rather than the needs of a single firm.

Faculty and Staff. The school anticipates that integration of faculty into the global campus network will occur over three phases, of which the school is currently in transition between the first and second.

In the first phase, the faculty network projected primarily from its "home base" in Durham, North Carolina. The school made an effort to ensure that a significant percent of faculty members based in Durham spent time engaging in other regions—delivering courses or conducting research. The primary objectives of this phase were to globalize the school's operating/ intellectual model and to globalize the curriculum model.

The second phase of implementation will involve adding faculty members in more permanent roles at each of the campus locations in order to form a sustainable core in each region. To do so, the school has focused on hiring individuals from regional diasporas who have a desire to return to their home region but who do not want to give up a tenured faculty position to do so. The final stage of the evolution is intended to strike a balance between a regional focus and cross-regional integration. In this stage, Sheppard foresees faculty members with a "heavy foot" in one region, and a "light foot" in either Durham or one of the other host regions.

Staff support in each region will consist initially of three or four permanently placed individuals serving as a regional director, program manager(s), and a regional assistant. The intent is to have enough staff in each location to provide day-to-day support for operations and strategic development but also to retain dependency on the core staff located in Durham in order to ensure that the campuses function as parts of a network rather than as independent entities.

Funding. Sheppard estimates that the establishment of the global campuses requires an ongoing $125 million operating budget. The university does not provide financial support for the program; instead, funding is expected to come from successful operations in each region, the business school, or from other sources in the various regions. So far, the school has successfully secured funding to cover the construction of all needed structures. Sheppard attributes this achievement to the school's ability to convey a genuine desire to be a "good citizen" of each region, to work collectively with local stakeholders, and to truly be embedded within the region. The main funding challenges that remain concern the management of cash flow to ensure the availability of funds for operating costs and working capital.

Outcomes

Fuqua's ambitious vision of creating a global campus network has already gained significant media attention as well as attention from prospective students and regional organizations that call the new Fuqua locations home. While the effects of the Fuqua "global campus" initiative will doubtless take time to be fully realized, the initiative is likely to continue to serve as a learning experience both for Fuqua and for those individuals who are monitoring the initiative's outcomes.

ESSEC BUSINESS SCHOOL PARIS-SINGAPORE

For decades, ESSEC Business School has taken a series of successive steps, some small and some large, to increase its international orientation, relevancy, and reputation.[18] The school has expanded its global footprint from two campuses in and near Paris, France, to include a physical presence in Singapore. It has adopted objectives for the recruitment of internationally representative students and faculty, and it has invested in the strategies necessary to achieve these objectives. Basic-level partnerships with other schools have expanded and, when appropriate, have been cultivated to form deeper relationships that provide new opportunities for students and faculty to cross borders, physically and intellectually. A focus on creating value through synergies—both among existing resources and through partnerships with other schools with similar values and complementary capabilities—has guided the approach.

Development of ESSEC-Singapore

When Pierre Tapie joined ESSEC as the school's president in 2001, he joined a school that already had a substantial level of involvement in Asia. Since 1984, the school had operated a permanent office in Japan. Through this office, ESSEC coordinated student and faculty exchanges and assisted students who sought internships with Japanese firms. As of 2008, ESSEC students have participated in more than 1,100 internships in Japan.[19] The school also has maintained long-standing partnerships with numerous institutions in Japan, China, South Korea, India, and Singapore. Through these partnerships and other activities—which primarily involved faculty and student exchanges, the delivery of executive education, and some

---

[18]Each case study was prepared with the purpose of illustrating an interesting variation in approach to the globalization of management education. Inclusion in this report does not constitute an endorsement of this approach for all schools.

This case study was developed through conversations and e-mail correspondence with Pierre Tapie (Groupe ESSEC president), review of a presentation by Tapie at the AACSB World Class Practices Conference in Beijing (2007), review of the ESSEC Business School website, and review of accounts of the school's activities in press releases, periodicals, etc. Errors and omissions are the sole responsibility of the authors.

[19]ESSEC Business School and Keio University, "ESSEC Business School & Keio Business School launch a MBA-level dual degree program," press release, September 12, 2008, electronic document, http://econtent.essec.fr/mediabanks/ESSEC-PDF/Actualites/CP_2008/CP_Keio_ ANG .pdf, accessed August 31, 2009.

collaborative research—the faculty and staff at ESSEC has included numerous individuals with Asian connections and experiences.

Tapie himself arrived with a strong conviction that Asia was a region of the world that needed to be incorporated within the minds and strategic thinking of those at ESSEC. He launched a series of "missionary trips" to Hong Kong, Shanghai, Tokyo, and Singapore during which small teams of key administrators and faculty explored each location and began to develop a corresponding business plan. Meanwhile, the Singapore government had reached out to ESSEC as part of its intention, announced in 1997, to attract 10 "world-class" higher education institutions to set up shop in Singapore within 10 years, in addition to the investment made in the three local universities.

After two years of assessment and business plan development, the dean presented the ESSEC Board of Directors with a proposal that a) ESSEC open a campus in Asia and b) the new campus should be located in Singapore. The selection of Singapore as the most ideal location for the new campus was based on several factors. First, as a melting pot of a variety of Asian and other cultures, Singapore was ethnically diverse. Second, the stability of the Singaporean government and regulations made the country an attractive setting for a long-term initiative of the scale that ESSEC was anticipating. Third, the location's easy accessibility and connectivity to other parts of Asia would lessen the burden of travel between the Paris and Singapore campuses as well as between the Singapore campus and other parts of Asia. Finally, though not a major reason for the selection of Singapore, the Singapore Economic Development Board (EDB) offered some funds toward initial costs of the initiative, which reduced the financial risk of the investment. The ESSEC Board accepted the proposal in the spring of 2004.

A dean of the Singapore campus was appointed, and he began working full-time in Singapore in September 2004. Beginning in early 2005, the ESSEC Asian Center began receiving students and faculty in temporary space while construction on the new building for the Singapore National Library, where ESSEC had secured space, was completed. The new campus was officially launched in October 2005. By 2009, the Center had educated 1,530 students and participants.

Broadening Support for the Decision

While the reasons for the decision to open a Singapore campus had been widely communicated and generally supported, Tapie observed that individual faculty members developed their own perceptions of the "true" reasons behind the initiative based on their own experiences. The diversity of geopolitical perceptions among what was believed to be a rather international team of faculty and staff became apparent as a substantial rift emerged between those individuals who had strong convictions about ESSEC's Asia initiative and were enthusiastic about supporting the new campus and those for whom Asia remained a distant, strange place.

To broaden support for the initiative and ensure a widespread understanding of the complementary roles played by the Singapore and Paris campuses, Tapie initiated a plan to send teams of faculty and staff from the Paris campus on "learning expeditions" to Singapore and other parts of Asia, also providing the opportunity to visit longstanding academic partners in the area. Still ongoing, each trip enables approximately 25 faculty and staff (representing all academic departments and staff support areas) to "discover very intensively and free of charge another continent or area." The expeditions have been enthusiastically embraced, and the result, according to Tapie, has been "transformational." He believes the expeditions have provided one of the best returns on investment during his tenure as dean.

As of September 2009, the Singapore campus became home to a "core" support team of 10 faculty members and approximately 12 to 15 staff members. Faculty members based in Singapore are selected as a function of the school's need for expertise in various disciplinary areas, as well as the faculty members' willingness to live and work in Singapore. Some faculty members are based in Singapore for long-term, unlimited periods; others are semi-permanent, spending between one and three years at the campus. Newly hired faculty members at the Paris campuses are hired with the understanding that they will spend time at the Singapore campus. Faculty at the Singapore campus, regardless of whether they have permanent or semi-permanent status, are encouraged to spend between one and three months at the Paris campus. This movement between campuses facilitates opportunities for faculty to socialize with their colleagues and share ideas, and it helps create the feeling of a single faculty body across locations.

Faculty who travel to the Singapore campus to teach are compensated at a level that Tapie says is attractive, but fair, compared to their other colleagues. He strongly believes that he must send a message that all faculty, regardless of the campus at which they are based, are compensated fairly. Singapore's location within Asia is also appealing for many reasons, and thus compensation does not need to serve as the sole incentive that entices faculty members to go there.

The Role of the Singapore Campus Today

Courses offered at the Singapore campus are a combination of courses from the standard ESSEC catalog as well as those distinctly oriented to focus on the Asian business, economic, and cultural environment. Students enrolled in ESSEC's MBA, MS in Strategy and Management of International Business, or MS in Financial Techniques have the option of pursuing an "Asian track," thereby completing approximately half of their courses at the Singapore campus. The campus also serves as a partner campus for the ESSEC-Mannheim EMBA program, hosting students for two-week residencies as well as for learning expeditions for other Paris-based programs (especially the advanced master's programs).

In addition to providing support for degree programs, the Singapore campus hosts custom executive education courses and programs for managers in Asia, hosts seminars and conferences on special topics, and provides a base location to support faculty research in the Asian region. After just five years of operations, it now hosts a total of 400 students per year. The opening of the Singapore campus has, according to Tapie, increased international awareness of ESSEC and its programs even more than had been initially anticipated.

International Student Recruitment

Another key aspect of ESSEC's globalization strategy is to place an emphasis on international student recruitment. Launched in the spring of 2004, ESSEC's current platform for international recruitment includes a full-time team of 12 staff members located at ESSEC's main campus in France and in local recruitment offices in India, South Korea, China, Japan, and Brussels. Locations for the satellite offices were chosen based on analyses of demographic trends and indications of an expanding potential student population in the surrounding region. The satellite offices establish relationships with local schools and otherwise seek to reach the local student population. Their efforts are reinforced by support from staff members in France who assist with the planning of big recruitment fairs and presentations. The effects of the initiative are clear. In the 2003–04 academic year, 550 of 3,600 students (15 percent) were from countries other than France. By 2009–10, the student population itself had grown to 4,200, of which 1,350 (32 percent) were international. The vast majority of international students study at the master's level.

The school's targeted international recruitment efforts have been enhanced by recent changes in French policy that have made the country more appealing to foreign students who hope to find employment within the country upon graduation. ESSEC's leaders were active, through efforts led by the Conférence des Grandes Ecoles (an association of the leading French business and engineering schools), in influencing government policy makers to adopt new laws in 2006 that enabled foreign master's-level students to remain in the country for up to six months upon graduation in order to seek full-time employment (meeting a minimum standard of qualifications and salary) and that provided assurance that a working visa would be provided if such a job opportunity should arise.

The motivations behind the international student recruitment platform and the institution's emphasis on attracting foreign students are grounded in the philosophy that student diversity encourages reciprocal learning experiences. By proactively seeking to diversify the mix of students across a variety of dimensions (including industry background), ESSEC aims to enrich both the academic and nonacademic learning experiences of the students during their time at the school.

Faculty Recruitment

In recent years, ESSEC has also increased the priority it places on the international diversity of its faculty. Of the 45 new faculty members hired by ESSEC in the past four years, 32 have originated outside France, resulting in the current total of 57 faculty out of 135 that are of non-French origin. The school's 57 international faculty members represent 33 nationalities, with no more than four from any one country. The diversity of the faculty has accelerated the intercultural dimensions of the school's research and has created new opportunities for connections to other universities (and their faculty) that otherwise likely would not have existed. ESSEC complements its international faculty recruitment efforts by assigning dedicated staff to provide the services and support needed to help foreign faculty members integrate into the school's culture and environment.

Pedagogy/Content

ESSEC's portfolio of degree programs reflects the school's international focus. The MBA IMHI (MBA/Masters in International Hospitality Management) was established in 1981, in partnership with Cornell University, and since that time, several programs have been added with a strong international focus (e.g., the MS in international supply management, international food industry management, international business law and management, and strategy and management of international business) as well programs offered abroad through collaborative agreements with other schools. The MBA in International Luxury Brand Management, in particular, has been a powerful vector for globalization since 1995, with the proportion of international students in the program varying between 80 and

95 percent. The Executive MBA, launched in 1994, has been developed in different formats through a partnership with the University of Mannheim. The BBA program also involves a substantial international dimension in its courses, requiring each student to spend at least one full year in a partner institution or company internship abroad before graduating. The PhD in Business Administration, developed with international standards, attracts a majority of international students (93 percent in the last recruited cohort).

Faculty members are under strong pressure to show pedagogical innovation and to regenerate courses from one year to the next. Financial support, an extensive network of international faculty connections, and a culture that encourages and fosters an international orientation all provide support for efforts to represent more internationally diverse case studies, examples, and perspectives into the curriculum.

ESSEC also places a high priority on multilingualism among its students. As early as the 1960s, approximately 60 percent of business students were also studying foreign languages.[20] Today, MBA students are expected to demonstrate proficiency in three languages, and undergraduate students are expected to demonstrate proficiency in four languages.

Additionally, all students of MBA and BBA programs are required to have an international experience that lasts at least nine months. This experience can take the form of an internship, an academic exchange, a dual-degree program, or a humanitarian mission.

The format of the PhD program was recently restructured to be more international in scope and more internationally accessible. The new program, created in 2006 and offered solely in English, involves two years of full-time classes preceding two years of dissertation work and combines both French and Western European characteristics. Ninety percent of students are of international origin; within just three years of its inception, applications to the program had risen to more than a 500 per year, for only 20 seats.

Partnerships

Over the years, ESSEC has developed an extensive portfolio of partnerships and strategic alliances with business schools in other countries and regions. The partnerships represent a variety of activities and, accordingly, various levels of commitment by the partner schools.

---

[20]Steinborn, Deborah, "ESSEC Wins High Marks," *Wall Street Journal*, September 17, 2007, electronic document, http://online.wsj.com/article/SB118999998309629531.html?mod=googlewsj, accessed August 31, 2009.

All decisions to partner with another school, regardless of the level of the partnership, are based on two primary assessments: the quality of students and the quality of faculty. The information needed to make this assessment at a confidence level appropriate for a basic-level partnership, says Tapie, is relatively easy to obtain. Over time, the experiences of the two schools working together foster a reciprocal learning process that enables both schools to assess the appropriateness of additional levels of engagement.

For ESSEC, the least risky and costly partnerships are those that solely support student exchange. ESSEC currently has 80 student exchange agreements for students in MBA and MS programs. Undergraduate (EPSCI BBA) students may choose from exchange opportunities with 70 universities. These partnerships support ESSEC's requirement that all undergraduate and graduate students spend time abroad, either on an internship, a university exchange, a double-degree program, or a humanitarian mission.

When the research priorities of ESSEC and the research interests of its faculty also converge with the same elements at another institution, collaborative research opportunities are presented. As mentioned before, the international recruitment of faculty has been a major factor that has helped create research connections between ESSEC and other schools. At times, these are ad hoc relationships between individual faculty members; at other times, the relationships become more institutionalized and contribute to a deeper connection between the two schools. Initiatives such as the opening of the Asian office in Japan in the 1980s and the subsequent Singapore campus in 2005 were designed, in part, to support collaborative faculty research on topics of relevance to the Asian region.

In partnership with a relatively small number of foreign institutions, ESSEC has extended its level of engagement to offer dual-degree programs for its students. Undergraduate-level dual degrees are available through seven of the university's partner schools, and graduate-level dual degrees are available through eight partner schools.[21] The most recently developed dual-degree program is a dual-MBA degree from ESSEC and Keio University in Japan, which was launched in September 2008 and began in September 2009. ESSEC has made a point to engage with schools of elite reputations in their region for these dual-degree programs in order to ensure that students are provided outstanding learning opportunities in a similarly demanding, rigorous program.

---

[21]Nanyang Technological University (Singapore), University of Mannheim (Germany), IIM-Ahmedabad (India), Seoul National University, GSIS and GSB (South Korea), Peking University, Guanghua School of Management (China), Tecnológico de Monterrey-EGADE (Mexico), and Keio University (Japan).

Strategic Alliances

In particular, years of building collaborations and a strong convergence of goals and priorities has led to relationships with three schools that ESSEC views as "strategic alliances." These alliances with the University of Mannheim (Germany), the Indian Institute of Management (IIM)-Ahmedabad (India), and Keio University (Japan) involve a variety of activities and the highest level of commitment by ESSEC and the partner institution toward the achievement of mutual goals.

For example, the long-term vision driving the alliance between ESSEC and Mannheim is to create a European academic institution with a global vision. However the vision and the alliance to achieve it were not created overnight. The seed for the alliance was planted in the early 1980s when the two institutions agreed to facilitate student exchanges. The growing strength of the exchange program evolved into the delivery of a dual-degree program in 1992, the development of a European Research Center to facilitate faculty exchange and collaborative research, collaboration between the two schools and Warwick Business School to offer a European MBA in 2002, and finally in 2003, the formation of the strategic alliance. Today, the two schools also jointly offer an Executive MBA program with courses in Mannheim, Cergy-Pontoise, and Singapore. The alliances with Keio University and IIM-Ahmedabad similarly emerged from many years of growing engagement, mutual esteem, and trust.

Building a Portfolio of Options

Overall, the portfolio of partnerships enables ESSEC to offer substantial variety to students who seek international experiences as part of their degree programs. For example, the Advanced Master's degree in Strategy and Management of International Business offers students seven "tracks" to choose from. Two of the seven tracks enable the degree program to be completed entirely at ESSEC's Cergy-Pontoise campus, but with courses either all in English or in a mix of English and French. Students on the American, Latin American, or Canadian track take half of their courses at the Cergy-Pontoise campus and half at a partner institution in the respective region (Thunderbird School of Global Management, Tecnológico de Monterrey-EGADE, and Queen's University, respectively). Participants in the 50 percent Asian track take half of their courses at ESSEC's Cergy-Pontoise campus and half at the Singapore campus, while students in the 100 percent Asian track take two-thirds of their courses at ESSEC's Singapore campus and one-third at Nanyang Technological University. Thus, ESSEC is able to provide "custom" variations of an existing program that meet varied student interests for study in a particular world region while at the same time benefiting from the local/regional expertise of faculty in its partner schools.

Reflecting on the network of partnerships that ESSEC has developed, Tapie underscores the importance of taking small, successive steps toward building an overall mix of collaborations that supports the mission of the school and adds value where needed. ESSEC's partnership arrangements have been successful, says Tapie, because they have been based on the gradual building of mutual esteem, trust, and, even more important, a growing confidence between the partners in their shared values and objectives. He remarks that not all schools have the shared values, objectives, and complementary capabilities that would support strategic alliances at the level of ESSEC's relationships with Mannheim, IIM-Ahmedabad, and Keio, adding that relationships of that level are themselves self-limiting because of the substantial commitment involved.

Additionally, Tapie notes that this approach has not insulated the school from challenges. Among the challenges the schools in the alliances have been faced with are the influences of different environments (e.g., different governmental priorities, organizational constraints, academic formats, and internal processes). The schools have had to address differences in faculty models (e.g., the status of full professors) and differences in faculty salaries, as well as varying levels of financial resources. However, the institutions' shared belief in a mutual goal, and the mutual esteem and trust acquired over a long-term relationship, enabled them to work through those issues successfully.

International Accreditation

The process of seeking international accreditation has done much to enhance ESSEC's international awareness and to provide a means for ESSEC to benchmark itself against other well-known international business schools. Since becoming the first school outside of North America to be accredited by AACSB (in 1997), ESSEC has experienced increased visibility on the international scene, according to Tapie. Reciprocally, the accreditation has enabled ESSEC to be very knowledgeable of, but also influential in, various important networks that shape business school environments globally.

Looking Ahead

Few major changes are planned to the school's international strategy in the near future. So far, says Tapie, the school's "triple strategy of internationalization, raising quality, and increasing intensity has increased finances, human capital, and reputation simultaneously," and the school and its stakeholders are content with those outcomes. Thus, the goal for ESSEC going forward will be to enhance its recent improvements "in a sustainable way," and to continue to accelerate growth of the Singapore campus. Additionally, Tapie foresees that, as more and more business schools increase their own international activities, ESSEC will seek to leverage its traditional values of innovation and humanism as "*the* characteristic institutional identity*" that differentiates it from other institutions with a global reputation.

Guidance regarding the school's international activities is provided by an International Advisory Board created in May 2006 and is comprised of world-class figures from academia, politics, and economics. This consultative committee is charged with "examining strategic decisions taken by ESSEC in terms of education and development, anticipating the needs of the business world, and planning pedagogical innovations in response to these needs."

Tapie also adds that the school consistently tries to remain open to new possibilities, even if the initial reaction to an idea is that it could never work. He says that a private school that is interested in innovation must "dare to risk on experimental mode—even without complete consensus," but must know full well that the glory of a successful initiative is shared with everyone, while a failed initiative will likely be viewed as entirely one's own.

FUNDAÇÃO GETULIO VARGAS-SÃO PAULO, ESCOLA DE ADMINISTRAÇÃO DE EMPRESAS DE SÃO PAULO (FGV-EAESP)

The Escola de Administração de Empresas de São Paulo (FGV-EAESP) is a private school affiliated with the Fundação Getulio Vargas, which is headquartered in Rio de Janeiro and which maintains five other schools and five strategic units.[22] Though some other schools/units also focus on management education and/or research, most are relatively autonomous; the focus of this case study is restricted to EAESP.[23]

EAESP was founded in 1954 with the support of the Brazilian government and business community and the assistance of faculty members from Michigan State University (United States). It was one of several schools in the second half of the 20th century to be developed with financial assistance from the United States Agency for International Development (USAID).[24] USAID, as part of its commitment to help create the first business school in Brazil, provided financial support for the building. A team of Michigan State University faculty members remained in Brazil for the first 12 years of the school's operation.

Since its founding, the school's strategy has changed from having an almost sole emphasis on the local business environment to having an increasing emphasis on being a global player in the management education industry, primarily through linkages with partner institutions abroad. In particular, given the school's presence in Brazil (one of the so-called "BRICs economies"[25]), the school has committed to the study of emerging markets,

---

[22]Each case study was prepared with the purpose of illustrating an interesting variation in approach to the globalization of management education. Inclusion in this report does not constitute an endorsement of this approach for all schools.

This case study was developed through conversations and email correspondence with Maria Tereza Fleury (dean, FGV-EAESP) and Ligia Maura Costa (associate dean, International Programs, FGV-EAESP), review of the FGV-EAESP website, and review of accounts of the school's activities in press releases, periodicals, etc. Errors and omissions are the sole responsibility of the authors.

[23]Other schools include: Escola de Economia de São Paulo (EESP), Escola de Direito de São Paulo (EDESP), Escola Brasileira de Administração Pública e de Empresas (EBAPE), Escola de Direito de Rio de Janeiro (DIREITO RIO), and Escola de Pós-Graduação em Economia (EPGE). Strategic units include: EDITORA, Centro de Pesquisa e Documentação de História Contemporânea do Brasil (CPDOC), Instituto Brasileiro de Economia (IBRE), Instituto de Desenvolvimento Educacional (IDE), and FGV PROJETOS.

[24]USAID was not officially established until 1961; the funding for FGV was through one of its predecessor organizations.

[25]The BRICs economies are generally understood to include Brazil, Russia, India, and China.

thus placing its focus on the local environment within a broader global context.

Globalization Strategy

The following policy guidelines lead the school's globalization efforts:

- Expand, without compromising quality, the partner network, seeking broad geographical coverage to represent different cultures, business atmospheres, and economic realities;
- Engage in international strategic alliances with top schools for joint projects and degrees;
- Preserve its local, national, and regional identity;
- Provide a friendly and high-quality interface for leading international schools that envision the establishment of joint projects that include a Brazilian, a Latin American, and a BRICS component; and
- Establish itself as the leading business school in Brazil, providing world-class quality education from its main campus located in a meaningful node of the global network (the City of São Paulo).[26]

The school's globalization efforts began in 1975, when FGV-EAESP became a member of the Partnership in International Management (PIM), a global business school consortium. The PIM network facilitates benchmarking among member schools and provides a foundation for student and faculty exchanges, joint programs, and other collaborative initiatives among members. In the case of FGV-EAESP, the network also facilitated relationships with other schools that would evolve to include dual-degree programs. Since joining PIM, FGV-EAESP has established double-degree programs with four other PIM members: HEC Paris (France), University of Texas at Austin (U.S.), Universidade Nova de Lisboa (Portugal), and Universidad Torcuato di Tella (Argentina). According to Associate Dean Ligia Maura Costa, the school would agree to engage in a dual-degree program with another school only after having cultivated a relationship with the school over many years.

In 1998, the school established an International Relations Office (CRI) to support its goal to expand the number of partner schools around the world,

[26]Fleury, Maria Tereza, personal interview, March 20, 2009. The "BRICS component" refers to the school's participation in the Association of BRICS Business Schools (ABBS), which includes select business schools in the emerging BRICs economies as well as South Africa.

with a focus on student exchanges. Soon after, in 2001, FGV-EAESP became an associate academic member of CEMS, a global alliance of business schools and corporations that offers a dual-degree program for select students from its member schools and also serves as a foundation for other collaborative initiatives.

Outcomes from Participation in the CEMS Alliance

The CEMS Alliance's Master's in International Management degree program is offered by the community of the consortium's full academic members as a dual-degree program. (As an associate member, FGV-EAESP was able to send students to other schools in the CEMS network, but could not host students from other schools who were working toward the CEMS degree.) Students complete the first year of their master's program at their home institution and then spend each of two remaining semesters at different member schools. Corporate members of the CEMS alliance provide internship opportunities for participating students. Students who complete the requirements for the CEMS MIM program as well as those of the degree program at their home institution may receive two degrees. Each partner school that hosts students in the program undergoes a peer review by other members every few years, with a focus on ensuring that the implementation of the program is of the quality expected by the CEMS community.

Since the school joined the consortium in 1998, FGV-EAESP has continued to renew its membership in CEMS, sending a total of sixteen students to the CEMS MIM program between 2002 and 2008. One student per year is funded by a scholarship offered by L'Oréal, one of the alliance's numerous corporate partners. In early 2009, FGV-EAESP was accepted, upon completion of an application and review process, into full membership with CEMS. With this status, FGV-EAESP can now serve as one of the host institutions for individuals who seek the CEMS MIM diploma.

Outcomes from Participation in the Sumaq Alliance

In 2002, FGV-EAESP, Instituto de Empresa (Spain), Universidad San Andrés (Argentina), Universidad de Los Andes (Colombia), ITESM (Mexico), IESA (Venezuela), Pontificia Universidad Católica de Chile (Chile), and INCAE (Costa Rica) established an alliance with the (initial) aim to pool together capabilities for the purpose of delivering executive education. The Sumaq Alliance, which remains exclusive to its original members, today facilitates a variety of activities that include summer programs; international research, training, and teaching opportunities for faculty members; development of in-house executive education programs for corporations; case development and undergraduate case competitions; and numerous outreach activities. According to Dean Maria Tereza Fleury, the Sumaq Alliance is the "largest executive training platform in Spanish and Portuguese-speaking countries." As a result of involvement with this alliance, FGV-EAESP hosts a faculty chair supported by Spain-based Software AG to promote research, analysis, and debate that concerns new trends related to the development of e-Government, e-Administration, and e-Democracy projects in order to improve the quality of public services and customer service in Brazil and Latin America. It also has led to the institution's involvement in 10,000 Women, an initiative launched in 2008 by Goldman Sachs, aimed at increasing access to business and management education among women in underserved regions of the world.

Another outcome of the school's participation in the Sumaq Alliance was the development of a joint PhD Program with the Instituto de Empresa Business School. Doctoral students who seek dual PhD degrees must find a faculty member at each institution who is willing to serve as an advisor. Ultimately, the student may present his/her thesis independently to the juries at the respective institutions or to the two juries simultaneously, depending on the topic and the arrangements made with the mentors at each school. (Sometimes, the thesis that is presented to each school may differ slightly). Each jury must accept the thesis for the degree to be awarded by its respective school. Participants in the program are few, but the ability to earn two degrees is appealing for individuals who seek ease of mobility between academic positions in Europe and Brazil.

Other Initiatives

In early 2009, a Dean for International Affairs was appointed to oversee the further strengthening and coordination of the school's international activities. The school maintains a network of more than 90 partner schools,[27] and FGV-EAESP's identified priority is to make its relationships with existing partners deeper and stronger. This focus on existing relationships has resulted in increased numbers of students who participate in exchange opportunities, the establishment of several double-degree programs, and enhanced engagement with the school's international networks, such as with Sumaq and CEMS, as described above.

---

[27]FGV-EAESP, International Partner Institutions web page, 2009, electronic document, http://eaesp.fgvsp.br/pt/atividadesinternacionais/escolas, accessed December 11, 2009.

Also in January 2009, FGV-EAESP participated in the first conference of the Association of BRICS Business Schools (ABBS), which includes select business schools in the emerging BRICs economies as well as South Africa. The purpose of the BRICS Business School network is to facilitate cooperation among business schools whose primary markets, though geographically distant, are in similar stages of economic development. The founding schools[28] will serve as the board of directors for the consortium and will determine policies and criteria for admitting additional schools based in the BRIC countries or South Africa. The group intends to focus on research and case study development that targets the common economic and business realities in their respective countries, and it hopes to eventually facilitate faculty exchange among the member schools.

FGV-EAESP maintains student exchange agreements with more than 70 universities in 30 countries. MBA students may choose to spend the program's last three-month module at any one of the PIM member schools. Numerous other opportunities exist for students in other programs, and these opportunities have grown substantially. In 2000, for example, 80 students from FGV-EAESP took part in exchange opportunities with 51 international partners; by 2009, 231 students participated in exchange opportunities with 85 international partners.

Because many student exchange agreements are reciprocal, incoming exchange students often represent countries and schools that Brazilian students will visit in a later semester. Therefore, incoming exchange students are asked to present seminars that discuss the political, cultural, and socio-economic issues of their home countries in "Pipoca com Guaraná" (Popcorn and Guaraná) sessions. Exchange students also provide advice to Brazilian students on what to do in the cities they will visit, how to take advantage of opportunities at the partner school, how to arrange accommodations, etc. The sessions, which used to be organized by the school's international relations department, are now organized by the student union, and Dean Fleury says the change in ownership has succeeded in making them even more popular among the students.

FGV-EAESP has also made a concerted effort in recent years to expand agreements with partner schools to include more opportunities for faculty members who wish to teach, conduct research, or study in other countries. Faculty members are encouraged to engage in international professional development opportunities, such as a four-week, regionally oriented

---

[28]Founding institutions include FGV-EAESP; State University for Management, Moscow; Xavier Institute of Management & Entrepreneurship, Bangalore; Renmin University of China, Beijing; and University of KwaZulu-Natal, Durban, South Africa.

program for professors from across Latin America that enables exchange of concepts, research plans, and methodology in a variety of business fields. The school also runs a foreign visitors program that hosts scholars, post-doctoral students, and researchers from around the world for a semester or year at a time.[29] During the school's short winter term, in July of each year, FGV-EAESP invites visiting professors from partner institutions to teach elective courses in business administration, public administration, and economics. Faculty members who travel abroad with funding from FGV-EAESP are expected to present seminars to other professors upon their return to share what they have learned (and many of those who travel with independent funds do so voluntarily). This knowledge may include the contents of a professional development session or insights into the country or region's business environment.

To promote the learning of foreign languages, FGV-EAESP encourages students to attend French language courses, the Cours de Français Blaise Cendrars, which are offered through French government subsidies. More than 90 students were enrolled in 2009, many of whom intend to complete courses at French-speaking partner schools.

Still, language barriers remain a challenge for FGV-EAESP in its efforts to attract foreign students to Brazil. In response, the school has begun to offer intensive Portuguese language training for foreign students as well as a variety of English-language programs. These programs include the Master's in International Management (MPGI), International Program in Management (IPM), the OneMBA Global EMBA Program, and the Doing Business in Brazil course, each of which is discussed in greater detail below.

Doing Business in Brazil. In 2000, FGV-EAESP launched a two-week, intensive executive education program designed to familiarize foreigners with the business culture in Brazil. Courses are taught by FGV-EAESP faculty and Brazilian executives, and students conduct site visits to a Brazilian firm, a multinational firm, and a financial institution. In the program's first nine years, a total of 175 students participated in the program. Additionally, FGV-EAESP has developed a total of 35 customized versions of the program for business schools in the U.S. and Europe.[30]

OneMBA Global Executive MBA program. In 2002, FGV-EAESP joined the Tecnológico de Monterrey Graduate School of Business Administration

---

[29]FGV-EAESP, Foreign Visitors Program web page, 2009, electronic document, http://www.eaesp.fgvsp.br/default.aspx?pagid = JLGCSPPN, accessed December 11, 2009.
[30]Fleury, Maria Tereza, personal interview, March 20, 2009.

and Leadership (EGADE) in Mexico, The University of North Carolina at Chapel Hill's Kenan-Flagler Business School in the U.S., the Faculty of Business Administration at The Chinese University of Hong Kong (CUHK), and the Rotterdam School of Management at Erasmus University in the Netherlands to offer an MBA program for high-level executives called the OneMBA Global Executive MBA program. The schools collaborate on development of a curriculum that can be delivered at each of their campuses, seeking to incorporate perspectives and best practices from their own experiences in their respective world regions. Program participants continue their careers while attending classes at the OneMBA partner university most convenient to them. At FGV-EAESP, for example, the majority of students are Brazilian, but generally up to 20 percent of students are from other countries.

The program's English-language courses are offered in three modules of five sessions each. Class sessions last three to four full-time days, including exams, and the entire program spans 21 months. In the program, approximately 100 participants from the five schools (who generally represent corporations based in the local region) come together four times for mandatory week-long residencies in the U.S., Europe, Latin America, and Asia. Participants from the various schools also are required to work together between residencies in three different project teams (each of which represent students from all the regions). In all, 160 of the total 624 teaching hours are spent in "coordinated courses" (courses that are the same at all campuses), 272 teaching hours are spent in "regional courses" (developed by and unique to the host school), and 192 teaching hours are spent in the global residencies. Upon completing the program, executives receive the OneMBA certificate issued by the five partner universities, as well as an MBA from their home university.

Linking the MPGI Program and the CEMS MIM Diploma Program. To accommodate foreign students who participated in the CEMS MIM diploma program in the second half of 2009, FGV-EAESP launched an English-language MPGI Program (Mestrado Profissional em Gestão Internacional, or Master's in International Management). The foundation for design of the program was a six-month, English-language diploma program for senior undergraduate and junior graduate students, known as the International Program in Management (IPM). Courses in that diploma program, which were later integrated into the school's undergraduate and MPGI programs, were intended to develop cross-cultural aptitudes and to prepare students for careers in a global business context through case studies, games, and role-playing. Students admitted into the new MPGI program are expected to spend six to 12 months abroad, either through the CEMS program or at one of the school's other partners: Università

Commerciale Luigi Bocconi (Italy), Universidad Nova de Lisboa (Portugal), Universität St. Gallen (Switzerland), HEC Paris (France), Sciences Po (France), or the School of International and Public Affairs (SIPA) at Columbia University (U.S.). Students also are required to present a thesis at the conclusion of the program.

Unlike the dual-degree programs at the MBA level, dual-degree programs at the MSc level are based on reciprocal exchange of students. Thus, all students, regardless of the dual-degree partner, pay the same rate of tuition (approximately $28,000) directly to FGV-EAESP. This rate includes the cost of courses taken at the partner institutions, but it excludes travel and living expenses. Students who participate in the dual-degree programs at the MBA level, on the other hand, pay tuition to whichever school offers the course, and therefore, an equal exchange of students from one partner to the other is not necessary.

Outcomes and Future Plans

FGV-EAESP has succeeded in achieving substantial increases in the number of agreements with international business schools as well as increases in the number of students who participate in international exchanges, joint programs, and other opportunities oriented toward providing students with a more global perspective. According to Dean Fleury, the international orientation of the school's MSc and PhD programs and the success of faculty in disseminating their research in international publications are both important competitive advantages for the school in the Brazilian context. She also cites enrollment growth in the OneMBA program, by 53 percent between the class of 2004 and the class of 2010, and the program's inclusion in international MBA rankings as evidence of the program's success.

Still, the school faces several challenges in its globalization efforts. Given the size of Brazil, and given Portuguese as the predominant language of instruction, the school as a whole remains primarily "a domestic player," according to Dean Fleury. Programs such as the MPGI and the IPM have taken steps toward addressing that limitation, and the school hopes to continue to increase the number of incoming and outgoing students in the future, in particular by offering more English-language courses.

The school also is working to establish more multidisciplinary double-degree programs, such as those currently offered in partnership with Columbia University SIPA and Sciences Po, believing that multidisciplinary degrees at the international level are important factors in increasing the number of opportunities available to the school's own students as well as to foreign students interested in Brazil.

As mentioned earlier, the school's primary focus going forward is to strengthen its relationships with existing partners, with a focus on 1) increasing opportunities for short-term exchange programs at the undergraduate and MBA levels, 2) increasing opportunities for faculty exchange, and 3) establishing agreements that will facilitate internships with Brazilian firms for foreign students as well as internships with foreign companies for Brazilian students. Dean Fleury notes that "reciprocity is an important value in international programs" and that the school's efforts to honor this value with its partners have provided a foundation for future development of those relationships.[31]

---

[31]FGV-EAESP, International Relations Office web page, electronic document, http://eaesp.fgvsp.br/en/BusinessCommunity/InternationalRelationsCoordination, accessed December 11, 2009.

HONG KONG UNIVERSITY OF SCIENCE AND TECHNOLOGY (HKUST), SCHOOL OF BUSINESS AND MANAGEMENT

The vision of the Hong Kong University of Science and Technology, School of Business and Management is to be the leading global business school in Asia.[32] This vision is reflected in the three components of the school's mission: to advance the frontiers of global business knowledge, to develop business leaders in Asia for the world, and to contribute to the social and economic transformation of the region.

The school's focus on Asia is apparent in its program offerings, which primarily are hosted at the school's Hong Kong campus with some additional offerings in Mainland China and other cities in Asia. However, the importance of global perspectives is evident in the school's emphasis on international faculty recruitment, international student recruitment, and its reliance on partnerships with foreign schools both to deliver joint programs and to offer student exchange opportunities. Each program offered by the school is tailored for a niche audience, with curriculum content and delivery methods adapted to best fit different contexts and cultures.

Establishing the Kellogg-HKUST Joint-EMBA Program (1998)

In 1996, at an AACSB conference that was focused on business school alliances, Steve DeKrey, then the Director of MBA Programs at the University of Florida, met the dean of the HKUST School of Business, Yuk-Shee Chan. DeKrey, formerly an assistant dean and faculty member at the Kellogg School of Management of Northwestern University, also found time to catch up with his former Kellogg dean, Don Jacobs, who was chairing the conference.

Soon after the conference, DeKrey found himself on his way to a new position at HKUST, a five-year-old school with a keen interest in enhancing

---

[32]Each case study was prepared with the purpose of illustrating an interesting variation in approach to the globalization of management education. Inclusion in this report does not constitute an endorsement of this approach for all schools.

This case study was developed through conversations and email correspondence with Leonard Cheng (dean, HKUST School of Business and Management), Steve DeKrey (senior associate dean and director of the Kellogg-HKUST EMBA program and HKUST-NYU MS in Global Finance Program), and Kate Chan (associate dean and director of the school's Bilingual EMBA Program), as well as through a review of the School of Business and Management website, and review of accounts of the school's activities in press releases, periodicals, etc. Errors and omissions are the sole responsibility of the authors.

its global reputation. Kellogg was also making strides to enhance its international reach, working to establish international joint EMBA programs with partners in various world regions. Given the shared international objectives of both schools, their common emphasis on faculty scholarship, and DeKrey's relationship with the two institutions, the Kellogg School of Management and the HKUST School of Business decided to offer a joint EMBA program with plans to graduate its first class in 1998.

The goal of the Kellogg-HKUST EMBA was "to foster a new network of leaders with global insights and local sensitivities."[33] DeKrey acknowledges that a primary goal of the HKUST Business School also was to use the partnership as a starting point to build the school's global reputation. The lack of detail in the memorandum of understanding between the two institutions was unusual, but it has thus far not been an impediment to the success of the partnership.

The program primarily is managed by DeKrey and his colleagues at the HKUST Business School, with support from Kellogg. The high level of trust between the two partner schools allows DeKrey and his colleagues to have substantial decision-making autonomy in the day-to-day management of the program, which substantially reduces the time and effort that are often required when multiple parties must weigh in on a decision. Also important is the high level of commitment by both schools to the original objective of the program—to produce a quality program designed to prepare global leaders. The program, which is entirely dependent on tuition revenue, took eight years to reach capacity, and DeKrey notes that if revenue had been one of the motivations for the program, it likely would have been ended after the initial few years. Instead, the two partner schools had a shared belief in short-term sacrifices to ensure long-term gain.

Extending the Global Focus to Undergraduates (2001)

In 2001, HKUST opened the undergraduate student experience to the globalizing world when it launched its three-year BBA in Global Business (GBUS). Aside from receiving the broad-based management education for which HKUST is known, students of the program are expected to specialize in a second major from among the other business disciplines that are offered. GBUS students take business communication courses both in

---

[33]Northwestern University Kellogg School of Management, Kellogg-HKUST Executive MBA Program web page, 2009, electronic document, http://www.kellogg.northwestern.edu/Programs/EMBA/Global_Partner_Programs/HKUST.aspx, accessed November 4, 2009.

English and in Putonghua (Mandarin Chinese), as well as an additional elementary foreign language course in a language of their choice (e.g., French, German, Greek, Japanese, Latin, Spanish, etc.). Due to the intensive nature of the program, the target intake quota is 45 GBUS students per cohort.

The BBA GBUS program includes several courses that are aimed specifically at providing students with an understanding of the complexities inherent in a global business environment. The "Global Business Analysis" course, for example, exposes students to each of the various disciplines of business and functional areas of an organization and to various economic and social factors that may influence an organization's operations. A "Global Perspectives on Contemporary Issues" course addresses students' capacity for critical reflection by exposing them to differing viewpoints on issues that extend beyond those in the business field. To complement the use of cases in other courses, a "Global Business Case Studies" course focuses on the analysis of cases involving international corporations and serves as a means of identifying students for participation in international case competitions.[34]

International experiences are also an important aspect of the GBUS program. In the spring semester of their second year, GBUS students are required to undertake an exchange semester at one of HKUST's 109 partner schools from all over the world. In addition, a number of summer internships with international (and locally based transnational) firms are available to GBUS students. Finally, since 2007, HKUST has arranged for shorter, two-to three-week study trips to foreign partner schools for undergraduate students during their winter and summer holiday breaks. Each one-credit study trip consists of a minimum of 42 contact hours and covers the following elements: 1) lectures delivered by faculty members at the host institution, 2) company visits, and 3) cultural adventure in the host country.[35] Such study trips are not limited to GBUS students, however; any undergraduate student at HKUST Business School is welcome to partake in them.

Expanding the Global Reach of the MBA and EMBA Programs (2002)

Both the Kellogg-HKUST EMBA program and HKUST's traditional full-time and part-time MBA programs involved a diverse mix of students and

---

[34]HKUST Business School, HKUST BBA Global Business Course Descriptions web page, 2010, electronic document, http://publish.ust.hk/univ/coursecat2010/showcourses.asp? deptcode= BMGB&pagenum=1, accessed October 1, 2010.

[35]HKUST Business School, "A Trip to Remember – The Study Trip to UK for Business School Undergraduates," web posting, 2008, electronic document, http://www.bm.ust.hk/ug/cms/web/ NewsDetail.aspx?NewsId = 180, accessed November 9, 2010.

faculty, which is a benefit of the diverse population within Hong Kong and the school's efforts to recruit international faculty. Still, says Kate Chan, associate dean and director of the School's Bilingual EMBA Program, around the year 2001, HKUST Business School began to receive an increasing number of requests from companies in China for executive education programs on the Chinese mainland. Consequently, in 2002, HKUST launched its international EMBA and Shenzhen MBA programs, thereby expanding its program delivery beyond Hong Kong.

The international EMBA (IEMBA) program is based at the Hong Kong campus, but 12 of the 15 required modules also are offered in other cities such as Beijing, Shanghai, Hainan, and Shenzhen. Classes are offered either in Putonghua or in English with subsequent Putonghua interpretation. The IEMBA program objectives are four-fold: 1) to develop corporate leaders with global perspectives, 2) to provide participants with cutting-edge business management knowledge and concepts, 3) to foster cross-cultural and cross-disciplinary strategic thinking, and 4) to network and share experiences with experts from different fields and professions.[36]

Chan says that the IEMBA program was modeled after the highly successful Kellogg-HKUST EMBA program, but that, in addition to the obvious location and language differences, the program model was adapted in further, subtle ways. For example, she says, given the speed and scale of development in China, Chinese students are on a different learning curve than are students from the West, or areas with substantial Western influence. "Chinese students are interested in learning how things work in the West, but are also concerned about their own legal, political, and economic environment," says Chan, "thus, it is important that the curriculum balance both contexts."

The Shenzhen MBA is similar to the part-time MBA program offered at HKUST's Hong Kong campus, but it is offered entirely at the school's Shenzhen campus. The program is advertised as one that is "designed to develop your ability to operate successfully in a global economy, and manage effectively in the Asian context."[37] Just as with the part-time and full-time MBA programs in Hong Kong, courses are arranged in three tiers—foundation, function, and integration—to provide a basis for further study in chosen areas.

---

[36]HKUST Business School, HKUST EMBA for Chinese Executives web page, 2009, electronic document, http://www.bm.ust.hk/iemba/program_over_en.html, accessed April 4, 2009.
[37]HKUST Business School, HKUST Part-time MBA Program web page, 2010, electronic document, http://www.bm.ust.hk/szmba/prog/curriculum.html, accessed December 29, 2010.

Differentiating via the HKUST-NYU MS Global Finance (2007)

Around 2006, the Finance Department of the HKUST School of Business began to consider opportunities to offer a specialized program for finance professionals living in or working in the Asia region. The school wanted to avoid development of a program that would compete with the Kellogg-HKUST EMBA program, but also it wanted to use the joint program model to offer a program that would "balance the technical and global dimensions of finance in a way that is not generally achieved in MBA programs."[38] The result was a partnership with the New York University Stern School of Business to offer a one-year, part-time HKUST-NYU Master of Science in Global Finance. The program welcomed its first class of students in the fall of 2007 and was touted as "the first executive format finance-specific master degree program in the Asia Pacific."[39]

Like the partnership between Kellogg and HKUST that enables the joint-EMBA program, the partnership between HKUST and the NYU Stern School of Business was enabled in part through an existing relationship between the two schools. George Daly, who was dean of NYU Stern at the time the partnership was first discussed, had at one time been a member of the HKUST advisory board. The NYU dean who helped make the partnership happen was Dean Thomas Cooley.

However, unlike the partnership between Kellogg and HKUST, says DeKrey, the HKUST-NYU partnership is based on a more detailed agreement between the two schools that outlines with greater specificity the expected contributions of the two partners. Aside from a two-week module in New York, classes (which are taught by both local HKUST faculty and visiting faculty from NYU) are held at the HKUST's downtown facility in Hong Kong. However, the administration of the program is more evenly split between the two schools. DeKrey notes that, because both schools are equally involved in the program's administration, and because of the resulting needs for coordination and consensus on many decisions, more time and effort is needed to administer the HKUST-NYU MS in Global Finance than to administer the Kellogg-HKUST EMBA. Still, he says that the program benefits immensely from the commitment of both schools, their shared commitment to quality and achievement of stated objectives, and the

---

[38]HKUST Business School, HKUST-NYU Stern Master of Science in Global Finance web page, 2009, electronic document, http://globalfinance.bm.ust.hk/webpage_view.asp? pageID=3, accessed April 4, 2009.
[39]HKUST Business School, HKUST Master of Science in Global Finance web page, 2010, electronic document, http://globalfinance.bm.ust.hk/schedule_view.asp, accessed December 29, 2010.

enthusiastic and collaborative nature of the faculty and administrators who support it.

Executive Programs

HKUST also offers non-degree executive education programs in various locations within the Asian region, including its home campus in Hong Kong. The majority of executive education programs are custom programs for small- to medium-sized companies, and thus the size and scope of these programs are heavily demand-driven. The school also provides a global executive program for the pharmaceutical company Merck, with modules in three locations: Hong Kong (HKUST), the U.S. (Kellogg), and France (INSEAD).

Exchange Partners

The HKUST School of Business also maintains more than 100 exchange partners at the undergraduate level and more than 50 exchange partners at the MBA level. Many of these partnerships, says DeKrey, have existed for between 10 and 15 years. He notes that the school is frequently solicited to engage in new partnerships, but he acknowledges that, given the large number of existing relationships, the school is very selective of potential options and does not anticipate much growth, if any, in the number of exchange partnerships it maintains. Though not the sole purpose for exchange partnerships, notes DeKrey, a benefit of such relationships is their potential to help generate attention for the school among faculty, students, and others who may not otherwise be familiar with the institution.

Faculty Management

The HKUST School of Business has approximately 140 full-time faculty members and sometimes uses part-time adjuncts to provide additional support as needed. Dean Leonard Cheng states that "it has been the institution's policy since its establishment to recruit internationally for its faculty and senior administrators." The result is that 90 percent of the school's full-time faculty members are considered international based on their nationality. Additionally, the joint programs with Kellogg and Stern are supported by visiting faculty from the respective schools.

Cheng notes that securing the financial resources necessary to pay the salaries that are required to attract international faculty is a challenge that the school will continue to face. MBA and EMBA programs in Hong Kong are 100 percent tuition dependent and ineligible for government funding. What is less of a challenge, according to Chan, is managing their existing faculty across the numerous program locations in Asia. The HKUST Business School uses the same pool of faculty to support its programs across all locations, yet, with all locations within a four-hour flight of Hong Kong, Chan says that faculty mobility across locations is relatively easy to facilitate. A more difficult task, she says, is just managing faculty resources across the numerous programs offered—a challenge for any school that balances a variety of programs, regardless of the programs' locations. DeKrey affirms this position, adding that the faculty management challenges faced by the school have little to do with its international diversity or the geographic spread of programs offered. Rather, the school places an emphasis on both quality research and capable instruction, and these are sometimes competing qualities. "Some of our best researchers are not a good fit for the MBA program," he says. The challenge they face, like many other schools, is therefore to balance faculty talents with the program needs.

International Perspectives in Curriculum Content and Delivery

"Consistency and adaptation" is the mantra that Chan says guides the school's approach to program delivery. Curriculum content is similar across programs but is adapted to suit the respective audience/culture (see the earlier example of how the Kellogg-HKUST EMBA curriculum was adapted for the IEMBA). Additionally, delivery techniques vary based on location. As an example, Chan notes that U.S. students are accustomed to interactive learning while Chinese students generally take some time to adjust to this approach; thus, in a class with primarily Chinese students, instructors may introduce this type of learning in the classroom gradually. DeKrey notes that adapting learning delivery to a diverse student audience comes somewhat naturally when the professors themselves are accustomed to diversity. This quality is a benefit of the emphasis the school places on international faculty recruitment. The school also now has a case center to write new cases that are oriented toward Asian companies and markets. Still, adaptation to local contexts is a challenge—one that DeKrey notes is especially true for schools that offer programs in another country/region without a local partner.

The school is constantly serving stakeholders that are connected to various markets. The speed of change in those markets, and particularly in China, is a constant driver for modifications to the curriculum. The school regularly surveys its faculty and other stakeholders to identify opportunities to make the curriculum more relevant. Additionally, regular campus-wide quality audits under Hong Kong's outcome-based education model also offer insights into opportunities for improvement. As a result, HKUST currently is in the process of making major revisions to some of its programs, including the EMBA. The curriculum change for the EMBA program is run by a 10-person committee that is coordinated by a former McKinsey consultant. The committee includes administrators, adjunct faculty, and tenured faculty and is chaired by Dean DeKrey. The school also plans to launch a new program next year that will offer more content that is relevant to the Chinese market.

The fact that the MBA and EMBA programs do not receive government funding allows the programs to be exempt from a Hong Kong regulation that stipulates that no more than 20 percent of students can be non-local. As a result, DeKrey reports, nearly 90 percent of students in the full-time MBA and the Kellogg-HKUST EMBA programs are outside of Hong Kong.

Expectations

Since it first opened in 1991, HKUST wanted to become a leading school in Asia, and with that ambition came the need to strive to be a global player. As Dean Cheng notes, "the intention of the School [of Business and Management] to globalize is enshrined in the School's mission" to:

- advance the frontiers of global business knowledge,
- develop business leaders in Asia for the world, and
- contribute to the social and economic transformation of the region.

Cheng believes that the outcomes of the school's activities and strategy thus far have met their expectations, "mainly in the areas of reputation, recruitment of faculty and students and research opportunities for faculty." He considers the most important assets to this success to be the international background of the faculty members, the general consensus of the School [of Business] in support of globalization, support from the larger institution, the English-speaking working and learning environment, and the attractiveness of their location, Hong Kong, as a "gateway" to China.

STANFORD UNIVERSITY, GRADUATE SCHOOL OF BUSINESS

Over the past 15 years, the international dimension of business practice has become progressively and increasingly integrated into the curricula of Stanford University's Graduate School of Business and the mindset of its students.[40] An integral part of the educational philosophy at the school is that a global outlook is one of four critical components necessary to a complete general management education. Today, the Graduate School of Business (GSB) has created centers to focus work around each of these four areas, and of the four, the Center for Global Business and the Economy has the largest number of senior faculty attached to it. Additionally, adjustments to the curricular requirements themselves that emphasize the importance of international aspects of business have served as a powerful signal, within the academic community and to prospective students, of the Stanford GSB's dedication to and appreciation of global mindsets among business leaders.

A Formal Globalization Strategy Begins to Take Shape

The Stanford University Graduate School of Business has been engaged in internationally oriented activities for many years, though not until 1994 did a more formal globalization strategy begin to take shape. Prior to that time, the school had enabled international study trips for students, provided electives with a global or international orientation, and collaborated with the National University of Singapore to deliver an executive education program in Singapore (the latter since 1983).[41] However, early efforts were fragmented and there was no overarching emphasis on the incorporation of

---

[40]Each case study was prepared with the purpose of illustrating an interesting variation in approach to the globalization of management education. Inclusion in this report does not constitute an endorsement of this approach for all schools.

This case study was developed through conversations and email correspondence with John Roberts (John H. Scully Professor of Economics, Strategic Management and International Business, and former senior associate dean, Stanford GSB), review of the Stanford GSB website, and review of accounts of the school's activities in press releases, periodicals, etc. Errors and omissions are the sole responsibility of the authors.

[41]*New Straits Times*, "The 5th Annual Stanford-NUS Executive Program," advertisement in Malaysia's *New Straits Times*, April 6, 1987, electronic document, http://news.google.com/newspapers?id = trkTAAAAIBAJ&sjid=XpADAAAAIBAJ&pg=6703,1188660&dq=executive + stanford + national + university + singapore, accessed August 26, 2009.

international perspectives into the curriculum or engagement in international activities.

This situation changed in 1994 when a group of students approached the dean and proposed that students who took a series of internationally oriented elective courses be awarded a certificate to recognize their focus on the international dimensions of business.[42] They also asked that more internationally oriented extracurricular activities be developed and available for students. The school responded by establishing the Global Management Program (GMP), which functioned as an optional certificate program for master's-level students, and served as a foundation for further development of a variety of academic and immersive international learning opportunities for students. Furthermore, the Global Management Program (the term used to refer to student-oriented international opportunities) today is just one component of the school's broader globalization efforts—which also include faculty research and learning, course development, and outreach to the business community.

The "Global Center" at Stanford GSB

The Center for Global Business and the Economy (the Global Center) at Stanford GSB was established in 2004 through gifts from the BP Foundation, Steve and Roberta Denning, Cemex, and John A. and Cynthia Fry Gunn. It is one of four centers supported by the school in areas it considers to be the cornerstones of general management education (entrepreneurship, global business, leadership, and social innovation).

The objective of the Global Center is to promote both course development and research in international business and economics. It aims to facilitate dialogue that involves students, faculty, and global business leaders and to integrate global awareness into the school's teaching, research, and outreach activities. Funding for the center is generated through an endowment of more than $2 million (generating income of approximately $100,000 per year) and from the GSB's general funds.

Rather than drive the school's globalization activities, the Global Center's primary role is to enable Stanford GSB to prioritize, support, and coordinate activities that are proposed and driven by individual faculty

---

[42]Byrne, John A., and Lori Bongiorno, "The Best B-Schools," *BusinessWeek*, October 24, 1994, electronic document, http://www.businessweek.com/1989-94/pre94/b339564.htm, accessed August 26, 2009.

members and groups of faculty. Approximately one-quarter of Stanford GSB faculty are involved directly with the Global Center.

Global Business in the Curriculum

Since the establishment of the GMP certificate program in 1994, substantial changes have occurred in the Stanford GSB's approach to integrating global perspectives into its MBA curriculum.

In 1999, the internationally oriented elective courses were supplemented by a course on global management that was required for all students, and that followed completion of a strategy course. According to Senior Associate Dean John Roberts, although the intellectual underpinnings of the course were heavily dependent on the content of the strategy course, the timing of the two courses was not well coordinated, and the courses incorporated overlapping content. The fledgling global management course also was not as well received as its more established prerequisite.

To resolve this issue, the school decided to integrate the two courses and to embed the content from the global management course within the strategic management course, which was lengthened from four hours per week to six hours per week. Most of the cases used in the revised strategy course involved international companies. However, new issues arose with this new format, primarily due to staffing challenges that were caused by the lengthened course and the more intense international focus. The original architect of the strategy course, Garth Saloner, was asked once again to revise the course, and the result was to pare it back down, eliminating much of the international content that had been integrated into it.

Several years later, in 2006, an overhaul of the MBA curriculum led by Saloner brought international content back to a prominent role with the inclusion of a course titled The Global Context of Management as a required first-quarter course and one of only a few required courses in a highly customizable program. The inclusion of this course at the beginning of the curriculum was intended to signal the importance of international perspectives as a necessary component of management education. The heavily structured course, which involves lectures, written team projects, and case analysis, focuses on introducing students to the process of learning about an unfamiliar economy, heightening their awareness of cultural differences and their implications for international business, and helping students to appreciate the complexities involved in managing a business in an international environment.

Many of the case studies used in the course come from a library maintained by the Global Center, which seeks to support content development for the 36 internationally oriented MBA core and elective courses at the GSB.

A Required Global Experience

As part of the curriculum revision, MBA students also are required to fulfill a Global Experience Requirement (GER) in their first year of the program. The requirement stipulates that students spend some minimal time in a structured, academically and managerially relevant context in a country that is new to the students. The GER can be met through participation in the GMIX, a student-initiated study trip, an international internship, or a student exchange with the school's partners in China and India.

GMIX. One option available to students to fulfill the global experience requirement is the Global Management Immersion Experience (GMIX), a program introduced in 2000 that places students in short-term, project-based internships in countries around the world. Interested students may select from and apply to opportunities provided by companies, nongovernmental organization, or other not-for-profit organizations with a local presence in countries other than the U.S. The organizations that participate in the program are recognized as "Global Affiliates" by Stanford University.

In 2008, 57 organizations in 28 countries around the world participated in the GMIX program, with substantial proportions of students traveling, in particular, to Asia and Central/Eastern Europe.[43] The internships generally take place in the four-week period between completion of a traditional summer internship and the start of the fall academic semester. Student participants are expected to seek opportunities in countries in which they have not lived before and to share their experiences with their colleagues at Stanford GSB upon their return. They also are given the opportunity to earn two course credits in return for completion of a research paper on an international business topic related to their GMIX experience.

Global Study Trip. Students also have the option to develop and participate in student-led global study trips. Groups of students, typically with experience and/or connections in a particular world region, may, at the end of their first year of study, propose itineraries for study trips that they will lead and that the next class of students will take in order to learn more

---

[43]Stanford Graduate School of Business, Global Management Immersion Experience (GMIX) 2009 Sponsor Guide, electronic document, http://www.gsb.stanford.edu/gmp/career/documents/GMIX2009SponsorGuide.pdf, accessed August 26, 2009.

about the business environment in that region. Stanford GSB staff review the students' proposals and determine whether the trips are feasible and likely to have the intended value. Students who submit accepted proposals receive feedback on how to enhance the value of the trip as well as additional support from the GSB staff toward the trip preparations. The bulk of the responsibility for planning the trip, however, falls to the student organizers.

In preparation for the trip, for example, students might host speakers on topics such as macroeconomic policy and political history in the region, and they might facilitate discussions on culture and business etiquette. Each group also is responsible for securing a faculty member to accompany the trip in an advising capacity. The study trips themselves involve student-initiated meetings with business, government, and nongovernmental organization leaders in the region. Upon returning to campus, students complete a report and share their experiences and key takeaways with the business school community.

Student Exchange. A third option for students who seek to fulfill the global experience requirement is to participate in one of two school-sponsored student exchange programs. While many business schools have exchange programs that send students for a term to take courses at one of numerous partner institutions, Stanford GSB has opted for an approach that involves a limited number of exchange partners and a highly structured, project-oriented exchange program.

The first of the two student exchange options is the Stanford-Tsinghua Exchange Program, or STEP. The program was launched in 2005–06 at the direction of the deans of each school, but it grew out of a relationship that had existed between the two schools for several years. Stanford had for some time provided training to faculty members of Tsinghua University's School of Economics and Management (SEM) in the areas of entrepreneurship and human resources. According to Roberts, Tsinghua SEM proposed that the schools deepen their relationship by establishing a student exchange agreement, but Stanford was uninterested in operating a traditional student exchange. The student profile at Stanford was already internationally diverse, and the curriculum model was not conducive to traditional student exchange opportunities.

Instead, Charles Holloway, Stanford GSB's Kleiner Perkins Caufield & Byers Professor of Management, Emeritus, and Director of the Center for Entrepreneurial Studies, suggested the establishment of a project-oriented exchange program that involves approximately 15 to 20 students from each school each year. In the program, small teams of two students from each school define and complete a research project under the supervision of a faculty member. Stanford GSB program participants attend lectures and participate in case discussions regarding the business environment in China, and Tsinghua SEM students receive similar exposure to the U.S. business environment.

A key component of the program is the students' participation in reciprocal one-week visits. Stanford GSB students spend one week visiting Tsinghua SEM, where they meet and attend classes with their project partners, visit local companies, and engage in social and cultural experiences. A few weeks later, the Stanford GSB students host their Tsinghua SEM counterparts for a similar weeklong experience.

The success of the program has since led both schools to replicate the program with other partners. In the fall of 2007, Stanford GSB and the Indian Institute of Management-Bangalore (IIM-B) launched the Stanford-Indian Institute of Management (Bangalore) Link, or SAIL. The two schools connected through a Stanford alumnus who was chairing IIM-B's advisory board and, according to Prakash G. Apte (then director of IIM-B), through the schools' shared philosophies and respective locations "in the technology and entrepreneurship centers" of the U.S. and India.[44] The SAIL program follows a similar model to that of the STEP program.

According to Roberts, the objectives of both exchange programs are similar: to enable students to build networks with future business leaders in other regions of the world, to enable students to deepen their insight into another country's business environment through the eyes of a local student, and to provide students experience working in a culturally diverse team.

Student Body

In addition to increasing the international content of its MBA program, Stanford GSB also has consciously increased the proportion of foreign students who participate in the program. Thirty-four percent of the MBA classes of '09 (741 enrolled) and '10 (739 enrolled) were from countries other than the U.S., while nearly 60 percent of the Sloan Master's students in the classes of '08 and '09 were from countries other than the U.S. (56 and 57 enrolled, respectively).

According to Roberts, the recent change in the MBA program curriculum (beginning with the class that entered in the fall of 2007) may have affected the profile of the students who apply to the school. The required Global Context of Management course at the beginning of the program and the required global experience, he believes, have served as a

---

[44]Stanford Graduate School of Business, "Student Exchange Program Links Stanford Business School and IIM Bangalore," Stanford GSB press release, January 2007.

signal to would-be applicants that the school places a heavy emphasis on global perspectives, which results not only in an internationally diverse applicant pool but also more students who truly "understand the importance of the international economy and of connecting to it."

Given its students' international focus and the program's emphasis on the global business environment, the school seeks to provide special assistance with international student job searches. Among the class of 2008, for example, 21 percent of students entered careers that were based outside of the United States.

Additionally, in an effort to encourage graduates to contribute to the economic development of developing countries, Stanford GSB offers an International Loan Forgiveness Program for graduates who are not U.S. citizens and who find employment in developing countries. On the model of similar programs available to U.S. federal aid recipients, the GSB covers a portion of its graduates' GSB loan obligations as long as they are employed in a developing country.

Faculty

As mentioned previously, the Global Center supports a variety of initiatives beyond those that are oriented directly toward students, such as organizing conferences, seminars, and speaker events; supporting faculty research; and assisting in development of case studies and other course materials.

The GSB (at times through the Global Center) provides financial support for international research and case writing as well as attendance at international events in the form of travel stipends, and it also provides faculty members with the flexibility to spend time away from campus obligations. In this way, and through the support network provided by the Global Center, the school actively encourages the incorporation of international perspectives into faculty members' research, course development, and outreach activities. Faculty members also have opportunities to participate in international study trips, both the student-organized trips and trips that are put together specifically for faculty members. Previously, faculty also could receive paid leave for a term if they spent the time overseas. Few were able to take advantage of this option, however, because of the disruption to spouses' careers and family life, and consequently the program was halted.

Other Initiatives

Stanford University supports a variety of international centers that are external to the business school, including the Walter H. Shorenstein

Asia-Pacific Research Center (Shorenstein APARC). In January 2007, the Shorenstein APARC developed the Stanford China Program, which is intended to "facilitate multidisciplinary, social science-oriented research on contemporary China, with a dual emphasis on basic and policy-relevant research."[45] Stanford GSB faculty members have opportunities to work with the Stanford China Program and to utilize the teaching and research space that the program has acquired on the campus of Peking University.

Stanford GSB also currently engages in three collaborative executive education programs, each of which is designed to capitalize on the strengths of the two partner institutions. These programs include one for executives on corporate social responsibility in collaboration with ESADE (Spain), an executive program in international management with the National University of Singapore, and the Cisco Supply Chain Leadership Institute (taught in Mandarin) with Fudan University (China). In addition to these collaborative executive education programs, Stanford GSB also develops custom executive education programs for firms based around the world, and markets its open-enrollment executive education programs internationally to attract a diverse group of students. Many of these programs enroll more international participants than Americans.

Outcomes and Future Plans

Stanford GSB's approach toward globalization has evolved substantially over the past decade, as faculty and administrators have increased their appreciation of the need for international perspectives to permeate teaching, research, and outreach activities, and as the school has experimented with different approaches to globalizing its curricula.

The result, according to Roberts, is that "faculty are contributing to the creation of knowledge that addresses problems with international scope," and "students are more aware of global issues and better prepared to manage in the global economy." He also notes that the recent restructuring of the MBA curriculum has had an important "signaling" effect for potential students—both in attracting applicants with an appreciation for the complexities of the global economy and, for admitted students, in

---

[45]Stanford University, Walter H. Shorenstein Asia-Pacific Research Center, About the Stanford China Program web page, 2009, electronic document, http://chinaprogram.stanford .edu/docs/about_scp/, accessed August 26, 2009.

stressing the importance of approaching the entire educational experience with a global mindset. At the same time, Roberts notes, a challenge to the school's ability to do as much as it might want to do "in the global arena" is that it is "always short of faculty."

In September 2009, the school welcomed Garth Saloner as its new dean. Saloner, who was instrumental in the development and implementation of the revised curriculum and is a staunch advocate of the school's globalization efforts, is expected to build upon the momentum created under the tenure of his predecessor, Robert Joss.

THE UNIVERSITY OF CHICAGO, BOOTH SCHOOL OF BUSINESS

The mission of the Booth School of Business is to "[produce] ideas and leaders that shape the world of business," and in doing so, the school has clearly striven to develop and maintain a global reputation as a leader in management education and research.[46] The school's intention is to achieve a global brand with *one* University of Chicago MBA degree, even though the degree program is available in several formats (full-time, evening, weekend, and executive). Efforts to create a global brand for the North American-based business school and its MBA program have been supported, in recent years, by the establishment of permanent campuses in both Europe and Asia. In addition to providing facilities for the delivery of the Executive MBA Program and non-degree executive education, the European and Asian campuses have enabled the school to diversify its connections to potential students, companies, and alumni beyond its home in North America.

A Second Campus is Considered

In 1991, The University of Chicago Booth School of Business (then known as the Graduate School of Business) was approached by a government representative of the country of Andorra, which was seeking a business school partner that was interested in establishing a campus in that tiny country on the border of France and Spain. Though the meeting failed to convince the school's leadership that Andorra would be the right location for such an endeavor, the representative's solicitation generated serious discussions among the school's administration and faculty led by former dean Bob Hamada. What would be necessary to establish a campus in Europe? What benefits might arise from such a move? The school soon found itself buying into the possibilities that such a move might offer: increased visibility, the opportunity to expand the reach of the program to

---

[46]Each case study was prepared with the purpose of illustrating an interesting variation in approach to the globalization of management education. Inclusion in this report does not constitute an endorsement of this approach for all schools.

This case study was developed in 2009–10 through conversations and e-mail correspondence with Ted Snyder (then dean, The University of Chicago, Booth School of Business) and Bill Kooser (then associate dean for Executive MBA Programs, Booth School of Business), review of the Booth School of Business website, and review of accounts of the school's activities in press releases, periodicals, etc. Errors and omissions are the sole responsibility of the authors.

new sets of students, and the chance for faculty to interact with other regions and business environments.

Determining the Program and Location. The school secured the assistance of a consulting firm to identify the most appropriate location and program type. It was agreed that if the second campus were to offer a University of Chicago degree, the program necessarily should be delivered by the school's own faculty. This imperative meant that the program would have to follow a modular format that would allow faculty to travel between the two locations. The school settled on the Executive MBA program as the most logical program to offer in this format, as its cohort model would be efficient to teach in the bi-campus structure.

The school wanted the program to be designated as a pan-European program that would attract students from outside Europe rather than a national program, and the location needed to facilitate that orientation. Ultimately, Barcelona, Spain, was selected as the location for the new campus. The city had recently hosted the 1992 Olympic Games and therefore had benefited from substantial international visibility as well as enhancements to the city's infrastructure and airport. Furthermore, Corporación Bancaria de España SA, a large bank holding company that was partly owned by the Spanish government, offered to rent a newly refurbished building to the school at "an attractive rate," according to the school's then deputy dean, Robin Hogarth.[47] Thus, the business school opened its Barcelona campus in 1994. At the time, other U.S. schools offered executive MBA programs in Europe, but this program would be the first to be offered without a local partner.

The Barcelona campus offered the same EMBA program that was delivered to students in Chicago by the same set of faculty. Classes were taught in fourteen intense weeks that were spread over eighteen months. In the program's first year, students in the Chicago and Barcelona programs had an optional opportunity to spend a week in the other location. This "exchange" was determined to be so valuable that it became a mandatory part of the program (for students in both Chicago and Barcelona) in the program's second year.[48]

---

[47]De Aenlle, Conrad, "Great Expectations from an American MBA Program: Building Better Businesses," *New York Times*, June 15, 1994, electronic document, http://www.nytimes.com/ 1994/06/15/news/15iht-mbabarc.html, accessed September 15, 2009.

[48]Shears, Toni, and Charles Wasserburg, "Going global: GSB in Barcelona" *The University of Chicago Chronicle*, Vol. 15, No. 4, October 26, 1995, electronic document, http:// chronicle.uchicago.edu/951026/gsb.shtml, accessed September 15, 2009.

Expansion

News of the Barcelona campus soon caught the attention of the school's alumni who were living and working in Asia and who began expressing their interest in an Asian campus that would offer the EMBA program to executives in the region. In 1997, the school began a process of investigating the possibility. This time, with the experience of the Barcelona site selection to rely on, the school did not enlist the support of a consulting firm. Many of the same objectives guided the process: the site needed to support a pan-Asian program and have a good airport and quality infrastructure. Singapore, which had the added benefit of a large English-speaking population, ultimately was selected. Additionally, Singapore was a location with which several faculty members were familiar, having participated in non-degree executive education programs that were delivered there in the 1980s. The Singapore campus opened in 2000.

Relocation

With the EMBA program now operational in two locations beyond Chicago, the business school was in a better position to recognize the influence of location on various aspects of the program. What soon became apparent was the fact that Singapore, a major regional business center, drew in more guest speakers and media attention than did Barcelona. In 2003, the school began to assess whether the Barcelona program might benefit from being relocated to a city more recognized as a "business center" for the European continent. The result was former dean Ted Snyder's decision to move from Barcelona to London in 2005.

One Program, Three Cities

"One Program. One Faculty. Three Campuses. The same distinctive approach. Where you learn how to think, not what to think. In or out of the box. In any situation."[49]

Those words welcome visitors to the EMBA program's website today, and this philosophy guides the management of the EMBA program. EMBA

---

[49]The University of Chicago, Booth School of Business, Executive MBA Program web page, 2010, electronic document, http://www.chicagobooth.edu/execmba/, accessed December 29, 2010.

students at each of the three campuses (approximately thirty at each location) follow the same set of classes, in the same order. They begin the program in June with a week of classes and other activities together in Chicago, and, through the course of the 22-month program, they will spend a total of four weeks together in the three campus locations. The vast majority of students return to Chicago for the formal graduation in March. Snyder and Deputy Dean Mark Zmijewski referred to the program as a global learning system that involves three cohorts of executive MBA students.

The school remains committed to its original objective of using the same core of faculty, based in Chicago, to deliver the programs in the three locations. It strives to avoid the creation (whether actual or perceived) of three sets of faculty who are specific to any one location. "As soon as you separate faculty for a long period of time, they no longer operate as 'one,' and you see a decrease in both collegiality and collaboration," notes former associate dean Bill Kooser. Faculty members are generally enthusiastic about opportunities to teach in the London and Singapore campuses, and the school has not been challenged to find faculty who are willing to teach beyond Chicago. Kooser attributes this success to the program format, which reduces the amount of time that faculty must be away from Chicago. Faculty members who travel are not given extra pay (though their expenses while traveling are covered). They do, however receive extra teaching credit. For example, one credit of teaching in London or Singapore would be considered 1.5 credits when determining a faculty member's teaching load.

Though students in the three locations follow the same classes in consecutive order, slight differences in scheduling enable faculty to travel between the three locations to teach. Chicago students attend class on Friday and Saturday, every other week. Students in both London and Singapore attend class Monday through Saturday roughly once a month. Thus, a typical faculty member might spend a week in London, take a week off, spend a week in Singapore, and then return home for four to five weeks before repeating the rotation.

The basic curriculum is the same in all locations. Says Kooser, "What we teach is at a level that is consistent around the world." While professors may adjust the examples they use in class or use cases that involve regional firms, and while each location may bring in guest speakers to focus on regional issues, no substantial variations are implemented in the program across locations.

In fact, consistency across the campuses extends beyond the faculty and curricula. Kooser reports that a constant challenge for the school is to ensure consistent quality in facilities and technology. "When students from Singapore visit the Chicago or London campus[es], for example," he says, "it is only natural for them to compare the facilities and services available in the other locations with what they have experienced at their home campus." This consistency also is important for faculty who travel between the locations so as to ensure that, as they travel from one location to another to deliver a course, they do not have to adapt to unfamiliar technology or processes.

While the London and Singapore campuses do not have permanent faculty, each has its own set of "permanent" staff (approximately 11.5 and 10.5 full-time equivalency, respectively) that help manage the location's day-to-day operations. Led by the managing director for each location, staff members manage local marketing and recruitment efforts, on-site registration, catering and A/V needs, and student services such as course registration and materials. In addition, the school's Career Services Office and Alumni Office both host staff in the two cities to provide program support as needed. Five staff members support the program in Chicago, but the program also relies on other staff members in the business school and university. The program's three managing directors each report to an associate dean for executive MBA programs, who is based in Chicago and reports to the deputy dean for part-time MBA programs.

Beyond the EMBA

The Chicago Booth MBA also is offered for non-executive students in either a full-time, weekend, or evening format at the Chicago campuses. These MBA students have several options for adding an additional international element to their degree programs.

MBA students have an opportunity to pursue one of several joint-degree programs by combining the MBA with a MA in International Studies or area studies in one of five geographic regions (including East Asia, East Europe/Russia, Latin America and the Caribbean, the Middle East, or South Asia). In addition to completing 24 to 28 courses, including language study, students who pursue a joint degree also must submit an integrated master's thesis.

The International MBA (IMBA) Program is a two-year program that is offered at the Chicago campuses for students "who want to gain a deeper understanding of global business issues."[50] The IMBA builds on the standard MBA curriculum by including five international business courses,

---

[50]The University of Chicago, Booth School of Business, International MBA web page, 2010, electronic document, http://www.chicagobooth.edu/fulltime/academics/international/imba.aspx, accessed December 29, 2010.

one academic term of study abroad, and a second language proficiency. This program is administered by the Booth School's International Programs Office.

Students enrolled in the full-time, evening, and weekend MBA programs, as well as PhD students, are given the opportunity to study abroad through the International Business Exchange Program (IBEP). Through the IBEP, which also is managed by the International Programs Office, students may choose to take courses at one of 33 partner schools in 21 countries. Approximately 65 to 75 Booth students travel abroad through the IBEP program each year, either for full-semester exchange programs or short-term programs of two to three weeks.

Part-time MBA students may participate in the International Entrepreneurship Lab, which allows students to gain an understanding of the critical aspects of building a business in China. The lab consists of 10 class sessions in Chicago followed by a weeklong trip to China, wherein the participants meet with representatives from local businesses.

The Global Leadership Series involves forums in cities around the world where members of the international business community gather to learn and share insights into issues they face every day in their careers. Speakers in the series include Chicago Booth faculty experts and business leaders from around the world, often who will take their presentations to cities in multiple regions. The series is viewed by the school as "a natural outgrowth of Chicago Booth's role as a leader in international business education."[51]

Chicago Booth supports 10 research and learning centers that are focused on a variety of business topics. One of these centers is the research Initiative on Global Markets (IGM), which is designed to improve financial and economic decision-making around the world by enhancing the understanding of business and financial market globalization. Originally launched with a founding grant from the Chicago Mercantile Exchange (CME) Group Foundation, the IGM's ongoing operations are funded through the support of four (current) business partners. In addition to supporting research by Booth faculty and visiting fellows, the IGM sponsors numerous forums and conferences. One of these conferences is the annual U.S. Monetary Policy Forum (USMPF), which brings international academics, market economists, and policy makers together to discuss U.S. monetary policy and produce a report on a critical medium-term issue confronting the

---

[51]The University of Chicago, Booth School of Business, Chicago Booth Global Leadership Series web page, 2010, electronic document, http://www.chicagobooth.edu/gls/, accessed December 29, 2010.

Federal Open Market Committee (FOMC). The IGM is administered by an executive director and a five-member executive board that includes two additional co-directors.

The Chicago and London campuses also support non-degree and custom executive education programs. A planned expansion to the Singapore campus will allow Chicago Booth to offer non-degree executive education programs, including programs by its Polsky Center for Entrepreneurship, and the campus will provide an opportunity for other parts of the university to offer programs in Singapore.[52]

Program Outcomes

Former dean Ted Snyder reports that the school hoped to accomplish four main objectives by opening and operating the London (previously Barcelona) and Singapore campuses:

- raise the school's global profile
- expand the school's network
- offer the Executive MBA outside the U.S. on a profitable basis
- support faculty development

He and Kooser both agree that the program has met these objectives, and more. One unanticipated positive outcome was the building of "a global learning system" across the three campuses. Another was the school's ability, through the three campuses, to provide better support for and strengthen ties to Booth School alumni who live and work in Europe and Asia. A third benefit was the enhanced ability for the school to work with its corporate partners to meet their needs, such as to provide EMBA graduates who have familiarity with European and Asian business contexts.

---

[52]The University of Chicago, Booth School of Business, "Larger Singapore campus to be built by University of Chicago Graduate School of Business," The University of Chicago press release, February 28, 2008, electronic document, http://www.chicagobooth.edu/newsmedia/releases/2008-02-28_singapore.aspx, accessed September 15, 2009.

UNIVERSITY OF MINNESOTA, CARLSON SCHOOL OF MANAGEMENT

For several years, the Carlson School of Management at the University of Minnesota has followed an international strategy that focuses on the maintenance of deep relationships with a few key partner schools, yet it supports a widespread global presence.[53] The Carlson School's International Programs Office centrally operates the funding and management of a wide range of international programs. The school's international activities are driven by a widely shared belief that expanding the global perspectives and competencies of students, faculty, and staff is central to the school's success. This commitment is manifest most clearly in a requirement that all undergraduate students, beginning with the fall 2008 freshman class, must have participated in some kind of international experience abroad prior to graduation. For the school to enable the approximately 450 freshman and 150 transfer students who enter the school each year to fulfill this requirement, while also supporting international activities for graduate students and faculty, a well-planned and well-executed effort is required by the business school's faculty and staff.

The Evolution of the School's Globalization

The Carlson School first began its focus on building the international capabilities of students, faculty, and staff in the mid-1980s, when it appointed Mahmood Zaidi as the school's first International Program Development Director. Since that time, the International Programs Office (IPO) has grown from a staff of two to a staff of 12 who operate under the direction of an Assistant Dean of International Programs, Anne D'Angelo King, and an Associate Dean of International Programs, Dr. Michael Houston. As he reflects on the early years, Zaidi recounts the initial steps he took to build momentum for this new area of focus. "Our first priority was

---

[53]Each case study was prepared with the purpose of illustrating an interesting variation in approach to the globalization of management education. Inclusion in this report does not constitute an endorsement of this approach for all schools.

This case study was developed through conversations and email correspondence with Dr. Michael Houston (associate dean for International Programs, University of Minnesota Carlson School of Management) and Anne D'Angelo King (assistant dean for International Programs, University of Minnesota Carlson School of Management), as well as a review of the Carlson School of Management website, and review of accounts of the school's activities in press releases, periodicals, etc. Errors and omissions are the sole responsibility of the authors.

to earn the support and respect of faculty, students, and staff. We focused on internationalizing the curriculum, establishing student and faculty exchanges, and developing study abroad programs. We also encouraged faculty research via small research and travel grants. In order to support development activities, we created fee-for-service programs such as the summer programs in Lyon and Vienna."[54] These initial steps formed the foundation for the inclusive, multidimensional approach that Zaidi, Houston, and D'Angelo King believe has made the international programs both successful and sustainable.

Establishing the Global Executive MBA Programs

In the early 1990s, the school brought greater focus to its international strategy, having decided to work on developing and maintaining deep relationships with a few key partner schools while complementing those efforts with a more widespread global presence. Thus began efforts to develop what Zaidi terms a "constellation of partnerships" that involved a few key institutions. In 1994, the Carlson School and the Warsaw School of Economics in Poland welcomed the first class of students into the Warsaw Executive MBA Program (WEMBA). In May 1999, the Carlson School received a $1.25 million gift from a German businessman and MBA program alumnus. The bulk of the donation went to support tuition fellowships for MBA students who were concentrating in international management. However, $250,000 was given as seed money to help develop the EMBA programs that were then being planned in Vienna and China.[55]

The Vienna Executive MBA (VEMBA) program began in 1999 in partnership with Wirtschaftsuniversität Wien. Two years later, in 2001, the China Executive MBA (CHEMBA) began in partnership with Lingnan (University) College of Sun Yat-sen University. According to a press release at the time, "the signed agreement was the culmination of more than two years of negotiations that, with the assistance of 3 M Corporation in Hong Kong, gained the approval of China's Ministry of Education."[56] China was seen as an appropriate location for the program given the university's

---

[54]University of Minnesota, Carlson School of Management, "Building International Bridges," *Going Global* newsletter, Spring 2008 edition, p. 2, electronic document, http://www.carlsonschool.umn.edu/assets/114759.pdf, accessed April 4, 2009.

[55]*The Minnesota Daily*, "Alumnus Donates Millions," February 11, 2009, electronic document, http://www.mndaily.com/2009/02/11/alumnus-donates, accessed April 4, 2009.

[56]*PR Newswire*, "Carlson School Dean Signs Agreement in China for New MBA Program Abroad," PR Newswire Association LLC, June 22, 2000, electronic document, http://www.accessmylibrary.com/coms2/summary_0286-27965272_ITM, accessed April 4, 2009.

tradition of enrolling Chinese students at its main campus and given the large number of university alumni who lived in Asia.

The Carlson School refers to the three joint-EMBA programs (WEMBA, VEMBA, and CHEMBA) together as the Global Executive MBA programs. Each program (in Warsaw, Vienna, and Guangzhou, respectively) has an on-site program director at the campus of the partner school. These directors report to a Global Executive MBA Academic Director at the partner school. All programs are financially sustainable.

The school's four EMBA programs (including a more traditional EMBA program on the Minnesota campus) run simultaneously and follow similar curricula, though the actual course structure varies among programs, as do course materials, discussions, and guest speakers. This freedom to adapt enables each program to focus on the business context in the region (e.g., the Warsaw program on Eastern Europe, the China program on South China, and the Vienna program on Europe), thereby allowing a global-local perspective in each program. While the four programs were originally designed to run independently of each other, today participants in all four programs collaborate with each other through a virtual team project. EMBA students in each of the four locations connect online to develop business plans for the introduction of a new product to the global marketplace. The four programs culminate in sync with each other as students from each location come to the University of Minnesota for an "Integrated Residency" where they meet the participants of the other EMBA programs and present their business plans prior to a common graduation ceremony.

The partnerships with the Warsaw School of Economics, Wirtschaftsuniversität Wien, and Lingnan (University) College also extend beyond delivery of the Global EMBA programs. Each school is a part of a much larger network of partner schools with which the Carlson School engages in semester exchanges, short-term study abroad programs, summer programs, faculty exchanges, and joint-faculty appointments.

Adopting an Undergraduate International Experience Requirement

In July 2006, soon after Alison Davis-Blake began her term as dean of the business school, she convened a team of administrators and faculty from peer institutions to review the school's programs. The team identified the school's international activity as one of its core strengths and suggested that the school consider ways to invest in and augment that activity. Based on this suggestion and subsequent exploration and analysis, the school's undergraduate program curriculum committee presented the faculty with a revised undergraduate curriculum that included a recommendation that all Carlson undergraduate business students be required to complete an international activity prior to graduation. Faculty overwhelmingly supported the proposal, which was then forwarded to the International Programs Office with the directive to "make it happen."

Driving the international experience requirement and its implementation is the belief that business school graduates must be globally competent members of the workforce. As he acknowledges the differences in how being "globally competent" might be defined depending on one's industry, environment, and responsibilities, Houston stresses that the "task [of the Carlson School of Management] is not to make the students globally competent, but to motivate them to want to become competent." Accordingly, though students are encouraged to take advantage of one of the business-oriented international programs offered by the business school, they may also fulfill the requirement by participating in non-business international programs that are coordinated at the university-level.

Prior to the implementation of the undergraduate requirement, approximately 50 percent of undergraduate business students studied abroad. Thus, the school also acknowledged that implementing the policy would require essentially doubling the level of international activity among that group of students; since then each year has seen incremental expansion in the number of available international program options. Houston also notes that, critical to the program's implementation was an acknowledgement that the 450 freshman who enter the business school each year vary substantially in their level of readiness for international exposure. Some have traveled extensively outside the U.S., while others have not ventured beyond Minnesota. Consequently, the available international program options vary in terms of location, length, subject matter, and academic content.

Also with the new requirement comes a more "guided approach" to utilizing international experiences than was in place before, says D'Angelo King. Guidance to students is provided in the form of an orientation program (IE 101) that all undergraduate students are required to attend. The orientation is attended by representatives from the university's Office of International Programs, the Carlson School's Undergraduate Programs and International Programs offices, and the University's Financial Aid Office, all of which collectively provide students with an overview of the various programs available and information regarding financial resources, the application process, and how to choose a program that aligns with their interests and career goals. IE 101 can also be completed online.[57] The

---

[57]University of Minnesota, Carlson School of Management, International Experience 101 Overview web page, 2009, electronic document, http://www.carlsonschool.umn.edu/page9322.aspx, accessed November 13, 2009.

International Programs Office holds walk-in advising hours during four afternoons per week in order to provide one-on-one assistance to students who are planning their international experience.

Student Exchange

Like many other business schools, the Carlson School of Management has partner/exchange agreements with more than 25 schools to support student exchange opportunities at the undergraduate and graduate levels. The geographic locations of partnerships are based on the importance of a country/region from a business perspective (which recently has led to more partnerships within Asia) and periodic surveys of students' location preferences. The choice of institutional partners is based on several factors, including the volume of courses taught in English, the school's experience with partnerships, and the institution's reputation among business school peers.

Short-Term Global Enrichment Programs

For students who prefer not to go on semester-long exchanges, the Carlson School offers a range of short-term global enrichment programs and summer programs. Short-term programs typically involve two weeks of travel following approximately eight weeks of classes, generally in the second half of the spring or fall semester. Graduate short-term programs result in four credits (most are graded on a letter scale, a few are graded pass/fail), and undergraduate programs may consist of either three- or four-credit courses. Summer programs range in length from two to six weeks and are hosted at partner institutions around the world.

Short-term programs may either focus on a special topic or take a "live-case" approach. Special topics at the graduate level include The Ethical Environment of Business (Brussels/London); Corporate Social Responsibility: A Scandinavian Approach (Norway, Sweden, and Denmark); Doing Business in Brazil (Brazil); Managing in a Global Environment (India); and Business and the Environment: Lessons from Central America (Costa Rica). Undergraduate students may pursue special topics such as Managerial Accounting—An International Perspective (Argentina); Business and the Environment, Lessons from Central America (Costa Rica); International Human Resources Management (Brisbane and Sydney); and An Introduction to Global Entrepreneurship (Shanghai and Beijing).

Students who participate in short-term enrichment programs on special topics pay a program fee that covers tuition, insurance, and some other program-related expenses. During the portion of the program in which students spend time abroad, they attend classes, conduct site visits with local firms, and experience some of the local culture.

Live-case programs follow a similar format of classroom preparation prior to the two weeks of travel, but they require students to work with actual companies on a real business problem. To deliver these programs, the Carlson School relies on its partnerships with the Warsaw School of Economics, Wirtschaftsuniversität Wien, Lingnan (University) College, and a second Chinese partner school, the Cheung Kong Graduate School of Business. For each program (one undergraduate and three graduate programs), students from the Carlson School and the partner school engage in readings, assignments, and research prior to coming together for a two-week "seminar" in the partner school location. Students from each school form teams to address a "live-case" regarding a company with operations in the region. When the students come together for the final two weeks of the program, in addition to combined lectures and site visits to regional firms, they collaborate to finalize their case recommendations and then present their recommendations to company executives. The companies that students work with include 3 M (Vienna Seminar), Cargill (Warsaw Seminar), and Toro and International Dairy Queen (China Seminars).

The short-term global enrichment programs also provide the school with an opportunity to contribute to the mission of globalizing the campus by encouraging staff members to apply to be Travel Coordinators for the various programs. As Travel Coordinators, the staff members serve as liaisons between the partner institution and the Carlson School IPO. They also provide support to students and faculty members in the program and facilitate the on-site schedule and site visits. The global enrichment programs are managed by a program director in the International Programs Office, with support from an associate program director and program managers.

The Global Discovery Program for MBAs

Beginning with the MBA Class of 2011, the Carlson School incorporated an international business requirement for its graduate students as well. The Carlson MBA Global Discovery Program is a required MBA course that takes place during the fall semester of the second year of the full-time MBA program, and it continues with a two-week international component in the following January. The class is divided into groups, each of which travels to a different global location and undertakes activities aligned with local business. Upon completion of the course, the separate groups return to the Carlson School and engage in a comparative analysis of the different regions to which they traveled.

According to D'Angelo King, the school felt that the international experience was just as salient to graduate students as to undergraduates, if not more so, but the model needed to be modified in order to reflect the greater academic understanding expected of students at the graduate level. With a typical graduate cohort of approximately 100 students being much smaller than the undergraduate cohort, the model of the Global Discovery Program is easier to achieve. MBA students who wish to enroll in additional global enrichment programs above and beyond this required course are free to do so as well.

Faculty

The Carlson School's focus on the international aspects of business attracts faculty with international backgrounds or interests to the school. Thus, while the school does not pursue the globalization of its faculty as a strategy, it has noted that the school's focus and culture tend to attract a globally diverse set of faculty candidates.

The International Programs Office works to provide a variety of means by which faculty can expand their international perspectives and competencies. These options include teaching opportunities in the global enrichment programs, the Global Executive MBA programs, and faculty exchanges (for research, study, and occasional lectures) with Keio University in Japan and l'Université Jean Moulin Lyon 3 in France. A Small Research Grant Program has provided funding to support faculty research activities that address global business issues and reflect an international or cross-national scope. Faculty members are encouraged to partner with faculty from foreign institutions, especially those schools that have existing relationships with the Carlson School.

The school also relies heavily on clinical faculty to assist in the delivery of its international programs, particularly the short-term global enrichment programs. Clinical faculty tend to be disproportionately more interested than the school's full-time tenure-track faculty in the international programs, and the school has found that using the clinical faculty for the short-term programs assists in the management of faculty resources across the core degree programs and courses that support the international experience requirement.

Contributing to a University-Wide Objective

In 2006, the broader set of University of Minnesota faculty and administration made the decision that "internationalization" would be a strategic objective at the university level. A statement from a university strategic planning document articulates that achievement of its vision to become a global university "demands that internationalization, diversity, and academic excellence be inextricably intertwined and central to the University's core mission." This aim has led to new initiatives at the university level that are focused on globalization, including a goal to have 50 percent of all undergraduate students study abroad.

Dr. Michael Houston, Associate Dean for International Programs, writes, "The Carlson School, rather than being affected by this strategy, was consulted as one of the units with an existing strong international effort which, in turn, helped the task force develop its recommendations." The fact that the university shares a commitment to globalization in turn ensures that the Carlson School has many internal "partners" at the University of Minnesota. The staff members of the IPO have a close working relationship with numerous university-level offices and committees that operate as part of the university's Office of International Programs. These establishments include a Learning Abroad Center (facilitates student exchange programs on a variety of subjects), the International Student and Scholar Services (provides support and assistance to visiting students and scholars), the International Scholarship Committee (guides and funds the university's international research agenda), the International Programs Council, and the International Data Base/Process Committee (tracks and provides data related to all of the university's international operations).

Outcomes

Houston and D'Angelo King cite several key outcomes of the school's approach to globalization. The International Programs Office originally operated using funds that were allocated from the business school, but the program array has developed in such a way that the portfolio of activities is largely self-sustaining. In past years, the portfolio has provided a net financial contribution back to the business school. More recently, this contribution has been reinvested in international programs to support the growth necessary to support the new undergraduate and MBA requirements.

The school has also benefited from an enhanced reputation as a school with an international focus and with innovative international programs. School representatives are frequently consulted by other business schools as well as by others within the University of Minnesota. The school has leveraged its proximity to and reputation among companies that operate in the local Minneapolis/St. Paul metropolitan area as well as in Central and

Eastern Europe and China. Corporate support for the programs has resulted in the provision of donations to support scholarships for students (an increasingly large need with the new requirements) who participate in the international programs and in the active engagement of firms in providing site visits, case studies, and "live-case" projects.

The Global Executive MBA programs have created an extensive international network of students and alumni. Additionally, for the part-time MBA students in particular, the short-term programs create a sense of community among the students that helps enhance their connections to each other and to the school as alumni.

The centralized management of the school's international activities through the International Programs Office has enabled the school to coordinate its activities, look for opportunities to engage partners in a variety of ways, and incorporate students, faculty, and staff from across the business school. These efforts are augmented by strong support from the business school administration and faculty, aligned objectives and a supportive culture at the university level, and excellent working relation-ships between the staff of the Carlson School's International Programs Office and the staff of the university-level international programs offices.

Future

Given the recent implementation of the university's undergraduate international experience requirement, the Carlson School is actively engaged in planning for further expansion in the number and types of international experiences available to students, which also may include internship and service-learning opportunities, or the school may allow students to create their own international experiences. The school also is committed to continuing to seek scholarship funding to alleviate the incremental cost to undergraduate students that is associated with the requirement.

Additionally, the school is exploring means to assess, empirically, the impact of the various international experiences on the global competencies of the students. Though in a very initial, exploratory stage, the school hopes to rely on these measures to further refine and develop programs to increase their effectiveness in achieving intended objectives.

UNIVERSITY OF SOUTH CAROLINA, MOORE SCHOOL OF BUSINESS

The Darla Moore School of Business at the University of South Carolina has a long history of attracting scholars who are focused on the international dimensions of business and on the delivery of educational programs that make use of that expertise.[58] Led by the Sonoco International Business Department, the school's Center for International Business Education and Research (CIBER), and a committed faculty and administration, the school has developed an array of programs that expose students of all levels—from undergraduates to graduate students and executives—to the complexities of conducting business across borders.

A Tradition Built over Decades

The Moore School of Business at the University of South Carolina has a history of focusing on international business that dates back to the early 1970s. In 1974, the school established a new Master's in International Business Studies (MIBS) program that was designed to prepare students from the school's regional market to conduct business across borders. Two years later, in 1976, the school established an International Business Department to help build the school's capacity to deliver international business education. This new department did more than provide the necessary capacity to continue development of the new master's program. According to William R. Folks, Jr., Associate Dean of International Activities, over time the department has been "the critical variable in the School's long-term success" in international business.

In 1988, the U.S. Congress passed an act that enabled the establishment of Centers for International Business Education and Research (CIBERs) at U.S. business schools, and the Moore School was selected as one of the first five schools to receive funding to host a center. The CIBERs, of which 33 currently exist, are intended to "increase and promote the nation's

---

[58]Each case study was prepared with the purpose of illustrating an interesting variation in approach to the globalization of management education. Inclusion in this report does not constitute an endorsement of this approach for all schools.

This case study was developed through conversations and e-mail correspondence with Dr. William R. Folks, Jr. (associate dean, International Activities, University of South Carolina, Moore School of Business), review of the Moore School of Business website, and review of accounts of the school's activities in press releases, periodicals, etc. Errors and omissions are the sole responsibility of the authors.

capacity for international understanding and competitiveness" through international education, research, and training.[59] Funded through grants that are administered by the U.S. Department of Education, each CIBER must apply for competitive grants (up to $450,000) every four years. According to Folks, the Moore School CIBER devotes as much as 30 percent of its budget to support faculty research—a percentage that is much higher than at many other CIBERs.

In 2004, the pivotal role of the International Business Department was recognized through a $3 million-gift from Sonoco, a global packaging company based in Hartsville, South Carolina. The gift established an endowed fund that provides substantial financial support for the Sonoco International Business Department's mission "to develop and disseminate leading-edge knowledge concerning the practice of global business."[60] Today, the department plays a role in a range of educational programs that include an International Business major within the Bachelor of Science in Business Administration (BSBA) program, a Master of International Business (MIB), an International Master of Business Administration (IMBA) program, an Executive International Master of Business Administration (EIMBA), a PhD in International Business, and a PhD in International Finance.

Globalizing the Undergraduate Curriculum

According to Folks, the philosophy behind development of the undergraduate international business curriculum is based on the assumption that every student, regardless of educational level, should graduate with at least an awareness of the impact of globalization on business. Thus, all business majors are required to complete at least nine credit-hours of courses with an international orientation, including at least one "international business" course offered through the Moore School. Faculty members who teach various functional courses (e.g., finance, marketing, etc.) are expected to infuse their courses with international content so that students graduate with an understanding of the international dimension of that functional field. Students interested in gaining a deeper understanding of international business outside the classroom can join the Global Business Council, a

---

[59]Centers for International Business Education and Research, About CIBERs web page, 2010, electronic document, http://www.ciberweb.org/about.asp, accessed April 24, 2010.
[60]University of South Carolina, Darla Moore School of Business, International Business web page, 2010, electronic document, http://mooreschool.sc.edu/facultyandresearch/departments/internationalbusiness.aspx, accessed December 29, 2010.

student organization that coordinates guest speakers, workshops, and international outreach projects.

For many years, undergraduate students at the Moore School of Business also had an opportunity to pursue a certificate in International Business. About seven years ago, however, the school converted the certificate program into an International Business (IB) major, which aims to develop students with a greater level of expertise in international business. IB students are expected to complete 15 hours of international business courses, participate in an overseas experience, and study a foreign language. In a design that is rather unique among business schools, students in the International Business major are also expected to pursue a major in another field.

Admission to the International Business major is highly competitive. Historically, students have applied to the major in the spring semester of their second year, and under this model, admission levels have been restricted—originally limited to 50 students per year and recently increased to 90 students per year. A recent decision to allow top newly admitted undergraduate students (those admitted to the university's South Carolina Honors College or Capstone Scholars program) to enroll directly in the major is expected, according to Folks, to increase the number of admitted students to as many as 150 to 200 per year by 2014.

All International Business majors are expected to complete a "Globalization and Business" course that focuses on "the business opportunities and threats for individuals, companies, and countries created by the growth of globalization, and how companies must operate in diverse foreign environments and engage in specialized transactions."[61] Students in the undergraduate International Business major also complete two functional courses that focus on the international components of a specific managerial function, such as finance or marketing. Additionally, they are required to complete one or two thematic courses that focus on a specific international business issue (such as foreign market entry or strategic management in developing markets) from a multidisciplinary perspective. Yet another requirement is to complete a regionally focused course that addresses business in and with a particular world region from a multidisciplinary basis.

The language requirement is rigorous compared to that for many undergraduate business programs in the U.S. Students are expected to take at least four courses in a foreign language, yet most take more in pursuit of a

---

[61]University of South Carolina, Darla Moore School of Business, International Business Courses web page, 2010, electronic document, http://mooreschool.sc.edu/facultyandresearch/departments/internationalbusiness/internationalbusinesscourses.aspx, accessed January 3, 2011.

minor in that language. Language education opportunities for undergraduate students are offered based on the capacity of the university's language departments, and they include Arabic, Chinese, French, German, Italian, Japanese, Portuguese, Russian, and Spanish. Given limited capacity in some languages, such as German, Portuguese, and Russian, students who pursue these languages may need to use a term of study abroad in order to pursue more advanced courses.

The Moore School of Business has agreements with several schools in other countries to facilitate study abroad opportunities for its students. Students who major in international business are required to spend at least one study period in another country, and many other business majors take advantage of study abroad opportunities as well. Beginning with the class admitted in 2011, International Business majors will be required to spend the spring semester of their junior year at a partner institution. Given the increases in the number of students who major in international business, and given that other undergraduates take three "internationally oriented" courses, the school is in the process of expanding the options it provides for student exchange. The school also is considering the possibility of requiring specific overseas learning experiences that are aligned with the student's area of study.

Undergraduate International Business and Chinese Enterprise (IBCE) Track

In the 2009–10 academic year, the first cohort of students began a new Bachelor of Science in Business Administration track offered by the Moore School in collaboration with the Chinese University of Hong Kong (CUHK). Named the International Business and Chinese Enterprise (IBCE) track, its primary objective is "to develop undergraduate students into professionals who can operate and succeed in the Chinese business environment."[62] The program brings together a cohort of students from the two schools on a rigorous course of study that is split between each campus. Though not required, most students are expected to enter the Moore School's one-year Master of International Business program immediately upon completion of the undergraduate degree program.

The idea for the program first arose approximately three years ago. A long-time faculty member of the Moore School, who also happened to be a

---

[62]University of South Carolina, Moore School of Business, IBCE Track web page, 2010, electronic document, http://mooreschool.sc.edu/undergrad/globalexperience/ibcetrack.aspx, accessed April 24, 2010.

CUHK alumnus, had been regularly traveling to Hong Kong as a visiting professor. Then, a second faculty member also began taking visiting assignments at CUHK. Meanwhile, since 2005, CUHK had been participating in a three-campus undergraduate program—Global Learning Opportunities in Business Education (GLOBE)—with Copenhagen Business School (CBS) and The University of North Carolina at Chapel Hill (UNC), and was gaining confidence in the success of the model. CUHK proposed the development of a similar program with the Moore School.

According to Folks, the complex nature of the program and the desire by both schools for the program to be of high quality meant that the plan did not evolve overnight. The development team went through about four different iterations of a potential program structure before finally settling on one that would meet the expectations and educational structures of both schools. Ultimately, three separate documents were needed to fully outline the responsibilities of each school and the processes for program delivery: a memorandum of understanding, an exchange agreement, and an operating document.

Each school admits 20 students per year into the program. As the Moore School and CUHK undergraduate degree programs are four years and three years in length, respectively, the Moore School admits students one year earlier than CUHK for the same cohort. Students from both schools are expected also to pursue another major field of study in addition to the IB major that is part of the IBCE program.

In the first year, students from South Carolina take two semesters of classes in Mandarin Chinese in addition to other courses needed to fulfill the Moore School requirements. Over the summer, they travel to Hong Kong to take an intensive language training course at CUHK. The students remain in Hong Kong during the second year, where they take courses together with the newly admitted CUHK students. Students from South Carolina continue to take courses in Mandarin Chinese during the spring and fall semesters of the second year, and they follow these courses with another intensive language training course in their second summer. In the third year, both sets of students return to Columbia, South Carolina, for two semesters of courses including a special section of the "Globalization and Business" course. The third summer is designated for students from both schools to pursue internships in the U.S. In the fourth year, all students take two semesters of courses at CUHK, including two special courses on Chinese business. At the conclusion of this year, each set of students receives an undergraduate degree from their respective institutions.

The summer immediately following graduation is designated for students to pursue an internship in China before moving on to the Master of International Business curriculum in the final year of the program (see below).

Undergraduate MENA & International Business: Middle East and North Africa (MENA) Track

In the 2011–12 academic year, the first cohort of students are scheduled to begin the latest Bachelor of Science in Business Administration track offered by the Moore School, in collaboration with the School of Business at American University in Cairo, Egypt (AUC). Named the MENA & International Business: Middle East and North Africa (MENA) track, its objectives and methodology are modeled after those of the ICBE track outlined above, but with a focus on the business environment of the Middle East and Northern Africa region.

As with the ICBE track, twenty students from both collaborating universities advance through the MENA program as a cohort. Students spend their freshman and junior years at the Moore School, and their sophomore and senior years at AUC. Moore School students participate in intensive study of Modern Standard Arabic during the summer semesters prior to and following their second year in Cairo. Moore School students will be expected to pursue a second business major in addition to the MENA track program. Additionally, the partner schools plan for internships to be offered both in the U.S. and the MENA region, with linked opportunities for graduate study.[63]

Master of International Business Program

The Master of International Business (MIB) program was introduced in 2009 as a pre-experience degree program limited to individuals with an undergraduate degree in international business. The school will introduce, in the Summer 2011 term, a pre-MIB summer program that focuses on the fundamentals of international business. This program would enable other business undergraduates "who otherwise meet admissions requirements, which include substantial foreign language skills and overseas experience" to be admitted into the program.

The MIB program is interdisciplinary in nature, with contributions from the Moore School, the College of Arts and Sciences (Political Science Department), and the School of Law, and focuses on the intersection of business and government in cross-border business operations. The

---

[63]University of South Carolina, Moore School of Business, MENA track web page, 2010, electronic document, http://moore.sc.edu/undergrad/globalexperience/menatrack.aspx, accessed November 8, 2010.

curriculum includes 15 hours of core courses, six hours of international business electives, six hours of international studies electives, and three hours of foreign policy that focuses on a particular world region. Among other considerations in the design of the program, an important goal was to structure it in a way that would coordinate well with master's programs that were emerging in Europe in alignment with the Bologna Accord. This direction, says Folks, will enable the school to pursue opportunities for double-degree programs with partners in Europe and elsewhere.

International Master of Business Administration Program

The post-experience International MBA (IMBA) program is the current iteration of the original Master's in International Business Studies program that was launched in the 1970s. All students take a series of courses that are included in the core curriculum, pursue an international internship, and take two semesters of elective courses (sometimes at an international partner institution). Additionally, students choose between two track options: a Language Track and a Global Track.

Students in the Language Track gain intensive training in a foreign language in preparation for an internship in a country where that language is spoken. Folks characterizes the Language Track as one in which "students enter a specific language track, develop or exhibit competence in that language, study overseas in a country where that language is a primary language, and intern in a country where that language is a primary language." Of the eight language options (Arabic, Chinese, French, German, Italian, Japanese, Portuguese, and Spanish), most require a 20 to 22 month curriculum, though Arabic, Chinese, and Japanese require 29 to 34 months of training to prepare students for the internship experience.

In lieu of language courses, Global Track students select from a set of regional business courses that focus on the political, economic, and business factors that affect the investment and operating climates in a particular geographic area. They also choose from a set of global topics courses such as International Taxation or Global Business Strategy. The curriculum includes a two-week immersion experience in a location in Europe or Asia.

Folks said the need for the school to maintain relationships in countries where each of the languages is spoken has been a major driver for the school's globalization efforts over the past several decades, which has served as a catalyst for continued development of connections between the school, its faculty, and students with other parts of the world. Still, Folks acknowledges that convincing students who enroll in a post-experience graduate program of the need for language training can be difficult.

Executive International Master of Business Administration (EIMBA) program

The Moore School offers a dual-degree Executive International Master of Business Administration (EIMBA) program in partnership with Tecnológico de Monterrey-EGADE in Guadalajara, Mexico. With the exception of two international seminars, weekend classes are held in Guadalajara every three weeks and are taught to an equal degree by the faculty of each university. The program's weekend course structure enables faculty members from the Moore School to easily travel to Guadalajara while still teaching at the Columbia campus.

Research and Outreach

What drives the delivery of each of these programs is a faculty who is passionate about international business research and a departmental research strategy. The Sonoco Department of International Business houses 13 tenure-track faculty members in a setting that Folks says "provides a home for cross-disciplinary scholars and allows the creation of cross-disciplinary teams." Research tends to focus on the institutional context of international business and how institutions and business evolve, both in the macro sense and with a deeper focus on specific regions.

Folks recounts that "faculty research has been a major component of the School's strategy since it first became involved globally in the early 1970s." Each faculty department at the Moore School has its own promotion and tenure policies, and therefore the Sonoco Department of International Business is able to set policies that encourage output that is focused on international business, either in publications such as the *Journal of International Business Studies* or other discipline-specific journals.

Faculty members are also encouraged to engage in international consultancies and pursue overseas teaching opportunities. Most overseas teaching is done on a contract basis between the faculty member and the host school, though, currently, the Moore School sponsors three trips in which faculty members take students with them to another country. Other international teaching opportunities are presented through the arrangement with Tecnológico de Monterrey-EGADE to provide the EIMBA in Guadalajara.

In 2009, The Columbia U.S. Export Assistance Center (USEAC) relocated its offices to USC's Darla Moore School of Business. The move is intended to create many opportunities for synergy between the international business faculty and USEAC, which is charged with "helping

SMEs export their goods and services by providing comprehensive counseling and advice, finding qualified international buyers, and providing market intelligence to firms interested in entering new markets."[64]

Academic programs and their curricula correspond closely with the research interests of the faculty. Most international business courses are taught by tenure-track faculty, meaning that substantial opportunity exists for research findings to influence the design of the program and course content. Folks notes that this practice is evident in the "institutional flavor" of the MIB program and the focus of some courses on specific geographic regions.

The research emphasis of the faculty also supports two doctoral programs: one in international business and another in international finance—whose graduates are well-regarded. Students who concentrate in international business are expected to demonstrate proficiency in at least one foreign language and to spend at least three months in overseas research, teaching, working, and/or studying.

The focus on international dimensions of business extends to faculty outside of the Sonoco Department of International Business as well. According to Folks, faculty in other departments often share similar areas of focus and also influence course and program development. The Department of Management Science established a Center for Global Supply Chain and Process Management in 2005 to provide education and training for students, solutions to client organizations, and to encourage practice-based research.

Finally, through the CIBER, the Moore School faculty help share their expertise with faculty members at other schools who are preparing to teach international business or who are seeking to enhance their capabilities. This knowledge-sharing takes place during a six-day workshop, Faculty Development in International Business, with tracks that focus on the international dimensions of different functional areas. Moore School faculty also lead two CIBER related regional Faculty Development in International Business (FDIB) programs to Sub-Saharan Africa and to the MENA region, and faculty from all departments participate in such cross-border study trips.

---

[64]International Trade Administration, U.S. Department of Commerce, "International Trade Administration and Columbia Mayor Join USC's Darla Moore School of Business for International Education Week," International Trade Administration press release, November 20, 2009, electronic document, http://www.trade.gov/press/press_releases/2009/iew_112009.asp, accessed April 24, 2010.

Outcomes

According to Folks, the outcomes of the school's efforts over the past three decades have been "an immeasurable order of magnitude," greater than the school had originally expected when it launched the MIBS program in the 1970s. The school has established a reputation as a leader in the field of international business, as evidenced by a continued strong showing in various related rankings. Its success has also enabled the school to influence the University's own globalization strategy through the expertise it has developed and the international relationships it has established. A key contributor to success, he notes, has been the "continued support through the CIBER and other sources for International Business related research," which has provided fuel for the school's expanded efforts.

At the same time, the continued development of the program has not been without challenges. Folks notes that changes in leadership have meant that levels of interest in international activities have fluctuated among the university's central administration over the past several decades, which in turn has influenced the pace and direction of development. Additionally, like many U.S. public schools, the University of South Carolina has been responding to substantial budget constraints that are largely due to declining levels of state funding, with effects across all schools and departments. Historically, federal funding through the CIBER has been a welcome supplement for the international business programs, which had enabled the school to focus on curriculum development and research support that it might not otherwise have been able to afford. Without this revenue grant funding and the revenue stream from popular undergraduate and graduate international business programs, Folks notes that the Moore School's financial situation could be "far worse."

Next Steps

As previously mentioned, the Moore School anticipates an expansion of the undergraduate international business major over the next several years as well as continued development of the master's program structure in order to facilitate dual-degree opportunities with partner schools. These plans, coupled with the school's interest in having greater influence on the specific courses that students take when they study abroad, call for the school to seek to establish deeper relationships with certain international partners. Given the importance of any partnership being a good fit for both schools, however, this charge has not been something the school has taken lightly; in fact, Folks notes that the school has developed a comprehensive set of criteria that it uses to guide partner selection and related decisions.

Additionally, Folks believes that the future will bring "an increased market for cross-border educational experiences that are more targeted to students' career aspirations" as well as "more need for students to learn languages and understand cultures, not less." Thus, the school plans to maintain its focus on developing language capabilities in tandem with international business expertise. It is in the process of developing additional cohort programs with partner schools (similar to the undergraduate ICBE and MENA tracks) with language training in German and potentially other, less commonly taught languages where the partner school has "substantive capability" and where a substantial corporate market exists for speakers of those languages.

Finally, in December 2009, the Moore School entered into an agreement with Cisco to use the company's TelePresence technology, which creates live, face-to-face meeting experiences for individuals in different locations, to support the delivery of graduate- and executive-level courses globally. Though still under development, plans include a technology-enabled degree program for executives that will be offered through collaboration with other business schools located around the globe.

Behind all of these plans, emphasizes Folks, is a constant effort not to "confuse global activity with global business education." Thus, the school's main priority remains its international business research—particularly that which seeks to better understand the implications of national borders for multinational enterprises—and the infusion of that knowledge into the content of the learning experiences it provides.

Bibliography of Works Cited

AACSB International, AACSB Member Collaboration Survey 2008, Internal survey data, 2008.

AACSB International, Business School Faculty Trends 2008, Report from AACSB International Knowledge Services, 2008.

AACSB International, *Business Schools on an Innovation Mission: Report of the AACSB International Task Force on Business Schools and Innovation*, 2010.

AACSB International, Business School Questionnaire, 2009–10.

AACSB International, *Eligibility Procedures and Standards for Business Accreditation*, revised January 31, 2010.

AACSB International, Spotlight: Business Schools and Doctoral Education, Featured School: Tulane University, 2010, electronic document, http://www.aacsb.edu/resources/doctoral/spotlights/TulaneLatinAmerican.pdf, accessed November 1, 2010.

AACSB International, Canadian Federation of Business School Deans, and European Foundation for Management Development, 2004–05 Alliances Survey Results, internal communication to survey participants, 2005.

Alderman, Geoffrey, "Bordering on the bureaucratic," *The Guardian*, September 2, 2008, electronic document, http://www.guardian.co.uk/education/2008/sep/09/internationalstudents.visas, accessed August 27, 2010.

ALFA Tuning Latin America, "Tuning Latin America Project" Web page, electronic document, http://tuning.unideusto.org/tuningal/, accessed June 10, 2010.

Altbach, Philip, "Globalization and the University: Myths and realities in an unequal world," *Tertiary Education and Management*, Vol. 10, No. 1 (2004), pp. 3–25.

Altbach, Philip, "Open Door in Higher Education: Unsustainable and Probably Ill-Advised," *Economic and Political Weekly,* Vol. 45, No. 13 (2010), pp. 13–14.

Altbach, Philip, Liz Reisberg, and Laura E. Rumbley, "Tracking a Global Academic Revolution," *Change*, Vol. 42, No. 2 (2010), pp. 30–39.

Alvarez, Paz, "Las Escuelas de Negocios, Contra las Cuerdas," CincoDías.com, April 4, 2009, electronic document, http://www.cincodias.com/articulo/Directivos/escuelas-negocios-cuerdas/20090404cdscdidir_1/cdspor/, accessed January 31, 2010.

Anderson, Bethanie L., "From Data to Strategy: Understanding Worldwide Trends in Graduate Management Education," Conference Paper for GMAC Annual Industry Conference 2007, electronic document, http://www.gmac.com/NR/rdonlyres/78E0448D-5D01-4E1A-B439-574E4A101B7C/0/Worldwide_Trends_small_v2.pdf, accessed December 28, 2009.

Andersson, U., and M. Forsgren, "In search of centre of excellence: Network embeddedness and subsidiary roles in multinational corporations," *Management International Review*, Vol. 40, No. 4 (2000), pp. 329–50.

Andersson, U., M. Forsgren, and U. Holm, "The strategic impact of external networks: subsidiary performance and competence development in the multinational corporation," *Strategic Management Journal*, Vol. 23 (2002), pp. 979–96.

Antunes, Don, and Howard Thomas, "The Competitive (Dis)Advantages of European Business Schools," *Long Range Planning*, Vol. 40, No. 3 (2007), pp. 382–404.

Arain, F.M., and S.A.A. Tipu, "Emerging Trends in Management Education in International Business Schools," *Educational Research and Review*, Vol. 2, No. 12 (2007), pp. 325–31.

Asalioğlu, Ibrahim, "YÖK seeks to attract foreign students to Turkish universities," *Today's Zaman*, October 7, 2008, electronic document, http://www.todayszaman.com/tz-web/detaylar.do?load=detay&link=155186&bolum=101, accessed August 27, 2010.

Associated Press, "With Help of Russian Business Leaders, M.B.A. School Opens in Moscow," *The New York Times*, September 30, 2009, electronic document, http://www.nytimes.com/2009/10/01/business/global/01iht-mba.html, accessed January 31, 2010.

Augier, Mie, and James G. March, "The Pursuit of Relevance in Management Education," *California Management Review*, Vol. 49, No. 3 (2007), pp. 129–46.

Australian Education International, "Transnational Education in the Higher Education Sector," Research Snapshot Series, 2009, electronic document, http://aei.gov.au/AEI/PublicationsAndResearch/Snapshots/2009073120_pdf.pdf, accessed August 18, 2010.

Beamish, P.W., "Internationalization as strategic change at the Western business school," in S. Tamer Cavusgil (ed.), *Internationalizing Business Education: Meeting the Challenge*, International Business Series, Michigan State University Press, East Lansing, MI, 1993.

Becker, Rosa, *International Branch Campuses: Markets and Strategies*, Report for the Observatory on Borderless Higher Education (OBHE), London, 2009.

Becker, Rosa, "International Branch Campuses: New Trends and Directions," *International Higher Education*, Vol. 58, Winter 2010, electronic document, http://www.bc.edu/bc_org/avp/soe/cihe/newsletter/Number58/p3_Becker.htm, accessed July 22, 2010.

Beinhocker, Eric, Ian Davis, and Lenny Mendonca, "The 10 Trends You Have to Watch," *Harvard Business Review*, Vol. 87, No. 7/8 (2009), pp. 55–60.

Bhagwati, Jagdish, *In Defense of Globalization*, Oxford University Press, Oxford, 2004.

Bhalla, Surjit S., "Second Among Equals: The Middle Class Kingdoms of India and China," 2007, electronic document, http://www.oxusinvestments.com/files/pdf/NE20090106.pdf, accessed August 23, 2010.

Birkinshaw, J., and N. Hood, "Multinational subsidiary evolution: capability and charter change in foreign-owned subsidiary companies," *Academy of Management Review*, Vol. 23, No. 4 (1998), pp. 773–95.

Bisoux, Tricia, "Global Immersion," *BizEd,* Vol. 6, No.4 (July/August 2007), pp. 46–47.

Bloland, H.G., "Whatever Happened to Postmodernism in Higher Education?: No Requiem in the New Millennium," *Journal of Higher Education,* Vol. 76, No. 2 (2005), pp. 121–50.

Bosma, Niels, and Jonathan Levie, *2009 Global Report,* Global Entrepreneurship Monitor, 2009, electronic document, http://www.gemconsortium.org/download/1282653102864/GEM%202009%20Global%20Report%20Rev%2020140410.pdf, accessed August 24, 2010.

Bradshaw, Della, "Canada eases work rules for graduates," *Financial Times,* July 28, 2008, electronic document, http://www.ft.com/cms/s/2/f65d3e04-5a80-11dd-bf96-000077b07658,dwp_uuid = 02e16f4a-46f9-11da-b8e5-00000e2511c8.html, accessed June 12, 2010.

Bradshaw, Della, "CEIBS inaugurates Ghana programme, *Financial Times,* May 19, 2009, electronic document, http://www.ft.com/cms/s/0/22f5d4e0-449f-11de-82d6-00144feabdc0,dwp_uuid = 87c504f8-2b20-11dc-85f9-000b5df10621.html, accessed August 23, 2009.

Bradshaw, Della, "Chinese school expands into African campus" *Financial Times,* April 6, 2008, electronic document, http://www.ft.com/cms/s/2/eaaedbb2-024c-11dd-9388-000077b07658.html, accessed August 23, 2009.

Brannen, Mary Yoko, and David C. Thomas, "Bicultural Individuals in Organizations: Implications and Opportunity," introduction to special issue, *International Journal of Cross-Cultural Management,* Vol. 10, No. 1 (April 2010), pp. 5–16.

Broughton, Philip D., "Harvard's Masters of the Apocalypse," *The Times of London,* March 1, 2009, electronic document, http://www.timesonline.co.uk/tol/news/uk/education/article5821706.ece, accessed January 31, 2010.

Byrne, John A., and Lori Bongiorno, "The Best B-Schools," *BusinessWeek,* October 24, 1994, electronic document, http://www.businessweek.com/1989-94/pre94/b339564.htm, accessed August 26, 2009.

Cantwell, J.A., "The globalisation of technology: What remains of the product cycle model?" *Cambridge Journal of Economics,* Vol. 19 (1995), pp. 155–74.

Cantwell, J. A., and L. Piscitello, "The emergence of corporate international networks for the accumulation of dispersed technological competencies," *Management International Review,* Vol. 39 (1999), pp. 123–47.

Centers for International Business Education and Research, About CIBERs Web page, 2010, electronic document, http://www.ciberweb.org/about.asp, accessed April 24, 2010.

CertifiedMBA.com, CMBA_Exam_Overview_and_Objectives, 2010, electronic document, http://www.certifiedmba.com/exam/CMBA_Exam_Overview_and_Objectives.pdf, accessed May 19, 2010.

China Europe International Business School, About CEIBS Web page, 2010, electronic document, http://www.ceibs.edu/africa/aboutceibs/index.shtml, accessed December 29, 2010.

China Europe International Business School, CEIBS Case Development Centre Web page, 2010, electronic document, http://www.ceibs.edu/cases/centre/index.shtml, accessed December 29, 2010.

China Europe International Business School, CEIBS Comes of Age Web page, 2009, electronic document, http://www.ceibs.edu/link/latest/36702.shtml, accessed October 5, 2009.

China Europe International Business School, "CEIBS Holds Africa Programme Inauguration Ceremony," CEIBS press release, May 19, 2009, electronic document, http://www.ceibs.edu/media/archive/40160.shtml, accessed August 23, 2009.

Chisholm, Alex, and Courtney Defibaugh, Asian Geographic Trend Report for GMAT Examinees, 2004–2008, Graduate Management Admission Council, McLean, VA, 2009.

Chisholm, Alex, and Courtney Defibaugh, World Geographic Trend Report for GMAT Examinees, 2004–2008, Graduate Management Admission Council, Reston, VA, 2009.

Chisholm, Alex, Courtney Defibaugh, and Hillary Taliaferro, Asian Geographic Trend Report for GMAT Examinees, 2005–2009, Graduate Management Admission Council, McLean, VA, 2010.

Chisholm, Alex, Courtney Defibaugh, and Hillary Taliaferro, World Geographic Trend Report for GMAT Examinees, 2005–2009, Graduate Management Admission Council, McLean, VA, 2010.

Clark, Tony, OECD Thematic Review of Tertiary Education, Country Report: United Kingdom, 2006, electronic document, http://www.education.gov.uk/research/data/uploadfiles/RR767.pdf, accessed March 31, 2010.

Cort, Kathryn T., Jayoti Das, and Wonhi J. Synn, "Cross-Functional Globalization Modules: A Learning Experience," *Journal of Teaching in International Business*, Vol. 15, No. 3 (2004), pp. 77–97.

Council of Graduate Schools, Findings from the 2008 CGS International Graduate Admissions Survey: Phase II: Final Applications and Initial Offers of Admission, CGS Research Report, August 2008, electronic document, http://www.cgsnet.org/portals/0/pdf/R_IntlAdm08_II.pdf, accessed August 27, 2010.

Cremer, Rolf, "Effective Practices: Asian Management Education Pedagogy," presentation at AACSB International World Class Practices Conference, Shanghai, China, June 2, 2009.

Cremer, Rolf, personal interview, 2009.

Damast, Alison, "Duke Rethinks Idea of a Global Campus," *BusinessWeek*, September 15, 2008, electronic document, http://www.businessweek.com/bschools/content/sep2008/bs20080914_756410.htm?chan = bschools_bschool + index + page_the + education + business, accessed June 29, 2009.

Damast, Alison, "U.S. Business Schools: Why Foreign M.B.A.s are Disappearing," *BusinessWeek*, August 3, 2009, electronic document, http://www.businessweek.com/bschools/content/aug2009/bs2009083_042666.htm?link_position = link1, accessed June 11, 2010.

Daniels, John D., "Specialization to infusion: IB studies in the 1990s," in Alan M. Rugman (ed.), *Leadership in international business education and research*, Elsevier Ltd, Oxford, 2003.

Datar, Srikant M., David A. Garvin, and Patrick G. Cullen, *Rethinking the MBA: Business Education at a Crossroads*, Harvard Business School Press, Cambridge, MA, 2010.

De Aenlle, Conrad, "Great Expectations from an American MBA Program: Building Better Businesses," *New York Times*, June 15, 1994, electronic document, http://www.nytimes.com/1994/06/15/news/15iht-mbabarc.html, accessed September 15, 2009.

DeKrey, Steve, personal interview, 2009.

Deutsch, Karl W., and Alexander Eckstein, "National Industrialization and the Declining Share of the International Economic Sector, 1890–1959," *World Politics*, Vol. 13 (1961), pp. 267–99.

Donham, W. B., "Business Teaching by the Case System," *American Economic Review*, Vol. 12, No. 1 (1922), pp. 53–65.

Doz, I.L., and G. Hamel, "The use of alliances in implementing technology strategies," in Tushman, M.L., and P. Anderson (eds.), *Managing Strategic Innovation and Change*, Oxford University Press, New York, 1997, pp. 556–80.

Duke University, The Fuqua School of Business, About Fuqua Web page, 2009, electronic document, http://www.fuqua.duke.edu/about/, accessed June 29, 2009.

Duke University, The Fuqua School of Business, Global Executive MBA Web page, 2010, electronic document, http://www.fuqua.duke.edu/programs/duke_mba/ global_executive/, accessed December 29, 2010.

Duke University, The Fuqua School of Business, International Locations Web page, 2009, electronic document, http://www.fuqua.duke.edu/about/locations/, accessed June 29, 2009.

Earley, P.C., and E. Mosakowski, "Cultural intelligence," *Harvard Business Review*, Oct. (2004), pp. 139–46.

Education Bureau of the Hong Kong SAR Government, Non-Local Higher and Professional Education (Regulation) Ordinance, List of Exempted Courses, 2010, electronic document, http://www.edb.gov.hk/index.aspx?langno = 1&nodeID = 1247, accessed July 23, 2010.

Education Bureau of the Hong Kong SAR Government, Non-Local Higher and Professional Education (Regulation) Ordinance, List of Registered Courses, 2010, electronic document, http://www.edb.gov.hk/index.aspx?langno = 1&nodeID = 1438, accessed July 23, 2010.

Edwards, R., G. Crosling, S. Petrovic-Lazarovic, and P. O'Neill, "Internationalisation of Business Education: Meaning and implementation," *Higher Education Research and Development*, Vol. 22, No. 2 (2003), pp. 183–92.

ESSEC Business School and Keio University, "ESSEC Business School & Keio Business School launch a MBA-level dual degree program," press release, September 12, 2008, electronic document, http://econtent.essec.fr/mediabanks/ ESSEC-PDF/Actualites/CP_2008/CP_Keio_ANG.pdf, accessed August 31, 2009.

European Commission, Erasmus Statistics, 2010, electronic document, http:// ec.europa.eu/education/erasmus/doc920_en.htm, accessed July 22, 2010.

European Commission, Study in Europe Web portal, electronic document, http:// ec.europa.eu/education/study-in-europe/, accessed December 30, 2010.

European Ministers of Education, The Bologna Declaration of 19 June 1999, joint declaration of the European Ministers of Education, 1999, electronic document, http:// www.ond.vlaanderen.be/hogeronderwijs/bologna/documents/MDC/BOLOGNA_ DECLARATION1.pdf, accessed June 10, 2010.

Executive MBA Council, "2006 Executive MBA Council Survey Results Offer Industry Insights," EMBA Council press release, electronic document, http://www.emba.org/pdf/pressroom/2006_research_results_11_18.pdf, accessed August 17, 2010.

FGV-EAESP, Foreign Visitors Program Web page, 2009, electronic document, http://www.eaesp.fgvsp.br/default.aspx?pagid = JLGCSPPN, accessed December 11, 2009.

FGV-EAESP, International Partner Institutions Web page, 2009, electronic document, http://eaesp.fgvsp.br/pt/atividadesinternacionais/escolas, accessed December 11, 2009.

FGV-EAESP, International Relations Office Web page, electronic document, http://eaesp.fgvsp.br/en/BusinessCommunity/InternationalRelationsCoordination, accessed December 11, 2009.

Fine, Philip, Wagdy Sawahel, and Maya Jarjour, "GLOBAL: Women no longer the second sex," University World News, October 25, 2009, electronic document, http://www.universityworldnews.com/article.php?story = 20091023110831548, accessed August 20, 2010.

Finkelstein, M.J., E. Walker, and Rong Chen, "The internationalization of the American faculty: Where are we? What drives or deters us?" unpublished manuscript, College of Education and Human Services, Seton Hall University, South Orange, NJ, 2009.

Fischer, Karin, "East Carolina U. Uses Simple Technology to Link Its Students With Peers Overseas," *The Chronicle of Higher Education,* May 7, 2009, electronic document, http://chronicle.com/free/v55/i35/35a02302.htm, accessed May 7, 2009.

Fischer, Karin, "Professors Get Their Own Study-Abroad Programs," *The Chronicle of Higher Education,* October 31, 2008, electronic document, http://chronicle.com/article/Professors-Get-Their-Own-St/21290/, accessed August 30, 2010.

Fischer, Karin, "U.S. Academics Lag in Internationalization, New Paper Says," *The Chronicle of Higher Education,* February 2, 2009, electronic document, http://chronicle.com/daily/2009/02/10660n.htm, accessed June 30, 2010.

Fleury, Maria Tereza, personal interview, 2009.

Folks, William R., personal interview, 2010.

Forsgren, M., U. Holm, and J. Johanson, "Internationalization of the Second Degree: The Emergence of the European-Based Centres in Swedish Firms," in Stephen Young and James Hamill (eds.), *Europe and the Multinationals: Issues and Responses for the 1990s,* Edward Elgar, Aldershot, England, 1992.

Friedman, Thomas L., *The World is Flat: A Brief History of the 21st Century,* Picador Press, New York, 2007.

Gabel, Medard, and Henry Bruner, *Global Inc.: An Atlas of the Multinational Corporation,* The New Press, New York, 2003.

Gallagher, Michael, Abrar Hasan, Mary Canning, Howard Newby, Lichia Saner-Yui, and Ian Whitman, "OECD Reviews of Tertiary Education: China," OECD Publishing, 2009, pp. 41–42, electronic document, http://www.oecd.org/dataoecd/42/23/42286617.pdf, accessed February 2, 2010.

Gavetti, Giovanni, and Jan W. Rivkin, "How Strategists Really Think: Tapping the Power of Analogy," *Harvard Business Review* Vol. 83, Apr. (2005), pp. 54–63.

Gerhard, A., K. Hansen, S. Keuchel, M. Neubauer, S.H. Ong, N. Tapachai, and C. Mueller, "Cross-cultural Learning Styles in Higher Education," *International Journal of Learning*, Vol. 12, No. 5 (2005), pp. 247–56.

Ghemawat, Pankaj, "Bridging the Globalization Gap at Top Business Schools: Curricular Challenges and a Response," Chapter 2.3 in Canals, Jordi (ed.), *The Future of Leadership Development*, Palgrave Macmillan, Houndmills, Basingstoke, Hampshire, UK, 2011.

Ghemawat, Pankaj, "Distance Still Matters: The Hard Reality of Global Expansion," *Harvard Business Review*, Sept. (2001), pp. 137–47.

Ghemawat, Pankaj, *Redefining Global Strategy: Crossing Borders in a World Where Differences Still Matter*, Harvard Business School Press, Cambridge, MA, 2007.

Ghemawat, Pankaj, "The globalization of business education: through the lens of semiglobalization," *Journal of Management Development*, Vol. 27, No. 4 (2008), pp. 391–414.

Ghemawat, Pankaj, *World 3.0: Global Prosperity and How to Achieve It*, Harvard Business School Press, Cambridge, MA, 2011.

Gill, John, "Malaysia: Full of Western Promise," *Times Higher Education*, August 27, 2009, electronic document, http://www.timeshighereducation.co.uk/story.-asp?sectioncode = 26&storycode = 407873&c = 2, accessed July 22, 2010.

Gillard, Julia, Speech at Universities Australia conference, March 4, 2009, electronic document, http://www.deewr.gov.au/Ministers/Gillard/Media/Speeches/Pages/Article_090304_155721.aspx, accessed August 23, 2010.

Global Business School Network, Entrepreneurship web page, 2011, electronic document, http://www.gbsnonline.org/component/option,com_fjrelated/Itemid,76/id,80/layout,blog/view,fjrelated/, accessed January 5, 2011.

Global Business School Network, Goldman Sachs' 10,000 Women Initiative web page, 2011, electronic document, http://www.gbsnonline.org/programs/current/goldman-sachs-10000-women-initiative.html, accessed January 5, 2011.

Global Foundation for Management Education, "A Global Guide to Management Education 2006," 2006, electronic document, http://www.gfme.org/global_guide/index.htm, accessed January 31, 2010.

Global Foundation for Management Education, "The Global Management Education Landscape: Shaping the future of business schools," 2008, electronic document, http://www.gfme.org/landscape/reportonlineversion.pdf, accessed January 31, 2010.

Goldman Sachs, "10,000 Women" press release, electronic document, http://www2.goldmansachs.com/china/citizenship/10000women/press-releases/332.pdf, accessed on January 5, 2011.

Gordon, Robert Aaron, and James Edwin Howell, *Higher Education for Business*, Columbia University Press, New York, 1959.

Green, Charles H., "Wall Street Run Amok, Why Harvard's to Blame," *BusinessWeek*, October 5, 2009, electronic document, http://www.businessweek.com/bschools/content/oct2009/bs2009105_376904.htm, accessed January 31, 2010.

Green, Madeleine F., and Kimberly Koch, U.S. Branch Campuses Abroad, Issue Brief Series, American Council on Education, September 2009.

Gregersen, H.B., A.J. Morrison, and J.S. Black, *Global Explorers: The Next Generation of Leaders*, Routledge, New York, 1999.

Gupta, A., and V. Govindarajan, "Knowledge flows and the structure of control within multinational corporations," *Academy of Management Review*, Vol. 16, No. 4 (1991), pp. 768–92.

Gupta, Vipm, and Kamala Gollakota, "Critical Challenges for Indian Business Schools as Partners in Development," *Decision*, Vol. 32, No. 2 (2005), pp. 35–56.

Gürüz, Kemal, *Higher Education and International Student Mobility in the Global Knowledge Economy*, State University of New York Press, Albany, NY, 2008.

Håkanson, L., and R. Nobel, "Technology Characteristics and Reverse Technology Transfer," *Management International Review*, Special Issue 40, No. 1 (2000), pp. 29–48.

Harvard Business Review, "How to Fix Business Schools," compendium of commentaries, electronic documents, http://blogs.hbr.org/how-to-fix-business-schools/, accessed January 31, 2010.

Hazelkorn, Ellen, "Globalization, Internationalization, and Rankings," *International Higher Education*, No. 53 (Fall 2008), pp. 8–10.

Higher Education for Development, "Missouri Southern State University to Provide Accounting and Finance Expertise in Haiti," *HED Articles*, June 2, 2008, electronic document, http://www.hedprogram.org/tabid/225/itemid/164/Missouri-Southern-State-University-To-Provide-Acco.aspx, accessed June 20, 2010.

HKUST Business School, "A Trip to Remember – The Study Trip to UK for Business School Undergraduates," Web posting, 2008, electronic document, http://www.bm.ust.hk/ug/cms/Web/NewsDetail.aspx?NewsId = 180, accessed November 9, 2010.

HKUST Business School, HKUST BBA Global Business Course Descriptions Web page, 2010, electronic document, http://publish.ust.hk/univ/coursecat2010/showcourses.asp?deptcode = BMGB&pagenum = 1, accessed October 1, 2010.

HKUST Business School, HKUST EMBA for Chinese Executives Web page, 2009, electronic document, http://www.bm.ust.hk/iemba/program_over_en.html, accessed April 4, 2009.

HKUST Business School, HKUST Master of Science in Global Finance Web page, 2010, electronic document, http://globalfinance.bm.ust.hk/schedule_view.asp, accessed December 29, 2010.

HKUST Business School, HKUST-NYU Stern Master of Science in Global Finance Web page, 2009, electronic document, http://globalfinance.bm.ust.hk/webpage_view.asp?pageID = 3, accessed April 4, 2009.

HKUST Business School, HKUST Part-time MBA Program Web page, 2010, electronic document, http://www.bm.ust.hk/szmba/prog/curriculum.html, accessed December 29, 2010.

Holland, Kelley, "Is it time to retrain business schools?" *New York Times*, March 14, 2009, electronic document, http://www.nytimes.com/2009/03/15/business/15school.html, accessed January 31, 2010.

Hvistendahl, Mara, "China Moves up to Fifth as Importer of Students," *The Chronicle of Higher Education*, September 19, 2008, electronic document, http://chronicle.com/article/China-Moves-Up-to-Fifth-as/8224/, accessed February 2, 2010.

IESE Business School, Colloquium on the Globalization of Business Education, Barcelona, Spain, October 4–6, 2007.

Institute of International Education and Freie Universität Berlin, Joint and Double Degree Programs in the Transatlantic Context: A Survey Report, 2009, electronic document, http://www.iienetwork.org/file_depot/0-10000000/0-10000/1710/folder/80205/TDP + Report_2009_Final21.pdf, accessed June 30, 2010.

International Association of Universities, IAU Online Databases, Higher Education Systems, 2010, electronic document, http://www.iau-aiu.net/onlinedatabases/index.html, accessed April 27, 2010.

International Monetary Fund, World Economic Outlook Database, April 2010 edition, electronic document, http://www.imf.org/external/pubs/ft/weo/2010/01/weodata/index.aspx, accessed August 25, 2010.

International Trade Administration, U.S. Department of Commerce, "International Trade Administration and Columbia Mayor Join USC's Darla Moore School of Business for International Education Week," International Trade Administration press release, November 20, 2009, electronic document, http://www.trade.gov/press/press_releases/2009/iew_112009.asp, accessed April 24, 2010.

Jain, Dipak, keynote speech, Annual Conference of CLADEA, Cartagena, Colombia, November 4, 2010.

Jaschik, Scott, "International Campuses on the Rise," *Inside Higher Ed*, September 9, 2009, electronic document, http://www.insidehighered.com/news/2009/09/03/branch, accessed July 22, 2010.

Jaschik, Scott, "International 'Leapfrogging,'" *Inside Higher Ed*, October 5, 2009, electronic document, http://www.insidehighered.com/news/2009/10/05/global, accessed August 20, 2010.

Javidan, M., "Global Mindset: Why is it important for Global Leaders?" 2010, electronic document, http://www.tobiascenter.iu.edu/conferences/documents/GlobalMindset-presentation3609.ppt, accessed on June 6, 2010.

Johanson, J., and J. Vahlne, "The internationalization process of the firm: a model of knowledge management and increasing foreign market commitments," *Journal of International Business Studies*, Vol. 7 (1977), pp. 22–32.

Jones, Christopher G., Rishma Vedd, and Sung Wook Yoon, "Employer Expectations of Accounting Undergraduates' Entry-Level Knowledge and Skills in Global Financial Reporting," *Journal of Business Education*, Vol. 2, No. 8 (2009), pp. 85–102.

Kedia, Ben L., and Shirley Daniel, "U.S. Business Needs for Employees with International Expertise," conference paper, Conference on Global Challenges and U.S. Higher Education, Duke University, Durham, NC, January 2003, pp. 5, 12–14, and 17, electronic document, http://ducis.jhfc.duke.edu/archives/global-challenges/pdf/kedia_daniel.pdf, accessed August 17, 2010.

Khanna, T., K. Palepu, and J. Sinha, "Strategies that fit emerging markets," *Harvard Business Review*, Vol. 83 (2005), pp. 63–76.

Khanna, Tarun, Rakesh Khurana, and David Lane, "The Globalization of HBS," HBS Case 9-703-432, pp. 1–23.

Khurana, Rakesh, *From Higher Aims to Hired Hands: The Social Transformation of American Business Schools and the Unfulfilled Promise of Management as a Profession*, Princeton University Press, Princeton, NJ, 2007.

Kim, C.S., and A.C. Inkpen, "Cross-border R&D alliances, Absorptive Capacity and Technology Learning," *Journal of International Management,* Vol. 11 (2005), pp. 313–29.

Knight, J., "Internationalisation of higher education," in J. Knight (ed.), *Quality and Internationalisation in Higher Education,* OECD, Paris, France, 1999.

Kooser, Bill, personal interview, 2009.

Kotabe, Maasaki, "To kill two birds with one stone: Revising the integration-responsiveness framework," in M. Hitt and J. Cheng (eds.), *Managing transnational firms,* Elsevier, New York, 2002, pp. 59–69.

Kragh, Simon U., and Sven Bislev, "Business School Teaching and Democratic Culture: An International and Comparative Analysis," *Research in Comparative International Education,* Vol. 3, No. 2 (2008), pp. 211–21.

Kragh, Simon U., and Sven Bislev, "Political Culture And Business School Teaching," Academy of Management "Best Conference Paper," 2005.

Krieger, Zvika, "Build It And They Will Learn," *Newsweek,* August 8, 2008, electronic document, http://www.newsweek.com/2008/08/08/build-it-and-they-will-learn.html, accessed June 12, 2010.

Kuemmerle, W., "The drivers of foreign direct investment into research and development: an empirical investigation," *Journal of International Business Studies,* Vol. 30, No. 1 (1999), pp. 1–24.

Kwok, Chuck C.Y., and Jeffrey S. Arpan, "Internationalizing the Business School: A Global Survey in 2000," *Journal of International Business Studies,* Vol. 33, No. 3 (2002), pp. 571–81.

Lee, Sang M., and Silvana Trimi, "Transforming Albanian Business Education," *International Journal of Entrepreneurship and Small Business,* Vol. 2, No. 1 (2005), pp. 27–33.

Leven, Bozena, "Poland's Transition in Business Education," *American Journal of Business Education,* Vol. 3, No. 1 (2010), pp. 53–60.

Lloyd, Marion, "Mexico Will Offer Online-Degree Programs to Citizens Living Abroad," *The Chronicle of Higher Education,* August 8, 2010, electronic document, http://chronicle.com/article/Mexico-Will-Offer/123854/, accessed December 30, 2010.

Love, Julia, "Globetrotting: Fuqua's Global Journey," *The Duke University Chronicle,* January 28, 2009, electronic document, http://dukechronicle.com/node/148142, accessed June 29, 2009.

Lovett, Clara M., "American Business Schools in the Post-American World," *The Chronicle of Higher Education,* September 10, 2010, p. A22.

Luo, Y., "Toward coopetition within a multinational enterprise: a perspective from foreign subsidiaries," *Journal of World Business,* Vol. 40, No. 1 (2005), pp. 71–90.

Maddux, W.W., and A.D. Galinsky, "Cultural Borders and Mental Barriers: The Relationship between Living Abroad and Creativity," *Journal of Personality and Social Psychology,* Vol. 96, No. 5 (2009), pp. 1047–61.

Malnight, T., "The transition from decentralized to network-based MNC structures: an evolutionary perspective," *Journal of International Business Studies,* Vol. 27, No. 1 (1996), pp. 43–65.

Martell, Kathryn, e-mail correspondence, April 1, 2010.

Maslen, Geoff, "GLOBAL: Huge Expansion in Overseas Campuses," *University World News*, November 22, 2009, electronic document, http://www.university-worldnews.com/article.php?story = 20091120103411843&mode = print, accessed July 23, 2010.

Maslen, Geoff, "SOUTHEAST ASIA: Bold plan to duplicate Bologna," *University World News*, November 23, 2008, electronic document, http://www.university worldnews.com/article.php?story = 20081120154941889, accessed December 31, 2010.

Massachusetts Institute of Technology, Sloan School of Management, Global MIT Sloan website, 2011, electronic document, http://mitsloan.mit.edu/globalmitsloan/ initiatives.php, accessed January 5, 2011.

Mavin, Duncan, "Harvard Business School Won't Open Asia Campuses," *The Wall Street Journal,* August 2, 2010, electronic document, http://online.wsj.com/ article/SB10001424052748704905004575404960728487290.html?KEYWORDS = management + education, accessed August 2, 2010.

MBA Roundtable, Insights into Curricular Innovation, electronic document, http:// mbaroundtable.org/members_events.html, accessed March 17, 2010.

McNeill, David, "Enrollment Crisis Threatens Japan's Private Colleges," *The Chronicle of Higher Education*, October 25, 2009, electronic document, http:// chronicle.com/article/Enrollment-Crisis-Threatens/48909/, accessed July 22, 2010.

McNeill, David, "No Looking Back: KAIST's President Fights for His Legacy of Change in South Korea," *The Chronicle of Higher Education*, June 20, 2010, electronic document, http://chronicle.com/article/No-Looking-Back-Kaists-Pr/ 65974/, accessed August 27, 2010.

Middlehurst, Robin, Steve Woodfield, John Fielden, and Heather Forland, *Universities and international higher education partnerships: making a difference,* project report, Million + , London, 2009, electronic document, http://www. millionplus.ac.uk/file_download/7/INT_PARTNERSHIPS_summaryReportfinal_ 003.pdf, accessed August 30, 2010.

Mills, Andrew, "Reforms to Women's Education Make Slow Progress in Saudi Arabia," *The Chronicle of Higher Education*, August 3, 2009, electronic document, http://chronicle.com/article/Saudi-Universities-Reach/47519/, accessed July 22, 2010.

Morrison, Terry, and Wayne A. Conaway, *Kiss, Bow or Shake Hands, 2nd edition*, Adams Media, Avon, MA, 2006.

Murray, E., and J.F. Mahon, "Strategic Alliances: Gateway to the New Europe?" *Long Range Planning*, Vol. 26, No. 4 (1993), pp. 102–11.

Murtha, Thomas P., Stefanie Ann Lenway, Richard P. Bagozzi, "Global Mind-sets and Cognitive Shift in a Complex Multinational Corporation," *Strategic Management Journal*, Vol. 19, No. 2 (1998), pp. 97–114.

Naidoo, Vikash, "International Education: A Tertiary-level Industry Update," *Journal of Research in International Education*, Vol. 5, No. 3 (2006), pp. 323–45.

Neelakantan, Shailaja, "Indian Higher Education Minister to Court Top U.S. Universities," *The Chronicle of Higher Education*, October 24, 2009, electronic document, http://chronicle.com/article/Indian-Higher-Education/48926/?sid = at& utm_source = at&utm_medium = en, accessed June 11, 2010.

New Straits Times, "The 5th Annual Stanford-NUS Executive Program," advertisement in Malaysia's *New Straits Times,* April 6, 1987, electronic document, http://news.google.com/newspapers?id = trkTAAAAIBAJ&sjid = XpADAAAA IBAJ&pg = 6703,1188660&dq = executive + stanford + national + university + singapore, accessed August 26, 2009.

Nohria, N., and S. Ghoshal, *The differentiated network: organizing multinational corporations for value creation,* Jossey-Bass, San Francisco, 1997.

Norberg, Johan, *In Defense of Global Capitalism,* Cato Institute, Washington, D.C., 2003.

Northwestern University Kellogg School of Management, Kellogg-HKUST Executive MBA Program Web page, 2009, electronic document, http://www.kellogg.-northwestern.edu/Programs/EMBA/Global_Partner_Programs/HKUST.aspx, accessed November 4, 2009.

NSF/NIH/USED/NEH/USDA/NASA, 2007 Survey of Earned Doctorates, custom report.

Obama, Barack, Address to Joint Session of Congress, February 24, 2009, electronic document, http://www.whitehouse.gov/the_press_office/Remarks-of-President-Barack-Obama-Address-to-Joint-Session-of-Congress/, accessed August 23, 2010.

O'Donnell, S.W., "Managing foreign subsidiaries: agents of headquarters, or an interdependent network?" *Strategic Management Journal,* Vol. 21, No. 5 (2000), pp. 525–48.

O'Rourke, Kevin H., and Jeffrey G. Williamson, "Once more: When did globalisation begin?" *European Review of Economic History,* Vol. 8, No. 1 (2004), pp. 109–17.

Otero, Manuel Souto, and Andrew Mc Coshan, 2006 Survey of the Socio-Economic Background of ERASMUS Students, ECOTEC Research and Consulting, Ltd., Birmingham, U.K., August 2006, electronic document, http://ec.europa.eu/education/erasmus/doc922_en.htm, accessed August 31, 2010.

Page, Scott E., *The Difference: How the Power of Diversity Creates Better Groups, Firms, Schools, and Societies,* Princeton University Press, Princeton, NJ, 2008.

Pan African University Enterprise Development Services, Women's Enterprise & Leadership Program web page, 2011, electronic document, http://www.pau.edu.ng/eds/index.php?option = com_content&view = article&id = 49&Itemid = 124, accessed on January 5, 2011.

Parker, John, "Burgeoning bourgeoisie," *Economist,* February 12, 2009, electronic document, http://www.economist.com/node/13063298, accessed February 1, 2010.

Parkhe, A., "Building Trust in International Alliances," *Journal of World Business,* Vol. 33, No. 4 (1998), pp. 417–37.

Peng, Mike W., and Hyung-Deok Shin, "How Do Future Business Leaders View Globalization?", *Thunderbird International Business Review,* Vol. 50, No. 3 (May/June 2008), pp. 175–82.

Peyton, Johnette, Asian Geographic Trend Report for GMAT Examinees, 2003–2007, Graduate Management Admission Council, McLean, VA, 2008.

Peyton, Johnette, Asian Geographic Trend Report for GMAT Examinees, 2002–2006, Graduate Management Admission Council, McLean, VA, 2007.

Peyton, Johnette, Asian Geographic Trend Report for GMAT Examinees, 2001–2005, Graduate Management Admission Council, McLean, VA, 2005.

Peyton, Johnette, Geographic Trend Report for Examinees Taking the GMAT, 2001–2005, Graduate Management Admission Council, McLean, VA, 2006.

Peyton, Johnette, Geographic Trend Report for Examinees Taking the GMAT, Graduate Management Admission Council, McLean, VA, 2005.

Peyton, Johnette, Geographic Trend Report for Examinees Taking the GMAT, 2000–2004, Graduate Management Admission Council, McLean, VA, 2005.

Peyton, Johnette, World Geographic Trend Report for GMAT Examinees, 2003–2007, Graduate Management Admission Council, McLean, VA, 2008.

Peyton, Johnette, World Geographic Trend Report for GMAT Examinees, 2002–2006, Graduate Management Admission Council, McLean, VA, 2007.

Pfeffer, Jeffrey, and Christina R. Fong, "The Business School 'Business': Some Lessons from the U.S. Experience," *Journal of Management Studies*, Vol. 41, No. 8 (2004), pp. 1501–20.

Pfeffer, Jeffrey, and Christina R. Fong, "The end of business schools? Less success than meets the eye," *Academy of Management Learning and Education*, Vol. 1, No. 1 (2002), pp. 78–95.

Pisani, N., "International Management Research: Investigating its Recent Diffusion in Top Management Journals," *Journal of Management*, Vol. 35, No. 2 (2009), pp. 199–218.

Plumer, Bradford, "The MBA Frayed," *The New Republic*, April 1, 2009, electronic document, http://www.tnr.com/article/politics/mba-frayed, accessed January 31, 2010.

Polanyi, Karl, Conrad M. Arensberg, and Harry W. Pearson (eds.), *Trade and Market in the Early Empires; Economies in History and Theory*, Free Press, Glencoe, IL, 1957.

Porter, Lyman W., Lawrence E. McKibbin, and the American Assembly of Collegiate Schools of Business, *Management Education and Development: Drift or Thrust into the 21st Century?* McGraw-Hill Book Company, New York, 1988.

Porter, M., *Competition in Global Industries*, Harvard Business School Press, Cambridge, MA, 1986.

Porter, M.E., *The competitive advantage of nations*, Macmillan, London, 1990.

Prahalad, C.K., and Yves L. Doz, *The Multinational Mission, Balancing Global Integration with Local Responsiveness*, Free Press, New York, and Collier Macmillan, London, 1987.

PR Newswire, "Carlson School Dean Signs Agreement in China for New MBA Program Abroad," PR Newswire Association LLC, June 22, 2000, electronic document, http://www.accessmylibrary.com/coms2/summary_0286-27965272_ITM, accessed April 4, 2009.

Raydt, Herm (ed.), "Zur Begründung einer Handels-Hochschule in Leipzig" (To Justify a Trade School in Leipzig), memorandum on behalf of the Leipzig Chamber of Commerce, 1897.

Rodrigués, Lucia Lima, Delfina Gomes, and Russell Craig, "The Portuguese School of Commerce, 1759–1844: A reflection of the 'Enlightenment,'" *Accounting History*, Vol. 9, No. 3 (2004), pp. 53–71.

Rouen Business School, History: From 1871 until today, electronic document, http://www.rouenbs.fr/en/rouen-business-school/history, accessed May 6, 2010.

Rumbley, L.E., I.F. Pacheco, and P.G. Altbach, *International Comparison of Academic Salaries: An Exploratory Study*, Boston College Center for International Higher Education, Chestnut Hill, MA, 2008.

Saiz, Albert, and Elena Zoido, "Listening to What the World Says: Bilingualism and Earnings in the United States," *Review of Economics & Statistics*, Vol. 87, No. 3 (2005), pp. 523–38.

Sassen, Saskia, *Territory, Authority, Rights: From Medieval to Global Assemblages*, Princeton University Press, Princeton, NJ, 2006.

Scherer, R., S. Beaton, M. Ainina, and J. Meyer (eds.), *A Field Guide to Internationalizing Business Education: Changing Perspectives and Growing Opportunities*, Center for International Business Education and Research, Austin, TX, 2000.

Schulich School of Business, Creating Canada's Global Business School, 2010, electronic document, http://www.schulich.yorku.ca/ssb-extra/ssb.nsf/docs/Transnational, accessed August 30, 2010.

Schwertfeger, Bärbel, "CEIBS: MBA in Ghana," *MBA-channel.com*, April 16, 2009, electronic document, http://www.mba-channel.com/channel/article/ceibs-mba-in-ghana/, accessed December 28, 2009.

SCImago Research Group, SCImago Institutions Rankings (SIR): 2009 World Report, Report Number 2009–003, 2009, electronic document, http://www.scimagoir.com/pdf/sir_2009_world_report.pdf, accessed June 20, 2010.

Scott, Peter, "Reflections on the Reform of Higher Education in Central and Eastern Europe," *Higher Education in Europe*, Vol. 27, Nos. 1–2 (2002), pp. 137–52.

Shanghai University of Finance and Economics, History of SUFE, 2010, electronic document, http://www.shufe.edu.cn/structure/english/AboutSUFE/HistoryofSUFE.htm, accessed August 17, 2010.

Shears, Toni, and Charles Wasserburg, "Going global: GSB in Barcelona" *The University of Chicago Chronicle*, Vol. 15, No. 4, October 26, 1995, electronic document, http://chronicle.uchicago.edu/951026/gsb.shtml, accessed September 15, 2009.

Sheppard, Blair, personal interview, 2009.

Sheppard, Blair, Santiago Iniguez de Onzono, and James W. Dean Jr., "Alliances and Global Collaboration," presentation at AACSB International Deans Conference, San Francisco, California, February 5, 2009.

Smith, Peter B., Mark F. Peterson, and David C. Thomas, *The Handbook of Cross-Cultural Management Research*, Sage Publications, Inc., Thousand Oaks, California, 2008.

Snyder, Edward A., Globalization of Management Education: A Conversation with AACSB Deans, AACSB Deans Conference presentation, February 2010.

Snyder, Edward A., "The Party's Over: The Coming B-School Shakeout," *BusinessWeek*, April 2, 2009, electronic document, http://www.businessweek.com/print/bschools/content/apr2009/bs2009042_773939.htm, accessed June 12, 2010.

Social Enterprise Knowledge Network, SEKN Home Web page, 2010, electronic document, http://www.sekn.org/en/index.html, accessed June 20, 2010.

Sölvell, Ö., and I. Zander, "Organization of the Dynamic Multinational Enterprise: The Home Based and the Heterarchical MNE," *Journal of International Studies of Management & Organization*, Vol. 25, Nos. 1–2 (1995), pp. 17–38.

Soros, George, *New Paradigm for Financial Markets: The Credit Crisis of 2008 and What it Means*, PublicAffairs, New York, 2008.

Stanford Graduate School of Business, Global Management Immersion Experience (GMIX) 2009 Sponsor Guide, electronic document, http://www.gsb.stanford.edu/gmp/career/documents/GMIX2009SponsorGuide.pdf, accessed August 26, 2009.

Stanford Graduate School of Business, "Student Exchange Program Links Stanford Business School and IIM Bangalore," Stanford GSB press release, January 2007.

Stanford University, Walter H. Shorenstein Asia-Pacific Research Center, About the Stanford China Program Web page, 2009, electronic document, http://chinaprogram.stanford.edu/docs/about_scp/, accessed August 26, 2009.

Steinborn, Deborah, "ESSEC Wins High Marks," *Wall Street Journal*, September 17, 2007, electronic document, http://online.wsj.com/article/SB118999998309629531.html?mod = googlewsj, accessed August 31, 2009.

Stewart, Matthew, "RIP, MBA," *The Big Money*, March 25, 2009 electronic document, http://www.thebigmoney.com/articles/judgments/2009/03/25/rip-mba, accessed January 31, 2010.

Stiglitz, Joseph E., *Globalization and Its Discontents,* W.W. Norton & Company, New York, 2002.

Swedish National Agency for Higher Education, OECD Thematic Review of Tertiary Education, Country Background Report for Sweden, 2006, electronic document, http://www.oecd.org/dataoecd/20/29/37524407.pdf, accessed March 31, 2010.

Tae-gyu, Kim, "Seoul Aims to Attract Top Business School," *Korea Times*, January 22, 2009, electronic document, http://www.koreatimes.co.kr/www/news/biz/2010/07/123_38322.html, accessed June 12, 2010.

Taiwan Central News Agency, "Taiwan's Universities See Record High Vacancies," *Taiwan News*, August 7, 2009, electronic document, http://www.etaiwannews.com/etn/news_content.php?id = 1025483&lang = eng_news, accessed July 22, 2010.

The Minnesota Daily, "Alumnus Donates Millions," February 11, 2009, electronic document, http://www.mndaily.com/2009/02/11/alumnus-donates, accessed April 4, 2009.

The Open University Business School, History and Milestones web page, 2011, electronic document, http://www8.open.ac.uk/business-school/about/history-milestones, accessed January 5, 2011.

The University of Chicago, Booth School of Business, Chicago Booth Global Leadership Series Web page, 2010, electronic document, http://www.chicago-booth.edu/gls/, accessed December 29, 2010.

The University of Chicago, Booth School of Business, Executive MBA Program Web page, 2010, electronic document, http://www.chicagobooth.edu/execmba/, accessed December 29, 2010.

The University of Chicago, Booth School of Business, International MBA Web page, 2010, electronic document, http://www.chicagobooth.edu/fulltime/academics/international/imba.aspx, accessed December 29, 2010.

The University of Chicago, Booth School of Business, "Larger Singapore campus to be built by University of Chicago Graduate School of Business," University of Chicago press release, February 28, 2008, electronic document, http://www.chicago booth.edu/newsmedia/releases/2008-02-28_singapore.aspx, accessed September 15, 2009.

Toyne, Brian, "Internationalizing Business Education," *Business and Economics Review*, Jan.-Mar. (1992) pp. 23–27.

UNESCO, International Standard Classification of Education 1997, electronic document, http://www.unesco.org/education/information/nfsunesco/doc/isced_1997.htm, accessed October 28, 2010.

UNESCO, "UNESCO World Conference on Higher Education opens With Call to Address Global Challenges," press release, July 7, 2009, electronic document, http://www.unesco.org/new/en/media-services/single-view/news/unesco_world_conference_on_higher_education_opens_with_call_to_address_global_challenges/browse/6/back/18276/, accessed March 30, 2010.

UNESCO Institute for Statistics, *Global Education Digest 2009: Comparing Education Statistics Across the World*, Montreal, Quebec, Canada, 2009, electronic document, http://www.uis.unesco.org/template/pdf/ged/2009/GED_2009_EN.pdf, accessed January 31, 2010.

UNESCO Institute for Statistics, "New Trends in International Student Mobility," electronic document, http://www.uis.unesco.org/template/pdf/ged/2009/UIS_-press_conference_presentation.pdf, accessed March 30, 2010.

Universities Australia, "The Nature of International Education in Australian Universities and its Benefits," 2009, electronic document, http://www.universitiesaustralia.edu.au/resources/285/2009-09%20-%20Intl%20Educ%20Benefits_-SPRE_FINAL.pdf, accessed August 18, 2010.

University of Cambridge, "Cambridge Launches Centre for India & Global Business," press release, March 10, 2009, electronic document, http://www.admin.cam.ac.uk/news/dp/2009030903, accessed March 11, 2009.

University of Evansville, Institute for Global Enterprise in India website, 2010, electronic document, http://www.globalindiana.com/about/, accessed December 30, 2010.

University of Minnesota, Carlson School of Management, "Building International Bridges," *Going Global* newsletter, Spring 2008 edition, p. 2, electronic document, http://www.carlsonschool.umn.edu/assets/114759.pdf, accessed April 4, 2009.

University of Minnesota, Carlson School of Management, International Experience 101 Overview Web page, 2009, electronic document, http://www.carlsonschool.umn.edu/page9322.aspx, accessed November 13, 2009.

University of North Carolina at Chapel Hill, Kenan-Flagler Business School, Global Business Project Web page, 2010, electronic document, http://www.kenan-flagler.unc.edu/ki/ciber/GBP/, accessed December 30, 2010.

University of Phoenix, Global Division web page, electronic document, http://www.phoenix.edu/colleges_divisions/global.html, accessed January 5, 2011.

University of South Carolina, Moore School of Business, IBCE Track Web page, 2010, electronic document, http://mooreschool.sc.edu/undergrad/globalexperience/ibcetrack.aspx, accessed April 24, 2010.

University of South Carolina, Moore School of Business, International Business Web page, 2010, electronic document, http://mooreschool.sc.edu/facultyandresearch/departments/internationalbusiness.aspx, accessed December 29, 2010.

University of South Carolina, Moore School of Business, International Business Courses web page, 2010, electronic document, http://mooreschool.sc.edu/facultyandresearch/departments/internationalbusiness/internationalbusinesscourses.aspx, accessed January 3, 2011.

University of South Carolina, Moore School of Business, MENA track web page, 2010, electronic document, http://moore.sc.edu/undergrad/globalexperience/menatrack.aspx, accessed November 8, 2010.

Van Auken, Stuart, Ludmilla G. Wells, and Daniel Borgia, "A Comparison of Western Business Instruction in China With U.S. Instruction: A Case Study of Perceived Program Emphases and Satisfaction Levels," *Journal of Teaching in International Business*, Vol. 20, No. 3 (2009), pp. 208–29.

Verbik, Line, and Lisa Jokivirta, "National Regulatory Approaches to Transnational Higher Education," *International Higher Education*, No. 41 (Fall 2005), pp. 6–8.

Vernon, R., "Contributing to an international business curriculum," *Journal of International Business Studies*, Vol. 25, No. 2 (1994), pp. 215–28.

Vienna University of Economics and Business, "WU History," 2009, electronic document, http://www.wu.ac.at/strategy/en/history/, accessed August 18, 2010.

Warrington, T., N. Abgrab, and H. Caldwell, "Building trust to develop competitive advantage in e-business relationships," *Competitiveness Review*, Vol. 10, No. 2 (2000), pp. 160–68.

Werner, S., "Recent developments in international management research: A review of 20 top management journals," *Journal of Management*, Vol. 28, No. 3 (2002), pp. 277–305.

Wildavsky, Ben, *The Great Brain Race: How Global Universities Are Reshaping the World*, Princeton University Press, Princeton, NJ, 2010.

Williams, K.Y., and C.A. O'Reilly, "Demography and diversity in organizations: A review of 40 years of research," *Research in Organizational Behavior*, Vol. 20 (1998), pp. 77–140.

Wilson, Dominic, and Roopa Purushothaman, "Dreaming With BRICs: The Path to 2050," *Global Economics Paper No: 99*, The Goldman Sachs Group, Inc., 2003, electronic document, http://www2.goldmansachs.com/ideas/brics/book/99-dreaming.pdf, accessed August 17, 2010.

Wolf, Martin, *Why Globalization Works*, Yale University Press, New Haven, CT, 2004.

Wood, V., "Globalization and higher education: Eight common perceptions from university leaders," Institution of International Education, electronic document, http://www.iienetwork.org/page/84658/, accessed June 19, 2009.

World Bank, World Development Indicators and Global Development Finance online database, 2010, electronic document, http://databank.worldbank.org/ddp/home.do?Step = 1&id = 4, accessed August 26, 2010.

World Education Services, "University Deregulation Measures Welcome News for Potential Foreign Campuses," *Korea Herald*, September 16, 2008, electronic document, http://www.wes.org/ewenr/PF/08oct/pfasiapacific.htm, accessed June 11, 2010.

World Trade Organization, Services Database Web page, 2010, electronic document, http://tsdb.wto.org, accessed August 5, 2010.

Yip, G., and A. Dempster, "Using the Internet to enhance global strategy," *European Management Journal*, Vol. 23, No. 1 (2005), pp. 1–13.

AACSB International Board of Directors

AACSB International Committee on Issues in Management Education

Jan R. Williams, Chair, Dean and Stokely Foundation Leadership Chair, College of Business Administration, University of Tennessee at Knoxville ♦ Shahid Ansari, Provost and Dean of Faculty, School of Management, Babson College ♦ Timothy Brailsford, Executive Dean, BEL Faculty, The University of Queensland ♦ Robert F. Bruner, Dean and Charles C. Abbott Professor of Business Administration, Darden Graduate School of Business Administration, University of Virginia ♦ Alison Davis-Blake, Dean, Carlson School of Management, University of Minnesota ♦ Stuart I. Feldman, Vice President, Engineering, Google, Inc. ♦ John J. Fernandes, President and CEO, AACSB International ♦ Ellen J. Glazerman, Executive Director, Ernst & Young LLP, Ernst & Young Foundation ♦ William H. Glick, Dean, Jesse H. Jones Graduate School of Business, Rice University ♦ Jaime A. Gomez, Distinguished Professor of International Strategy and Management, Instituto Tecnológico y de Estudios Superiores de Monterrey-Campus Monterrey ♦ Thierry Grange, Dean, Grenoble Ecole de Management ♦ Yash P. Gupta, Dean, Carey Business School, Johns Hopkins University ♦ Richard K. Lyons, Dean, Haas School of Business, University of California, Berkeley ♦ Michel Patry, Director, HEC Montréal ♦ Susan M. Phillips, Professor of Finance and Former Dean, School of Business, The George Washington University ♦ Andrew J. Policano, Dean, The Paul Merage School of Business, University of California, Irvine ♦ Christopher P. Puto, Dean, Opus College of Business, University of St. Thomas-Minneapolis ♦ Yingyi Qian, Dean and Professor, School of Economics and Management, Tsinghua University ♦ Robert S. Sullivan, Dean and Stanley and Pauline Foster Endowed Chair, Rady School of Management, University of California, San Diego ♦ Howard Thomas, Dean and LKCSB Chair in Strategic Management, Singapore Management University ♦ David A. Wilson, President and Chief Executive Officer, Graduate Management Admission Council ♦ Mark A. Zupan, Dean and Professor of Economics and Public Policy, William E. Simon Graduate School of Business Administration, University of Rochester.

About AACSB International

Mission

AACSB International advances quality management education worldwide through accreditation, thought leadership, and value-added services.

AACSB International—The Association to Advance Collegiate Schools of Business—is a not-for-profit association of more than 1,200 educational institutions, corporations, and other organizations in nearly 80 countries and territories. Founded in 1916, members are devoted to the promotion and improvement of higher education in business and management.

AACSB International established the first set of accreditation standards for business schools, and for more than 90 years it has been the world leader in encouraging excellence in management education. Today, close to 600 business schools in more than 35 countries maintain AACSB accreditation.

In addition to accrediting business schools worldwide, AACSB International is the business education community's professional development organization. Each year, the association conducts a wide array of conferences and seminars for business school deans, faculty, and administrators at various locations around the world.

The organization also engages in research and survey projects on topics specific to the field of management education, maintains relationships with disciplinary associations and other groups, interacts with the corporate community on a variety of projects and initiatives, and produces a range of publications and special reports on trends and issues within management education.

AACSB's world headquarters is located in Tampa, Florida, USA and its Asia headquarters is located in Singapore.

For more information, please visit www.aacsb.edu.

About Emerald Group Publishing

Emerald is a leading independent publisher of global research with impact on business, society, public policy, and education.

Emerald is well-known as a leading publisher in management research, and works closely with business schools worldwide. We publish over 250 journals and 150 books per year, with authors from all the institutions listed in the 2010 *FT Top 100* business school ranking disseminating their work through Emerald.

Emerald was established in 1967 by a group of management academics from Bradford University, and since then we have published "research that you can use", a philosophy that bridges the gap between theory and practice throughout the globe. This approach demonstrates our belief in the value of academic research to the broader social environment.

We are committed to supporting emerging research trends through new journal launches and our growing book portfolio. We constantly strengthen our collections through publishing research focused on emerging economies, reflecting the globalization of management practice and the importance of culture in managing businesses and organizations.

Emerald is a global organization:

- We have regional offices and representation in the USA, UK, China, India, Japan, Australia, Malaysia, UAE, South Africa and Poland
- Our journals and e-journal collections are used by over 3,000 business schools and universities worldwide
- The *FT Top 100* business schools download over 1.4 million Emerald articles a year
- Over 23 million articles are downloaded from Emerald journals each year.
- Every year we publish authors from over 100 countries, and we have regular contact with 80,000 Emerald Literati Network members
- Thomson Reuters (ISI) impact factors for Emerald journals have improved dramatically over the last five years.

We are delighted to work with AACSB to publish *Globalization of Management Education*. The report identifies that "Business schools are part of a larger system and have a responsibility to take a leadership role in the globalization of business and society." Emerald is committed to working with the AACSB, its members, and key stakeholders (deans, researchers, course directors, and teachers) to publish, disseminate, and make available the research that flows from globalization, advancing management practice across the world.

For more information, please visit www.emeraldinsight.com.